The Borderlands of the American and Canadian Wests

The Borderlands
of the American *and* Canadian Wests

Essays on Regional History
of the Forty-ninth Parallel

Edited by Sterling Evans

UNIVERSITY OF NEBRASKA PRESS · LINCOLN AND LONDON

© 2006 by the
Board of Regents
of the
University of Nebraska
All rights reserved
Manufactured in the United
States of America
∞
Set in Sabon by Bob Reitz.
Designed by R. W. Boeche.

Library of Congress
Cataloging-in-Publication Data
The borderlands of the American and
Canadian Wests: essays on
regional history of the forty-ninth
parallel / edited by Sterling Evans.
p.   cm.
Includes bibliographical
references and index.
ISBN-13: 978-0-8032-1826-0
(cloth: alk. paper)
ISBN-10: 0-8032-1826-5
(cloth: alk. paper)
1. United States—Relations—Canada.
2. Canada—Relations—United States.
3. Regionalism—Northern
boundary of the United States.
4. Regionalism—West (U.S.)
5. Regionalism—Canada, Western.
6. Northern boundary of the United
States—Social conditions.   7. West
(U.S.)—Social conditions.   8. Canada,
Western—Social conditions.
9. Group identity—West (U.S.)
10. Group identity—Canada,
Western.   I. Evans, Sterling, 1959–
E183.8.C2B675   2006
303.48'2712078—dc22
2005029572

To Sheri, who has crossed many borders with me

Contents

Illustrations

Tables

Foreword

John Herd Thompson

No international boundary could have less physiographic reality than the forty-ninth parallel of latitude that divides the U.S. West from its Canadian counterpart. The boundary's inception was entirely political. In 1818, British and American diplomats who had never seen the forty-ninth parallel arbitrarily chose it to separate U.S. from British territory from Lake of the Woods to the Rockies. In 1846, another group of Anglo-American diplomats extended the line west from the mountains to the Pacific. No natural feature marks this 1,300-mile political frontier; on the contrary, identical landforms extend north and south across it. If this seems obvious on the northern plains, it is equally obvious west of the Continental Divide: the rugged terrain of British Columbia is impossible to tell apart from that of Montana, Idaho, or Washington, and the desert that crosses the parallel with Okanagan River continues south from British Columbia all the way to Sonora, Mexico. So identical is the landscape on either side that historians who reprint photographs of boundary surveyors at work must take care not to reverse the negatives.

In the half century after the surveyors marked the forty-ninth parallel with eight-foot iron mileposts, however, British-Canadian nationalists rapidly invested the boundary with ideological meaning. An evolving western myth became a fundamental building block of an emerging national identity in Canada, as it did in the United States. Each myth proclaimed each country's uniqueness and justified the conquest and dispossession of the Native peoples who lived in each West. But although the historical process that created the two Wests had been interconnected and essentially similar, Canadians and Americans told strikingly different stories about their Wests. The American narrative—so familiar that it requires no explication here—took little notice of the boundary and the Canadian West. The Canadian western myth, on the other hand, cast the United States as the villain in the black Stetson. In contemporary literary language, the U.S. West played binary opposite "other," the lawless "wild" West against which Canadian editorials, textbooks, cartoons, and novels contrasted Canada's supposedly peaceful version. In the Canadian narrative, Americans went west aggressively to fulfill their Manifest Destiny; Canadians did so defensively out of a manifest duty to protect the Native peoples north of the forty-ninth parallel from the cruel fate that Americans imposed south of it. The American West represented the apogee of autarchic individualism; the Canadian West apotheosized the orderly transplantation of community and government institutions. Vigilante justice misruled the American West; in Canada, the incorruptible North-West Mounted Police meted out the Queen's law evenhandedly to all.

Ironically, an American scholar best encapsulated this notion of two fundamentally dichotomous Wests: Wallace Stegner (1909–93), who spent 1914 to 1920 growing up in southwestern Saskatchewan. "The forty-ninth parallel ran directly through my childhood, dividing me in two," Stegner remembered in *Wolf Willow*. Stegner claimed (without evidence other than eloquent assertion) that Native peoples had called the parallel "the medicine line." Because of the contrasting coats of the U.S. Army and the Mounted Police, writes Stegner, "one of the most visible aspects of the international boundary was that it was a color line: blue below, red above, blue for treachery and unkept promises, red for protection and the straight tongue." Stegner did not present this as unvarnished "truth"; in his next sentence, he admitted, "this is not quite the way a scrupulous historian would report it." [1] But Stegner's caveat notwithstanding, the boundary remained an intellectual barrier that all too few scholars saw any reason to traverse.

Instead, most historians abbreviated their inquiries within their nation-states, to create what a young scholar has recently called "the narratives of exceptionalism that often characterize the histories of the Canadian and U.S. Wests." [2] Canadians made the boundary an intellectual barrier very consciously; too many histories of the Canadian West depicted the U.S. West in caricature, reduced to "the gunfighting, the lawlessness, and the bloody clashes with Indians." [3] Americans made the boundary an intellectual barrier simply by ignoring it. In the master narrative of the American West, the Canadian West was invisible. Two otherwise brilliant syntheses by "new" western historians provide examples. Patricia Nelson Limerick's *Legacy of Conquest: The Unbroken Past of the American West* (1987) and Richard White's *It's Your Misfortune and None of My Own: A New History of the American West* (1991) take no notice of Canada; neither has an index entry for "Canada," although three tangential references do sneak into White's 632 pages. [4] A map reprinted in White's book demonstrates the Canadian West's absence: the arrows that illustrate the northward "dispersion routes of the horse in North America" stop abruptly at the forty-ninth parallel! [5] This neglect of the northern boundary contrasts with the close attention paid to southern borderlands of the U.S. West. *The Oxford History of the American West* (1994) has only four references to Canada in its first 800 pages, but there are more than fifty index entries for "Mexico" and "Mexicans." [6]

The Borderlands of the American and Canadian Wests challenges the intellectual isolation and the national exceptionalism that has marked work on the U.S. and Canadian Wests. The contributors understand that the northern borderlands connect the Wests as surely as they divide them and that understanding the region's history is indispensable to understanding both countries' pasts. The chapters in *Borderlands* represent three interrelated approaches to studying this binational frontier. Some study the area as *one West* in which the forty-ninth parallel was almost without meaning, as it was until the late nineteenth century. [7] Other chapters adopt a *transnational* perspective to consider interactions that spanned the parallel. Finally, some chapters offer *comparative* history of difference and similarity on opposite sides of the border. Many of the chapters choose more than one of these approaches; several combine all three. All interrogate the central notion of the border as a "medicine line."

It is particularly encouraging that U.S. and Canadian scholars are almost equally represented in this collection and that many of the contributors are young. I hope to read much more of their transboundary scholarship and trust that they will accomplish the ambitious historical agenda implicit in this volume. Would that these chapters, and more like them from these and other authors, will find a place in the larger stories that Americans and Canadians tell about their Wests.

Notes

1. Wallace Stegner, *Wolf Willow: A History, a Story, and a Memory of the Last Plains Frontier* (New York: Viking Press, 1962), 81, 101–2.

2. Andrew Graybill, "Texas Rangers, Canadian Mounties, and the Policing of the Transnational Industrial Frontier, 1885–1910," *Western Historical Quarterly* 35 (Summer 2004): 168.

3. J. Arthur Lower, *Western Canada: An Outline History* (Vancouver: Douglas and McIntyre, 1983), 118, uses this phrase to summarize "the American western frontier." The phrase is typical of the twenty-six substantive references to the U.S. West in Lower's 310-page book.

4. See Patricia Nelson Limerick, *Legacy of Conquest: The Unbroken Past of the American West* (New York: Norton, 1987), and Richard White, *It's Your Misfortune and None of My Own: A New History of the American West* (Norman: University of Oklahoma Press, 1991). In fairness, a recent synthesis is a significant exception: Robert V. Hine and John Mack Faragher, *The American West: A New Interpretive History* (New Haven: Yale University Press, 2000).

5. White, *It's Your Misfortune*, 22. The map is reprinted from Warren A. Beck and Ynez D. Haase, *Historical Atlas of the American West* (Norman: University of Oklahoma Press, 1989).

6. See Clyde A. Milner II, Carol A. O'Connor, and Martha Sandweiss, eds., *The Oxford History of the American West* (New York: Oxford University Press, 1994). Again to be fair, a thoughtful essay by Walter Nugent on "Comparing Wests and Frontiers" concludes the *Oxford History*. But none of Nugent's insights have informed the multiple authors of the rest of the volume.

7. See also the essays in *One Myth, Two Wests*, a special issue of the *American Review of Canadian Studies* 33 (Winter 2003).

Preface

The idea to create an edited collection of essays on the history of the western U.S./Canadian borderlands stems not from the scarcity of published material on the subject but rather from how it has been a scattered literature. There has also been a lack of any such collection to bring together some of the new scholarship in what is an emerging discipline on the western U.S./Canadian borderlands. Its emergence has been made apparent to me at several conferences, especially at recent meetings of the Western History Association and at the 2001 American Historical Association–Pacific Coast Branch meeting in Vancouver, British Columbia, whose theme of cross-boundary interactions attracted a broad variety of papers on the region.

I decided there in Vancouver to compile this book and provide a venue for essays on the interdisciplinary nature of the region's history. Thus *The Borderlands of the American and Canadian Wests* joins together the works of twenty-three scholars from both sides of the border (eleven Canadians, twelve Americans) in the fields of history, geography, anthropology, criminal justice, sociology, and environmental studies. Interdisciplinarity is inherently awkward to a degree, but I hope it serves its purpose in this book by showing readers how truly multidimensional the borderlands are. Some of the writers are prominent scholars in their fields; others are newer to the academy, but their works will continue to add to our scholarship on the borderlands. Their essays, researched and written in the different styles of their disciplines, cast light on intriguing aspects of the history of the West—a transboundary West with many dimensions worthy of study.

These dimensions comprise what David Wrobel and Michael Steiner referred to in their edited book on the American West as "many Wests" and as the "extended Wests."[1] Not only are the borderlands of the Amer-

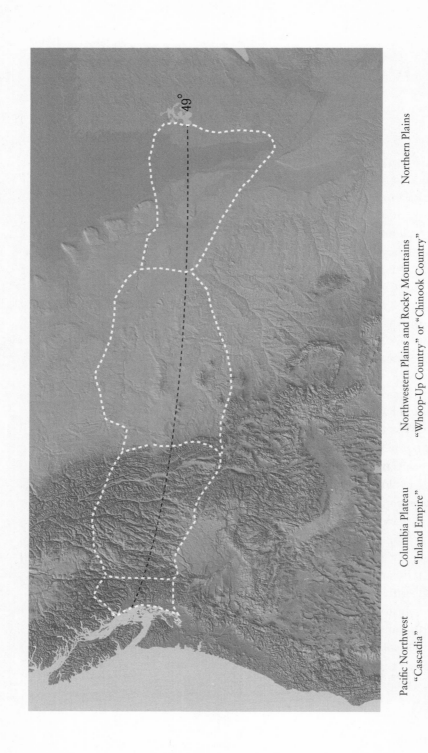

49°

Pacific Northwest   Columbia Plateau   Northwestern Plains and Rocky Mountains   Northern Plains
"Cascadia"   "Inland Empire"   "Whoop-Up Country" or "Chinook Country"

Figure 1. The four subregions of the borderlands of the American and Canadian wests. Map by Brian Ludy and Cassie Hansen of the Humboldt State University Cartography Lab.

ican and Canadian Wests an extended and overlapping region; there are four subregions in the area through which the forty-ninth parallel runs (see figure 1). Moving from east to west, the first subregion is the northern plains, which encompasses the borderlands of North Dakota, eastern Montana, and southern Manitoba and Saskatchewan. Next is the higher elevation Northwestern Plains and Rocky Mountain zone ("Chinook Country," or as it was often called in the nineteenth century, "Whoop-Up Country"), the borderlands area of central and western Montana, southwest Saskatchewan, and southern Alberta. To the west of that region is the Columbia Plateau (also called the Inland Empire)—the more arid borderlands of Idaho's panhandle, eastern Washington, and southeast British Columbia. The fourth subregion is the much wetter Pacific Coast borderlands (sometimes called Cascadia) of western Washington and British Columbia. (Often the Inland Empire and Cascadia are lumped together as the greater region of the Pacific Northwest, or as William Robbins labeled it, the "Greater Northwest.")[2] Each of these zones is covered in the readings that follow.

Unlike the historiography of the borderlands of the American Southwest/Mexican North, in which a robust scholarly presence and literature have existed for decades (especially within the larger history of the American West), the borderlands of the forty-ninth parallel have received scant attention. For example, in the *Journal of Borderlands Studies* only 5 out of 187 articles from 1986 through 1998 dealt with the U.S./Canadian borderlands, and only 2 of those dealt specifically with the West. The historian Paul Sharp lamented back in 1948 that "the forty-ninth parallel has been a far more formidable barrier to many historians than to the . . . institutions they have examined."[3] Only a few scholars have overcome the barrier in the past fifty years, but recently there has been new research that is helping to bring many angles of this region's history to light. Newer studies include emphasis on the environment, aboriginal history, frontier interactions and comparisons, gender history, agricultural and labor relations, various aspects of the borderlands as a region of refuge, and its history of natural resource use and conservation.

Those areas constitute the makeup of this book. Part 1 seeks to define the bordered region by examining questions of bioregionality, the impact of the border, and perceptions and implications of the boundary, particularly as they apply to West Coast Indians/First Nations, and especially with newer implications since the events of September 11, 2001. Part 2 addresses aspects of colonizing the region in the postnational period, especially with the region's history of colonization, ranching, and violence. Included here is a gendered analysis of this colonization process. Part 3 discusses how various groups sought sanctuary in the borderlands of the nineteenth century—how crossing the "medicine line" (both into Canada and into the United States) was perceived as a refuge alternative. Part 4 examines transnational agricultural, industrial, and labor interactions in the region. Part 5 concerns twentieth-century patterns of seeking refuge, but now as a south-to-north crossing zone for Americans fleeing U.S. policies. Part 6 deals with a variety of natural resource, conservation, and environmental issues that characterize the forty-ninth parallel borderlands.

The border itself has played an important role in the region's history. James Loucky and Donald Alper provide a useful working definition of the role of borders in general: "[B]orders are simultaneously sites of nexus and convergence as well as lines of delineation and disjuncture. They are alternately flexible and fixed, open and closed, zones of transition as much as institutional settings. As places where people meet, exchange, and change, the areas adjoining borders are as prone to hybridization as they are to separation and polarization."[4]

Historian Jeremy Mouat has written that the forty-ninth parallel "functions as a significant border . . . one of the more significant western structures. . . . Yet, it began as an imaginary line, born of Euclidean geometry and geopolitics, most notably for the way in which it imposed European definitions of space on the landscape. . . . Gradually this imaginary line became real, and today one can observe at least part of its length from outer space."[5] But that line also represents a political boundary separating people with a remarkably similar environment, culture, economy, and historical experience—a point that adds to the complexity of understanding the borderlands region.

Many studies point out that the forty-ninth parallel represents the longest such divider between any two nations in the world, that Canada is the largest country in the world to border only one other country, and that some 90 percent of all Canadians live within 250 kilometers (150 miles) of the United States. They suggest that these points have led to a Canadian identity that University of Calgary political scientist Roger Gibbons has labelled a "borderlands society"—tied to the United States in so many cultural and economic ways, yet trying desperately not to be just like the United States.[6] Loucky and Alper conclude that "the U.S.–Canada border has figured prominently only in the psyche of Canadians," but that "in the United States, people strain to realize that it even exists."[7] Albertan singer and songwriter k. d. lang artistically commemorated this Canadian characteristic in her album *Hymns of the Forty-ninth Parallel*, which was released in 2004 while I was compiling this borderlands book. The album pays tribute to a variety of well-known Canadian vocal artists, such as Neil Young, Joni Mitchell, Bruce Cockburn, and Leonard Cohen, who, like lang, had crossed the international boundary to enjoy success in both Canada and the United States. The songs she covers by those and other artists, including her own album, represent a very clear sense of place. "The geography seeps through the lyrics and through the melodies," lang mentioned in an interview. "I just think the vastness of the Canadian landscape is just so much a part of these songs."[8]

While invisible to the geography (except where marked or defined by a swath), the border does represent a divider for some noticeable cultural distinctions: metric and Celsius measurements to the north, standard to the south; bilingual road signs and product labels to the north, surprise at such from Americans entering from the south; British spellings and the letter "zed" to the north, American spellings and "zee" to the south; a unique Canadian accent to the north, compared with a U.S. northern accent (somewhat different than the Canadian) on the U.S. side only in the Upper Peninsula of Michigan, Wisconsin, Minnesota, and the Dakotas, but not in Montana westward to Washington; the widespread use of the ever-popular and useful interrogative "eh?" north of the border, without an equal, or use of the more awkward "isn't that right?" in the States; ketchup-flavored potato chips, gravy on french fries, and poutine north of the border—items not found in stores or on menus to the south; a passion by many for the sport of curling to the north, met by bewilderment as to why (or even what it is) to the south. There are numerous other simple differences, reflected when crossing the border, but finding explanations of their origins is more difficult. Still, they are small differences between two regions with so many geographic, linguistic, historic, and cultural similarities.

No discussion of the region's borders would be complete without mention of the American and Canadian Wests distant from the 49th parallel: the 141st meridian borderlands of Alaska, the Yukon, and northwest British Columbia. In first setting out on this project I considered covering both of these western U.S./Canadian border zones. However, I quickly realized that combining regions would add too greatly to the length of the book and would be outside the forty-ninth parallel scope, especially as much of the Far North's borderlands have a history and literature of their own. Likewise, there already exists an excellent collection of essays on the topic, although I am sure there are plenty of areas in the region's history that are in need of new research and analysis.[9]

Curiously, there are only a few original works and edited collections on the history of the U.S./Canadian borderlands. There are several excellent works on the entire borderlands of the two nations (primarily coming from the Canadian side), yet none of these deals specifically with the forty-ninth parallel West. For example, W. H. New's *Borderlands: How We Talk about Canada* (1998) is a narrative discussion of myths, stereotypes, and images from the perspective of a Canadian professor of English. Robert Lecker's anthology *Borderlands: Essays in Canadian-American Relations* (1991) includes a variety of excellent studies (including literary analysis), but it examines the entire U.S.–Canada border, with more essays on the eastern and maritime border than on the western boundary. *Borderlands Reflections: The United States and Canada* (1989), by geographers Lauren McKinsey and Victor Konrad, and Roger Gibbons's *Canada as a Borderlands Society* are both short monographs that deal with important border issues, but they are not specific to the West.

Other works are pertinent to the region, but they either cover the whole of U.S.–Canadian relations or are limited to one of the subregions of study here. Of note on the former are Seymour Martin Lipset's *Continental Divide: The Values and Institutions of the United States and Canada* (1990), Richard Gwyn's *The 49th Paradox: Canada in North America* (1985), and John Thompson and Stephen Randall's *Canada and the United States: Ambivalent Allies* (1997).

On the latter, five relatively recent books stand out: John Findlay and Ken Coates's edited collection *Parallel Destinies: Canadian-American Relations West of the Rockies* (2002), an excellent anthology, but it deals exclusively with the Pacific Northwest; Beth LaDow's *The Medicine Line: Life and Death on a North American Borderland* (2001), a seminal work on many facets of the borderland of Montana and Saskatchewan; Katherine Morrissey's *Mental Territories: Mapping the Inland Empire* (1997), although only one of its chapters deals with the transboundary Columbia Plateau in British Columbia; John Bennett and Seena Kohl's *Settling the Canadian-American West, 1890–1915* (1995), which is primarily a work of "historical anthropology"; and Hana Samek's *The Blackfoot Confederacy, 1880–1920: A Comparative Study of Canadian and U.S. Indian Policy* (1987), which is one of the best studies to date on transboundary Native American/First Nations history but is limited in scope to the Montana/Alberta area. Readers will find much more comprehensive reading lists at the end of each part introduction.

Thus, to this growing literature *The Borderlands of the American and Canadian Wests* is designed to add under one cover an interdisciplinary understanding of the region's transboundary history of interactions. The goal is for its contents and suggestions for further reading to be useful resources for scholars, students, and the interested public studying this North American area. They will discover, as Victor Konrad has so well defined them, that the borderlands "are distinctive regions of mitigating landscapes fading from the common edges of the boundary." And with the information here, readers will be able to add a western U.S./Canadian twist to Konrad's analysis of the borderlands as a whole: "Between Canada and the United States, borderland regions have emerged . . . among peoples with common characteristics, in spite of the political boundary delineated between them. . . . [B]orderlands exist when shared characteristics set a region apart from the countries that contain it, and residents share more with each other than with members of their respective national cultures. In the Canada–United States context particularly, borderlands are regions that have a tempering effect on the central tendencies of each society, and these regions reveal the ways in which the nation-states blend into each other." [10]

Notes

1. David M. Wrobel and Michael C. Steiner, eds., *Many Wests: Place, Culture, and Regional Identity* (Lawrence: University Press of Kansas, 1997), and especially part 4, entitled "Extended Wests."

2. As is titled the fourth part of William G. Robbins, ed., *The Great Northwest: The Search for Regional Identity* (Corvallis: Oregon State University Press, 2001).

3. Paul F. Sharp, *The Agrarian Revolt in Western Canada: A Survey Showing American Parallels* (Minneapolis: University of Minnesota Press, 1948), vii.

4. James Loucky and Donald Alper, "Pacific Borders, Discordant Borders: Where America Edges Together," paper, conference of the Association for Canadian Studies in the United States (ACSUS), Portland OR, Nov. 2003, 2.

5. Jeremy Mouat, "The Forty-ninth Parallel: Defining Moments and Changing Meanings," in Robbins, ed., *The Great Northwest*, 121.

6. Roger Gibbons, *Canada as a Borderlands Society* (Orono ME: Borderlands Project, 1989). See also W. H. New, *Borderlands: How We Talk about Canada* (Vancouver: University of British Columbia Press, 1998), and Robert Lecker, ed., *Borderlands: Essays in Canadian-American Relations* (Toronto: ECW Press, 1991).

7. Loucky and Alper, "Pacific Borders, Discordant Borders," 3.

8. "k. d. lang Looks Homeward on *Hymns*," National Public Radio, *Weekend Edition*, August 29, 2004 (at *www.npr.org/features/feature.php?wfld=3870950*).

9. See Yukon Historical and Museums Association, *Borderlands: The Conference on the Alaska-Yukon Border*, proceedings (Whitehorse YT: Yukon Historical and Museums Association, 1989).

10. Victor Konrad, "Common Edges: An Introduction to the Borderland Anthology," in Lecker, ed., *Borderlands*, viii.

Acknowledgments

Developing this anthology was made easier and more pleasant with the help and support of many individuals. First, it was made financially possible by grants from the Humboldt State University Foundation and the HSU Office of Research and Graduate Studies (a Research, Scholarship, and Creative Activity award). I express my sincere thanks to the directors of those organizations for appreciating the value of this project and for understanding the daunting task of encouraging faculty publications at Humboldt State. Their funds enabled the purchase of permissions to reprint the several previously published essays found here and to hire Sheri L. Evans to perform the tedious word-processing and reformatting duties. She did a superb job in typing every chapter, and her keen proof-reading skills caught the many errors that I inexplicably missed.

For organizing the project and improving the book, I received invaluable advice from both sides of the border, especially from Elizabeth Jameson (University of Calgary) and C. L. Higham (Davidson College). Betsy and Carol generously shared their time and suggestions with me—sometimes with quick kicks in the pants to make sure I understood in which direction this project should go! Their imprints are apparent here, and I have appreciated their counsel all along the way. Likewise, each of the scholars who contributed essays to the book was excellent to work with. I greatly appreciate their work to research, write, and revise their essays. I am especially indebted to Pete Morris for his comprehensive bibliographies, which helped me build the "For Further Reading" sections on the prairie borderlands. And to Sam Truett at the University of New Mexico, accomplished scholar of the Mexican/American borderlands, I express special thanks for his strong support and encouragement for this project as an avenue to advance greater understanding of the lesser studied western Canadian/American border region.

Others elsewhere deserve my thanks. I will always be grateful to Donald Worster for his advice and encouragement in (and after) graduate school at the University of Kansas and for reminding students to be mindful of the transnational aspects of western and environmental history. I also valued the encouragement I received from the late John D. Wirth (Stanford), who early on emphasized the need to look at the larger continental perspectives of North American history. When I taught at the University of Alberta, my colleagues Gerhard Ens, Ted Binnema, and John Herd Thompson (on leave from Duke at the time) were equally as supportive of my endeavors, and we shared many useful conversations on borderlands topics. I thank John for being willing to write the foreword here. I have also benefited from the enthusiasm and encouragement that Tom Isern (North Dakota State University) and Bruce Shepard (an independent scholar in Saskatoon, Saskatchewan) have given me on my research and ideas over the years. Thus it was only logical to invite that transboundary duo to write the introduction to this book, and I thank them for agreeing to do so. Their humor and anecdotes, especially on borderlands topics, are always, let's say, enriching.

While at Humboldt State I greatly benefited from the interest my departmental colleague Jason Knirck (now at Central Washington University) expressed in this project. He became a very useful springboard off of which to bounce ideas and frustrations, and his advice (given in his characteristically pithy manner!) was always most welcome. I also am indebted to geographer Dennis Fitzsimons, and his cartography students Brian Ludy and Cassie Hansen, who did an excellent job of creating the book's maps. And now at Brandon University, my Canadianist colleagues James Naylor and Morris Mott have given valuable suggestions and have lent their much-appreciated support to this project. The move to Manitoba coincided with the period when the final copyediting touches needed to be done on the manuscript. There were too many ironic moments that occurred while completing that task—reading, writing, and editing about past borderlands events and issues while on the same days making trips to the port of entry at Dunseith, North Dakota/Boissevain, Manitoba, to deal with work permits, vehicle imports, and the barrage of bureaucracy involved with conducting a transboundary move. But I have returned to the borderlands of my natal northern plains, and I wouldn't want to leave.

As Wallace Stegner wrote in *Wolf Willow*, "I may not who I am, but I know where I'm from."

I also thank the editorial staffs at the University of Nebraska Press and at the University of Calgary Press for taking such an instant interest in this project and for their efforts in advancing it along through the many stages of publication. Also, the suggestions from external reviewer Beth LaDow and two anonymous reviewers were extremely useful for improving the book as a whole.

My family deserves a great deal of credit for seeing this project through. My parents, who brought me into the world in Grand Forks, North Dakota, a mere ninety miles from the Canadian border, have provided constant emotional support for my research projects over the years. I thank Sheri (to whom the book is warmly dedicated) for always understanding why I take these kinds of projects on and encouraging me nonjudgmentally throughout the process. Our two daughters, Alex (who has been such a great sport in our various cross-border moves) and Shelby (whom I'll always remember as a three-year-old playing fascinating games in a big cardboard box underneath the computer desk in our loft while I worked!), have given me the loving and fun distractions I needed and have generously tolerated my time away from them when I was working on the book. To all involved, I extend my heartfelt gratitude.

Duty-Free

An Introduction to the Practice of
Regional History along the Forty-ninth Parallel

Thomas D. Isern and R. Bruce Shepard

On my first expedition to western Canada in 1985, I (Isern) commenced a study of the North American plains on an international basis. I exited the United States by auto via Portal, North Dakota, and entered Canada at North Portal, Saskatchewan, without incident. Traveling with me was my wife, a German citizen. The following year, this time traveling alone, I arrived at the same border crossing, intent on continuing my studies, and was met by the same border guard. I found myself delayed by endless questions, questions of the circular sort intended to expose inconsistencies and thus ensnare a traveler who has been deemed suspect. Suddenly I understood the problem and dealt with it easily. "My wife and I had a wonderful time in Saskatchewan last summer," I remarked. "She's going to fly in and meet me in Saskatoon in three weeks." That earned me a ritual "Enjoy your stay in Canada" and sent me on, marvelling at memory or monotony, whichever was responsible for the incident. A great lone land, indeed.

Fifteen years later I arrived at the same port of entry accompanied by the seminarians of "The Great Plains from Texas to Saskatchewan," a National Endowment for the Humanities Summer Seminar for School Teachers. Several of us paid for bottle purchases at the duty-free store in North Portal, after which we proceeded into no-man's-land, because a shack just short of the border, between the two ports of entry, was the pick-up point for duty-free purchases. There we piled out of the vans and, assembling by the obelisk marking the forty-ninth parallel, recited William Stafford's poem, "At the Un-National Monument along the Canadian Border."

> *This is the field where the battle did not happen,*
> *where the unknown soldier did not die.*
> *This is the field where grass joined hands,*
> *where no monument stands,*
> *and the only heroic thing is the sky.*
>
> *Birds fly here without a sound,*
> *unfolding their wings across the open.*
> *No people killed on this ground*
> *hallowed be neglect and an air so tame*
> *that people will celebrate it by forgetting its name.*

It was a summary ceremony of passage, for the obelisk perches on a slippery slough-bank, giving poor purchase to poets.

That night at Jack's Café in Eastend, Saskatchewan—boyhood home of Wallace Stegner, he of the conflicted Canadian American identity in *Wolf Willow*—we chatted with Sharon Butala, who came from the ranch for supper with us. We recited Stafford to her, right there in the Fancy Room at Jack's, and she said, "I like it, but it's all wrong." The wind is never still on the forty-ninth parallel, she said. The border is hardly a "place where the battle did not happen," but rather a point of continual contention. Later, exiting via the main dining room, we read our way around the four walls, every inch covered with historical murals painted by proprietress Angela Doulias—paintings depicting the Canadian saga of orderly development and peaceful progress, Mounties and all. .

It was the American historian Paul F. Sharp who remarked, "The forty-ninth parallel has been a far more formidable barrier to many historians than to the men and institutions they have examined." I'm not so sure. In the first place, the historians are creatures of their own national cultures. They like to think they shape their national narratives, but more often they are shaped by them. Without a doubt over the past half century those scholars who have attempted to practice a prairie history that crosses the border have been harassed by scholarly border guards, but my sense now is that those critics were merely designated hitters representing their constituents well. In the second place, the border never constituted a blockade to scholars, any more than it did to bootleggers. The border stopped nothing intellectual. Rather, what happened was that after freely crossing the border, the scholar found him- or herself walking in gumbo. The neighbor nation was big, as was its academic and literary establishment, and its gumbo stuck to the scholar's boots, picking up rocks and sticks and more gumbo, so that eventually the scholar was pulled down in exhaustion. Weary of the continual necessity of translation, accommodation, diplomacy, explanation, and defense, the transborder scholar went home.

Despite the experiences of such pioneers of the gumbo, in the 1990s scholars in numbers and talent sufficient to constitute a new school of regional practice have commenced crossing the border again, and they appear to be doing so with impunity, if not profit. Perhaps they are merely light on their feet, but we prefer to think that the ground has become better for travelers. This is a trend worth noting and examining. We propose, therefore, to trace the checkered past of cross-border studies in history and related disciplines of the social sciences and humanities. Second, we wish to examine the current crop of work in the region, sorting the theoretical approaches into three categories, which we term continental, comparative, and borderlands. Third, we make bold to critique the three approaches in a self-conscious attempt to chart directions for new work in the emerging field.

Regional history on a transborder basis holds antecedents in the 1940s with the work of Paul Sharp and American sociologist S. M. Lipset. There is a puzzling division here. They published works on agrarian radicalism in western Canada at about the same time—Sharp's *Agrarian Revolt in Western Canada* in 1948 and Lipset's *Agrarian Socialism* in 1950. Because it posited a potent American influence in western Canadian affairs, *Agrarian Revolt* was criticized by Canadian reviewers (with the notable exception of W. L. Morton). *Agrarian Socialism*, a more modest study limited to the Cooperative Commonwealth Federation in Saskatchewan, was treated more kindly, although not canonized in Canada. We do not wish to encourage conspiracy theory in the academy, but there is something yet to be explained about the cordiality of historical sociologist S. D. Clark toward the work of Lipset and his animus toward that of Sharp. Sharp went on to write the essential text for transborder studies in the Canadian-American West, *Whoop-Up Country*, a selection of which follows in chapter 4. Much later, Lipset penned the notable comparative work *Continental Divide* without any citation of Sharp's main works. Sharp, on the other hand, praised *Continental Divide* publicly and fulsomely.

Although we just referred to *Whoop-Up Country* as the essential text for transborder studies, we don't mean to say that it was well understood and universally acclaimed. Both Canadian and American readers failed to grasp the work's thesis and importance. The work was essentially a test of Walter P. Webb's Great Plains thesis, which posited a cultural integrity for the entire plains region on the basis of adaptation to environment. Somewhat to his surprise, Sharp found that on the northern plains, Canadian nationality was more powerful than the environment in shaping regional history and identity. Canadian reviewers were too blinkered to see the significance of Sharp's work for their own developing historiography. So what if Sharp refuted Webb? They had never heard of Webb. American reviewers (with the exception of Abe Nasatir) were likewise unaware of the Canadian importance of Sharp's work; they missed its point and thought the work an extension of American historical interpretation into Canada, rather than a qualification of such thought. Sharp moved on to a wonderfully successful career in higher educational administration, and transborder studies of the prairies languished for a generation.

If we relax slightly the definition of the decade, then we can say that the renewal of the practice of prairie scholarship on a transborder basis in the 1990s commences with Bob Thacker's *The Great Prairie Fact and Literary Imagination* in 1989. It continues at close of decade with the reopening of debate on the historical origins of Canadian ranching and with a promising lot of other studies in progress on both sides of the border. Before looking specifically at items in this burgeoning catalog, allow us first to delineate the three approaches we discern in both earlier and current studies.

The first approach is that of the continentalist. Let's begin discussion of this intellectual approach with appropriate disclaimers. We have nothing to say for or against the continentalist annexationists of the nineteenth century. Nor do we have any truck with unthinking Americans who assume western Canadians would like to be Americans or with political flakes in places like Alberta who still brandish the American wild card. We are speaking rather of an intellectual approach to regional studies that begins with the assertion of a regional integrity that crosses national lines. Commonly, in line with the (often overstated but nevertheless real) environmental determinism of Walter P. Webb, continentalist scholars treat a North American plains region comprising level, semiarid prairies. The region of study may be defined as less than the entire plains. Both Canadian and American scholars often prefer to deal only with the northern plains, for reasons that may be intellectually grounded but that we suspect also have something to do with their common prejudice against all things southern, especially Texan. Even within the northern plains study, areas may be more closely circumscribed. The region of study may also be defined in terms other than the physiographic—in cultural or economic terms, for instance—but this is an underdeveloped aspect of the approach.

It was the continentalism of *Agrarian Revolt* that ran Sharp afoul of the Canadian scholarly fraternity. In *Whoop-Up Country* he converted to a comparative approach. The comparative approach is intellectually simple but logically essential to transborder studies. As any open-minded, inductive scholar of the prairies will observe, there are matters where the regional overrides national difference, and there are matters where nationality overrides region. Invoking the classic comparison-contrast format, adherents of the comparative approach sort out the similarities and differences and generally emphasize the differences—as did Lipset and Sharp. Such comparative studies offer aid and comfort to Canadian nationalists and can be made acceptable to American exceptionalists. Comparative studies are a relatively safe occupation.

For those who enjoy extreme sports, there is the borderlands approach to Canadian-American regional studies. The intellectual roots of this approach lie in two distinct soils. The first grounding is the school of borderlands history founded by Herbert E. Bolton, which focused first on the Hispanic-American borderlands of southwestern North America and then broadened to encompass the multinational history of the Americas. The second grounding for the borderlands approach stands the Boltonian school, with its emphasis on colonization, on its head. It is the literature of postcolonialism. Knowingly or not, practitioners of the borderlands

Table 1. Three approaches to the practice of forty-ninth parallel history

Approach	Emphasis	Intellectual Roots	Strengths	Weaknesses
Continental	Integrity of the Great Plains as an international region	Environmental determinism Grounding in natural sciences	Applicability to history of agriculture and natural resources Strong regional identity	Disregard of importance of nationality Weak treatment of political economy
Comparative	Importance of nationality (or nationalism)	Nationalist historiographies (and mythologies) Social scientific method	Strong national identity Counterbalance to environmental determinism	National chauvinisms Disregard of environmental influences
Borderlands	Historical agency of the border; emergence of a border culture	Southwestern borderlands historiography Post-Colonialism	Foregrounding of liminal peoples Deconstruction of determinisms	Marginality of the field Is there a border culture along the 49th Parallel?

approach to the Canadian-American plains, with their focus on terrains and peoples previously liminal, are linking up with postcolonialism as an international phenomenon. In general, the borderlands approach dwells geographically on lands and peoples physically adjacent to the international boundary or in some way associated with it. More specifically, the borderlands approach proposes that the border has agency in history and that it forms border cultures and constitutes its own historical themes distinct from, and perhaps subversive of, national cultures (see table 1).

In practice the three approaches to transborder studies may resemble one another, blend, and alternate within a given corpus. At such times, though, they still may be recognized through DNA analysis. Continentalists generally spring from nationalist lines, and the borderlands gang boasts Boltonian or postcolonial blood.

Cutting across the three approaches to regional history, and to some extent correlating with them, are certain tendencies corresponding to nationality. Scholars on each side of the border had their own fundamental problem that constrained understanding of the regional situation. On the Canadian side, the problem was defensive nationalism. On the American side, the problem was smug complacency. Only to a degree have these constraints on inquiry eased, as Canadians have felt comfortable laying down the burden of national defense and Americans have become curious as to what they might learn from Canadian experience. Still in the 1990s, both Canadian and American scholars have continued to exhibit mossy intellectual anachronism at the same time they produce stimulating new findings.

For instance, anthropologists John W. Bennett and Seena B. Kohl, in *Settling the Canadian-American West,* use new readings of old sources to produce an international/regional synthesis. Their focus is the "heritage concept" in "remembered experience" recorded in "autobiographical materials" and "published local histories." In both the United States and Canada, they find values of frontier egalitarianism instilled by common origins, experiences, hardship, and myth making. There is, they argue, a common identity throughout the "Canadian-American West Heartland"; the border matters little. Their continentalist argument, while possessing considerable merit, ultimately lacks credibility because the authors appear thoroughly steeped in American interpretive frameworks but exhibit no knowledge of alternative Canadian readings of their materials.

On the other hand is *With Scarcely a Ripple,* by Randy Widdis, a population geographer from the University of Regina. The most intriguing part of Widdis's study of Anglo-Canadian migration back and forth across the border is the section devoted to migration into Saskatchewan from Ontario directly and from American states in a second-stage migration. Widdis remains committed to that great liberal immigration fantasy, the "returning Canadian." Despite all that, the work triumphs as defensive nationalism, operating on the venerable principle that the best defense is a good offense. Sensing the coming deluge of dissertations and books pursuing prairie topics across the international border, Widdis gets ahead of them all with his troublesome tour de force. Here is the gist of his position. Most Canadians live near the border, but that is not a sign of weak national identity. Canadians are a border people who, because they know it, command the border and use it for their own purposes.

They do not need to have the border culture delineated for them by new borderlands scholars; they *are* the border culture; they *are* the liminal underdogs who, postcolonially, will survive and inherit the earth. Widdis is a chess master who co-opts the postcolonial impulse of borderlands scholarship in service of the most hidebound nationalism, who co-opts the co-opters. He goes so far as to maintain that only Anglo-Canadian nationalism can offer safe sanctuary for Canadian prairie regionalism by defending it against ravaging Americanism—a brazen case of assigning guardianship of the chicken house to the foxes in order to repel the coyotes.

Given the lineage of transborder studies, and inspired by the upsurge of interest in the field over the past decade, we think it timely to offer some remarks on the relative merits of the various approaches employed in regional history. It is vanity and a conceit to think that one may direct the development of a dynamic new field of study. Our purposes are more modest: to initiate a critical discussion, to encourage practitioners in the field to be aware of their approaches, and to help us learn from one another.

What is to be done with the practice of regional history? Three things, we think. The first thing is to decide whether what we have here is a viable field of inquiry. That is a question in two parts. The first part is, does the field have an academic future? Will practitioners of this sort of regional history be able to survive and thrive in their respective academies? We don't know; we invite discussion of the issues. The other part is, does the field have use and appeal to our publics? Can we advance understanding of our regional condition and cultivate a constructive regional identity or identities by doing this sort of history?

The second thing to do is to continue what we have begun here, that is, make our assumptions and aims clear, smoke out the phony problems, identify the genuine barriers, figure out who the players are, and start acting like a credible and self-conscious school of inquiry. All of us may continue to make contributions to other fields, but we can acquaint ourselves with the work in transborder history, encourage its advancement, and claim membership in the movement.

The third thing we must do requires that we test the ground that used to be gumbo but that now, we hope and sense, is firming up. Let us cross the permeable border, north and south, duty-free, conducting the basic research that will ground our emerging field. We will truly know one another only when we have met in the archives and in the field; no symposium can accomplish it for us. Let us, too, make partnerships, individual and institutional, that produce concrete works—collaborations that result in books defining the field and students trained to advance it.

Are we witnessing the birth of an exciting new field of international scholarship? Or is the current crop of studies merely an ephemeral congruence of individual investigations? We are not so naïve as to think we can make a coherent field emerge by the power of our resolution. If, however, this development is as potent and timely as we think it is, then we want to be in the club car when the train pulls out.

Part 1: Defining the Region, Defining the Border

The borderlands of the American and Canadian Wests are made up of four distinct subregions: the Northern Great Plains, the Northwestern Plains and Rocky Mountains (Chinook Country), the Columbia Plateau (or Inland Empire), and the Pacific Coast (sometimes referred to as Cascadia). (See the map in the preface, p. xvi, for more specific descriptions.) Each subregion has specifically different environments, Native peoples, and histories through which the forty-ninth parallel arbitrarily runs. As environmental historian Theodore Binnema writes in the opening chapter, there is a strong case to be made for understanding each of these areas as "bioregions," and his essay addresses how that can be accomplished for the grasslands of the northwestern plains.

It is fitting to begin this book with this kind of environmental analysis, as the landforms and weather of each bioregion certainly played a large role in how they would be viewed and eventually developed economically. In that, they are indeed cultural as well as geographic regions. Geographers Leonard Evenden and Daniel Turbeville assess the cultural and economic components of the Pacific Northwest borderlands in chapter 2. They also evaluate "the distinction between boundary and frontier" and discuss "issues of border regional development and cooperation" that occurred in the 1980s.

But the forty-ninth parallel itself (the "border," the "boundary," the "line") has also played a significant role in the borderlands. Established by the Treaty of Ghent in 1814 and finalized by the Convention of London in 1818 between British North America and a young United States, the line ran from Lake of the Woods in Minnesota/Ontario to the Continental Divide of the Rocky Mountains. West of there to the Pacific Ocean was

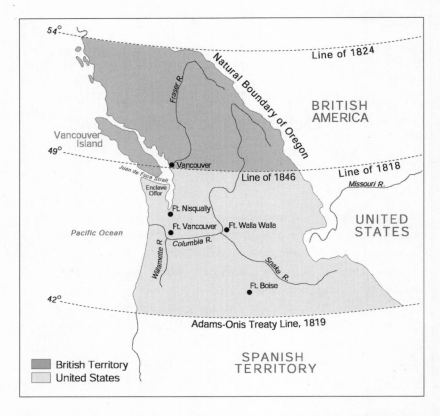

Figure 2. Oregon Country and the extension of the forty-ninth parallel from the Rockies to the Pacific, 1819–46. Map by Brian Ludy and Cassie Hansen.

Oregon Country, a jointly occupied British/American territory (approved by the Rush-Bagot Agreement of 1818) that extended from the northern border of the Mexican territory of California north to 54°40', which runs through the center of what is today British Columbia (see figure 2).

By the middle of the nineteenth century, however, many Americans were clamoring for territorial expansion. Others had started to move into the region, causing expansionist president James Knox Polk and his supporters to want to secure Oregon Country for the United States. Although many in Congress were ready to go to war against Great Britain for the entire territory ("54°-40'or Fight"), saner heads prevailed. Unlike soon thereafter when the United States waged war against Mexico for what became the American Southwest, the American and British governments enacted a compromise in 1846 that extended the forty-ninth parallel as the international border from the Rockies to the Strait of Juan de Fuca, cutting Oregon Country virtually in half. (Space constraints prevent more discussion of these geopolitical negotiations here, but for a thorough review of the 1818 boundary-making treaty, readers should consult the seminal essays of Max Savelle and William Lass or the number of excellent works dealing with the Oregon Compromise of 1846, listed below.)

But there have been other than political ways to conceive of the boundary and its impact in the region and on local identities in the "bordered lands," as historians Jeremy Adelman and Stephen Aron offered in their comprehensive essay on the topic in "From Borderlands to Borders" in the *American Historical Review* (June 1999). What kinds of perceptions influenced regional identity in the borderlands? Another historian, Katherine Morrissey, found that in the Columbia Plateau—that dry inland region of northeastern Washington, the panhandle of Idaho, and southeastern British Columbia—residents created "mental territories" that weighed heavily on regional identity, their understanding of a sense of place, and their role in it. In *Mental Territories: Mapping the Inland Empire* (1997), a landmark work on the topic and region from which unfortunately there was insufficient space to include an extract here, Morrissey details the transboundary history of the area's settlement, economic development, and the establishment of Spokane, Washington, as its economic and cultural hub.

In a similar vein but about the Pacific Coast subregion, Donald Alper wrote "The Idea of Cascadia: Emergent Transborder Regionalisms in the Pacific Northwest–Western Canada" (*Journal of Borderlands Studies*, 1996), and in "Excavating the Future in Cascadia" (*BC Studies*, Autumn 2000), Matthew Sparke discussed the Northwest in terms of "imagined geographies of a cross-border region." Here anthropologist Bruce Miller writes in chapter 3 about "Conceptual and Practical Boundaries" in the Pacific Northwest. His essay is an important contribution to our understanding of the historic and more recent pasts of First Nations who have had to negotiate the forty-ninth parallel in creative ways to continue cultural and salmon-based economic traditions. And, as he shows, with the advent of tighter border security since the events of September 11,

2001, cross-boundary Native peoples have had to adjust once again to policies outside their control.

At the end of each part introduction, readers will find suggestions for further reading on topics covered in the chapters. However, the list below is quite a bit longer to include the many introductory dimensions: on the "border, borderlands, and comparing the Wests," on the borderlands of the Plains, Rockies, and Pacific Northwest (including the Inland Empire), on issues concerning Pacific Coast American Indians/First Nations (works on Native peoples of the Rockies and Plains borderlands are listed in part 3), and on changes stemming from 9/11. And although it is beyond the scope of this book, included is a list of works on the Alaska/Yukon/northwestern British Columbia borderlands (the 141st meridian boundary area) for readers who may want to extend their borderlands insights northward.

For Further Reading

On the Border, Borderlands, and Comparing the Wests
On the Borderlands Regions of the Prairies and Rockies
On the Borderlands Region of the Pacific Northwest (Inland Empire
    and Cascadia)
On Native Americans/First Nations in the Pacific Northwest Border-
    lands
On Post-9/11 Border and Security Issues
On the Alaska–Yukon–British Columbia Borderlands

On the Border, Borderlands, and Comparing the Wests

Abbott, Carl. "That Long Western Border: Canada, the United States, and Economic Change." In John M. Findlay and Ken S. Coates, eds., *Parallel Destinies: Canadian-American Relations West of the Rockies*, 203–17. Seattle: University of Washington Press, 2002.

Adelman, Jeremy, and Stephen Aron. "From Borderlands to Borders: Empires, Nation-States, and the Peoples in Between in North American History." *American Historical Review* 104 (June 1999): 814–41.

Anderson, Stuart. "British Threats and the Settlement of the Oregon Boundary Dispute." *Pacific Northwest Quarterly* 66 (October 1975): 153–60.

Baker, Marcus. *Survey of the Northwestern Boundary of the United States, 1857–1861.* Bulletin of the U.S. Geological Survey, no 174. Washington: Government Printing Office, 1900.

Birdsall, S. S., and J. W. Florin. *Regional Landscapes of the United States and Canada*. New York: John Wiley, 1978.

Blaise, Clark. "The Border as Fiction." In Randall Bass, ed., *Border Texts: Cultural Readings for Contemporary Writers*, 509–18. Boston: Houghton Mifflin, 1999.

Brown, Russell. *Borderlines and Borderlands in English Canada: The Written Line*. Orono ME: Borderlands Project, 1990.

Browne, Ray B. "The Border through Canadian Detective Field Glasses." *Journal of American Culture* 9 (Spring 1986): 7–10.

Careless, J. M. S. *Frontier and Metropolis: Regions, Cities, and Identities in Canada before 1914*. Toronto: University of Toronto Press, 1989.

Carroll, Francis, M. *A Good and Wise Measure: The Search for the Canadian-American Boundary, 1783–1842*. Toronto: University of Toronto Press, 2001.

Conaty, Gerry. "The Many Myths of the Borderland." Paper, symposium "One West, Two Myths: Comparing Canadian and American Perspectives," Calgary, October 2002.

Cook, Ramsay. "Frontier and Metropolis: The Canadian Experience." In Ramsay Cook, ed., *The Maple Leaf Forever: Essays on Nationalism and Politics in Canada*. Toronto: Macmillan, 1977.

Deutsch, Herman J. "A Contemporary Report on the Forty-ninth Parallel Boundary Survey." *Pacific Northwest Quarterly* 53 (January 1962): 17–33.

————. "The Evolution of Territory and State Boundaries in the Inland Empire of the Pacific Northwest." *Pacific Northwest Quarterly* 51 (July 1960): 115–31.

————. "The Evolution of the International Boundary in the Inland Empire of the Pacific Northwest." *Pacific Northwest Quarterly* 51 (April 1960): 63–79.

Dippie, Brian W. "American Wests: Historiographical Perspectives." In Patricia Nelson Limerick, Clyde A. Milner II, and Charles E. Rankin, eds., *Trails: Toward a New Western History*, 112–38. Lawrence: University Press of Kansas, 1991.

————. "The Borderless West: Continuity in Western Art." Paper, symposium "One West, Two Myths: Comparing Canadian and American Perspectives," Calgary, October 2002.

Dunbabin, J. P. D. "Red Lines on Maps: The Impact of Cartographical Errors on the Border between the United States and British North America, 1782–1842." *Imago Mundi: International Journal for the History of Cartography* 50 (1998): 105–25.

Fish, Andrew. "The Last Phase of the Oregon Boundary Question." *Quarterly of the Oregon Historical Society* 22 (June 1921): 161–224.

Fountain, Steven M. "Voyageurs, Mountain Men, and Country Wives: Contesting Empire and Making Borders in North America." Paper, conference of the Association for Canadian Studies in the United States, Portland OR, November 2003.

Fowler, Albert G. "The Other Gulf War: The Tale of a Pig, an Island, and Two Neighbors." *Beaver* 72 (Winter 1992–93): 24–31.

Friesen, Gerald. *The West: Regional Ambitions, National Debates, Global Age*. Toronto: Penguin Books, 1999.

Garreau, Joel. *The Nine Nations of North America*. New York: Avon Books, 1982.

Gibbons, Roger. *Canada as a Borderlands Society*. Orono ME: Borderlands Project, 1989.

————. "Meaning and Significance of the Canadian-American Border." In *Border Regions in Functional Transition: European and North American Perspectives on Transbound-*

ary Interaction, 227–37. Berlin: Institute for Regional Development and Structural Planning, 1996.

Gough, Barry M. "British Policy in the San Juan Boundary Dispute, 1854–72." *Pacific Northwest Quarterly* 62 (April 1971): 59–68.

Graebner, Norman A. "Politics and the Oregon Compromise." *Pacific Northwest Quarterly* 52 (January 1961): 7–14.

Gwyn, Richard. *The 49th Paradox: Canada in North America*. Toronto: Totem Books, 1985.

Harrison, Dick. "Fictions of the American and Canadian Wests." *Prairie Forum* 8 (Spring 1983): 89–97.

Heaton, Herbert. "Other Wests than Ours." *Journal of Economic History* 6 (May 1946): 50–62.

Higham, C. L., and Robert Thacker, eds. *One West, Two Myths: A Comparative Reader*. Calgary AB: University of Calgary Press, 2004.

———, eds. *One West, Two Myths: Essays on Comparison*. Calgary: University of Calgary Press, forthcoming.

Holman, Andrew. "Playing Offside: Meanings and Use of Hockey in the Canada–U.S. Borderlands, 1895–1939." Paper, conference of the Association for Canadian Studies in the United States (ACSUS), San Antonio TX, November 2001.

Hudson, John C. *Across This Land: A Regional Geography of the United States and Canada*. Baltimore: Johns Hopkins University Press, 2002.

Jameson, Elizabeth, and Jeremy Mouat. "Telling Differences: The Forty-ninth Parallel and Historiographies of the West and Nation." *Pacific Historical Quarterly*, forthcoming.

Jones, Sharon. "U.S./Canada National Border Issues/Policies and the Porous Nature of the 4000 Miles." Paper, ACSUS, San Antonio TX, November 2001.

Klotz, Otto. "The History of the Forty-ninth Parallel Survey West of the Rocky Mountains." *Geographical Review* 3 (May 1917): 382–87.

Konrad, Victor. "Borderlands: A Concept for Reinterpreting North America." *Association of American Geographers Annual Meeting and Abstracts*, 1990, 27.

———. "The Borderlands of the United States and Canada in the Context of North American Development." *International Journal of Canadian Studies* 4 (Fall 1991): 77–95.

LaDow, Beth. "Drawing the Line." Chap. 1 of *The Medicine Line: Life and Death on a North American Borderland*. New York: Routledge, 2001.

Lass, William E. "How the Forty-ninth Parallel Became the International Boundary." *Minnesota History*, Summer 1975, 209–19.

———. *Minnesota's Boundary with Canada*. St. Paul: Minnesota Historical Association Press, 1980.

———. "The North Dakota–Canada Boundary." *North Dakota History* 63 (Fall 1996): 2–23.

Laxer, James. *The Border: Canada, the United States, and Dispatches from the Forty-ninth Parallel*. Toronto: Doubleday Canada, 2003.

Lecker, Robert, ed. *Borderlands: Essays in Canadian-American Relations*. Toronto: ECW Press, 1991.

Linton, Patricia W. "Border Crossings and the Space of Subjectivity." Paper, ACSUS, San Antonio TX, November 2001.

Lipset, Seymour Martin. *Continental Divide: The Values and Institutions of the United States and Canada*. New York: Routledge, 1990.

Long, John W., Jr. "The Origin and Development of the San Juan Island Water Boundary Controversy." *Pacific Northwest Quarterly* 43 (July 1952): 187–213.

Lower, J. Arthur. *Western Canada: An Outline History*. Vancouver: Douglas and McIntyre, 1983.

Lumsden, Ian, ed. *Close the 49th Parallel, Etc.: The Americanization of Canada*. Toronto: University of Toronto Press, 1973.

McKinsey, Lauren, and Victor Konrad. *Borderlands Reflections: The United States and Canada*. Orono ME: Borderlands Project, 1989.

McKnight, Tom L. *Regional Geography of the United States and Canada*. Englewood Cliffs NJ: Prentice Hall, 1992.

McManus, Sheila. "Making the 49th Parallel: How Canada and the United States Used Space, Race, and Gender to Turn Blackfoot Country into the Alberta-Montana Borderlands." In Higham and Thacker, eds., *One West, Two Myths*, 109–32.

Merk, Frederick. "The Oregon Pioneers and the Boundary: A Reprint." *Oregon Historical Quarterly* 28 (December 1927): 359–88.

————. *The Oregon Question: Essays in Anglo-American Diplomacy and Politics*. Cambridge MA: Belknap Press of Harvard University Press, 1967.

Merrit, Chris. *Crossing the Border: The Canada–United States Boundary*. Orono ME: Borderlands Project, 1991.

Morris, Peter S. "When Maps Fail: Straight-Line Metaphors and the Borders and Regions of the Canadian-American Plains." Paper, conference of the American Historical Association, New York, January 1997.

Mouat, Jeremy. "The Forty-ninth Parallel: Defining Moments and Changing Meanings." In William G. Robbins, ed., *The Great Northwest: The Search for Regional Identity*, 121–44. Corvallis: Oregon State University Press, 2001.

Murphy, Thomas. "Seeking a True Flag of Freedom: African Americans and the San Juan Boundary Dispute, 1859–1872." Paper, conference of the Association for Canadian Studies in the United States; Portland OR, November 2003.

Murray, Keith. *The Pig War*. Tacoma: Washington State Historical Society, 1968.

Neal, Arthur G. "Symbolism of the Canadian–U.S. Border." *Journal of American Culture* 9 (Spring 1986): 2–6.

New, W. H. *Borderlands: How We Talk about Canada*. Vancouver: University of British Columbia Press, 1998.

Nord, Douglas C. "Canada Perceived: The Impact of Canadian Tourism Advertising in the United States." *Journal of American Culture* 9 (Spring 1986): 23–30.

Nugent, Walter. "Comparing Wests and Frontiers." In Clyde A. Milner II, Carol A. O'Connor, and Martha Sandweiss, eds., *Oxford History of the American West*, 803–33. New York: Oxford University Press, 1994.

Paullin, Charles O. "The Early Choice of the Forty-ninth Parallel as a Boundary Line." *Canadian Historical Review* 4 (December 1923): 127–31.

Perkmann, Markus, and Ngai-Ling Sum, eds. *Globalization, Regionalization, and Cross-Border Regions.* New York: Palgrave Macmillan, 2002.

Poteet, Maurice. "Stopping at the Border." *Journal of American Culture* 9 (Spring 1986): 17–22.

Robbins, William G. "The American and Canadian Wests: Two Nations, Two Cultures." Chap. 3 of *Colony and Empire: The Capitalist Transformation of the American West.* Lawrence: University Press of Kansas, 1994.

Savelle, Max. "The Forty-ninth Degree of North Latitude as an International Boundary, 1719: The Origin of an Idea." *Canadian Historical Review* 38 (September 1957): 183–201.

Scott, Leslie M. "Influence of American Settlement upon the Oregon Boundary Treaty of 1846." *Oregon Historical Quarterly* 29 (March 1928): 1–19.

Shanahan, Daniel E. "The Concept of a Border in North America." *Journal of American Culture* 9 (Spring 1986): 11–16.

Sharp, Paul F. "Three Frontiers: Some Comparative Studies of Canadian, American, and Australian Settlement." *Pacific Historical Review* 24 (November 1955): 369–77.

Stanley, George F. G. "Western Canada and the Frontier Thesis." Canadian Historical Association, *Report of the Annual Meeting,* 1940, 105–14.

Stevenson, Garth. "Canadian Regionalism in Continental Perspective." *Journal of Canadian Studies* 15 (Summer 1980): 16–28.

Thompson, Don. "The 49th Parallel." *Geographical Journal* 134 (June 1968): 209–15.

Thompson, John Herd. "The Limits of North American Cultural Convergence." Paper, ACSUS, Portland OR, November 2003.

Thompson, John Herd, and Stephen J. Randall. *Canada and the United States: Ambivalent Allies.* 2nd ed. Athens: University of Georgia Press, 1997.

Tunem, Alfred. "The Dispute over the San Juan Islands Water Boundary." *Washington Historical Quarterly* 23 (July 1932): 196–204.

United States–Canada Boundary Treaty Centennial, 1846–1946. Seattle: Department of Conservation and Development, State of Washington; and Victoria: Province of British of Columbia, 1946.

Van Herk, Aritha. "Beyond Borders: Invisible Geographies and Their Invented Space." Paper, ACSUS, San Antonio TX, November 2001.

Vibert, Elizabeth. "Border Crossings: A Review Essay." *BC Studies* 119 (Autumn 1998): 97–103.

Weeks, Kathleen. "Monuments Mark the Boundary." *Canadian Geographical Journal* 31 (September 1945): 120–33.

Widdis, Randy W. "Borderland Interaction in the International Region of the Great Plains: An Historic-Geographical Perspective." *Great Plains Research* 7 (Spring 1997): 103–37.

———. "Borders, Borderlands and Canadian Identity: A Canadian Perspective." *International Journal of Canadian Studies* 15 (Winter 1997): 49–66.

———. "A Canadian Geographer's Perspective on the Canada-United States Border." In Donald Janelle, ed., *Geographical Snapshots of North America,* 45–48. New York: Guilford Press, 1992.

————. *With Scarcely a Ripple: Anglo-Canadian Migration into the United States and Western Canada, 1880–1920*. Montreal: McGill-Queen's University Press, 1998.

Winks, Robin. *The Myth of the American Frontier: Its Relevance to America, Canada, and Australia*. Leicester: Leicester University Press, 1971.

Worster, Donald. "Two Faces West: The Development Myth in Canada." In Paul W. Hirt, ed., *Terra Pacifica: People and Place in the Northwest States and Canada*, 71–91. Pullman: Washington State University Press, 1998.

Wrobel, David M., and Michael C. Steiner, eds. *Many Wests: Place, Culture, and Regional Identity*. Lawrence: University Press of Kansas, 1997.

On the Borderlands Regions of the Prairies and Rockies

Alm, Leslie R., and Leah Taylor. "Alberta and Idaho: An Implicit Bond." *American Review of Canadian Studies* 33 (Summer 2003): 197–218.

Binnema, Theodore. *Common and Contested Ground: A Human and Environmental History of the Northwestern Plains*. Norman: University of Oklahoma Press, 2001.

Francis, Douglas, and Howard Palmer, eds. *The Prairie West: Historical Readings*. Edmonton: University of Alberta Press, 1992.

Friesen, Gerald. *The Canadian Prairies: A History*. Toronto: University of Toronto Press, 1987.

————. *River Road: Essays on Manitoba and Prairie History*. Winnipeg: University of Manitoba Press, 1996.

Hildebrandt, Walter, and Brian Huber. *The Cypress Hills: The Land and Its People*. Saskatoon: Purich, 1994.

Hudson, John C. "Cross-Border Contrasts in the Rocky Mountains, United States and Canada." *Abstracts, Association of American Geographers, 93rd Annual Meeting*. Washington DC: Association of American Geographers, 1997.

Jones, Stephen B. "The Cordilleran Section of the Canadian–United States Borderland." *Geographical Journal* 89 (May 1937): 439–50.

LaDow, Beth. *The Medicine Line: Life and Death on a North American Borderland*. New York: Routledge, 2001.

Luebke, Frederick C. "Regionalism and the Great Plains: Problems of Concept and Method." *Western Historical Quarterly* 15 (January 1984): 19–38.

Maly, Stephen, Tom Shillington, and Lauren McKinsey. *Sharing the 49th Parallel: A Handbook on Canadian Relations for Montana Officials*. Bozeman: 49th Parallel Institute, Montana State University, 1983.

Manning, Richard. *Grasslands: The History, Biology, Politics, and Promise of the American Prairie*. New York: Viking Penguin, 1995.

McBane, J. Duncan, and Paul B. Garrison, eds. *Northwest Montana and Adjacent Canada: Field Conference and Symposium*. Proceedings. Billings: Montana Geological Society, 1984.

Morris, Peter S. "Disturbed Belt or Rancher's Paradise? Exploration and Place-Making in a Western Canadian–American Borderland." Paper, International Conference of Historical Geographers, Quebec City QB, August 2001.

————. "Don't Let the Smooth Line Fool You: The Borders and Regions of the Canadian-

American Plains." Paper, conference of the Association of American Geographers (AAG), Ft. Worth TX, April 1997

————. " 'Neighbor Ground' along the Medicine Line: The Canadian-American Plains as a Borderland." Paper, conference of the Western History Association (WHA), Denver, October 1995.

————. "Regional Ideas and the Montana-Alberta Borderlands." *Geographical Review* 89 (October 1999): 469–90.

————. "A Special Kind of Comparative History: Envisioning the Borderlands of the Northwestern Canadian–American Grasslands." Paper, conference of the Association for Canadian Studies in the United States, Minneapolis, November 1997.

————. "Whooping It Up in Chinook Country: Regional Ideas and the Montana-Alberta Borderlands." Paper, conference of the Association of Pacific Coast Geographers, Flagstaff AZ, October 1998.

Peltzer, Duane A. "Ecological and Ecosystem Functions of Native Prairie and Tame Grasslands in the Northern Great Plains." *Prairie Forum* 25 (Spring 2000): 65–82.

Potyondi, Barry. *In Palliser's Triangle: Living in the Grasslands, 1850–1930.* Saskatoon: Purich, 1995.

Rozum, Molly. "Grassland Grown: A Twentieth-Century Sense of Place on North America's Northern Prairies and Plains." PhD diss., University of North Carolina, 2001.

Sauchin, David J., and Alwynne B. Beaudoin. "Recent Environmental Change in the Southeastern Canadian Plains." *Canadian Geographer* 42 (Winter 1998): 337–53.

Sharp, Paul F. "The Northern Great Plains: A Study in Canadian-American Regionalism." *Mississippi Valley Historical Review* 39 (June 1952): 61–76.

Shortridge, James R. "The Expectations of Others: Struggles toward a Sense of Place in the Northern Plains." In David M. Wrobel and Michael C. Steiner, eds., *Many Wests: Place, Culture, and Regional Identity,* 114–36. Lawrence: University Press of Kansas, 1997.

Spry, Irene M. *The Palliser Expedition: The Dramatic Story of Western Canadian Exploration, 1857–1860.* Toronto: Macmillan, 1963.

————, ed. *The Papers of the Palliser Expedition, 1857–1860.* Toronto: Champlain Society, 1968.

Stegner, Wallace. *Wolf Willow: A History, a Story, and a Memory of the Last Plains Frontier.* New York: Viking Books, 1955.

Strom, Claire. *Profiting from the Plains: The Great Northern Railway and Corporate Development of the American West.* Seattle: University of Washington Press, 2003.

Thompson, John Herd. *Forging the Prairie West.* Toronto: Oxford University Press Canada, 1998.

Turner, C. Frank. *Across the Medicine Line.* Toronto: McClelland and Stewart, 1973.

Wardhaugh, Robert, ed. *Toward Defining the Prairies: Region, Culture, and History.* Winnipeg: University of Manitoba Press, 2001.

On the Borderlands Region of the Pacific Northwest (Inland Empire and Cascadia)

Alper, Donald K. "The Idea of Cascadia: Emergent Transborder Regionalisms in the Pacific Northwest–Western Canada." *Journal of Borderlands Studies* 9 (1996): 1–22.

Ashbaugh, James G. *The Pacific Northwest: Geographical Perspectives.* Dubuque IA: Kendall/Hunt, 1997.

Bennett, John W., and Seena Kohl. *Settling the American and Canadian West, 1890–1915: Pioneer Adaptation and Community Building.* Lincoln: University of Nebraska Press, 1995.

Boag, Peter. "Mountain, Plain, Desert, River: The Snake River Region as a Western Crossroads." In Wrobel and eds., *Many Wests,* 177–204.

Brown, Richard Maxwell. "The Other Northwest: The Regional Identity of a Canadian Province." In Wrobel and Steiner, eds., *Many Wests,* 279–314.

Coates, Kenneth S. "A Matter of Context: The Pacific Northwest in World History." In Hirt, ed., *Terra Pacifica,* 109–33.

Edwards, Thomas, and Carlos A. Schwantes, eds. *Experiences in a Promised Land: Essays in Pacific Northwest History.* Seattle: University of Washington Press, 1986.

Etulain, Richard W. "Inventing the Pacific Northwest: Novelists and the Region's History." In Hirt, ed., *Terra Pacifica,* 25–52.

Ewart, Eric. "Setting the Pacific Northwest Stage: The Influence of the Natural Environment." In Goble and Hirt, eds., *Northwest Lands,* 1–26.

Findlay, John M. "A Fishy Proposition: Regional Identity in the Pacific Northwest." In Wrobel and Steiner, eds., *Many Wests,* 37–70.

Findlay, John M., and Ken S. Coates, eds. *Parallel Destinies: Canadian-American Relations West of the Rockies.* Seattle: University of Washington Press, 2002.

Forward, Charles N., and George A. Gerbold, eds. *Environment and Man in British Columbia and Washington: A Symposium on Canadian-American Relations.* Proceedings. Bellingham: Western Washington State College, 1974.

Friesen, Gerald. "From 54°40'to Free Trade: Relations between the American Northwest and Western Canada." In Hirt, ed., *Terra Pacifica,* 93–108.

Goble, Dale, and Paul W. Hirt, eds. *Northwest Lands, Northwest Peoples: Readings in Environmental History.* Seattle: University of Washington Press, 1999.

Harris, R. Cole. "British Columbia, Cascadia, and Canada." Paper, conference of the American Historical Association–Pacific Coast Branch, Vancouver BC, August 2001.

Hirt, Paul W., ed. *Terra Pacifica: People and Place in the Northwest States and Western Canada.* Pullman: Washington State University Press, 1998.

Jetté, Melinda Marie. "Misremembering a Joint Colonial Past: Canadian and American Narratives of the Oregon Country prior to 1846." Paper, conference of the Association for Canadian Studies in the United States (ACSUS), Portland OR, November 2003.

Loucky, James, Donald Alper, and J. C. Day, eds. *Transboundary Policy Changes in Pacific Border Regions of North America.* Calgary: University of Calgary Press, forthcoming.

McDonald, Norbert. *Distant Neighbors: A Comparative History of Seattle and Vancouver.* Lincoln: University of Nebraska Press, 1987.

Meinig, Donald W. *The Great Columbia Plain: A Historical Geography, 1805–1910.* Seattle: University of Washington Press, 1968.

Morrissey, Katherine. *Mental Territories: Mapping the Inland Empire.* Ithaca: Cornell University Press, 1997.

Mouat, Jeremy. "Nationalist Narratives and Regional Realities: The Political Economy of Railway Development in Southeastern BC, 1895–1905." In Findlay and Coates, eds., *Parallel Destinies,* 123–44.

Murphy, Thomas. "Seeking a True Flag of Freedom: African Americans and the San Juan Boundary Dispute, 1859–1872." Paper, ACSUS, Portland OR, November 2003.

Murray, Keith A. "The Role of the Hudson's Bay Company in Pacific Northwest History." *Pacific Northwest Quarterly* 52 (January 1961): 24–30.

Peel, Bruce. "The Columbia River Drainage Basin in Canada: A Bibliographical Essay." *Pacific Northwest Quarterly* 52 (October 1961): 152–54.

Perras, Galen Roger. " 'Who Will Defend British Columbia?' Unity of Command on the West Coast, 1934–1942." *Pacific Northwest Quarterly* 88 (Spring 1997): 59–69.

Pomeroy, Earl S. *The Pacific Slope: A History of California, Oregon, Washington, Idaho, Utah, and Nevada.* New York: Alfred A. Knopf, 1965.

Reimer, Chad. "Borders of the Past: The Oregon Boundary Dispute and the Beginnings of Northwest Historiography." In Findlay and Coates, eds., *Parallel Destinies*, 221–45.

Robbins, William G. "The Cultural in Natural Landscapes: North America and the Pacific Northwest." *Journal of the West* 38 (October 1999): 8–14.

———, ed. *The Great Northwest: The Search for Regional Identity.* Corvallis: Oregon State University Press, 2001.

Robbins, William G., Robert J. Frank, and Richard E. Ross, eds. *Regionalism and the Pacific Northwest.* Corvallis: Oregon State University Press, 1983.

Samek, Hana. *The Blackfoot Confederacy, 1880–1920: A Comparative Study of Canadian and U.S. Indian Policy.* Albuquerque: University of New Mexico Press, 1987.

Schwantes, Carlos A. *The Pacific Northwest: An Interpretive History.* Lincoln: University of Nebraska Press, 1989.

Sparke, Matthew. "Excavating the Future in Cascadia: Geoeconomics and the Imagined Geographies of a Cross-Border Region." *BC Studies* 127 (Autumn 2000): 5–44.

Stratton, David H., ed. *Spokane and the Inland Empire: An Interior Pacific Northwest Anthology.* Pullman: Washington State University Press, 1991.

White, Richard. *Land Use, Environment, and Social Change: The Making of Island County, Washington.* Seattle: University of Washington Press, 1980.

Wrobel, David M., and Michael C. Steiner, eds. *Many Wests: Place, Culture, and Regional Identity.* Lawrence: University Press of Kansas, 1997.

Yarmie, Andrew. "A Cross-Border Comparison of Washington State and British Columbia, 1890–1935." *Pacific Historical Review* 72 (November 2003): 561–615.

On Native Americans/First Nations in the Pacific Northwest Borderlands

Ames, Kenneth M., and Herbert G. Maschner. *Peoples of the Northwest Coast: Their Archaeology and Prehistory.* London: Thames and Hudson, 1999.

Barman, Jean. "What a Difference a Border Makes: Aboriginal Intermixing in the Pacific Northwest." *Journal of the West* 38 (July 1999): 14–20.

Boxberger, Daniel L. "A Tale of Two Rivers: Indigenous Rights across the Borders." Paper, conference of the Association for Canadian Studies in the United States (ACSUS), San Antonio TX, November 2001.

———. *To Fish in Common: The Ethnohistory of Lummi Indian Salmon Fishing.* Lincoln: University of Nebraska Press, 1989.

Cote, Charlotte. "Historical Foundations of Indian Sovereignty in Canada and the United States: A Brief Overview." *American Review of Canadian Studies* 31 (Spring/Summer 2001): 15–23.

Elmendorf, William E. *Twana Narratives: Native Historical Accounts of a Coast Salish Community*. Seattle: University of Washington Press, 1993.

Findlay, John M., and Ken S. Coates, eds. *Parallel Destinies: Canadian-American Relations West of the Rockies*. Seattle: University of Washington Press, 2002.

Franks, C. E. S. "Indian Policy in Canada and the United States Compared." In Curtis Cook and Juan D. Lindau, eds., *Aboriginal Rights and Self-Government*, 221–63. Montreal: McGill-Queen's University Press, 2000.

Harmon, Alexandra. *Indians in the Making: Ethnic Relations and Indian Identities around Puget Sound*. Berkeley: University of California Press, 1998.

Hirt, Paul W., ed. *Terra Pacifica: People and Place in the Northwest States and Western Canada*. Pullman: Washington State University Press, 1998.

Lutz, John. "Inventing an Indian War: Canadian Indians and American Settlers in the Pacific West, 1854–1864." *Journal of the West* 38 (July 1999): 7–13.

———. "Work, Sex, and Death on the Great Thoroughfare: Annual Migrations of 'Canadian Indians' to the American Pacific Northwest." In Findlay and Coates, eds., *Parallel Destinies*, 80–103.

Marshall, Daniel P. "No Parallel: American Miner-Soldiers at War with the Nlaka'pamux of the Canadian West." In Findlay and Coates, eds., *Parallel Destinies*, 31–79.

Miller, Bruce G. *The Problem of Justice: Tradition and Law in the Coast Salish World*. Lincoln: University of Nebraska Press, 2001.

———. "The 'Really Real' Border and the Divided Salish Community." BC *Studies* 112 (1996–97): 63–79.

Miller, Christopher. *Prophetic Worlds: Indians and Whites in the Columbian Plateau*. New Brunswick NJ: Rutgers University Press, 1985.

Nicholls, Roger L. *Indians in the United States and Canada: A Comparative History*. Lincoln: University of Nebraska Press, 1998.

Raibmon, Paige. "Authentic Indians: Episodes of Encounter from the Late-Nineteenth-Century Northwest Coast." PhD diss., Duke University, 2000.

———. "Indians, Land, and Identity in Washington (or, Why Cross-Border Shop)." BC *Studies* 124 (Winter 1999/2000): 93–100.

———. "Theaters of Contact: Cultural Interaction on the Northwest Coast and at the World's Columbian Exposition, Chicago, 1893." *Canadian Historical Review* 81 (June 2000): 157–90.

Samek, Hana. "Evaluating Canadian Indian Policy: A Case for Comparative Historical Perspective." *American Review of Canadian Studies* 16 (Autumn 1986): 389–406.

St. Germain, Jill. *Indian Treaty-Making in the United States and Canada, 1867–1877*. Lincoln: University of Nebraska Press, 2001.

Woodcock, George. *Peoples of the Coast: The Indians of the Pacific Northwest*. Bloomington: Indiana University Press, 1977.

Wunder, John R. "Pacific Northwest Indians and the Bill of Rights." In Hirt, ed., *Terra Pacifica*, 159–88.

On Post-9/11 Border and Security Issues

Andreas, Peter, and Thomas J. Biersteker. *The Rebordering of North America: Integration and Exclusion in a New Security Context*. New York: Routledge, 2003.

Barry, Donald. "Managing Canada–U.S. Relations in the Post 9/11 Era: Do We Need a Big Idea?" Policy Paper in the Americas, Center for Strategic and International Studies 14, Study 11, November 2003.

Bradbury, Susan, and Daniel E. Turbeville. "Enhanced Trade or Enhanced Security? Post–9/11 Policy Conflicts on the Canada–U.S. Border." Paper, conference of the Association for Canadian Studies in the United States (ACSUS), Portland OR, November 2003.

Clarkson, Stephen. *Lockstep in the Continental Ranks: Redrawing the American Perimeter after September 11th*. Ottawa: Canadian Centre for Political Alternatives, 2002.

Cody, Howard, et al. *Perspectives on U.S. –Canada Relations since 9/11: Four Essays*. Orono ME: Canadian-American Center, University of Maine, 2003.

Collacot, Martin. *Terrorism, Refugees, and Homeland Security*. Kingston ON: Kashton Press, 2002.

Condon, Bradly J., and Tapen Sinha. *Drawing Lines in Sand and Snow: Border Security and North American Economic Integration*. Armonk NY: M. E. Sharpe, 2003.

Drache, Daniel. *Border Matters: Homeland Security and the Search for North America*. Black Point, Nova Scotia: Fernwood, 2004.

Jones, Sharon. "U.S./Canada Border Issues Pre– and Post–September 11." Paper, ACSUS, San Antonio TX, November 2001.

Small, Peter, and Christian Cotroneo. " 'We Don't Welcome You Anymore': Foreign-Born Canadians Find Trouble at U.S. Border." *Toronto Star*, 7 November 2002, A3.

On the Alaska–Yukon–British Columbia Borderlands

Alaskan Boundary Tribunal. *The Counter Case of the United States*. Washington: Government Printing Office, 1903.

Bellfly, Phil. "Indigenous People at the Alaska/BC Border: The Metlakatla Experience." Paper, conference of the Association for Canadian Studies in the United States (ACSUS), San Antonio TX, November 2001.

Coates, Kenneth S., and William R. Morrison. "Native People and the Alaska Highway." In Chad Gaffield and Pam Gaffield, eds., *Consuming Canada: Readings in Environmental History* (Mississauga ON: Copp Clark, 1995), 316–39.

————, eds. *Interpreting Canada's North: Selected Readings*. Toronto: Copp, Clark, Pittman, 1989.

Conn, Stephen. "Policing in Bush Alaska and in the Canadian North: Two Approaches with Two Results." Paper, ACSUS, San Antonio TX, November 2001.

Green, Lewis. *The Boundary Hunters: Surveying the 141st Meridian and the Alaska Panhandle*. Vancouver: University of British Columbia Press, 1982.

Frykman, George A. "The Alaska-Yukon-Pacific Exposition, 1909." *Pacific Northwest Quarterly* 53 (July 1962): 89–99.

Irvine, Amy. "Wild at Heart: The Tatshenshini River, Alaska, British Columbia, and the Yukon." Chap. 3 of *Making a Difference: Stories of How Our Outdoor Industry and*

Individuals Are Working to Preserve America's Natural Places. Guilford CT: Globe Pequot Press, 2001.

Lundberg, Murray. "The Alaska-Canada Boundary Dispute." *www.explorenorth.com/ library/weekly/aa103000a.htm*.

Madden, Ryan. "The Alaska Boundary Dispute: Changing Historical Interpretations over Time." *University of Vermont History Review* 1 (Spring 1987): 60–64.

Manning, Richard. *Inside Passage: A Journey beyond Borders*. Washington DC: Island Press, 2001.

McPhee, John. *Coming into the Country*. New York: Farrar, Straus and Giroux, 1976.

Mighetto, Lisa, and Marcia Montgomery. *Hard Drive to the Klondike: Promoting Seattle during the Gold Rush*. Seattle: University of Washington Press, 2002.

Morrison, William R. *True North: The Yukon and Northwest Territories*. Toronto: Oxford University Press Canada, 1998.

Pederson, Fran. "The Alaska-Canada Boundary." www.gi.alaska.edu/ScienceForum/ASF1/ 193.html.

Penlington, Norman. *The Alaska Boundary Dispute: A Critical Reappraisal*. Toronto: McGraw-Hill Ryerson, 1972.

Porsild, Charlene. *Gamblers and Dreamers: Women, Men, and Community in the Klondike*. Vancouver: University of British Columbia Press, 1999.

Pretes, Michael. "Northern Frontiers: Political Development and Policy-Making in Alaska and the Yukon." In Robert Lecker, ed., *Borderlands: Essays in Canadian-American Relations* (Toronto: ECW Press, 1991), 309–28.

Ratzlaff, Wayne A. "From Storekeeper to Prospector: The Experiences of a Klondike Gold Rush Party from Emporia, Kansas." *Journal of the West* 38 (October 1999): 75–82.

Ricketts, Bruce. "The BC–Alaska Boundary Dispute." *www.mysteriesofcanada.com/BC/bc alaska boundary dispute.htm*.

Riggs, Thomas. "Running the Alaska Boundary." *Beaver* 25 (September 1945): 40–43.

Rychetnik, Joseph S. "Law and Order Comes to the 49th State." *Journal of the West* 38 (January 1999): 77–84.

Shape, William. *Faith of Fools: A Journal of the Klondike Gold Rush*. Pullman: Washington State University Press, 1998.

Webb, Melody. *The Last Frontier: A History of the Yukon Basin of Canada and Alaska*. Albuquerque: University of New Mexico Press, 1985.

Yukon Historical and Museums Association. *Borderlands: The Conference on the Alaska-Yukon Border*. Proceedings. Whitehorse YT: Yukon Historical and Museum Association, 1989.

1. The Case for Cross-National and Comparative History

The Northwestern Plains as Bioregion

Theodore Binnema

In order to make their research projects manageable and their analysis and interpretation coherent, historians necessarily set boundaries around their studies. Most historical studies include temporal boundaries. Historians of aboriginal peoples often organize their studies around tribes. For example, there are fine histories written of the Crees, Blackfoot, Crows, Ojibwas, and so on. Historians also use political boundaries to limit the scope of their studies. Often they anachronistically project current political boundaries back in time. For example, almost every general history of Canada, the United States, Montana, or Alberta surveys the history of a place that was Canada, the United States, Montana, or Alberta when the author wrote the book, even though these boundaries were meaningless at earlier times.

Reflective scholars define their topics carefully because they understand that merely by defining their studies they can open themselves to insights that others have overlooked. Examples can be found in the many innovative historical studies whose contributions lie, in part, in the fact that they challenge widely accepted periodizations. On the other hand every organizing scheme will blind researchers to important evidence. I have argued elsewhere that by organizing so many of their studies around particular ethnic groups, historians of aboriginal peoples have downplayed vital interethnic links and important intraethnic dynamics in history.[1] Studies organized around tribes or ethnic groups are legitimate, but the organizing scheme creates certain images of aboriginal people that are misleading. Such studies subtly imply that these tribal or ethnic identities were unchanging or that tribes or ethnic groups were the inevitable product of historical forces. They suggest that aboriginal people two hundred or five hundred years ago identified themselves primarily as members of a certain tribe when that may not have been the case. Similarly, historical studies bounded by present-day political considerations subtly imply that these political entities are either timeless or the result of historical inevitability. Students might easily forget (especially given many textbook maps) that in 1800, Alberta and Montana had not been named, and the western borders of the political entities known as "Canada" and the "United States" were a very long ways away from present-day Alberta and Montana. The forty-ninth parallel may have become the border between the British Possessions (not Canada) and the United States in 1818, but in many places that border was irrelevant for many years thereafter. In sum, any organizing scheme tends to create blind spots, but whenever an organizing scheme dominates the historiography in a field, those blind spots become troublesome. The purpose of the following study is to explore the potential of environmentally defined studies, particularly in aboriginal and environmental history. It will do so by focusing on the northwestern plains, a bioregion that is bisected by an international boundary today. I will argue that by embracing historical studies based on bioregional foundations, particularly when these bioregions now span international boundaries, we increase the likelihood that we will understand the past in fresh ways.

Relatively rare, certainly among histories of aboriginal peoples and even among environmental histories, are studies that are organized around biological or ecological regions. In a cogent defense of such studies, University of Montana historian Dan Flores advocated the drawing of boundaries "in ways that make real sense ecologically and topographically." [2] Flores credited a Canadian, Allan Van Newkirk, with coining the word *bioregion*. A convincing case can be made that the forty-ninth parallel today bisects a major bioregion within the Great Plains: the northwestern plains. But in this case, and in many cases, organizing research around bioregions can only be done *in defiance* of international, state or provincial, county, or municipal boundaries. It often requires historians to defy the trail left by the documentary record. In other words, writing bioregional histories presents particular challenges because it complicates one of the central reasons we set limits on our studies: making the research project manageable. The obstacles present themselves immediately. Our first task is to identify and find suitable bioregions. Once we have done that we are almost certain to find that the number of documents we need to consult and the number of archives we need to visit will proliferate. Moreover, when we research the history of bioregions bisected by the Canada–United States border, we also confront the very different historiographical traditions of the two countries. The rewards, however, are very real. If we believe that the environment influences human history in very real ways, and if we organize our studies bioregionally, we are almost certain to read the documentary evidence in ways that others who read the same documents cannot.

In the eastern half of North America, natural environments seem generally to be aligned east-west. This meant that migrants from Virginia and North Carolina typically settled in Kentucky, Tennessee, and Missouri, while New England migrants more typically homesteaded in Michigan, Ontario, and Wisconsin, where they found environments that they could comprehend. Farther north, the Canadian Shield (also called the Pre-Cambrian or Laurentian Shield) made agricultural settlement impossible in all but a few places. In the western half of North America, however, environments seem to be oriented north-south. The high plains of western Alberta, eastern Colorado, and New Mexico present similar opportunities and challenges to ranchers. The northwestern plains of North America (figure 3) form a generally north-south environmental province of the Great Plains. The unique features of the topography, vegetation, and climate have shaped the unique human history of the region in many ways. The northwestern plains are not flat but undulating. In fact, in the shadow of the Rocky Mountains, they are dotted with rough and broken country. Most of the rivers of the northwestern plains find their sources in the glaciers and permanent snows of the imposing Rockies that divide the eastward flowing rivers from the Great Basin and the Pacific slope. While the Rocky Mountains unmistakably separate the northwestern plains from very different environments, another low divide runs across the region very near the forty-ninth parallel. Rivers to the north of this divide flow into the Saskatchewan River system on their way to the Hudson Bay; those to the south flow into the Missouri River, which drains eventually into the Gulf of Mexico. Highlands along this divide include the Milk River Ridge and the Cypress Hills, but in many places the divide is imperceptible. Many people today pass over it without ever noticing it. This divide is not a significant environmental border, although it has been significant in human history.

The Rocky Mountains both withhold and give the northwestern plains their meager water supplies. The mountains' rain shadow effect is responsible for the semiarid climate of much of the region, but the mountain snows also feed the many creeks and rivers that course through the high plains. As the glaciers receded after the last ice age, the torrents of meltwater carved deep and wide valleys through these plains. Today many of the larger rivers and their major tributaries still occupy these valleys. In a dry, windy, and exposed country prone to rapid weather changes, the deep sheltering valleys, cold clear waters, large stands of cottonwood (*Populus deltoids*), and luxuriant grasses once provided humans and animals with food, water, thermal cover, and protection from predators and enemies. In fact, such valley locations were so critical for the survival of aboriginal communities that, although (or rather because) the plains were vast and these sheltered areas small, and although (or perhaps because) aboriginal groups were present at these places only periodically, controlling a relatively few of these virtual oases was the linchpin to military control of the vast plains that surrounded them.

Along with the valleys, various highlands also figured prominently in the region's history. Most noteworthy among them are the Hand Hills, Cypress Hills, Sweetgrass Hills, Bearspaw Mountains, Highwood Mountains, Big Belt Mountains, Little Belt Mountains, Judith Mountains, and Snowy Mountains. They rise from a few hundred to a few thousand feet above the surrounding plains. Even the smaller hills are tall enough to cause orographic precipitation, particularly in May and June when cool, moist northeasterly winds are common. For example, in most years the Cypress Hills receive two or three more inches of precipitation during the growing season than do the surrounding plains. These highlands are often snow clad, even in September and May, while the surrounding plains are snow-free most of the winter. Cooler and wetter than the plains, they support lush vegetation. Even very low hills, like the Milk River

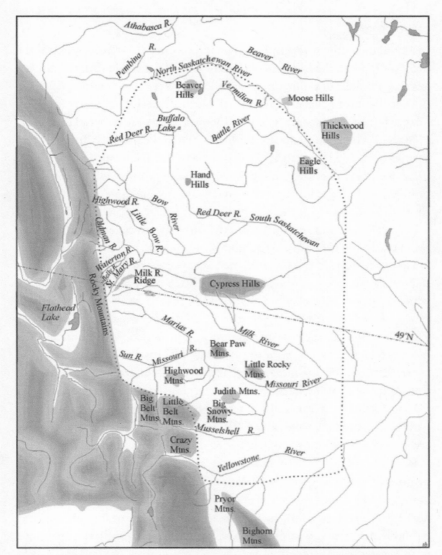

Figure 3. The northwestern plains of North America. Map by Ted Binnema.

Ridge, are often snow covered in winter. In July and August any observant traveler will be struck by the contrast between the dry, short, and sparse grasses, only a few inches tall, on the plains surrounding the highlands, and the verdant waist-high grasses, shoulder-high reeds, and substantial forests of lodgepole pines (*Pinus contorta*), jack pine (*Pinus banksiana*), white spruce (*Picea glauca*), and Douglas fir (*Pseudotsuga menziesii*) on the highlands only a few miles away. The springheads and creeks in the highlands and in the foothills of the Rockies also provide surface water to grazing animals and humans in an otherwise waterless landscape. (Bison do not live up to their reputation as North American camels. They are adapted to cold environments, not dry ones. Bison are tethered to sources of water.) The rough country with its sheltered areas, catchments, and springs provided excellent conditions for large grazing animals, including bison for many centuries, and they continue to do so today, although the bison's less hardy successors are much more vulnerable to the region's capricious climate.

The climate and vegetation of the northwestern plains are very much products of the geography. The northern mixed prairie, one of the main grassland regions of the Great Plains, dominates the northwestern plains (figures 4 and 5). In contrast to the short grass prairie farther south, which consists overwhelmingly of warm-season grasses, the northern mixed prairie consists of a mixture of cool- and warm-season species. There are two subregions, the xeric (or dry) mixed grasslands and the more productive mesic (or moist) mixed grasslands. In three directions the northern mixed prairie merges with the relatively luxuriant fescue prairie. The boundaries of these regions and subregions are related to topography but determined primarily by the ratio of precipitation to evaporation. Although ecologists have drawn discrete boundaries for each vegetative region, they recognize that each blends imperceptibly into the next as climatic and topographic conditions vary and change. Moreover, highlands or north facing slopes in the xeric mixed prairie region are likely to be dominated by grasses more typical of the mesic mixed prairie or the fescue grasslands, while a south facing slope in the fescue prairie region may resemble the xeric mixed prairie. The border between the two subregions is all the more imperceptible because all the grasses of the xeric mixed prairie are also found in the mesic mixed prairie, but tend to grow taller as the moister and cooler conditions allow. None of these grasslands is as productive as the tallgrass prairies of the eastern plains, but for various reasons the region may have sustained the densest bison populations on the plains.

The growing season begins as early as late March or early April in the region south of the Cypress Hills. In May and June growth peaked

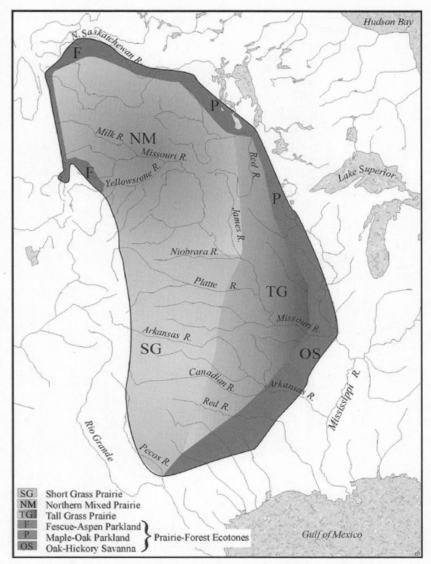

Figure 4. Climate patterns of the northwestern plains. Map by Ted Binnema.

and then declined as the soils dried and the summer temperatures rose. Thanks to the influence of climate and elevation, this is an earlier start to the growing season than is found farther north, east, or west. This early growth meant that the critical period of late winter and early spring when bison and other grazing animals were under the greatest stress ended

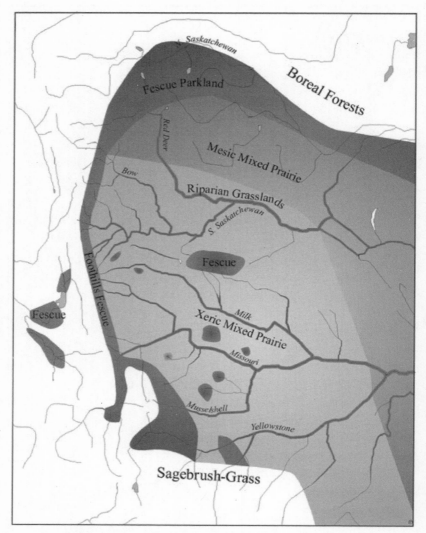

Figure 5. Grassland regions of the northwestern plains. Map by Ted Binnema.

earlier here than it did elsewhere on the northern plains. The grasses were sparse, but the tender new shoots were highly nutritious.

Many of the grasses in the xeric mixed prairie in this region are cool-season grasses, like the aptly named needle-and-thread (*Stipa comata*), which stops growing by early July. The dominant species, however, is the drought resistant, warm-season grass, blue grama (*Bouteloua gracilis*).

Blue grama and buffalo grass (*Buchloë dactyloides*) sprout about a month after the other grasses and in some areas may continue growing until mid-August. The xeric mixed prairies are not very productive, and warm-season grasses are generally less nutritious than cool-season grasses, but the cool-season grasses of the northern mixed prairie sprout early in spring, and the warm-season grasses recover well from the heavy grazing they experience in late spring and summer. Furthermore, blue grama grass—many plains dwellers will know this as the whimsical "eyebrow grass"—is an exceptionally nutritious warm-season grass that is known to be a particular favorite of bison.

The mesic subregion of the northern mixed prairie lies generally to the north of the xeric subregion. The two associations are classified as variations of one region because virtually all species found in the xeric prairie will also be found in the mesic prairie. (For example, the warm-season blue grama grass, Colorado's state grass, will be found growing on south-facing banks of the North Saskatchewan River in Saskatchewan, although its size will not impress visitors from Arizona or Colorado, while needle-and-thread, Saskatchewan's provincial grass, will also be found in the driest and warmest parts of the northwestern plains.) Still, there are important differences between the subregions. The dominant grasses in the mesic subregion are various heavier-yielding cool-season mid-grasses, including western porcupine grass (*Stipa curtiseta*), western wheatgrass (*Agropyron smithii*), needle-and-thread, and the very early June grass (*Koeleria cristata*). Although the cool-season grasses in the mesic prairie sprout at least a week later in the spring than they do on the xeric prairie, they grow and stay green longer in the summer because the region is cooler and wetter. As a result, the mesic grassland is substantially more productive than the dry subregion. Moreover, because the dominant species in the mesic prairie are early-growing cool-season grasses, its carrying capacity on average is already double that of the xeric prairie by the end of April.

The fescue prairies were the most productive grasslands on the north-western plains and the ones upon which bison herds were most reliant during the winter. These grasslands, which are dominated by foothills rough fescue (*Festuca campestris*) or its smaller cousin, plains rough fescue (*F. hallii*), thrive on the cooler summer temperatures (thus lower evaporation) and greater rainfall than the northern mixed prairie experiences. The fescue grasslands can be found in a nearly continuous arc in association with groves of aspen (*Populus tremuloides*) in the parkland belt along the northern rim of the plains west of the forks of the Saskatchewan Rivers, and as a narrow band of submontane vegetation along the foothills of the Rocky Mountains along the western margins of the plains, and along and between the Big Belt and Snowy Mountains of present-day Montana. Foothills rough fescue also penetrates the mountains in major valleys such as the Bow River valley, the Crowsnest River valley, the Waterton River valley, and the Missouri River valley where it occasionally occurs near subalpine meadows. Finally, fescue grasslands are scattered throughout the northwestern plains on highland areas, benchlands, and north-facing slopes in the mixed-grass prairie. The Milk River Ridge, Sweetgrass Hills, Cypress Hills, and Bearspaw Mountains are covered with rough fescue in almost pure stands that are nearly as productive as the northern parkland. In 1881 Duncan McNab McEachran, a visitor from eastern Canada, described the pasturage on the foothills near the Bow River valley not far from Calgary:

> There is an abundance of pine and cottonwood . . . besides numerous thickets of alder and willow . . . which afford excellent shelter for stock in winter. The grasses are most luxuriant, especially what is known as "bunch grass" [foothills rough fescue], and wild vetch or peavine [*Vicia americana* and *Lathyrus venosus*], and on the lower levels, in damper soil, the blue joint grass, which resembles the English rye grass, but grows stronger and higher [probably reed grasses, *Calamagrostis* spp.]. On some of the upland meadows wild Timothy [perhaps alpine timothy, *Phleum alpinum*] is also found. These grasses grow in many places from one to two feet high and cover the ground like a thick mat. Nowhere else has the writer seen such abundance of feed for cattle.[3]

While exploring the Oldman River valley on the southern extremes of the Porcupine Hills, McEachran wrote that "there is an inexhaustible growth of rich nutritious grass. In some places it is so thick and so long as to impede the progress of the horses."[4] He visited after the buffalo were extirpated from these lands and before cattle replaced them, so what he saw may not represent the typical state of the grasslands, but the descriptions do suggest that the foothills grasses were remarkably productive and nutritious. George M. Dawson of the Canadian Geological Survey echoed this opinion. Dawson wrote of the Porcupine Hills that "within the Porcupines and their northward and southward extensions some of the best cattle ranching country of the entire North-west is situated."[5] Other early observers wrote as enthusiastically about some of the other highlands. Captain John Palliser, when visiting the Cypress Hills during the dry late 1850s, described the Cypress Hills as "a perfect oasis in the desert" marked by an "abundance of water and pasture."[6] When John Macoun visited the Cypress Hills in the much wetter early 1880s, he noted that "no better summer pasture is to be found in all the wide North-west than exists on these hills, as the grass is always green, water of the best quality is always abundant, and shelter from the autumnal and winter storms always at hand."[7] Captain W. J. Twining, chief astronomer and surveyor for the United States during the boundary survey of the 1870s, wrote of the Sweetgrass Hills region that "these three Buttes are the center of the feeding ground of the great northern herd of buffaloes. The herd, which ranges from the Missouri River north to the Saskatchewan, made its appearance, going south, about the last of August. The number of animals is beyond all estimation." George Dawson noted that the hills were marked by copious springs that supported wooded valleys and grassy foothills. Even much smaller hills, like the Hand Hills, supported richer vegetation than the surrounding plains. According to John Palliser, "The plain all around the base of the [Hand] hills is bare and arid, but the high level of the hill bears a fair and almost rich pasture, being 680 feet higher than the plain; it also contains lakes of pure fresh water, and gullies with a small growth of poplar."[8]

Like the foothills and uplands, the wide valley bottoms and depressions were important to bison during the winter, and like the fescue grasslands, the valleys and depressions supported abundant grasses, particularly where influenced by the activities of beavers. Valleys usually supported healthy stands of western wheatgrass, the most productive species on the northern mixed prairie (and today the state grass of Wyoming and North Dakota). As a result, the valley flats were about as productive as the fescue prairie. Meriwether Lewis at the Great Falls of the Missouri noted in his journals that "the grass and weeds in this bottom are about 2 feet high; which is much greater hight [*sic*] than we have seen them elsewhere this season. . . . the grass in the plains is not much more than 3 inches high."[9] Sedges (*Carex atherodes*), a favorite food of bison, also grew in moist depressions and swamps.

The fescue grasslands, like other tall grasses along the margins of the plains, begin growing as much as a month later than the mixed prairies, making them poor forage during the critical period in early spring when bison are weak. Rough fescue, like other grasses of the aspen parklands, responds poorly to heavy grazing during the growing season. In the south and on the highlands like the Cypress Hills, however, the fescue grasslands are more species-rich than in the north, and the additional species found in the foothills region render that area more resistant to overgrazing than fescue grasslands to the north. Equally important, however, is the fact that on the northwestern plains, especially in the foothills region, the fescue grasslands, xeric mixed prairie, and mesic mixed prairie are often very near one another physically, thus requiring bison herds to move only a short distance between them. The early growth of adjacent grasslands and the later growth of the fescue grasslands induced major concentrations of buffalo to move onto the mesic mixed prairie in spring, allowing the fescue to complete most of its growth cycle relatively undisturbed by grazing. Fescue grows robustly in June and July, and it is markedly more productive than other grasses on the northwestern plains, producing two· or three times as much forage per acre as the xeric, and almost twice as much as the mesic mixed prairie. Thus the carrying capacity of land for large ungulates on the northwestern plains generally increases toward the north as the climate becomes cooler and wetter but also increases toward the west and southwest as elevation increases. The various highlands of the northwestern plains, more common in the west than the east, also support more luxuriant prairies because of the wetter, cooler weather (thus lower evapotranspiration). Slope breaks in upland regions, marked by freshwater springs, made surface water available to flora and fauna. Finally, rough topography and the river valleys, relatively deeper and wider than valleys to the east, provided areas of luxuriant grass growth and areas of shelter from winter storms for both bison and humans.

Because of the topography, various early growing and late maturing grass species were found in close proximity. Bison that depended on the abundant grasses of the fescue prairies all winter often had to move only a short distance to graze on the early spring growth of June grass or wheatgrass. Bison on the flatter eastern plains did not have this advantage. Other characteristics of the western grasses also sustained buffalo. It is a general rule that taller grasses consist of a higher proportion of cell wall and thus are less nutritious than shorter grasses, but this would probably not have been a major limiting factor for bison, which digest poor quality forage well. It might better explain why other ungulates like pronghorn antelopes (*Antilocapra americana*), which required higher quality forage, were most common on the western plains. More important was the relative tendency of various grasses to cure in the summer or fall. Curing is a process in which grasses retain high levels of digestible carbohydrates and a portion of their crude protein after their growth period ends. Although the grasses of the tallgrass prairie grow abundantly, few of their species cure on the stem. Their nutrition drops rapidly after the first fall frosts bring the growing season to an end. In contrast, many grasses of the northern mixed grass and fescue prairies cure well and remain erect, retaining much more of their carbohydrates and protein than eastern grasses even until the grasses resume growing in the spring. Unique characteristics of fescue grasses make them particularly good dormant season forage. Fescue grasses retain high crude protein levels exceptionally well, contain a very low percentage of lignin (a structural substance related to cellulose), and have a very low degree of cross-linking in the lignin-cellulose complex that forms the cell walls. Early ranchers had no scientific explanations, but they were quick to notice the superior quality of fescue grasses during the dormant season. McEachran noted that "these grasses do not wither and die as they do in a more humid climate . . . they cure on their roots and make excellent hay. They thus preserve all their nutritious qualities, and make excellent feed for winter, a fact which is proved by the fat condition of all stock wintered in that country." [10] Thus, although the northwestern grasslands may not have been as productive as those of the northeastern plains, the grasses were more nutritious during the critical period of the year when the quality of forage would be at its nadir. Given the significance of plains rough fescue in the history of the northwestern plains, it is very appropriate that in 2003 the Alberta legislature designated this grass, now retreating in the face of introduced grasses, as the provincial grass of Alberta.

Not only did the northwestern plains, especially the fescue prairie regions, provide more abundant forage than most neighboring areas on the Great Plains, and not only did the quality of its forage in winter and early spring exceed that of other neighboring areas, but average climatic conditions on the northwestern plains also were more likely to sustain buffalo populations during the winters.

The Rocky Mountains generally block the flow of mild Pacific air, and the northern plains have a continental climate, with long cold winters and short warm summers. The Rocky Mountains produce a rain shadow to their east, with precipitation, both in the form of rain and snow, being lighter on the northwestern plains than on the northeastern plains. Still, Pacific air moderates temperatures in the west more than it does in the east. More important, although the Rocky Mountains block the flow of moist Pacific air, they also engender foehn winds known along the eastern slopes of the Rocky Mountains as chinooks. Chinook winds occur when a low pressure system over the plains draws mild, moist Pacific air over the Rocky Mountains. As the air rises over the mountains, water vapor and water droplets condense, releasing heat (heat of condensation). Then, as the air sweeps down the eastern side of the mountains, the air is compressed by adiabatic compression, sometimes producing higher air temperatures east of the Rocky Mountains than west. These warm, dry winds affect regions closest to the mountains most, and because grasslands adjoin the Rockies from the Bow River south into the Missouri basin, chinooks are most important in this area. In many of these areas chinook winds are so strong and frequent that they have been more important than water in shaping the landscape. One study, for example, shows how the alignment of coulees in southwestern Alberta is related to the direction of the prevailing chinooks. [11] The warm, dry chinook winds from the southwest generally keep the southwestern part of the region (the chinook belt) free of snow and quite warm for much of the winter (figure 6). In fact, on average the present-day city of Lethbridge, Alberta, has temperatures above 5° C (40° F) on thirty-five days during the coldest three months of the year (December, January, and February), while

Winnipeg, at nearly the same latitude, averages fewer than two such days. On his first visit with the Peigan Indians in the winter of 1787–88, David Thompson recorded, "Our guide also told us that as we approached these [Rocky] mountains of snow we should find the weather become milder. This we could not believe, but it was so and the month of November was fully as mild as the month of October at the trading house we left to the eastward. For the cold of these countries decreases as much by going westward as by going south." [12] A passage in the journals of Alexander Henry the Younger illustrates the effects of a typical chinook. On the morning of January 19, 1811, at Rocky Mountain House (in present-day Alberta), the temperature was 17° F, the wind was out of the northwest, and two feet of snow covered the ground. Then Henry heard a noise "towards the Southward as if a strong gale of wind was passing. . . . Upon meeting with the face it was warm and gentle, but very soon increased to a [?] gale. . . . at 1 Oclock the Thermometer stood at 56 above Zero, having rose 16 degrees in the course of ¾ of an hour. . . . the wind increased in a most violent manner which continued during the night . . . and to our great surprise we found the snow all melted away, and nothing but a few ponds of water remaining. Not one speck was to be seen in the plains, nor anywhere were [*sic*] the wind could reach it." [13]

The result of chinooks is that in most years the forage is easily accessible to grazing animals most of the year. The drying winds help to cure the grasses, ensuring that the nutritive value of plants in this region remains higher than in moister regions of the prairie. The survival of contemporary feral horse herds over the long term in both the foothills of the Rocky Mountains and on the Suffield Military Experimental Range in southeastern Alberta is attributable to these factors. Bison, which are better adapted to the harsh climate and limited forage of the region than horses, were better able to maintain their numbers than horse herds were.

North of the Bow River, a wedge of forest separates the grasslands from the mountains. Therefore the chinook winds affect the northern prairie less than the southern grasslands. In the North Saskatchewan River basin, snow cover, although not usually deep, is more or less constant from November to March. Above-freezing temperatures are considerably less frequent than they are in the south. Still, compared with the Red River region of the eastern prairies, which is farther south and lower

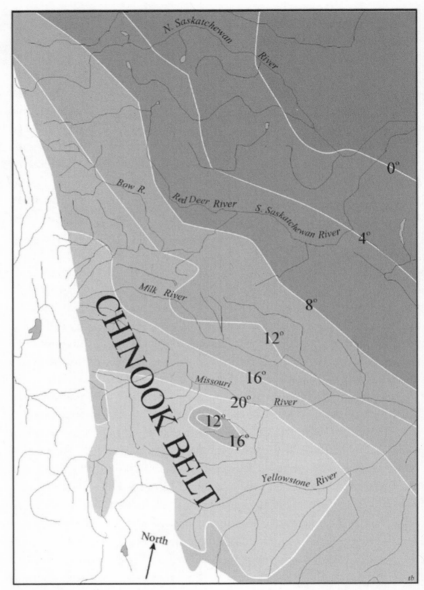

Figure 6. The chinook belt of the northwestern plains. Map by Ted Binnema.

in elevation, the North Saskatchewan basin has higher average winter temperatures and no greater average depth of snow cover. The parkland region, characterized by plains rough fescue and by many wet meadows of luxuriant sedges, is more extensive in the extreme northwestern plains than it is anywhere else. Even there, bison were likely to find plentiful forage during the winter.

And so the northwestern plains' unique combination of topography, geography, climate, and vegetation makes it a bioregion. The bioregion has changed substantially over the years. The bison were almost completely extirpated, and none are now free-roaming; the grizzly bears and wolves have been driven to mountain refugia. Exotic species have moved in. Each year, aggressive introduced plants supplant more of the rough fescue and other native grasses.[14] Over the years the significance of the forty-ninth parallel has grown and waned. The histories of southern Alberta, southern Saskatchewan, and western Montana are different in some very important ways. It is appropriate that historians have studied the history of the Canadian prairies, the U.S. West, Alberta, and Montana. Using political boundaries to define our studies not only makes projects feasible by limiting the number of archives we have to visit and files we have to consult. It also opens us up to insights about certain places. Still we ought to consider at what expense we write a history of the "Canadian prairies" or "American West" during a time when the forty-ninth parallel had little or no meaning, or even during a subsequent time, since the international boundary between Canada and the United States remains very porous. The environment shaped the human history of the northwestern plains before the era of reserves, reservations, borders, and cities, and it continues to shape life on either side of that line. In both cases, where the histories of Montana and Alberta have diverged, and where they have been similar, comparative and cross-national approaches offer great promise.

Given the environmental unity of the northwestern plains, and given the long-standing permeability of the boundary that has bisected the region, cross-national studies will hold tremendous promise. Cross-national studies straddle international boundaries because they assume that there are forces that have given a binational region a certain unity. I have argued that environmental forces have done so. Paul F. Sharp's *Whoop-Up Country* (1955) explores the whiskey trade of the late 1860s and 1870s, when the international border grew in importance. The international dimensions of that trade were not incidental but central to the story, as traders used the international boundary to evade law-enforcement authorities. Hugh Dempsey has recently published a detailed reexamination of this trade.[15]

Since the histories of both the environment and aboriginal people long antedated the boundary, they are particularly relevant topics for cross-national study. Various aboriginal communities are divided by the international boundary or have moved from one side of the forty-ninth parallel before or after it became an international boundary. Among these are the Blackfeet (known as Blackfoot in Canada). John C. Ewers's book *The Blackfeet: Raiders on the Northwestern Plains* (1958) remains the finest history of the Blackfeet.[16] It surveys the history of communities that now live on reserves and reservations in both Canada and the United States. Curiously, some groups with very interesting histories on either side of the forty-ninth parallel seem to have been ignored as a result. The Gros Ventre are an example. They live on a reservation in Montana, but they lived north of the forty-ninth parallel during most of their history. We do not have a good study focused on the Gros Ventre before they came to the United States.[17] Sitting Bull, who fled to Canada after the Battle of the Little Bighorn, has attracted considerable attention from scholarly and popular historians.[18] Those Crees who fled to Montana after the North-West Rebellion are not as well known, but they are a fascinating study. Some who were forced to return to Canada are now known as the Montana Cree band near Hobbema. Others eventually got a reservation in northern Montana. Because the history of these people has been at the center of claims and litigation on both sides of the border, this history was explored early.[19] More recently, this history has been explored from many perspectives. Larry Burt's article was published in 1987 by the *Great Plains Quarterly*, which, thanks to the influence of longtime editor Frances W. Kaye, has been the most important publisher of comparative and cross-national articles on plains topics. Today the best introduction to the Crees in the borderlands is through the work of Michel Hogue (see chapter 9), completed at the University of Calgary, whose history department has moved to the forefront in promoting comparative research in the history of the Canadian-American West.[20]

While cross-national histories underscore the international dimensions of historical developments, comparative histories are geared toward an exploration of the similarities and differences of historical developments in two countries. Naturally, comparative history holds the greatest promise when historians can compare metaphoric apples with metamorphic apples. This would suggest that historians would rush to compare Canadian and U.S. history, but that has not happened. There are surprisingly few comparative environmental or aboriginal histories of the northwestern plains. For example, John C. Ewers's *The Blackfeet* is not a comparative history. It makes little attempt to compare the experience of Blackfeet in Canada and the United States. Indeed, impressive as the book is, it is not particularly international. Although Ewers spoke with some elders in Canada, most of his informants and all of his archival sources were in the United States.

A few very promising comparative histories have appeared in the field of aboriginal history. Their rarity, however, is surprising because the potential value of such comparisons seems so obvious that they hardly need defense. Furthermore, one might think that the long-standing belief, in both Canada and the United States, that Canadian Indian policy has been much more benevolent than U.S. policy might have encouraged comparative study. (Canadian historians now reject this image of Canadian policy.) However, there are remarkably few comparative studies. Some of the better studies have dealt with the northwestern plains. Hana Samek's comparison of the effects of Indian policy among the Blackfeet in Canada and the United States is an interesting study with some intriguing conclusions. Jill St. Germain's *Indian Treaty-Making Policy in the United States and Canada, 1867–1877* also contributes to a field of study that has tremendous potential to improve our understanding of the history of Indian policy in both countries.[21] Comparative historians should avoid the temptation to find out which country had the better Indian policy, or the most positive relationship with its aboriginal population, but should instead seek to understand the reasons for the similarities and differences in aboriginal history, and aboriginal-nonaboriginal relations, and Indian policies in the two countries.[22] Given the immaturity of the field and the different historiographical traditions in Canada and the United States, it is probably not surprising that the most successful comparative studies have been those in which scholars have tried to immerse themselves in the primary evidence relating to narrowly defined topics. [23] Still, it is truly remarkable, given the number of unresolved issues in aboriginal-state relations in Canada and the United States, that scholars and policy makers in each country seem to be so ill-informed about the history in the other. Given the degree to which Indian policy in each country was evidently influenced by Indian policy in the other and by international trends, some familiarity with Indian policy in one country seems essential for a proper understanding of policy in the other. Yet Indian policy history in both countries is often written as if it were unique.

While comparative historians attempt to compare aspects of the history of two countries, borderland histories are those studies which examine the historical significance of international borders upon the people who have lived near such borders. [24] The residents of the northwestern plains have had changing, varying, and ambivalent relationships with the border. Aboriginal communities have been divided by the line, but aboriginal people have also used the border to their advantage. Many nonaboriginal people and communities are divided by the border today, and many continue to use the border to their advantage. The permeability of the border is enhanced by the remarkable similarities of people on either side of the border. Little about the appearance or behavior of a Lethbridgian in Great Falls will give him away as a foreigner—at least until he finishes his first sentence, eh? Economic, social, religious, cultural, and recreational activities link people on either side of the border, and the frequency and ease by which these activities are conducted ensure that families continue to straddle the border. [25] While borderlands histories are few, we are blessed with some very fine studies. Wallace Stegner's beautiful and evocative *Wolf Willow* (1955) is a classic, not only in northwestern plains writing but in North American writing more generally. His story is based on his memories of life in the area of southwestern Saskatchewan and northern Montana near his family's homestead, which literally ended at the Saskatchewan-Montana border. In *The Medicine Line* (2002), Beth LaDow has recently explored the same area in a similar combination of story and history. And Sheila McManus's recent book and other publications are also worthy of note (see chapter 7). [26]

Cross-national, comparative, and borderlands historians will face

significant obstacles. One of those obstacles will be the different historiographical traditions in Canada and the United States. During the last
twenty years, the field of western United States history has been revital-
ized, but western Canadian historiography has been largely unaffected
by this surge of interest. The standard textbook in western Canadian
history is now fifteen years old. Nor do western historians in Canada
and the United States perceive their Wests similarly. Over a hundred
years have passed since Frederick Jackson Turner advanced his "frontier
thesis." [27] For many decades, his thesis dominated interpretations of the
American West and inspired many comparative studies, including studies
of Canada, although the frontier thesis never influenced the historiography on western Canada the way it did the scholarship in the United
States. [28] Today historians of the western United States can still get hot
under the collar about the significance of the frontier in U.S. history. Most
Canadian historians watch this debate with a mixture of amusement and
amazement. If there is one question upon which we do not need more
comparative study, it is the question of the usefulness of the frontier
thesis for understanding the past. It seems as though the underlying and
lingering assumptions that United States history generally, and the history
of the western United States in particular, is exceptional do not encourage
comparisons with western Canada. The myth of United States exceptionalism is no longer quaint. As James Belich has argued, "Most neo-Britains
have the same list of 'unique' national characteristics: egalitarianism,
pragmatism, anti-intellectualism, 'colonial ingenuity,' and the like. This
stems in part from a very common human fallacy: the tendency to confuse
separate identity with uniqueness." [29] We should welcome comparisons
between the western United States and Australia or South Africa, but at
the same time we should question why there are not more cross-national
and comparative studies between Canada and the United States. [30]

Different historiographical traditions have produced very different
historical narratives. Comparative historians will have to wonder, when
they perceive differences in the United States and Canada, to what extent
their perceptions are rooted in different historical realities and to what
extent they are rooted in different scholarly traditions. A cursory discussion of historical surveys will reveal this. In *The Canadian Prairies*, Gerald
Friesen devotes 87 pages to the fur trade before 1870 and 61 pages to the

Métis (the history of the Métis of the Canadian West is underexamined in the growing and cross-national study of hybridity, but see chapter 8). By contrast, he requires only one paragraph to discuss the arrival, spread, and significance of the horse. Horses apparently do not warrant an entry in the index. Richard White's history of the U.S. West devotes 3 pages and a full-page map to the arrival and spread of the horse (although only to the forty-ninth parallel).[31] White's index identifies 21 scattered pages that discuss the fur trade. Neither the Métis nor guns warrant an index entry. These books reinforce the idea that Native-European trade and intermarriage and the spread of European weaponry through trade are quintessentially Canadian stories. The history of the Canadian plains, if you will, is the legacy of trade. On the other hand, the spread of the horse was a U.S. story. So was the constant struggle between Plains Indians and invading empires and nations. U.S. western history is the legacy of conquest. In narrower fields similar historiographical differences exist. In Canada, for example, the literature on the aboriginal role in the fur trade is very well developed. Literature on the role of aboriginal people in the fur trade in the northern plains of the United States is less well developed. On the other hand, the literature on Indian policy history in the United States is far more developed than the literature on Canada, and it is guided by different questions.

Those who contemplate undertaking cross-national, comparative, and borderlands Canada–United States historical research face significant challenges, but they have an exceptional opportunity to contribute to our understanding of the past. Alternatives to the studies defined by present-day boundaries will help us to better understand the uncertainties, contingencies, and concerns of those who lived in the past. Almost inevitably, comparative and cross-national studies will also disabuse us of the notions that the history of the West in one country was wholly unique and distinctive or that the history in the two countries was virtually identical. Here, perhaps more than anywhere else, researchers are likely to feel that they are comparing apples and apples—McIntosh and Delicious perhaps. Almost inevitably, by comparing phenomena in two countries we will arrive at richer understandings of the international trends and environmental factors that influenced developments in both countries and the many links that connected communities on both sides of the border. We can be so bold as to predict that comparative studies will almost certainly help us understand contemporary problems better and perhaps help us avoid repeating the mistakes already made elsewhere. The rewards of comparative, cross-national, and borderlands research are worth striving for.[32]

Notes

This paper is an expanded version of a paper presented at the conference of the Western History Association, Portland OR, October 1999.

1. Theodore Binnema, "Old Swan, Big Man, and the Siksika Bands, 1794–1815," *Canadian Historical Review* 7 (1996): 1–32; Binnema, *Common and Contested Ground: A Human and Environmental History of the Northwestern Plains* (Norman: University of Oklahoma Press, 2001).

2. Dan Flores, "Place: An Argument for Bioregional History," *Environmental History Review* 18 (1994): 6.

3. Duncan McNab McEachran, "Description of a Journey from Fort Benton to Bow River, NWT," archives, Glenbow-Alberta Institute, Calgary, Alberta, M736, 23.

4. McEachran, "Description," 28.

5. George M. Dawson, "Report on the Region in the Vicinity of the Bow and Belly Rivers," Geological Survey of Canada *Report of Progress, 1882–1884*, 10–11c.

6. Irene M. Spry, ed., *The Papers of the Palliser Expedition, 1857–1860* (Toronto: Champlain Society, 1968), 420, 19.

7. In R. G. McConnell, "Report on the Cypress Hills Wood Mountain and Adjacent Country," Geological Survey of Canada *Annual Report 1885*, 10c.

8. Twining quoted in archives, Glenbow-Alberta Institute, M736, 32; Dawson, "Report on the Region," 17c; Palliser in Spry, *The Papers of the Palliser Expedition*, 406.

9. Gary E. Moulton, ed., *Journals of the Lewis and Clark Expedition*, 13 vols. (Lincoln: University of Nebraska Press, 1983–2001), July 14, 1805, 4:380.

10. MacEachran, "Description of a Journey," 23–24.

11. Chester B. Beaty, *The Landscapes of Southern Alberta: A Regional Geomorphology* (Lethbridge: University of Lethbridge Printing Services, 1975).

12. Richard Glover, ed., *David Thompson's Narrative, 1784–1812* (Toronto: Champlain Society, 1962), 47.

13. Barry Gough, ed., *The Journal of Alexander Henry the Younger, 1799–1814* (Toronto: Champlain Society, 1992), January 20, 1811, 583.

14. We do not yet have a cross-national or comparative history on this topic, but Clinton L. Evans has written *The War on Weeds in the Prairie West: An Environmental History* (Calgary: University of Calgary Press, 2002).

15. Binnema, *Common and Contested Ground*; Paul F. Sharp: *The Canadian-American West* (Minneapolis: University of Minnesota Press, 1955); Sharp, *Whoop-Up Country*; Sharp, "When Our West Moved North," *American Historical Review* 55 (1950): 286–300; Hugh Dempsey, *Firewater: The Impact of the Whisky Trade on the Blackfoot Nation* (Calgary: Fifth House, 2002).

16. John C. Ewers, *The Blackfeet: Raiders of the Northwestern Plains* (Norman: University

of Oklahoma Press, 1958). For the twentieth century see Paul Rosier, *Rebirth of the Blackfeet Nation, 1912–1954* (Lincoln: University of Nebraska Press, 2001).

17. One article pretends to trace the history of the Gros Ventre while they were north of the forty-ninth parallel. See Thomas F. Schilz, "The Gros Ventres and the Canadian Fur Trade, 1754–1831," *American Indian Quarterly* 12 (1988): 41–56. However, I have argued that this article is unreliable. See Theodore Binnema, "The Gros Ventre in the Canadian Fur Trade: A Response to Thomas F. Schilz," *American Indian Quarterly* 18 (1994): 533–42. Unwisely I chose to copy my title from Schilz's. During the years 1754–1831 the Gros Ventre were not involved in the "Canadian" fur trade, since Rupert's Land at that time was not part of Canada.

18. Grant MacEwan, *Sitting Bull: The Years in Canada* (Edmonton: Hurtig, 1973). Sitting Bull's time in Canada is also discussed in Beth LaDow, *The Medicine Line: Life and Death on a North American Borderland* (New York: Routledge, 2002); and Sharp, *Whoop-Up Country*. An important study is David G. McCrady, "Living with Strangers: The Nineteenth-Century Sioux and the Canadian-American Borderlands" (PhD diss., University of Manitoba, 1998).

19. J. Verne Dusenberry, *The Rocky Boy Indians: Montana's Displaced Persons* (Helena: Montana Historical Society Press, 1954); Floyd W. Sharrock and Susan R. Sharrock, *Ethnological Report on the Chippewa Cree Tribe of the Rocky Boy Reservation and the Little Shell Band of Indians, by John C. Ewers: History of the Cree Indian Territorial Expansion from the Hudson Bay Area to the Interior Saskatchewan and Missouri Plains* (New York: Garland, 1974).

20. Larry Burt, "Nowhere Left to Go: Montana's Crees, Metis, and Chippewas and the Creation of Rocky Boy's Reservation," *Great Plains Quarterly* 7 (1987): 195–209; Michel Hogue, "Crossing the Line: The Plains Cree in the Canadian–United States Borderlands, 1870–1900" (MA thesis, University of Calgary, 2002), and Hogue, "Disputing the Medicine Line: The Plains Crees and the Canadian-American Border, 1876–1885," *Montana: The Magazine of Western History* 52, no. 4 (Winter 2002): 2–17.

21. Hana Samek, *The Blackfoot Confederacy, 1880–1920: A Comparative Study of Canadian and U.S. Indian Policy* (Albuquerque: University of New Mexico Press, 1987); Hana Samek "Evaluating Canadian Indian Policy: A Case for Comparative Historical Perspective," *American Review of Canadian Studies* 16, no. 3 (1986): 293–99; Jill St. Germain, *Indian Treaty-Making Policy in the United States and Canada, 1867–1877* (Lincoln: University of Nebraska Press, 2001). A promising start in comparative history can be found in a general survey: Roger L. Nichols, *Indians in the United States and Canada: A Comparative History* (Lincoln: University of Nebraska Press, 1998).

22. Those wishing to undertake comparative studies would do well to read Deborah Montgomerie, "Beyond the Search for Good Imperialism: The Challenge of Comparative Ethnohistory," *New Zealand Journal of History* 31 (1997): 153–68.

23. This is something predicted by Raymond Grew in "The Comparative Weakness of American History," *Journal of Interdisciplinary History* 16 (1985): 93.

24. For a fine defense of borderlands studies, see Michiel Baud and Willem Van Schendel, "Toward a Comparative History of Borderlands," *Journal of World History* 8 (1997): 211–42.

25. This point was driven home to me on a sunny Sunday afternoon during the autumn

of 2000 when I crossed the border from Montana to Alberta at Sweetgrass Hills. The border guard remarked that I was the first person to cross the border that day who was not simply crossing the border to have coffee with a friend or family member on the other side of the line.

26. Wallace Stegner, *Wolf Willow: A History, a Story, and a Memory of the Last Plains* (Lincoln: University of Nebraska Press, 1955); LaDow, *The Medicine Line: Life and Death on a North American Borderland* (New York: Routledge, 2001); "Mapping the Alberta-Montana Borderlands: Race, Ethnicity, and Gender in the Late Nineteenth Century," *Journal of American Ethnic History* 20 (2001): 71–87.

27. Frederick Jackson Turner, "The Significance of the Frontier in American History," *Annual Report of the American Historical Association for 1893* (1894): 199–227.

28. New France and Upper and Lower Canada have been foci of this literature. A convenient introduction to the literature on Upper and Lower Canada can be found in Michael S. Cross, ed., *The Frontier Thesis and the Canadas: The Debate on the Impact of the Canadian Environment* (Toronto: Copp Clark, 1970). Given the circumstances under which the Canadian prairies have been settled, it is probably not surprising that the prairies have not been as thoroughly examined from the perspective of the frontier thesis. Despite its age, readers will still find the work of Paul F. Sharp worth reading. Consult his "Three Frontiers: Some Comparative Studies of Canadian, American, and Australian Settlement," *Pacific Historical Review* 24 (1955): 369–77. A very influential article in Canada, offering an alternative interpretation to frontierism, has been J. M. S. Careless, "Frontierism, Metropolitanism, and Canadian History, *Canadian Historical Review* 35 (1954): 1–21. Careless's article has been noted by a number of historians of the U.S. West, and anyone (the New Western Historians included) inclined to emphasize the role of the state and of the cities in the settlement and development of the U.S. West might find it interesting that an article of this kind was published fifty years ago. For a short historiographical article see Howard R. Lamar, "Coming into the Mainstream at Last: Comparative Approaches to the History of the American West," *Journal of the West* 35, no. 4 (1996): 3–5.

29. James Belich, *Making Peoples: A History of the New Zealanders* (Honolulu: University of Hawai'i Press, 1996), 277.

30. See Patricia Nelson Limerick, "Going West and Ending Up Global," *Western Historical Quarterly* 32 (2001): 5–23; Ann Stoler, "Tense and Tender Ties: The Politics of Comparison in North American History and (Post)colonial Studies," *Journal of American History* 88 (2001): 829–65; Thomas Dunlap, *Nature and the English Diaspora: Environment and History in the United States, Canada, Australia, and New Zealand* (New York: Cambridge University Press, 1999).

31. Gerald Friesen, *The Canadian Prairies: A History* (Toronto: University of Toronto Press, 1987), 38–39; Richard White, *"It's Your Misfortune and None of My Own": A New History of the American West* (Norman: University of Oklahoma Press, 1991), 19–24.

32. For this reason, we should be hesitant to criticize too heavily an impressive attempt to write a coherent general comparative history like Nichols, *Indians in the United States and Canada*.

2. The Pacific Coast Borderlands and Frontier

Leonard J. Evenden and Daniel E. Turbeville III

It took at least a century for the boundary between the United States and British North America, later Canada, to be established. In 1818, the forty-ninth parallel of latitude was established as the boundary in the West, but this agreement did not apply beyond the Rockies. Finally, in 1846, it was agreed by treaty that this line should be extended to the coast at the Strait of Georgia. Between these dates, however, settlement in the area known to Americans as the Oregon Country was open to people of both powers—a "joint occupation."

The establishment and subsequent character of this segment of the boundary illustrates the distinction between boundary and frontier: the one conventionally understood as a line of containment, the other a dynamic zone of predominantly outward movement.[1] To extend the boundary to the Pacific coast was imperative, a task made difficult by remoteness and the loose character of settlement in the West, "that shadowy belt of American occupation . . . where it met the corresponding nebulous outskirts of the far-away Canadian state on the St. Lawrence River."[2] The traumatic memory from the War of 1812, of fixing the boundary at the "Niagara frontier," was cautionary. Canadians considered the War of 1812 a victory in that the boundary at Niagara was maintained in the face of the advancing American frontier, and this experience may have represented a significant American frustration. But the circumstances of the boundary establishment in the far West are different from those at Niagara, and the United States "won the race for the effective settlement of the Oregon country."[3]

Frontier and Focus

The steady growth of American settlement in the Willamette Valley, the "garden of Oregon," stretching south from the lower Columbia, forged the focal point of the territory, a counterpoise to the (British) Hudson's Bay Company post on the lower Columbia. Americans were ambitious, not only to engage in the fur trade, but to own and reside on the land, develop farms, introduce American forms of government, and gain access to the Pacific. In 1843, in an increasingly tense atmosphere, the Hudson's Bay Company relocated its headquarters to a newly established fort at the southern tip of Vancouver Island, to be created a British crown colony in 1849. This fort was the nucleus around which would form the city of Victoria, capital of the colony. Thus the two principal foci had emerged of land-based American settlement and the British coastal fort and colonial capital.

Not long after, in 1858, thousands of Americans were attracted to Victoria and the Fraser River by the discovery of gold in the interior of British Columbia. The British responded by sending a regiment, the Royal Engineers, to the area and by establishing the mainland colony of British Columbia. The engineers built routes to the interior and established town-sites, the best known being New Westminster, positioned on the high right bank on the north side of the unbridged Fraser, a site protected by the expanse of the river from the possibility of invasion from the south.

The Americans felt no similar fear of land-based invasion. What they feared was the power of the Royal Navy, a substantial consideration, given that the boundary in Georgia Strait was still being contested. Hence they established a number of coastal forts, including one at Port Townsend at the entrance to Puget Sound (see figure 7). Just as New Westminster had become the dominant focus in the new mainland colony, so Port Townsend was ambitious to become the main economic center on the American side. As tensions eased, both places lost out to larger centers, namely, Vancouver and Seattle, which lay at a distance from the border. Thus a nascent settlement system, focused at the border for political and military reasons, yielded to a network of places that grew up in response to economic development and that drew the focus away from the border. This second network spatially anchors today's settlement.

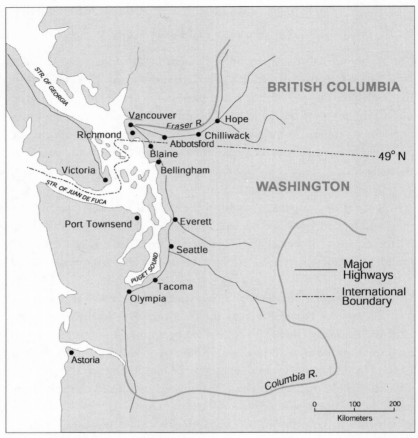

Figure 7. The Pacific Northwest borderlands, or Cascadia. Map by Brian Ludy and Cassie Hansen.

Unity and Separation at the Border: Contemporary Perceptions

To a Canadian who lives within a few minutes' drive of the border, the crossing represents not only an impediment but also an opportunity of access to a market with a wide range of favorably priced consumer goods. Recreational land is also comparatively cheap, considering its proximity to Vancouver, and development regulations have been permissive. To an American, the mounting pressures attending this spillover of people as shoppers, holiday residents, and curious neighbors is both welcome and irritating. Some development opportunities are stimulated in this region of historically marginal prosperity, but traffic line-ups in the small border towns at times render the streets almost impassable to residents, and queues at the checkout counters in the stores cause delays. Comparatively relaxed regulations concerning drinking and entertainment establishments can also result in behavior that local authorities are ill-equipped to handle. [4] As for purchasing recreational land, "Canadians now . . . are . . . condemned as alien interlopers and land-grabbers."[5] The boundary is clearly permeable, and the border region, most importantly in Whatcom County, is a place of mixing.

First-year university students in Vancouver, with only rudimentary geographical education, were asked in 1978 to draw an outline map of Canada from memory. Results are conventional, but in a few cases the far western boundary segment is modified or transgressed. Such perceptual permeability of the boundary perhaps suggests regional unity in the popular mind. In contrast, a study of popular regions based on the choice of regional names for metropolitan enterprises may suggest the opposite. In Zelinsky's study, the term "Northwest" coincides in large measure with the older notion of the Oregon territory. The boundary of "West" extends into Canada and intriguingly points out the region of historic Willamette Valley settlement. "Pacific" identifies not only distant California but also adjacent Canada. Thus literally nominal evidence points to popular regional boundaries that are spatially constricted in the border zone, emphasizing separation. Openness and closure appear to coexist in boundary perceptions in this region.

Perceptual ambiguity at the personal and popular levels, however, is complemented at the state level by spatially wide-ranging perceptions of regional unity. In the mid-1970s the elected legislators of Washington and British Columbia, without reference to national contexts, met in Bellingham, Washington, the compromise border location, to discuss regional issues of common interest.[6] Following the passage of the free-trade agreement, this discussion has been reopened around the idea of forming a new political and economic geographic unit. The Pacific Northwest Economic Region comprises five states and two provinces, and its aim is to promote cooperation in the region to become more competitive globally. Its core area comprises the Strait of Georgia and Puget Sound lowlands; the wider region combines the favored coast and an extensive resource hinterland. About one-third of its 15 million people live in the politically bisected core. How the aims of economic cooperation can be achieved must be negotiated, as has been the case for two centuries in matters pertaining to the border.

Unity and Separation at the Border: Contemporary Behavior

The United States, as the dominant power, is a looming presence in Canadian life. Paradoxically, the lesser power has a comparatively strong presence in the border regions. Nowhere does this imbalance have greater local effect than at the Pacific end of the forty-ninth parallel, that is in the lower Fraser River valley of British Columbia, including metropolitan Vancouver, and in adjacent Whatcom County, with its county seat of Bellingham.

Prices for consumer goods are generally lower on the American side, attracting Canadian shoppers, but Vancouver provides the closest major urban "downtown" for American border region residents. Cross-border tourism has grown, and Whatcom County has become a popular place for Canadians to purchase recreational property. Canadian travelers use the Bellingham airport for flights to destinations in the United States, and in this way the airport is developing an overflow function for Vancouver. Both Seattle and Vancouver have hosted world fairs, and it is now conventional to point to Expo '86 in Vancouver as the moment when a turning point was reached in the development of the border economy on the American side. Economic planning in the hitherto rural Whatcom County is now largely predicated upon the existence of the adjacent, numerous, and reasonably well paid Canadian population. Some Canadian firms, for example, in the wood-products industries, having found it increasingly difficult to compete in traditional American markets under current terms of trade, have relocated to the south side of the border to take advantage of domestic status and lower production costs, especially labor.

"Day-trippers" going to Bellingham and the border communities to shop have increased in number from 6.6 million in 1986 to more than 13 million in 1990. Spending in this region by British Columbian residents increased from nearly 67 million to almost 200 million Canadian dollars during the same period. Popular purchases include gasoline, groceries, clothing, and electronic items. The unprecedented demand for these goods is transforming the border towns from service centers for the traditional agricultural and fishing economies to suburban shopping center in a metropolitan economy, albeit centers dislocated from Vancouver by the spatial intervention of the international boundary. This "boom" in the development of shopping facilities on the south side of the border is matched by a decline in demand for such outlets and goods on the north side. Indeed, in 1990, certain British Columbian merchants, with failing businesses located near the border, brought a lawsuit against the Canadian government for failing to collect all payable duty on goods purchased by travelers in the United States.

With such pressures, and with a recent agreement that binds the two countries to the principle of mutual "free trade," it is difficult to foresee any abatement in these trends. Overall, nearly 9 million automobiles crossed this segment of the boundary in 1989, representing a threefold increase since 1985. This has prompted efforts to speed up cross-border traffic. But to expedite the flow of traffic is not universally regarded as desirable. The issue is difficult in both countries, for it means that local conditions must be understood in distant capitals. By the time national priorities are weighed and decisions made, the effect at the local level can be quite uncoordinated.

Together Yet Apart

In recognition of the peaceful settling of the boundary disputes in this area, Sam Hill of Seattle, a Quaker and entrepreneur, initiated the construction of the Peace Arch as a gesture of goodwill. Built astride the boundary, it was dedicated in 1921. A plaque on the east side of the structure displays the image of the *Mayflower*, recalling the long cultural memory of America to this point on the boundary. This is balanced on the west side by a plaque bearing the image of the *Beaver*, the first steamship on the northwest coast, in the service of the Hudson's Bay Company. These plaques are a study in the contrasts of the wider influences brought into focus at this point. The arch itself, its iron gate fixed in an open position and its classical imagery perhaps more American than Canadian, has come to symbolize the meeting of the two countries and local border communities in a spirit of friendship, even of kinship. Indeed, its south-facing inscription reads "Children of a Common Mother."

Since the Peace Arch was built, this region has come to face the Pacific world to a greater degree than ever before. It does so with increasing self-consciousness and perhaps self-assurance. The full ramifications of any movement to regional economic cooperation will not be known for some time, but it will force issues of border regional development and cooperation. No matter how separate or similar the national experiences, however, the essential unity of the region can never be completely denied. If it were to be composed today, the inscription on the Peace Arch might well be modified to read "Partners in a Common Destiny."

Notes

This essay originally appeared in Donald G. Janelle, ed., *Geographical Snapshots of North America* (New York: Guilford Press, 1992), 52–56, and is reprinted here with permission.

1. D. Kristof Ladis, "The Nature of Frontiers and Boundaries," *Annals of the Association of American Geographers* 49 (1959): 269–82.
2. Ellen C. Semple, *Influences of Geographic Environment* (New York: Henry Holt, 1911), 211.
3. Don W. Thomson, *Men and Meridians*, vol. 1 (Ottawa: Queen's Printer, 1966), 261.
4. Terry Simmons and Daniel E. Turbeville III, "Blaine, Washington: Tijuana of the North?" in Edgar L. Jackson, ed., *Current Research by Western Canadian Geographers: The Cariboo College Papers, 1984* (Vancouver: Tantalus Research, 1985), 47–57.
5. Gerard F. Rutan, "The Ugly Canadian: Canadian Purchase and Ownership of Land in Whatcom County, Washington," *Social Science Journal* 14 (1977): 7.
6. See Charles N. Forward and George A. Gerhold, eds., *Environment and Man in British Columbia and Washington: Symposium on Canadian-American Relations* (Bellingham: Western Washington State College, 1974).

3. Conceptual and Practical Boundaries

West Coast Indians/First Nations
on the Border of Contagion in the Post-9/11 Era

Bruce Granville Miller

A few years ago I wrote about the forty-ninth parallel, the international border between the United States and Canada or, more specifically, Washington State and the province of British Columbia, focusing on the largely invisible ways in which the border disrupted and bifurcated the communities of Coast Salish and adjacent Interior Salish peoples. I noted that the climate of the mid-1990s was "predisposed to the crossing of intellectual, disciplinary, political, and cultural boundaries," as part of a response to a modernist theory of society which was said to be a boundary-maintaining system, separating culture from nature, culture from society, culture from the individual, and "traditional" culture from "modern" culture.[1] Since the 1970s, "Boundary maintaining was out; adventurous, indeed necessary border crossings were advocated between science and literature, ethnography and biography, interpretation and imagination. The greatest challenge became to understand, and thereby overcome, the one border . . . between Us and the Other, the West and the Rest."[2] I observed that these efforts to connect the global and the local and to transcend boundaries posed the risks of becoming institutionalized into noncritical forms of producing knowledge. Nancy Scheper-Hughes put it this way:

> In the brave new world of reflexive postmodernists . . . everything local is said to dissolve into merged media images, transgressed boundaries, promiscuously mobile multinational industries and workers, and transnational-corporate desires

and fetishism. This imagined postmodern, borderless world is, in fact, a Camelot of free trade that echoes the marketplace rhetoric of global capitalism. . . .

The idea of an anthropology without borders . . . ignores the reality of the very real borders that confront and oppress "our" anthropological subjects. . . . These borders are as real as the passports and passbooks, the sandbagged bunkers, the armed roadblocks.[3]

Scheper-Hughes's comments regarding the ease of movement of goods, at least as it relates to the U.S.–Canadian border, now seems dated as the United States continues to pose significant new restrictions on the movement of commercial traffic from its major trading partner, Canada. Her focus on the "really real" borders and ways these oppress local communities, however, remains on target. I could not have imagined in 1996 the ways in which the events of September 11, 2001, and its aftermath would alter the circumstances facing the Salish peoples and disrupt the distinctive ways indigenous peoples manage life in a border zone. The American state, and a circumspect Canadian state, deeply troubled by developments in the United States, particularly the invasion of Iraq and the threats of American reprisals against Canada, have jointly created a new variant of the modernist border zone. This reconfigured zone focuses directly on images of contagion, profanity, danger, and corruption to support public policy. Today those problems faced by indigenous peoples since the mid-nineteenth century persist, but they are now joined with a new set as the government of the United States self-consciously cultivates a perception of a nation under siege and at war with terrorism.

In some ways the current dilemma is not new, and the British (and the successor Canadian) state and the United States have a long history of dispute and contention along the forty-ninth parallel, but there is a curious reversal. Canadians have long feared and indeed suffered from American intrusion into what is now British Columbia. For example, in 1858 some 30,000 unregulated, armed American and other foreign miners advanced into British Columbia, prompting fears of U.S. annexation of the territory. These miners attacked villages and killed an unknown number of indigenous peoples along the Fraser River in a display of "bold-faced, cross-border American aggression and vigilantism."[4] More recently, a member of the Washington State legislature proposed publicly that the U.S. fleet sail up the inside passage between Vancouver Island and the British Columbia mainland to intimidate Canadian negotiators into quickly resolving disputes over the harvest of salmon swimming through international waters. This time it is the Americans' turn to fear the penetration of their soil. The major development has been that in focusing on the twin and conceptually linked threats of terror and epidemic, U.S. policy has forced indigenous interests, particularly for those indigenous communities located directly on the international border, to be set aside once again. The hardening of the international boundary after September 11 poses yet another particularly difficult challenge to communities and continues a long process of making border crossing more difficult. Many Canadian First Nations peoples and American Indians report that ease of movement across the border was the norm until the 1970s. The United States has attempted to create in administrative law the terms of the 1794 Jay Treaty, which allowed for free passage but was voided by the War of 1812; however, Canada has not.

My argument is that the political border creates parallel conceptual and practical boundaries for the indigenous peoples of this region. Following a widely held indigenous perspective, I treat the international boundary as an arbitrary but potent fact of life that divides peoples and communities. I argue that in the present-day process of rearranging their relations to the state (the provincial, state, and federal governments) Salish peoples have intensified the development of strategies concerning the border in the pursuit of social justice. At present, First Nations in British Columbia are negotiating both land claims and treaties with the provincial and federal governments. The First Nations are also creating their own formal systems of governance, social services, education, legal systems, and other programs. Tribes in Puget Sound are considerably ahead in self-governance and institutional growth, a difference which itself puts a wedge between related communities. These activities are largely invisible and receive little public or academic attention, but reflect the perception that Salish identity and community cannot exist without those on the other side of the border.

In brief, these efforts include current legal challenges to the state to regain rights of free passage within traditional territories that overlap the international border. Also, indigenous-driven initiatives are under way to change the procedures whereby winter Spirit Dancers who are in a state of extreme spiritual danger are permitted to cross between British Columbia and Washington. There are attempts to promote a form of political unity between Coast Salish bands and tribes whose interests in the salmon fishery are split by residence within separate nation-states and efforts of individuals to find medical care within different regimes of service delivery. In addition, communities seek to control their membership by formally recognizing as tribal members those living on the other side of the boundary. Individual Salish people have exploited the difference in commodity prices and public health to gain personal security in their homeland on both sides of the border.

The Salish peoples are not alone in their responses to the border, and other indigenous peoples (or nations, in current discourse), too, are partitioned into more than one state. The Canadian-American border, for example, separates the Coast Salish and Interior Salish of British Columbia from relatives in Washington and Idaho, but also the Nuu-chah-nulth on Vancouver Island and related peoples of the adjacent Olympic Peninsula of Washington, Blackfoot/Blackfeet and Lakota in the plains, Ojibway/Chippewa in the Great Lakes region, Iroquois in the eastern woodlands, and Mi'qmac on the Atlantic coast are among the many divided peoples. My examination of these topics rests upon my own fieldwork with Coast Salish communities of Puget Sound and the Fraser River since the mid-1970s, interviews with members of these communities and public officials specifically for the study of the border, participation as a participant at various federal government–sponsored events, and a reading of the ethnographic and historical materials.

American Responses to the Events of September 11

The immediate American response along the forty-ninth parallel following the destruction of the twin towers in New York City and related events was to tighten the border, subjecting all traffic into the United States from Canada along the heavily traveled Vancouver to Seattle corridor to searches. The PACE lane program, a dedicated, preapproved lane for registered, regular travelers from both countries, was canceled. After several months, security was gradually relaxed and the waiting time for the lines of cars was reduced from several hours, in many cases, to an average of a half-hour, but with episodic longer waits during periods of heightened fear of terrorism known as "Orange Alerts."

As the United States developed its response to what government officials characterized as a war, initially with Osama bin Laden and Afghanistan, and later with Saddam Hussein and Iraq, the domestic focus was on "homeland security" and the attempt to seal the U.S. borders from danger. This effort at preventing intrusions of foreigners into American life took many forms, including the stationing of U.S. officials in the Port of Vancouver to stop the possible movement of weapons of mass destruction through containerized shipping and to catch terrorists hiding among the ships. During a period of intense negotiations over the effective closing of the border to vital Canadian exports, particularly lumber, through the imposition of tariffs, U.S. federal authorities pushed to negotiate the terms on which U.S. military personnel could operate on Canadian soil.

The implications of these policy initiatives for indigenous peoples became clear at a unique Tribal/County Criminal Justice Summit, held at Bow, Washington, on January 8–10, 2003. Here, state and federal officials, including Christine Gregoire, attorney general of the state of Washington, the Hon. Susan Owens of the Washington State Supreme Court, and federal officials representing U.S. Attorney General John Ashcroft, met with tribal and county officials principally to lay out plans for the war on terrorism. In three days of discussions, the argument was made that tribes on the international border were especially vulnerable to intrusion from Canada. According to federal officials, terrorists coming across the border had already established or were likely to establish methamphetamine labs on Indian reservations, and other terrorists were likely to pour in.

In an hourlong presentation, a senior official from the Washington State Department of Health graphically described the possible use of smallpox by terrorists and a new national program to inoculate front-line officials and large segments of the general population. The capturing of public health by political concerns did not go unnoticed, and tribal officials in the packed audience raised several questions. One asked cynically if the terrorists might borrow surplus infected blankets from the U.S. War

Department. Another noted that terrorists attempting to use smallpox "would have to be rather dumb." A third asked why the state budget was shifted to combating a hypothetical smallpox outbreak, given that there were health disasters already affecting Indians, including diabetes, AIDS, and TB.

Federal officials described a program for cross-deputizing tribal, county, and state police in order that all could respond immediately to the terrorists who were imagined to be crossing the international border through Indian country or anywhere else. This program held an inherent appeal for tribal police officials, who battle the perception that their officers are inferior to those in the mainstream society. The federal officials proposed a program to provide U.S. Border Patrol high-tech equipment to tribal police helping in the terrorist problem. Efforts were begun to coordinate the goals and objectives of the Border Patrol, the Bureau of Indian Affairs, and the new federal Homeland Security agency. Meanwhile, tribal attorneys noted in private that the FBI, legally responsible for dealing with a set of major crimes committed in Indian country, including murder and rape, had simply stopped doing so in order to concentrate on terrorism. Tribes' legal systems were left with the option of prosecuting murderers on their lands with a maximum sentence of one year or a fine of $5,000. Tribal borderlands became, in a sense, lawless.

Public policy shifts regarding American Indians after September 11 focused on recruiting tribal personnel into the war on terrorism. The long border with British Columbia was described as constituting a serious threat to tribes, and issues of tribal sovereignty were left unconsidered. Justice officials urged tribes, along with all other sectors of American society, to put their own interests aside and to pull together for the common good. In addition, the presentations of federal officials conjoined images of disease, epidemic, and contagion with images of violence, terrorism, disruption, and impurity in the form of alien people and diseases, all coming from Canada.

This effort to link diverse forms of contagion rested, by necessity, on the transformation of the image of British Columbia, and Canada generally. Canada had long been regarded as a docile, bucolic neighbor, as symbolized by the Peace Arch, a structure built directly at the forty-ninth parallel and on the major thoroughfare between the countries, which displays the texts "Children of a Common Mother" and "May These Gates Never Be Closed." But stories in the U.S. media suggested that terrorists involved in the September 11 disasters had entered the United States from Canada. Canada was depicted as a haven for terrorists, and British Columbia, in particular, was described on Seattle television and elsewhere in U.S. media as the home of pot growers and drug smugglers. The *Vancouver Sun*, for example, reported the comments of a New York talk radio show host who called Canada a "tin-pot, bankrupt country that has nothing to offer the world but drugs."[5]

Many accounts focused on what was taken to be an inadequate approach by the Canadian government to immigration and border inspection, and the U.S. government pushed negotiations to coordinate services and to coerce Canadian officials into adopting an American approach. Paul Cellucci, American ambassador to Canada, appeared on Canadian television directly to intervene in Canadian domestic policy and later criticized the Canadian prime minister's decision not to send troops to Iraq while intimating coming economic reprisals.[6] Canada's image was transformed to that of a country intent on polluting the United States through its illegal imported goods, its lax policies toward immigrants, especially those from the Middle East, and its ineffective socialist society. U.S. immigration agents began to detain, interrogate, and fingerprint nonwhite Canadian citizens born abroad who attempted to cross the border. The Canadian minimalist response to the threat of terrorism maddened U.S. officials, but held few implications for indigenes.

Although Salish peoples and communities retain interests in moving back and forth across the border for religious and other purposes, these interests were left unexplored in the rush to plug up the border. However, there remain particular social and cultural issues binding the Salish that have not attenuated with time and that become apparent in examining their patterns of affiliation and systems of meaning. I make a detour from the U.S. war on terrorism into the Salish world to draw out these connections.

Salish Affiliative Networks

The Coast Salish peoples, now grouped into some fifty bands in British Columbia and twenty-four tribes in Washington, are the descendents of speakers of Coast Salish languages who lived within Puget Sound and connecting areas, along the Fraser River and its tributaries, and on the southeastern portions of Vancouver Island and the adjacent mainland.[7] Other groups are located in Oregon. Their social organization in the early contact period was made up of fluid local groups, composed of one or more households, which interacted to form a regional structure.[8] Tribes did not exist prior to interaction with Europeans and state governments, but emerged as political entities following treaty negotiations, the establishment of the reserve/reservation systems, and as a response to the requirements of subsequent legal actions against the government. Before this, individuals closely identified with the local group with whom they were residing and with the larger "speech community" (composed of those who speak a common language). Kin ties created a network of relations that extended far beyond one's own river drainage.

These networks have persisted to the present and serve to organize activity in a variety of domains, thereby perpetuating the connectiveness of the larger Coast Salish community.[9] Persistent, regular activities bring together people from throughout the Coast Salish area for marriage and kinship, commercial fishing, winter ceremonial activity, and summer festivals emphasizing sporting contests and informal mingling. In addition there are regularly scheduled events on the Pow-Wow circuit of intertribal festivities that draw Salish peoples together.

The indigenous people who occupy a region drained by the Columbia and Fraser rivers east of the Cascade Mountains in Washington and the Coast Range in British Columbia are the descendents of speakers of seven Interior Salish languages. The Interior Salish peoples maintain a vast network of interpersonal ties constructed around kinship, friendship, and trade connections and, in earlier periods, created regional task groups for subsistence purposes. A further factor that promoted regional cooperation was the possibility of food shortage due to the thinness and wide dispersal of resources within their region.

Existence as a subordinated people and a common postcontact history has reinforced the connections between the various Salish peoples. So, too, has placement on reserves and reservations and attendance in common in government-imposed residential schools. Both in the precontact period and up to the present day, the broad network of affiliation between Salish peoples and communities has incorporated those on both sides of the border. Maintaining this system has grown difficult and prompted indigenous responses.

Indigenous Challenges to State-Imposed Borders

The case of *Robert Watt v. E. Liebelt and the Minister of Citizenship and Immigration*, on appeal to the Trial Division, Federal Court of Canada, is a case in which, to the Crown, the issue "is whether an aboriginal person who is neither a Canadian citizen nor a registered Indian has a right to remain in Canada because he belongs to a tribe whose traditional territory straddles the Canada–United States border."[10] Robert Allen Watt, a member of the Arrow Lakes (Sinixt) Tribe, an Interior Salish people, had been appointed by elders to come north into Canada to be "the guardian of a sacred burial site in British Columbia."[11] Watt, an enrolled member of the Colville Confederated Tribe, lived in the Slocan Valley, British Columbia, for most of the period between 1986 and 1993 in carrying out his guardian role.

In the nineteenth century the Arrow Lakes peoples moved within a district of lakes from the vicinity of Revelstoke, British Columbia, to Colville, Washington. Following the establishment of the forty-ninth parallel to mark the boundary between U.S. and British territories west of the Rockies in 1846, it became difficult for the Arrow Lakes people to continue traditional patterns of seasonal movement. Many members of the Arrow Lakes community moved to the Washington Territory in 1872 after the establishment of the Colville Reservation where they were offered land allotments together with other indigenous peoples. In 1953 the Arrow Lakes people were declared extinct by Canada, even though more than 250 were enrolled members of the Colville Confederated Tribes and were continuing to use traditional territories in British Columbia.[12]

In 1993 an adjudicator of a hearings board within the Ministry of Citizenship and Immigration ruled that, under the terms of the Canadian Immigration Act and because Watt was not a registered Canadian Indian under the Indian Act, he was to leave Canada within thirty days. The Watt case directly calls into question federal government conventions concerning who and what "aboriginal peoples of Canada" are. Legal counsel for Watt argued, "The definition of 'aboriginal peoples of Canada' . . .

infers that there may be other peoples who could raise a reasonable claim that they ought to be considered 'aboriginal.' "[13] The passage in question reads, "In this Act, 'aboriginal peoples of Canada' *includes* [emphasis added] the Indian, Inuit, and Métis peoples of Canada." Furthermore, counsel argued that given an open-ended definition and that the Supreme Court of Canada had held that Section 35 of the Constitution Act is to be interpreted generously and liberally, aboriginal peoples all along the U.S.–Canada boundary should be included within Section 35 as being aboriginal peoples of Canada. In addition, counsel argued that Subsection 35 (1) "protects the long-standing aboriginal right to move freely throughout their traditional territories." The Immigration Act, according to this argument, ought not to be interpreted in such a manner that "would eliminate the rights of the Arrow Lake or Sinixt people to move freely throughout their traditional territories."

The Watts case is not alone in querying the cross-border rights of First Nations along the international border; indeed, a series of related issues have arisen within the last few years. The issues include the rights of bands and tribes in the management of traditional territories that incorporate watersheds or other natural zones that straddle the border. In sum, recent activities by bands and tribes have questioned the role of the state in defining indigenous communities, in limiting access to territories, and in limiting any liability or trust responsibility to those on one side of the border. The First Nations claims constitute a proposal for a broader, more incorporative view that better accounts for the nature of their own community organization. Such claims occur in less conspicuous forms as well.

Indigenous Challenges to the Intrusiveness of the Border

In common with other indigenous peoples of the Americas, Coast Salish religious life focuses on the relationships between individuals and spirit beings who interact with humans and who provide humans access to powers of various sorts. Throughout Coast Salish territory, initiates into the society of Spirit Dancers spend a winter developing their relationship with their spirit helper. As initiates ("babies") they are spiritually reborn and experience a state of ritual liminality in which they are susceptible to spiritual and physical danger. Initiates travel to the several earthen-floor ceremonial longhouses, homes to other groups of babies, in Washington and British Columbia that collectively compose the ritual congregation. Babies travel in ceremonial costumes that provide a measure of spiritual protection; for example, headdresses largely cover their eyes to keep them from danger. In some cases, experienced Spirit Dancers carry masks in containers that cannot be opened except in a ceremonial context.

The immediate problem for Spirit Dancers traveling between Coast Salish communities located across the border is the incompatibility of inspection procedures associated with customs regulations and their own spiritual beliefs. Babies may be placed in spiritual danger if, for example, someone looks directly into their faces. Masks and other regalia cannot be handled by nondancers. The cedar costumes and headdresses and wooden staffs carried by black and red faced dancers sometimes appear bizarre and suspicious to border agents. [14] Another difficulty facing the Spirit Dancers is the cultural prohibition on the communication of specific information about Spirit Dancing. To reveal specifics could potentially place a dancer in spiritual danger and reduce the efficacy of their relationship with their spiritual helper.

Associate Chief Elva Caulkins, of what was then the U.S. Department of Treasury (Custom Service), told this author in 1995 that while Indian people may cross from north to south, this is not unproblematic and "at times we are going to look." Further, "we don't do an 'attitude check' even if they are lippy. But if they are *evasive* [emphasis mine], it can cause problems. Lots of time Indians won't tell us what country they're from. Coast Salish believe both countries are their country. Indians often say they are resident of both. We ask them, 'Where is your longhouse?' [in the attempt to determine residency]." [15] The new U.S. efforts at patrolling the border complicate the efforts to establish working agreements between the congregation of Spirit Dancers and border officials. The border staff is larger, and many officers, new to the area, are unaware of the practices of the local indigenous peoples. Detailed inspections heighten the risk of difficulty.

Canadian border officials have published articles describing ceremonial objects in internally circulated professional journals, but these have focused on the material culture of Native people outside of British Columbia. Caulkins noted to this author that "Indians are angrier at

Canadians than the United States, due to the failure of Canadian policy to allow largely unrestricted passage," a perspective that accurately reflected the view of many Canadian First Nations until September 11.

A related problem concerns the movement of goods intended for potlatches, ritual events that require the distribution of goods to people in attendance. Potlatch goods taken across the border are subject to duty. In one incident, a man's car was seized by U.S. officials following accusations of smuggling as he attempted to bring two hundred blankets across the border to a relative's potlatch. In addition, there are problems concerning the transport of other ceremonial or religious items across the border. The U.S. Fishery and Game Act prohibits transporting items such as eagle feathers, which indigenous peoples sometimes carry in their vehicles. These feathers are thought by border officials to be associated with the possession and use of drug paraphernalia. Both the duties imposed on goods and the restrictions on eagle feathers constitute a regulatory environment that increases the complexity of the regular conduct of Salish life.

The Salmon Fishery and Problems of Access and Identity

Among the most significant relationships of traditional Salish peoples are with the salmon beings that provide the food that defines Salish culture. In earlier periods, Salish villages were built along rivers or on the saltwater to facilitate salmon fishing. The relationship has never been solely material, however, and Salish maintain their spiritual connection with salmon through the conduct of First Salmon ceremonies in which salmon beings make themselves known and humans demonstrate their respect for the salmon. Salish social organization and cultural identity, then, are directly connected to the fishery, acknowledged in the nineteenth century by both Washington State and British Columbia. The treaties of western Washington specified that Indians would continue to have access to salmon and other species; in British Columbia, reserves were established in particular locations in part because of the proximity to fishing stations.

The eventual creation of separate national fishing policies has created significant difficulties for Salish people, especially given the extraordinary richness of the resources in the area along the international border.

Previously, access to resources was determined largely through kinship connection. Affiliative patterns were spread across what became the international border, and people from what is now Washington fished in the Fraser River and adjoining British Columbia waters, a circumstance which is explicitly acknowledged today. Ernie Crey, former director of Stó:lō Nation fisheries, for example, observed that Lummi Nation fishers of Washington traditionally fished salmon stocks that spawned on the Fraser River and its tributaries. In addition, fisheries around the Gulf Islands of British Columbia and the San Juan Islands of Washington formerly incorporated fishers from bands and tribes located now on both sides of the border.

However, contemporary Salish Indian fishers of Washington and British Columbia remain largely within separate camps, despite the memories of earlier management protocols. Although Indian fishers of Washington were excluded from the fishery by the 1950s, today they co-manage the salmon resource with the State Department of Fisheries. British Columbia bands were similarly excluded from a fishery that became progressively more capital-intensive through the twentieth century.[16] The Reasons for Judgment in the case of *Sparrow v. The Queen*, 1990, interpreted the Canadian Constitution Act of 1982, Section 35 (1) as protecting the aboriginal right to fish for social and ceremonial purposes, but was silent concerning commercial sales. Subsequently, the federal government created a trial policy, the Aboriginal Fisheries Strategy, to allow limited indigenous commercial fishing. In response, Salish First Nations have attempted to create their own commercial fisheries management programs.

As a consequence of these developments, Indian people and polities have ended up on opposite sides in the international negotiations over fisheries allocations that form the backdrop to the Pacific Salmon Treaty. Distinctive features of Indian fisheries management are thereby underplayed, and commonalities of interest between Salish peoples are obstructed. Some Coast Salish peoples have responded by attempting to create formalized links across the border through the creation of a Coast Salish "Treaty" recognizing a common heritage and interests, and others rely on more informal, individual exchanges of information between band and tribal fisheries officers and managers. The larger problem for the

Coast Salish remains in articulating a common vision that is compatible with the circumstances of particular bands and tribes.

Personal Accommodations to the Border

Other responses to the border do not take the form of overt political action. Rather, they can be seen as personal acts of accommodation to the partitioning of the community by the international boundary. One Coast Salish woman, for example, who was born in a Stó:lō community along the Fraser River in British Columbia and who married into a Coast Salish tribe of western Washington, monitors the available health care opportunities for her dependent with a debilitating ailment.[17] She uses the existence of two national policies concerning public health as an asset; as an enrolled tribal member she has available the services of the Indian Health Service, and as a Canadian citizen she is eligible for the provisions of a socialized medical system with a somewhat different array of specialty services for chronic children's diseases. It is significant that she has not violated the spirit or the letter of either Canadian or U.S. law in looking after her dependent, nor has she duplicated services. This strategy has required that the caregiver maintain active affiliations with the community of her birth and the community into which she married.

Other Salish people make use of the differences in the Canadian and American economies by movement across the border in an effort to find employment. Generally this requires activating a latent affiliation with a community across the border and relocating for some months or years. In other cases, for example, members of the Semiahmoo (Canada) community, this entails exploiting the job market of Whatcom County, Washington, and a daily return to their reserve. One member of the Semiahmoo Nation noted, "It's easier for the Semiahmoo. So many of us have worked in the United States for the past thirty, forty, fifty years. We've been working on and off since teenagers, commuting back and forth. They [government officials] know us at the border."[18] Since September 11 it has been uncertain whether crossing the border to work will remain a possibility.

In common with other Canadian citizens, indigenous people living on the border have previously made use of differences in pricing. Semiahmoo people shop in Blaine, Washington, bringing home milk, eggs, cheese, and other food products that are ordinarily cheaper in Washington. Others have taken advantage of differences in the value of American and Canadian currency through importing goods with Native content duty-free from the United States for sale on Canadian reserves. This circumstance, although the product of the differences between the two countries, has served to unite the larger Salish community. New restrictions impede this movement.

Indigenous Citizenship and the Border

Another distinct pattern is the appropriation and reshaping of federal notions of membership and citizenship. This takes two forms. In one, communities enroll as tribal or band members those people who maintain ancestral connections but who are formally citizens across the international boundary. Although federally recognized tribes of Washington State do not allow cross-enrollment (enrollment in more than one tribe or band), one tribe included on their roll Native people residing in Canada, holding Canadian citizenship, and eligible for enrollment with a Canadian band. Other Washington tribes may also have enrolled Canadian Native people. By doing this, the tribe can assert its existence as a legitimate tribe by employing aboriginal notions of affiliation and membership independent of criteria imposed by the state and, simultaneously, fulfill the desires for membership of those who claim affiliation and common descent but live across the international border.

A second means of reshaping federal notions of citizenship is by simply claiming existing categories of membership and acting on them. This is the case for members of the Semiahmoo First Nation who speak of themselves as "dual citizens," although they are not formally recognized by both the United States and Canada as such. They do this for a variety of reasons. Nineteenth-century Semiahmoo territory, as is the case with the Arrow Lakes, straddles the international boundary, and band members maintain their connection to place. Semiahmoo people act on their perceived rights by exploiting economic and educational opportunities in northern Washington. In addition, Semiahmoo maintain active connections to the 3,000-member Lummi Nation of Washington and are aware of the Semiahmoo presence within that tribe. Finally, Semiahmoo, who moved north away from a portion of their territories at the time of the settlement of the international border, have considered legal action for compensation for territory. These are all indications of a continued Semiahmoo presence within Washington.

Conclusions

Despite efforts at resistance and accommodation, the border imposes consequences on the Salish communities. There is some truncation of communication between groups despite the efforts to overcome the problems the border poses. Groups are not fully aware of the political circumstances and governmental forms of those on the other side. [19] It is clear that some ceremonial exchanges are altered or diminished, particularly those requiring the movement of goods across the border. There are also fears of intrusive claims to territory, cash settlements, and legal entitlements by Native communities across the border. These arise in part from the control of lands by bands or tribes other than those who occupied them in the middle of the nineteenth century when the international border was created. These fears reflect both a misunderstanding of the legal circumstances across the border and recognition of the capacity of large political entities to extend their reach across the line, to intervene, for example, in litigation. Some Semiahmoo, for example, have expressed concerns that the Lummi Nation of Washington will make land claims in Semiahmoo territory in British Columbia even though Lummi occupy former Semiahmoo grounds rather than vice versa. In this case the discrepancy in size and resources seems to be at play. The Lummi Nation numbers about 3,000 and is the preeminent fishing tribe in the United States. The Semiahmoo number in the sixties.

On a related note, some people find themselves of necessity residing on the wrong side of the border. This is particularly the case for members of tribes that are not federally recognized, such as the Arrow Lakes in British Columbia or previously the Samish in Washington (although the Samish were newly recognized by the federal government as an "official tribe" in 1996). In the Arrow Lakes case, there is a recognized tribe in Washington, the Colville Confederated Tribes, with whom they can affiliate, but none in British Columbia. In the case of members of the Samish Tribe living on Vancouver Island, the opposite is true. Finally, there is the sheer difficulty of legal challenges such as the Watt case. This case failed initially, and although the appeal has not yet been heard, it appears to be an uphill battle.

Nevertheless, Salish people are currently contesting and accommodating the international border in various ways in order to maintain their communities and to preserve their sense of common identity. Indigenous people on both sides of the border persist in thinking of the border as an intrusion and think of their responses to the border as efforts to gain social justice within the Canadian and American states. The difficulties of carrying out their lives and pressing their claims within two separate national legal systems remain a considerable barrier to the maintenance of community and the achievement of justice.

Both the activity and the conceptualizations are of importance. One might anticipate that border issues will grow in importance to Salish and other indigenous communities as they continue the processes of building their own governance and managing any resources over which they are able to regain control. This is especially so given the current policy initiatives linked to the U.S. war on terrorism that further bifurcate the Salish world and make passage considerably more difficult, time-consuming, fraught with the possibility of detention and arrest, and subject to increased surveillance. As is often the case, the fates of indigenous peoples and communities are determined by events and circumstances far away from their homes. U.S. policy makers, in their fixation on terrorism and the Middle East, are largely unconcerned with indigenous issues. To the U.S. government especially, the border zone, including the Indian reservations, is now characterized as a region of contagion and danger rather than as a region occupied by the descendents of the earliest inhabitants who still form a distinct, connected community lapping across the border.

Notes

This essay is an expanded and updated version of a paper presented at the conference of the American Historical Association–Pacific Coast Branch, Vancouver BC, August 2001.

1. See Bruce G. Miller, "The 'Really Real' Border and the Divided Salish Community," BC *Studies* 112 (1996–97): 63–79.

2. Johannes Fabian, "Crossing and Patrolling: Thoughts on Anthropology and Boundaries," *Culture* 13, no. 1 (1993): 52.

3. Nancy Scheper-Hughes, "Propositions for a Militant Anthropology," *Current Anthropology* 36, no. 3 (1995): 417.

4. Keith Thor Carlson, "The Power of Place, the Problem of Time: A Study of History and Aboriginal Collective Identity" (PhD diss., Department of History, University of British Columbia, 2003), 259.

5. *Vancouver Sun*, March 26, 2003, A6.

6. *Vancouver Sun*, March 26, 2003, A1; *Toronto Globe and Mail*, March 26, 2003, 1.

7. Bruce G. Miller, "Women and Politics: Comparative Evidence from the Northwest Coast," *Ethnology* 31 (October 1992): 367–84.

8. Bruce G. Miller and Daniel L. Boxberger, "Creating Chiefdoms: The Puget Sound Case," *Ethnohistory* 41, no. 2 (1994): 270–72.

9. See Michael J. E. Kew and Bruce G. Miller, "Locating Aboriginal Governments in the Political Landscape," in Michael Healey, ed., *Seeking Sustainability in the Lower Fraser Basin: Issues and Choices* (Vancouver: Institute for Resources and the Environment/Westwater Research, 2000), 47–63.

10. B. Justice Reed, *Reasons for Order* (IMM-6881–93, 1994), 1.

11. Zool K. B. Suleman, *Further Memorandum of Argument of the Applicant* (IMM-6881–93, 1994), 2.

12. See Paula Pryce, *"Keeping the Lakes' Way": Reburial and Re-creation of a Moral World among an Invisible People* (Toronto: University of Toronto Press, 1999).

13. Suleman, *Further Memorandum*, 16.

14. Personal communication, Doreen Maloney, member of the Council of the Upper Skagit Tribe, Washington State, February 1995.

15. Personal communication, Elva Caulkins, assistant chief, Department of the Treasury, U.S. Custom Service, Blaine WA, February 28, 1995.

16. See Dianne Newell, *Tangled Webs of History: Indians and the Law in Canada's Pacific Coast Fisheries* (Toronto: University of Toronto Press, 1999).

17. Notes from interviews with a woman who will remain unidentified here.

18. Personal communication, Eleanor Charles of Semiahmoo, January 1995.

19. See Bruce G. Miller, *The Problem of Justice: Tradition and Law in the Coast Salish World* (Lincoln: University of Nebraska Press, 2001).

Part 2: Colonizing the Borderlands with Trails, the Law, and Ranching

The four chapters in this section speak to various aspects of interactions in the borderlands of the American and Canadian Wests during the mid- to late nineteenth century when the region was being colonized by Euro-Americans and Euro-Canadians. Colonization was more than a westward-moving settlement process; it had south-to-north and north-to-south patterns across the forty-ninth parallel worthy of our inquiry here. Nor does the term "settlement" adequately address the process, since Anglo invaders worked to displace the many First Nations and Native American peoples in the region by colonizing it with their own ideologies, trade, ranching, and agriculture. Further, colonization required enforcement of policies to maintain the colonizers' sense of order that was played out in this region, albeit somewhat differently on either side of the border.

Thus the first essay, an extract from Paul Sharp's seminal work on the subject of transboundary interactions in the West, examines the south-north Whoop-Up Trail, which served the forts and trading posts established in northern Montana Territory and the southwestern part of what became Alberta. Marian McKenna's chapter deals with how the frontier was policed on both sides of the "Blue Line" to protect the interests of the colonizers. Her essay discusses the development of Canada's North-West Mounted Police, its role in policing the frontier region, and how it was both different from and similar to the efforts of the United States to enforce policies below the border.

Cattle ranching, following the destruction of native bison herds, became the first predominant business in the borderlands region (excluding the Pacific Coast area) upon Anglo colonization. Geographer Terry Jordan-Bychkov examines various transboundary dimensions of ranching in chapter 6. He concludes that the forty-ninth parallel did not mark a dividing line between American and Canadian ranching patterns, but that in the borderlands region as a whole there developed a similar ranching industry characterized by many significant south-to-north influences.

Finally, Sheila McManus adds a race, gender, and landscape analysis in chapter 7. From the writings of Anglo women in the frontier-era Montana/Alberta borderlands, McManus discerns how "perceptions of land and landscape" connected to the process of establishing "white, English-speaking settler societies east of the Rockies" as opposed to "social landscapes complicated by racial diversity."

For Further Reading

On Frontier Colonization and Ranching in the Borderlands
On Law and Order in the Frontier Borderlands
On Frontier-Era Women's History and Gender Issues in the American and Canadian Wests

On Frontier Colonization and Ranching in the Borderlands

Antle, James Jay. "Stewardship, Environmental Change, and Identity in the Judith Basin of Montana." PhD diss., University of Kansas, 2003.

Bennett, John W., and Seena B. Kohl. *Settling the Canadian-American West, 1890–1915: Pioneer Adaptation and Community Building.* Lincoln: University of Nebraska Press, 1995.

Berry, G. L. *The Whoop-Up Trail: Early Days in Alberta-Montana.* Lethbridge AB: Lethbridge Historical Society, 1953.

Breen, David H. *The Canadian Prairie West and the Ranching Frontier, 1874–1924.* Toronto: University of Toronto Press, 1983.

Cavanaugh, Catherine, and Jeremy Mouat, eds. *Making Western Canada: Essays on European Colonization and Settlement.* Toronto: Garamond Press, 1996.

Dempsey, Hugh A. *The Golden Age of the Canadian Cowboy: An Illustrated History.* Saskatoon: Fifth House, 1995.

Dobak, William A. "The Army and the Buffalo: A Demur." *Western Historical Quarterly* 26 (Summer 1995): 197–202.

———. "Killing the Canadian Buffalo, 1821–1881." *Western Historical Quarterly* 27 (Spring 1996): 33–52.

Elofson, Warren. *Cowboys, Gentlemen, and Cattle Thieves: Ranching on the Western Frontier.* Montreal: McGill-Queen's University Press, 2000.

———. "The Untamed Canadian Ranching Frontier, 1874–1914." In Simon M. Evans, Sarah Carter, and Bill Yeo, eds., *Cowboys, Ranchers, and the Cattle Business: Cross-*

Border Perspectives on Ranching History, 81–100. Calgary: University of Calgary Press, 2000.

Evans, Simon M. "American Cattlemen on the Canadian Range, 1874–1914." *Prairie Forum* 4 (1979): 121–35.

————. *The Bar U and Canadian Ranching History*. Calgary: University of Calgary Press, 2004.

————. "The End of the Open Range Era in Western Canada." *Prairie Forum* 8 (1983): 71–87.

————. "The Origin of Ranching in Western Canada: American Diffusion or Victorian Transplant?" In L. A. Rosenvall and Simon M. Evans, eds., *Essays on Historical Geography of the Canadian West*, 70–94. Calgary: University of Calgary, Department of Geography, 1987.

————. "Review Essay: Some Research on the Canadian Ranching Frontier." *Prairie Forum* 19 (Spring 1994): 101–10.

Evans, Simon M., Sarah Carter, and Bill Yeo, eds. *Cowboys, Ranchers, and the Cattle Business: Cross-Border Perspectives on Ranching History*. Calgary: University of Calgary Press, 2000.

Ewing, Sherm. *The Ranch: A Modern History of the North American Cattle Industry*. Missoula: Mountain Press, 1995.

————. *The Range*. Missoula: Mountain Press, 1990.

Fletcher, R. H. *Free Grass to Fences: The Montana Cattle Range Story*. New York: University Publishers, for the Historical Society of Montana, 1960.

Foran, Max. "Crucial and Contentious: The American Market and the Development of the Western Canadian Beef Cattle Industry to 1948." *American Review of Canadian Studies* 32 (Fall 2002): 451–76.

Fountain, Steven M. "Voyageurs, Mountain Men, and Country Wives: Contesting Empire and Making Borders in North America." Paper, conference of the Association of Canadian Studies in the United States, Portland OR, November 2003.

Higham, C. L. *Noble, Wretched, and Redeemable: Protestant Missionaries to the Indians in Canada and the United States, 1820–1900*. Albuquerque: University of New Mexico Press, 2000.

Jameson, Sheilagh. *Ranches, Cowboys, and Characters: Birth of Alberta's Western Heritage*. Calgary: Glenbow Museum, 1987.

Jordan, Terry. *North American Cattle-Ranching Frontiers: Origins, Diffusion, and Differentiation*. Albuquerque: University of New Mexico Press, 1993.

Klassen, Henry C. "Shaping the Growth of the Montana Economy: T. C. Power & Bro. and the Canadian Trade, 1869–1893." *Great Plains Quarterly* 11 (Summer 1991): 166–80.

LaDow, Beth. *The Medicine Line: Life and Death on a North American Borderland*. New York: Routledge, 2001.

McManus, Sheila. *"The Line That Separates": The Alberta-Montana Borderlands in the Late Nineteenth Century*. Lincoln: University of Nebraska Press, 2005.

Morris, Peter S. "Ft. McLeod of the Borderlands: Using the 49th Parallel on Southern Alberta's Ranching Frontier." In C. L. Higham and Robert Thacker, eds., *One West, Two Myths: A Comparative Reader*. Calgary: University of Calgary Press, 2004.

Regular, Keith. " 'Red Backs and White Burdens': A Study of White Attitudes toward Indians in Southern Alberta." MA thesis, University of Calgary, 1985.

Sharp, Paul F. *Whoop-Up Country: The Canadian-American West, 1865–1885.* Minneapolis: University of Minnesota Press, 1955.

Slatta, Richard W. *Comparing Cowboys and Frontiers.* Norman: University of Oklahoma Press, 1997.

———. *Cowboys of the Americas.* New Haven: Yale University Press, 1990.

Smits, Daniel D. "The Frontier Army and the Destruction of the Buffalo, 1865–1883." *Western Historical Quarterly* 25 (Autumn 1994): 313–88.

Starrs, Paul F. *Let the Cowboy Ride: Cattle Ranching in the American West.* Baltimore: Johns Hopkins University Press, 1998.

Stegner, Wallace. *Wolf Willow: A History, a Story, and a Memory of the Last Plains Frontier.* New York: Viking Press, 1955.

Vanderhaeghe, Guy. *The Englishman's Boy: A Novel.* Toronto: McClelland and Stewart, 1992.

———. *The Last Crossing.* Toronto: McClelland Stewart, 2002.

Vrooman, C. W., G. D. Chattaway, and Andrew Stewart. *Cattle Ranching in Western Canada.* Ottawa: Department of Agriculture, 1946.

Weir, Thomas R. *Ranching in the Southern Interior Plateau of British Columbia.* Ottawa: Geographical Branch, Mines and Technical Surveys, 1964.

On Law and Order in the Frontier Borderlands

Anderson, Frank W. *Sheriffs and Outlaws of Western Canada.* Calgary: Frontier, 1973.

Baker, William M., ed. *Pioneer Policing in Southern Alberta: Deane of the Mounties.* Calgary: Historical Society of Alberta, 1993.

Beahen, William, and Stan Horrall. *Red Coats on the Prairies: The North-West Mounted Police, 1886–1900.* Regina: Centax/Printwest, 1998.

Brown, Richard Maxwell. "Western Violence: Structure, Values, Myth." *Western Historical Quarterly* 24 (February 1993): 5–20.

Chapman, T. L. "Crime and Injustice in Medicine Hat, 1883–1905." *Alberta History* 39 (Spring 1991): 17–24.

Dawson, Michael. *The Mountie from Dime Novel to Disney.* Toronto: Between the Lines, 1998.

Deane, R. Burton. *Mounted Police Life in Canada: A Record of Thirty-one Years' Service.* London: Cassell, 1916.

DeLorme, Roland L. "Policing the Pacific Frontier: The United States Bureau of Customs in the Northern Pacific, 1849–1899." *Pacific Northwest Forum* 5/6 (Fall/Winter 1980–81): 54–67.

Dempsey, Hugh A., ed. *Men in Scarlet.* Calgary: McClelland and Stewart West, 1975.

Graybill, Andrew. "Instruments of Incorporation: Rangers, Mounties, and the North American Frontier, 1875–1910." PhD diss., Princeton University, 2003.

———. "Texas Rangers, Canadian Mounties, and the Policing of the Transnational Industrial Frontier, 1885–1910." *Western Historical Quarterly* 35 (Summer 2004): 167–92.

Hanson, Stanley D. "Policing the International Boundary Area in Saskatchewan, 1890–1910." *Saskatchewan History* 19 (Spring 1966): 61–73.

Harvie, Robert A. *Keeping the Peace: Police Reform in Montana, 1889–1918*. Helena: Montana Historical Society, 1994.

Knafla, Louis. "Violence on the Western Canadian Frontier: A Historical Perspective." In J. I. Ross, ed., *Violence in Canada: Sociopolitical Perspectives*, 10–39. Oxford: Oxford University Press, 1995.

LaDow, Beth. *The Medicine Line: Life and Death on a North American Borderland*. New York: Routledge, 2001.

Long, H. G., ed. *Fort Macleod: The Story of the North-West Mounted Police*. Fort Macleod AB: Fort Macleod Historical Association, 1993.

Macleod, Rod C. "Canadianizing the West: The North-West Mounted Police as Agents of the National Policy, 1873–1905." In Lewis H. Thomas, ed., *Essays on Western History*, 101–10. Edmonton: University of Alberta Press, 1976.

———. *The NWMP and Law Enforcement, 1873–1905*. Toronto: University of Toronto Press, 1976.

Sharp, Paul F. "Law in Scarlet Tunics." Chap. 5 of *Whoop-Up Country: The Canadian American West, 1865–1885*. Minneapolis: University of Minnesota Press, 1955.

Slotkin, Richard. *Regeneration through Violence: The Mythology of the American Frontier, 1600–1860*. Middletown CT: Wesleyan University Press, 1973.

Stegner, Wallace. "Law in a Red Coat." Chap. II-8 of *Wolf Willow: A History, a Story, and a Memory of the Last Plains Frontier*. New York: Viking, 1955.

Thorner, T. "The Not-So-Peaceable Kingdom: Crime and Criminal Justice in Frontier Calgary." In Anthony W. Rasporich and Henry C. Classen, eds., *Frontier Calgary: Town, City, and Region, 1875–1914*, 100–113. Calgary: McClelland and Stewart West, 1975.

Utley, Robert M. *Frontier Men in Blue: The United States Army and the Indian, 1848–1865*. New York: Macmillan, 1967.

———. *Frontier Regulars: The United States Army and the Indian, 1866–1891*. New York: Macmillan, 1973.

On Frontier-Era Women's History and Gender Issues in the American and Canadian Wests

Armitage, Susan, and Elizabeth Jameson, eds. *The Women's West*. Norman: University of Oklahoma Press, 1987.

Butler, Anne. *Daughters of Joy, Sisters of Mercy: Prostitutes in the American West*. Urbana: University of Illinois Press, 1987.

Embry, Jessie L. "Two Legal Wives: Mormon Polygamy in Canada, the United States, and Mexico." In Brigham Y. Card et al., eds., *The Mormon Presence in Canada*. Edmonton: University of Alberta Press, 1990.

Faires, Nora. "Constructing a Class and a Gender Outpost across the Border: The American Women's Club of Calgary." In Jameson and McManus, eds., *One Step over the Line*.

———. "Talented and Charming Strangers from Across the Line: Class Privilege, National Identity, and the American Women's Club of Calgary." Paper, conference of the Association of Canadian Studies in the United States, Portland OR, November 2003.

Gray, James H. *Red Lights on the Prairies.* Toronto: Macmillan of Canada, 1971.

Hopkins, Monica. *Letters from a Lady Rancher.* Halifax: Goodread Biographies, 1983.

Jameson, Elizabeth. "Connecting the Women's West." In Jameson and McManus, eds., *One Step over the Line.*

Jameson, Elizabeth, and Susan Armitage, eds. *Writing the Range: Race, Class, and Culture in the Women's West.* Norman: University of Oklahoma Press, 1997.

Jameson, Elizabeth, and Sheila McManus, eds. *One Step over the Line: Toward a History of Women in the North American Wests.* Forthcoming.

Jameson, Sheilagh. "Women in the Southern Alberta Ranch Community, 1881–1914." In Henry C. Classen, ed., *The Canadian West,* 63–78. Calgary: University of Calgary Comprint Publishing Co., 1977.

Jeffrey, Julie Roy. *Frontier Women: The Trans-Mississippi West, 1840–1880.* New York: Hill and Wang, 1979.

Jordan, Teresa. *Cowgirls: Women of the American West.* Reprint, Lincoln: University of Nebraska Press, 1992.

Kay, Jeanne. "Landscapes of Women and Men: Rethinking the Regional Historical Geography of the United States and Canada." *Journal of Historical Geography* 17 (1991): 435–52.

Kolodny, Annette. *The Land before Her: Fantasy and Experience of the American Frontiers, 1630–1860.* Chapel Hill: University of North Carolina Press, 1984.

Leger-Anderson, Anne. "Canadian Prairie Women's History: An Uncertain Enterprise." *Journal of the West* 37 (January 1998): 47–59.

Lindgren, H. Elaine. *Land in Her Own Name: Women as Homesteaders in North Dakota.* Norman: University of Oklahoma Press, 1996.

McManus, Sheila. "Making the Forty-ninth Parallel: How Canada and the United States Used Race, Ethnicity, and Gender to Turn Blackfoot Country into the Alberta-Montana Borderlands." In C. L. Higham and Robert Thacker, eds., *One West, Two Myths: A Comparative Reader,* 109–32. Calgary: University of Calgary Press, 2004.

————. "Mapping the Alberta-Montana Borderlands: Race, Ethnicity, and Gender in the Late Nineteenth Century." *Journal of American Ethnic History* 20 (Spring 2001): 59–74.

————. "Unsettled Pasts, Unsettling Borders: Women, Wests, Nations." In Jameson and McManus, eds., *One Step over the Line.*

Murphy, Mary. "Latitudes and Longitudes: Teaching the History of Women in the U.S. and Canadian Wests." In Jameson and McManus, eds., *One Step over the Line.*

————. "Searching for an Angle of Repose: Women, Work, and Creativity in Early Montana." In David M. Wrobel and Michael C. Steiner, eds., *Many Wests: Place, Culture, and Regional Identity,* 156–76. Lawrence: University Press of Kansas, 1997.

Myres, Sandra L. *Westering Women and the Frontier Experience, 1800–1915.* Albuquerque: University of New Mexico Press, 1982.

Pascoe, Peggy. "Western Women at the Cultural Crossroads." In Patricia Nelson Limerick, Clyde A. Milner III, and Charles E. Rankin, eds., *Trails: Toward a New Western History,* 40–58. Lawrence: University Press of Kansas, 1991.

Randall, Isabelle. *A Lady's Ranche Life in Montana.* London: W. H. Allen, 1887.

Riley, Glenda. *A Place to Grow: Women in the American West*. Wheeling IL: Harlan Davidson, 1992.

————. *Women and Indians on the Frontier*. Albuquerque: University of New Mexico Press, 1984.

Rozum, Molly. "Between Gender and Region: The Transnational Northern Grasslands Case." In Jameson and McManus, eds., *One Step over the Line*.

Savage, Candace. *Cowgirls: Real Cowboy Girls*. Vancouver: Greystone Books, 1996.

Schlissel, Lillian. *Women's Diaries of the Westward Journey*. New York: Schocken Books, 1983.

Schlissel, Lillian, Vicki L. Ruiz, and Janice Monk, eds. *Western Women: Their Land, Their Lives*. Albuquerque: University of New Mexico Press, 1988.

Smith, Charleen. " 'Crossing the Line': American Prostitutes in Western Canada, 1895–1910." In Jameson and McManus, eds., *One Step over the Line*.

4. The Trail to the North in Whoop-Up Country

Paul F. Sharp

Today's tourists traveling northward on U.S. Highway 91 [now Interstate 15] from Great Falls, Montana, to visit the Calgary Stampede or Banff and Lake Louise speed through a vast plain of wheat and grass. Though little remains to remind them of its past, they are passing through a region that pioneers called the Whoop-Up Country, and their modern hard-surfaced highway parallels the Whoop-Up Trail, a colorful and useful avenue of commerce and a high road of adventure in the years before the railways crossed the western plains (see figure 8).

Despite its rowdy name, this half-forgotten highway once brought trade and culture into a great interior market stretching northward from the Missouri River to the Bow River Valley. From Fort Benton on the Great Muddy to Fort Macleod on the Oldman, it reached into the North, writing history in whiskey, guns, furs, freight, and pioneer enterprise.

This trail commands attention, for it was an international highway, neatly bisected by the Canadian-American boundary that marches steadily westward along the forty-ninth parallel with the precision of the surveyor's chain. But to the first settlers on both sides of this man-made boundary, the trail symbolized the economic, social, and cultural ties that for many years defied a politically inspired division of the northern plains. C. E. D. Wood, editor of the *Fort Macleod Gazette*, expressed this sentiment in the first issue of his little newspaper: "And to our American cousins in Montana; to our brother frontiersmen over the way, whose boundary touches our own, and whose interests are so similar and allied to ours, to them we shall look for the patronage which they always extend

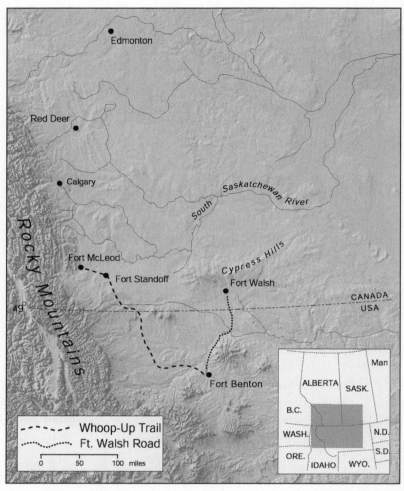

Figure 8. "Whoop-Up Country." Adapted from map in Paul F. Sharp, *Whoop-Up Country* (Minneapolis: University of Minnesota Press, 1955), 6.

to a new enterprise, trusting that the *Gazette* may make one more of the many bonds and ties already joining the two greatest countries in the world."[1]

Local historians in the United States have painstakingly searched out the stories of less important and less colorful thoroughfares, and highway commissions have proudly and expensively marked their routes. The Whoop-Up Trail, however, faded into obscurity as grass healed the deeply rutted wounds on the plains and as time dimmed the recollections of those who remembered.

The story of this northern trail disappeared beyond an international boundary where for many years it was only a chapter in western Canadian history. Yet for a quarter of a century it was a main artery into the western plains, carrying thousands of tons of freight to government installations, North-West Mounted Police posts, United States Army camps, cattle ranches, and Indian reservations. Along its dusty tracks rode Indians searching for game or plunder, scarlet-jacketed Mounties seeking enemies of the Queen, blue-coated United States cavalrymen preserving order, greedy whiskey traders violating laws of God and man in their lust for profits, and ambitious traders seeking likely sites for their short-lived trading posts. In its boom years between 1874 and 1885, this trail carried one-third of all the freight handled through Fort Benton and enriched Montana merchants with profits drained from Canada.[2]

The Whoop-Up Trail thus represented an economic intrusion and a "peaceful penetration" of cultural influence from the south that colored Canadian-American relations during these years. Many Americans hopefully viewed this development as a prelude to economic absorption and political annexation, while patriotic Canadians feared and resented it as a menace to their economic and political expansion. To them the trail symbolized a Manifest Destiny quietly penetrating the outer edge of the Empire, binding it with firm economic ties to the ambitious American republic.

Fort Benton in the post–Civil War years was the hub of an overland transportation network radiating as spokes in a giant wheel to the busy gold fields along the circumference of North American civilization. Through the treeless, dusty streets of this frontier village moved the commerce of the continental heartland.

To supply freight for these trails, toylike, shallow-draft sternwheelers fought their way up the Great Muddy, as capricious a watercourse as commerce ever forced to do its will. Senator Ingalls's famous description, "a little too thick for a beverage and a little too thin for cultivation," paid tribute to its dirty waters. The upper river was especially dangerous, for treachery lay under the shallow, murky waters in shifting sand bars, constantly changing channels, and the countless snags on which the fragile "Mountain" boats might be "stove in" without warning.

Perched at the head of navigation, Fort Benton was an unusual frontier town. "Chicago of the Plains" the village proudly called itself—"the door through which the country to the east, west, and north of it was entered."[3] Eastern pilgrims always watched with mingled emotions the motley crowds that greeted their boat as it nosed into the wharf, for there stood merchants in high-collared broadcloth coats, French Canadian and Creole rivermen wearing bright-colored sashes, tough trappers and traders heavily armed and wearing buckskin, bullwhackers and muleskinners in coarse, rough denim, and, in the background, Indians wearing leggings and blankets.

This diverse collection of humanity was eloquent testimony that Fort Benton was the most cosmopolitan city on the plains. Through this inland port passed pious missionaries and hunted desperadoes, merchants and gamblers, American soldiers and British policemen, hopeful land-seekers and speculators, miners, roustabouts, muleskinners, bullwhackers, and cowboys. Immigrants from nearly every nation of Europe visited it, as well as wanderers from China and African Americans from the Deep South.

The human stream pouring through Fort Benton was a constant reminder that the northern plains were the commercial hinterland of the proud little river town. With justifiable enthusiasm, the local editor could claim that his little village "commands the traffic of the country, holds the key to the business houses of the Territory . . . [is the] transportation center of Montana."[4] With the opening of the Canadian plains, the country to the north was regarded as an addition to Fort Benton's territory—"a vast expanse of country . . . extending into Her Majesty's dominions, its natural and permanent tributary."[5]

Two hundred and forty miles northwest of Fort Benton lay Fort Macleod, northern terminus of the Whoop-Up Trail. Snakelike, the trail crawled out of Benton along the banks of the Teton River to the Whoop-Up crossing on Captain Nelse's ranch; then it struck out across the plains, passing Pen d'Oreille Spring and Yeast Powder Flat, to cross the Marias River near old Fort Conrad. Northward the trail swept past Rocky Springs in northern Montana to enter Canada near present-day Sweetgrass. In Canadian territory the trail forded the Milk River and split into three routes: the eastern branch to Nicholas Sheran's coal banks at modern Lethbridge, the central route to Fort Hamilton or Fort Whoop-Up, and the western route across the St. Mary River at Slideout to Fort Macleod.

Fort Macleod was even less pretentious than Fort Benton, for it was but an atom of settlement in an empty grassland wilderness. Smothered under great clouds of dust from the wheels of busy wagon trains in the summer and buried in seas of mud in spring and autumn, the tiny village seemed the end of civilization to those who ventured up the Whoop-Up Trail to its extremity.

The island site originally selected for Fort Macleod was an unfortunate one, for the community annually faced destruction as high waters from the mountains threatened to wash everything down stream. "Each succeeding Springtime," dryly observed the *Gazette*, "the betting is almost even that the whole concern, Fort, town and inhabitants will form a stately procession on the watery road to Winnipeg."[6]

Despite these unpropitious surroundings, the little Canadian village was an important economic and political center. Here the Mounted Police made their first headquarters in the West and through its streets moved supplies for police, ranchers, and Indians of the Canadian plains. Up the trail from Fort Benton flowed the lifeblood of this western community.

Just as Whoop-Up Trail symbolized the unity of this northern grassland empire, its history demonstrates a centuries-long period of economic, cultural, and political interdependence imposed by geographic integrity. Here on the northern plains, the two great streams of Anglo-Saxon pioneering that had pushed across the continent finally reached their last West in the same environment.

But similarity does not imply identity. Environment never shapes advanced human societies entirely to its will. Other forces are equally important—and often more important. Certainly, significant differences marked the two national communities that developed along the Whoop-Up Trail. Though poured into the same plains environment, the two societies centered at Fort Benton and Fort Macleod retained their separate political and cultural identities.

Many extraregional relationships and many heritages from older societies were far too powerful to be affected by environment. National-ism, the most pervasive force in our modern world, was unaffected by its movement into this semiarid and treeless plains country. It created Canadian plainsmen to the north and American plainsmen to the south. Each possessed loyalties reaching outside the region that prevented a complete identification of common problems. Thus nationalism achieved in the generation following the American Civil War what nature could not accomplish in millenniums; it gave reality to a political line that bisected a region of geographic unity.

Nature created a grassland region possessing a unity and integrity that its aboriginal inhabitants respected. The white man's politics rent it asunder to create highly complex societies whose orientation was changed from a north-south to an east-west axis. The decades during which these great changes were in the making were the years of the Whoop-Up Trail. Its story is the exciting one of creating Canadian and American institu-tions cheek by jowl in the West. Two societies so similar, yet so different that only a most cautious judgment can calculate the parallels or measure the differences. Society on these northern plains, Canadian and American, was the heir of many cultures, the image and transcript of none.

Notes

Originally published as "Trail to the North," in Paul Sharp, *Whoop-Up Country: The Cana-dian and American West, 1865–1885* (Minneapolis: University of Minnesota Press, 1955), 1–9, copyright 1955 by the University of Minnesota Press; reprinted here by permission.

1. *Fort Macleod Gazette*, July 1, 1882.
2. Canada, *Sessional Papers*, no. 23, pt. III, 188, p. 22. See also Gerald L. Berry, *The Whoop-Up Trail: Early Days in Alberta-Montana* (Edmonton: Applied Art Products, 1953), and Charles M. MacInnes, *In the Shadow of the Rockies* (London: Rivington, 1930).
3. H. V. A. Ferguson, "Fort Benton Memories," manuscript in Historical Society of Montana Library, Helena.
4. *Fort Benton Record*, February 1, 1875.
5. *Fort Benton Record*, December 12, 1879.
6. *Fort Macleod Gazette*, November 14, 1882.

5. Above the Blue Line

Policing the Frontier in the Canadian and American West, 1870–1900

Marian C. McKenna

> *He [Gen. Nelson A. Miles] had heard his officers say that the line would never stop him when in pursuit of Indians. There wasn't a scout, muleskinner, or trader along the upper Missouri who would doubt that Miles would say, "To hell with the border." Who could stop him anyway? A handful of policemen in red jackets?*
>
> Frank Turner, *Across the Medicine Line*

Capt. Cecil Denny, who rode out with the first contingent of North-West Mounted Police (NWMP) in 1874 on its historic "march west," in his memoirs later asked, "Was the saddle over the Canadian?" According to his account, the country's western frontier was a composite of evils—battles, murder, plunder, and sudden death from the Red River to the Rocky Mountains. Year by year it exacted its toll—yes, even a grisly toll. Red men warred against red men, tribe against tribe, and white men warred and preyed upon them all. When homicide anywhere goes unpunished, unless [it is] privately avenged, he wrote, thieving and plundering are accounted virtues, and "life snuffed out is only one life less."[1]

This does not mean that the law was flouted: there was no law. At a few isolated settlements scattered around one of its trading posts on some northern lake or river, the Hudson's Bay Company officer might have occasionally held the semblance of a court, for he represented such authority as the country knew. But since there existed no legal machinery or law enforcement, decrees issuing from such a tribunal seldom had any effect on anything.

Farther out west, in the great treeless region drained by the Bow, Belly, and South Saskatchewan rivers, there were neither trading posts nor settlements to speak of, and such contact between the Natives and whites as existed were such a character as to inspire little faith among the tribesmen or any great respect for white men. Traders venturing into this territory risked losing not only their goods but also their scalps.

Those white men whose trading endeavors were mainly responsible for the frequent clashes and atrocities in this region operated chiefly along the international boundary. Some, though not all, were outlaws, fugitives from justice and the Montana courts, or deserters from the Civil War armies, with long records of crimes behind them. Their headquarters on the banks of the Belly River, not far from the present city of Lethbridge, Alberta, was a fort these whiskey traders from south of the border had built and nicknamed "Fort Whoop-Up."

The sale of liquor had a deleterious effect on the Native men, who became crazed by the poisonous concoction. They threw away their robes, fighting broke out, and terror and devastation spread throughout both Native and white traders' camps. The white traders did not hesitate to use their rifles on the Natives, whether wantonly or in drunken abandon. As Denny reports, they shamefully abused the men and debauched the women. By the 1870s, the situation was serious and constantly growing worse, so much so that it called for some immediate measures on both sides of the border and drastic means of repression.

Denny's portrayal of the scene as it was unfolding in the 1870s seems to mirror some of the current revisionist interpretations emerging in Canadian historiography, which hold that lawlessness on *both* sides of the border was a distinct and general characteristic of frontier society in popular culture before 1900. The time frame of this essay encompasses the period from 1870 to 1900. The NWMP were well secured in the Northwest and had already become for Canadians a "western icon." When the Liberal government in Ottawa attempted to eliminate the force in 1896, there was such an outcry that it had to abandon the idea.

In earlier accounts, the two frontiers are depicted as very different, the Canadians in the Northwest being seen as orderly, respectful, and law-abiding, while the Americans are invariably portrayed as raucous, unruly, and lawless. Historians in both countries have been wrestling with the task of comparing the two northwestern frontiers in efforts to enforce the law in their respective territories, anticipating an increase in white settlement. A flood of immigrants was expected to arrive on Canada's frontier once they could gain access to the region by train.

An examination of the institutions the two societies came to rely on to establish law and order and keep the peace inevitably reveals more differences than similarities. But while acknowledging the differences that certainly did exist, historians are revealing a new image of the Canadian frontier, a less distorted, mythical one than the long-standing portrayal of the past. Canadian law, it can be shown, was not the universal authority north of the border that many writers have made it out to be. What eventually emerges will be a far cry from the peaceful and law-abiding region portrayed in earlier literature.

This essay compares Alberta and Montana territory as they put in place a system of law and order on the two frontiers. A feature that makes any comparison risky is the fact that settlement in the Canadian Northwest Territories lagged well behind the United States. Canadians were years behind the westering American throng. The effect was a far less aggressive military policy required on the Canadian side of the border. In dealing with the western Indian tribes, for example, the Canadians were at a distinct advantage on account of the Native peoples' relatively small numbers. Canadians took inordinate pride in the fact that good relations with their Indian tribes distinguished them from the Americans.

If there was less racial violence between Natives and whites on the Canadian frontier, it resulted, at least in part, from the work of the North-West Mounted Police. The NWMP did a reasonably good job in establishing a benevolent policy toward Native peoples during a very difficult transition period from nomadic life as buffalo hunters, in settling the Native bands on reserves, and trying to cement tolerable relations with them. All this was in sharp contrast to the Indian policy pursued by the United States before 1900.

In spite of the problems involved, a comparison can be drawn between Canada's Northwest and Montana territories, looking at establishing law and order on both sides of the border. It should be kept in mind that in 1870 the two frontiers were at very different stages of development and maturity. An exploration of their evolution will demonstrate that the differences far outweigh the similarities. Nevertheless, it should be constructive to compare various aspects of law enforcement, legal institutions, and the general principles operating in the two frontier settings during this formative period.

❈

The two agencies most closely associated with ensuring the peace and safety of inhabitants were the NWMP and the U.S. Army, along with an American apparatus of legal and judicial institutions brought out on the frontier to cope with any substantial settlement. In Montana, Fort Shaw, built of adobe or sun-dried brick, was in the mid-1870s the largest military post in western Montana. Its commanding officer, Gen. John Gibbon, a friend of President Lincoln, was a Civil War veteran with a record of long service in Indian wars. Under him were some four hundred men, cavalry and infantry. Many of his officers had brought along their families.

Contrary to popular belief, both the NWMP and the U.S. Army were out on their frontiers in advance of white settlement. Between 1870 and 1880, they had to prepare the Indians for the painful arrival of whites. An experience common to both countries was recognizing that establishing law, order, and effective policing would hinge in large measure on how the authorities went about finding methods of pacifying the Natives. The social and physical environment of the frontier dictated that Canadian and American legal authorities would be forced to confront similar obstacles as well as many of the same difficulties in trying to deal with them. Different Indian policies were adopted by the two governments, and their modus operandi proved in most features to be in conflict at every stage.

"The tide of immigration in Canada has not been as great as along our frontier," observed Gen. Nelson A. Miles in his memoirs. "Canadians have been able to allow the Indians to live as Indians, which we have not, and [they] do not attempt to force upon them customs which to them are distasteful." Miles, who was made responsible for forcing the return of Sitting Bull and his three thousand Sioux to the United States after their flight into Canada following the battle at the Little Bighorn, became more sympathetic to the Indians in later life than he was in the 1870s. He said he would gladly have ignored the boundary on occasion, calling it "one of the troubles of this business."[2]

Certain common topographical characteristics united the northwestern frontiers of Alberta and Montana. One of them was their geographical similarity. They formed part of the vast northern plains region, divided by an artificial boundary. At midcentury the huge American interior between the tier of states bordering the Mississippi River on the east and the Rocky Mountains on the west remained comparatively unsettled by whites. Generations of pioneers had avoided the semiarid, treeless, interminable grasslands of the Great Plains for the more congenial expanses that lay beyond. It was considered a hostile environment, presenting obstacles to settlement. But by 1870, Canada began to view the plains and prairie region as a "Last Best West." Canadian nationalists feared that if they did not get on with exploiting this vast hinterland, it was inevitable that expansionists to the south who coveted it would move into the void.

In terms of climate and topography, the Canadian plains region, stretching from Manitoba to the prairies of Saskatchewan and Alberta, where it ran along the foothills of the Rockies and south to the American border, was similar to western Montana territory. Warm chinook winds, blowing across Alberta's flatlands from the eastern slopes of the mountains, melted winter snow, exposing grasslands available for winter pasture. Numerous coulees furnished natural shelter from the intense cold of the high latitude. The region contained an abundance of highly nutritious short grass vegetation and streams, available for watering stock.

The semiarid soil was not considered favorable for agriculture, with the result that settlement did not occur to present a barrier to early ranching, utilizing the open range. In the initial phase of settlement (1880–1900), agents of law enforcement would be concerned with developing techniques to cope with the increasingly complex kinds of criminality that accompany the arrival of ranchers, settlement of towns, and the beginnings of urbanization. Not until the 1880s did prospective farmers, called "sodbusters," begin to move into these territories, once dry farming techniques were introduced. But the plains' natural advantages attracted western adventurers. Fur and whiskey traders, moving north out of Fort Benton in Montana, saw the potential this country had to offer those interested in trade.

The population density on the two frontiers was not the same. But both covered vast, untamed areas, with wide open spaces extremely difficult to police. White men, whose activities were mainly responsible for the frequent atrocities in the region, operated chiefly along the international boundary. Some were outlaws. Comparative crime rates and lawless tendencies in the territories during these decades are impossible to document. Numerous crimes went unreported or unsolved, and like most appeals, they did not appear in existing court records. Circumstances on both frontiers were fluid, constantly changing.

An organized system of cross-border trade had developed during the early days of the River colony, but farther to the west, the territory peopled by the feared Blackfoot Confederation deterred all activity by white traders on both sides of the border. Even the powerful Hudson's Bay Company (HBC) was forced to operate far to the north of Fort Edmonton and Rocky Mountain House. Organized trade first began to move across the U.S.–Canadian border and into the heart of Blackfoot country in 1869. Historian Paul Sharp observed that the American frontier crossed the international boundary with the Yankee traders. The prairie and grasslands now part of southern Alberta and the rangelands of Montana to the south constituted what was known as "Whoop-Up country" (after Fort Whoop-Up, a notorious rendezvous for whiskey traders at the junction of the Bow and Belly rivers). Homemade American flags flew over this and other trading forts on the Canadian side of the line.

"Half-breed" traders, calling at the Wood Mountain post of the NWMP, told the story of a frontiersman who arrived at Fort Benton to buy supplies. "How's trade?" he was asked. "We're a whoopin' it up" was the reply. That, it is said, was how the whiskey fort, the focal point of lawlessness near the border, got its name. This country was made a part of the economic hinterland of Fort Benton on the Missouri River. (It was not until the 1840s that the Blackfoot were conciliated sufficiently to tolerate the construction of Fort Benton by the American Fur Company.) Merchants from Benton made sure that the area to the north was well supplied with trade goods, including whiskey.[3]

At that time, Montana Territory had a considerable white population made up mainly of cattle ranchers, miners, gamblers, adventurers, and "bad" men who came and went. Lawlessness was rife, and lynchings were routine. Vigilance committees dealt out summary justice to the tougher elements. It was reported that forty men were hanged by these committees for horse theft, murder, or other crimes in the town of Benton in less than three years. Recruits for the NWMP were brought into Alberta by way of Benton, and there was a good deal of travel and trade between Canada's Northwest Territories and points in Montana. Benton boasted a sheriff, his deputies, and a magistrate (a man who had led a Fenian raid on Canada in 1871 and harbored no love for Britishers). He is said to have measured the amount of any fine he imposed by the amount of money in the possession of a convicted prisoner.[4]

As early as the 1860s, suggestions were already being made for organizing some type of quasi-military force to bring law and order to the northwestern plains, even before the territory was formally annexed to Canada. One of the earliest ideas originated with Thomas Blackiston, an officer in the Royal Artillery, who accompanied the 1859 British expedition across the Canadian prairies led by Capt. John Palliser. In describing the condition of this territory, Blackiston observed the absence of any form of civil government or rule of law. He made notes on the demoralizing effect the liquor traffic was having on the Natives and the general lawlessness that prevailed in this wild land. Lawlessness arose in part out of the absence of any means of administering justice in a region where tribal warfare and violence between Indians and whites was a fairly common occurrence. He was among the first to recommend a military police force based in part on the Royal Irish Constabulary (RIC).

The RIC was established by Britain during the Napoleonic wars when militia and troops were deployed to the continent. It was feared that internal disorder in Ireland could result in inviting a French invasion. The constabulary, the model for colonial police forces in India and other parts of the British Empire, offered a solution to the problem Canada faced to provide cheap but effective law enforcement in its Northwest Territories. Its dual character combined the military capabilities of an armed force with the judicial functions of peace officers.[5] To Prime Minister John A. Macdonald, it seemed the kind of force particularly well suited to maintaining order under frontier conditions. He began making plans for units of about 200 men in the winter of 1869–70 in preparation for Canada's assuming control of the Hudson's Bay Company lands annexed to it. However, the need to deal with a Métis uprising in 1869–70 at Red River in opposition to Canada's impending takeover of their land forced postponement of plans for a domestic police force. The Métis rebellion directly affected the government's timetable for organizing the force.

By then, what little authority the HBC had left in the region had been lost. Local police and militia had performed miserably in Manitoba, where ethnic tensions between Métis and white settlers remained unresolved. The earlier failures of HBC's courts and police in Rupert's Land further encouraged the reversion by Ottawa to the British colonial model used in India, Ireland, and Australia.[6]

The HBC's long-standing inability to enforce its laws was a factor in Métis unrest. Governor William McTavish had proved unable to exercise the slightest influence before the transfer of HBC territory to the Dominion of Canada. This state of affairs was not lost on John A. Macdonald. In a letter in 1870 to Sir John Rose, his government's representative in London, he asked for more details about the organization of the RIC and explained: "The reason why I telegraphed for the organization of the Royal Irish Constabulary is that we propose to organize a mounted police force . . . for Red River purposes. We must never subject the Government there to the humiliation offered McTavish."[7] Macdonald came near to admitting that in 1869–70, federal or any other kind of control over law enforcement had been lost in the only populated part of the Canadian West.

A more systematic approach to deployment of a military force to Canada's Northwest was recommended by Capt. William F. Butler, a British army officer, who toured the former HBC territories in 1870 and then issued a voluminous report in 1871. To bring law and order to a country he found without security for life or property, Butler drew on

British experiences in Ireland and India. He recommended organizing a mounted police force of about 150 men under a civil magistrate or commissioner, to be stationed along a northerly line, occupying a chain of posts that included Fort Edmonton and Prince Albert. This would have utilized a route where trade and future settlement were expected to grow. Relying on their anticipated mobility, he expected police units to serve as a strike force, making quick response to any trouble spots on the plains to the south.[8]

Another proposal, quite different from Butler's, was put forward two years later by one of Canada's top military men, Col. Patrick Robertson-Ross, adjutant general of the Canadian Militia. He was sent west to carry out a reconnaissance of the situation and to survey military requirements in the Northwest. His report was on Macdonald's desk by December 1872. Butler noted that the illicit liquor trade between Fort Benton and the southwestern prairies was well established and growing, but he did not consider it much of a threat. However, by the time Robertson-Ross reached the area (he traveled farther south than Butler), he found that conditions were much worse. He cited Fort Whoop-Up as the single most notorious of the whiskey trading posts.

Robertson-Ross proposed locating the largest NWMP contingent considered so far (150 men) in what is now southern Alberta near the international boundary. The reason stated was the growing concern over activities of American whiskey traders in the area. His alarming report described the huge territory of Montana as being under the control of American renegades and businessmen of questionable ethics—army deserters, smugglers, gamblers, wolfers [professional wolf hunters], freebooters, and trading post bootleggers, peddling guns and red-eye liquor to Indians in return for horses, furs, and buffalo robes. His report recommended organizing a full regiment of 550 mounted riflemen to occupy a chain of posts stretching west from Manitoba to the Rocky Mountains.[9]

The government had reports from Thomas Blackiston, Captain Palliser, Captain Butler, Colonel Robertson-Ross, Sandford Fleming, a number of HBC officials, missionaries, and others. Butler's and Robertson-Ross's recommendations included two conflicting choices the Canadian government would have to consider in determining whatever kind of force would be organized to bring law and order to the western frontier. Butler proposed about 150 men stationed along a northerly line of posts, and Robertson-Ross recommended a much larger force of 550 mounted men with a heavy concentration in southern Alberta near the border. Ottawa authorities took their time deciding on a workable policy and plans for putting it into effect.

A defensive line of forts along a northerly route to be deployed on occasion as a strike force into the border country was not a workable option. It was unrealistic to think that with one blow, any force could eradicate the whiskey traffic, establish law and order, and introduce civil government into such a vast territory. The suggestion carried with it the possibility of a confrontation with whiskey traders, the Blackfoot Confederacy, or both. In contrast, U.S. Army policy favored pacification of frontier areas by establishing an advancing line of forts right through Indian territory, rather than concentration of forces at strategic locations.[10]

The Ottawa government's attention was riveted on the Northwest Territories after 1870, owing to alarming reports of sporadic outbreaks of Indian warfare, intertribal rivalries compounded by rapidly vanishing buffalo herds, and the sale of guns and whiskey to Native tribes in the region. While the Macdonald government debated the question of how best to establish a regime of law and order on the frontier without placing too heavy a burden on the treasury, it was jolted into action by alarming reports received from several sources. During the spring of 1873, rumors had been circulating about a massacre of Assiniboines in the Cypress Hills in Canadian territory by a party of American whiskey traders working out of Fort Benton. Confirmation of the atrocity appeared in Montana newspaper reports, and in May the Ottawa government was given official notification through diplomatic channels.

Word came from the British ambassador in Washington, Sir Edward Thornton, of the massacre of possibly as many as fifty Assiniboines by a group of vengeful whiskey traders from Montana. Their horses had been stolen one night, probably by Cree Indians, while the traders were making their way to Fort Benton after wintering along the border.

Fearing that the Canadian prairies would be inflamed in Indian wars like those raging south of the border, and seeking to bolster Canada's claim to sovereignty over its Northwest Territories, in May 1873 the Macdonald government introduced legislation regarding the administration of justice in the West, providing judicial machinery for the territories and establishing a force of policemen-soldiers. The bill was received in the House with marked disinterest but was passed that month without debate. Attention was focused on an impending public scandal growing out of charges that the Conservative Party had received upwards of $300,000 from Hugh Allan, president of the Canadian Pacific Railway Company, in return for the assurance that the company would be awarded the contract to build the transcontinental railroad. The Macdonald government's days in office were numbered.

In his original statement to the House on a police force, Macdonald had used the term "Mounted Rifles," but upon receiving adverse reactions, mostly from alarmists south of the border protesting that Canada was displaying "warlike tendencies," he crossed out the word "Rifles" and wrote in "Police." It was on balance a better term for units that would have the duties of a civilian police force but would be organized as a military force in form and discipline. Its mission was to establish law and order, preserve the peace, prevent crimes, arrest offenders, try and sentence offenders, and apply the letter of the law. NWMP officers (commissioners and superintendents) were made justices of the peace, or stipendiary magistrates. Macdonald wanted as little "gold braid" as possible.

He did not envision creating an elite cavalry division on the British model; he wanted an efficient, mobile constabulary to end outlawry and the whiskey trade, collect the customs, gain the Indians' respect, and pave the way for the white settlement of towns, farms, and villages. He had his heart set on eventual completion of a Pacific railway. The men's uniforms, with their redcoats, were designed to remind the Indians of a British tradition of law with which some of the older ones had already had experience. On his western tour, Robertson-Ross had observed that Natives associated the scarlet tunics of soldiers with the "Great White Mother" (Queen Victoria) and British justice that the soldiers supposedly represented.

Wallace Stegner, a writer and scholar of the West who grew up in southern Saskatchewan, later wrote: "Never was the dignity of the uniform more carefully cultivated and rarely has the ceremonial quality of impartial law and order been more dramatically exploited." Since the middle of the eighteenth century, the red coat of the British dragoons had signified to the Indians a force that was non- and sometimes anti-American. The contrast was doubly effective once the blue coats of the American cavalry had become an abomination to American Plains Indians. According to Stegner, one of the most visible aspects of the international boundary was that it was a color line: blue below, red above: blue for treachery and unkept promises, red for protection and the straight tongue.[11]

Prime Minister Macdonald replaced Manitoba's first lieutenant governor, Adams G. Archibald, with a fellow Conservative he believed would go far in easing the tensions in that strife-ridden province. He named Alexander Morris in the summer of 1872 as the first chief justice of the Court of Queen's Bench. His appointment was meant to strengthen the province's judicial system, which was not yet fully organized. Macdonald intended for Morris to succeed Archibald, which he did in December 1872. Morris was also lieutenant governor of the Northwest Territories and thus chief representative of the Ottawa government.

At the end of 1872, Macdonald assured Morris that legislation for the formation of a police force would pass at the next session of Parliament. Morris deserves the credit for convincing his chief of the need for such a force and the urgency of swift action to put it into use. He also pressed for a larger force than the fifty men contemplated. Not even double that number would suffice, in his opinion. Nor did he want the militia force diminished below its present strength. As for the choice of uniform worn by the new NWMP, in a letter to Macdonald he wrote that "the police should also be under military discipline and if possible be *red coated*—as fifty men in red coats are better than 100 in other colours."[12]

Macdonald's original intention for his police force was to recruit, organize, and train mounted units in eastern Canada during the winter of 1873–74, before sending them out to the prairies. Headquarters were to be in Winnipeg. But the alarming turn of events in the summer of 1873 forced him to change his timetable, speeding up orders to dispatch the force to the scene of trouble. Privy Council Order no. 114 of August 30, 1873, brought the NWMP into existence as a legally constituted body to bring law and order to Canada's Northwest Territories and patrol an area of about 500,000 square miles.

Late in August 1873, the Canadian government was stunned by a confidential report from Alexander Morris. From Fort Garry he described what was known of the circumstances of the Cypress Hills massacre, which he blamed on whiskey traders from Fort Whoop-Up. His report urged Ottawa to take immediate action against the traders. The government was not easily moved to take action. The minister of the interior, Alexander Campbell, in a bland reply to Morris, indicated that he did not consider the situation "grave enough" to send out a force immediately. Morris turned to other officials, including the governor general, to plead the case for dispatch of mounted police units at once, warning that the situation in the Cypress Hills could bring on a repeat of the 1869 Métis uprising or a major Indian war. He also contacted George A. French, the Royal Artillery officer named by Macdonald to be the first commissioner and commander of the NWMP.

At this critical juncture, Macdonald's government was voted out of office in January 1874. The new prime minister, Sir Alexander Mackenzie, had never liked Macdonald's ideas of a semimilitary force. If it had not been officially established while Macdonald still had the authority to do so, it might never have been formed at all. During the transition of governments, French informed the deputy minister of justice, Hewitt Bernard, that Lieutenant Governor Morris "has reliable information that there are five forts between Milk River and Edmonton, each containing 100 outlaws and mounting several guns." Apparently these men had boldly announced that they were prepared to fight it out with any force sent out to disturb them. French added, "I think it is possible that they mean what they say." [13]

Mackenzie's first impulse was to request assistance from the United States. He favored a joint expedition with American troops empowered to cross the border into Canadian territory. But Lord Dufferin, Canada's governor general, used his considerable influence to dissuade Mackenzie from taking such a course of action. He pointed out that not only would there be international complications but, by acting alone, Canadians would appear to the Indians as their allies against the American-based traders. Mackenzie finally agreed that the expedition should be "purely

Canadian," ordering the hastily organized detachments to go after the gang of "Yankee desperadoes" who had massacred the Assiniboines and had now established themselves at the juncture of the Bow and Belly rivers. [14] His report failed to mention that at least four Canadians were among the gang of wolfers who perpetrated the atrocity. Once the arrest and incarceration of the gang was accomplished, the force was to be broken up into smaller units, with the principal objective of abolishing the liquor trade.

In order for a combined force of some 275 men to reach the junction of the Bow and Belly rivers, they were to proceed west from Fort Dufferin, staying close to the border. But Morris opposed use of a southerly route, informing Ottawa in May that he had reliable information that 1,000 Sioux had crossed the Missouri River and were heading north toward the border. They were hostile toward the border survey and invasion of their hunting grounds. Fearing that the Mounted Police would become victims of an attack, Morris advised Ottawa to order the expedition to follow the northerly trade route to Fort Edmonton, from which it could then march south to Whoop-Up Country. [15]

Ottawa ignored this advice from the region's lieutenant governor. If French had followed initial orders to travel along the path of the Boundary Commission west, the force would have had a clearly marked trail as a guide and stations along the way for supplies and water. But to avoid any conflict with the Sioux, French was now ordered to proceed along the border for 150–200 miles and then strike north, continuing in a northwesterly direction toward Qu'Appelle, away from the border. Before reaching the turning point at Qu'Appelle, the force was ordered to move more directly westward toward the Cypress Hills. The final order was not settled upon until French was able to consult with Morris in Manitoba.

In July 1874, five companies of NWMP left Fort Dufferin to begin the march west to police Canada's new frontier. But by taking the mounted force away from the border, the route required them to move through hundreds of miles of semiarid country with no grass, no water, and poor supplies. French had been misinformed about the country through which he was to lead his green force. Paul Sharp, one of the first to deflate a romantic legend in Canadian history involving the NWMP, found that the famous 800-mile trek west was anything but romantic. As he wrote, this entire enterprise was nearly wrecked by a combination of misfortunes, inexperience, and ignorance.[16]

❀

In the early years of Montana's territorial history, law enforcement relied on the limited resources of elected county sheriffs and their deputies, in an attempt to maintain order on the vast northwestern ranges. Officially above the sheriff and his deputies there was a territorial marshal, appointed by and under the jurisdiction of the federal authorities in Washington. This position was normally held by a politician, appointed for his allegiance to the administration holding office. Frequently the marshal had little experience in law or its workings and usually he delegated some of his duties to one or two deputies. They had to devote much of their time to serving subpoenas, forming juries, conducting auctions or private sales, locating witnesses, and issuing writs or warrants. Urban centers like Helena, Miles City, and Great Falls appointed their marshals and constables, who were more directly involved in the prevention and control of crime. In other urban centers like Atchison, with only a city marshal and one police officer to patrol the entire town, advocates of law enforcement usually lost out against city taxpayers, who balked at footing the bill for more police protection in a town already overrun with pickpockets, thieves, and confidence men.[17]

Like Canada's Mounties, Montana's policing authorities faced staggering difficulties with the enormity of their task. In that day, the territory was the home of many warlike tribes—Gros Ventre, Sioux, Blackfeet, and others, who looked upon the "Long Knives" or "Bluecoats" (their names for U.S soldiers) as their enemies. The Americans were far more involved than Canadians in gunning down Indians on their frontiers, and there were numerous clashes in Montana. In a single region of that state, there were more than thirty Indian massacres after 1860.[18] In 1867, soldiers and civilians putting up hay near Fort Smith were attacked by Sioux warriors. By the end of the day eight Indians, two soldiers, and one civilian had been killed, and thirty more had been wounded.

Montana authorities had to police their frontier with the most skeletal of forces—a mere handful of lawmen trying to exercise control over thousands of square miles, while performing numerous other functions besides keeping the peace. Montana had more settlers, more cattle, more cattlemen, more Indians, and more outlaws than Canada's Northwest with its sparse population on the other side of the border.[19] Unlike Mounties, U.S. soldiers never went in force into an Indian camp. Many an unlucky army fellow caught alone by Indians was likely to be tortured or killed.

The Mounties had much greater policing and discretionary powers than their American counterparts in establishing law where none had existed before. Methods of law enforcement could be easily distinguished on either side of the border. The NWMP commissioner and superintendents, as ex officio justices of the peace, had authority to try most, if not all, the suspects they apprehended. They could then mete out fines and jail sentences to those they arrested and convicted. This was the kind of authority that the entire array of local sheriffs, federal marshals, and the U.S. Army lacked. Local American juries were reluctant to convict their liquor-trading neighbors.

On the two frontiers, the human obstacles to future white occupation were the Native peoples. In many cases, Canadian Indians occupying the buffalo plains without borders had the same tribal affiliations as their American counterparts. They included the Sioux and northern Cheyenne. The U.S. Army and the Mounties shared the task of attempting to keep the peace with and between the various tribes in the Northwest. At times they found themselves hamstrung in their endeavors, lacking adequate authority, especially in the case of the U.S. Army, whose pony soldiers occupied posts strung out across the entire western half of the continent, piercing through the heart of Indian country.

On both frontiers, white hunters and adventurers decimated the buffalo herds, depriving the Plains Indians of their livelihood, the bedrock of their culture, social organization, and way of life. (Some Native peoples, anxious to reap the reward for trading buffalo hides, contributed to the slaughter.) With the completion of the transcontinental railroads, promising an influx of settlers, both governments were forced to revisit their Indian policies. The pursuit by the United States of its ill-advised policy had the effect of plunging the Great Plains into decades of Indian warfare.

There may have been fundamental differences between the two countries in their methods of frontier policing, especially in their dealings with the Native peoples, but there were also similarities in attitudes on the part of white settlers, which produced some of the same tensions on the Canadian side that existed south of the border. If there was less racial violence in Alberta and the Northwest than in Montana, it did occur, and historians are beginning to find a surprising amount of it. The result of ingrained attitudes made for far less racial harmony than earlier historical accounts have acknowledged. Despite all their honest efforts and mostly worthy intentions, the NWMP had less success in maintaining peaceful relations with Native peoples over the long haul. Consider this editorial: "These Indians must be kept on their reserves else the indignant stockmen will some day catch the red rascals and make such an example of them that the noble red men will think h——'s a poppon, besides a probably attack of kink in the back of the neck [lynching] and we can't say that we should greatly blame them either. That a lot of dirty, thieving, lazy ruffians should be allowed to go where they will, carrying the latest improved weapons, when there is no game in the country, seems absurd."[20] Complaints by ranchers to the NWMP were often strident, but cattlemen were fortunate to have whatever protection could be offered by the force, especially once systematic patrols were introduced. Friction between Indians and white settlers would likely have escalated had not the Mounties attempted to enforce tougher liquor laws and managed to eliminate some, though not all, the liquor traffic to the Indians. The patrol system was set up by Lawrence W. Herchmer after he became commissioner in 1886. It proved to be partially effective with the establishment of a network of posts throughout the southern range's ranching communities on the prairies. Four of the largest cattle ranches in the Canadian West had such posts within a few miles of their home buildings.

Frontier police in Canada have been credited with frequent and effective patrolling of the region's ranching districts, but recent studies question how effective this system could have been encompassing such a huge expanse of territory. In April 1897, a newspaper writer noted: "The NWMP patrol under Inspector Jarvis, which went north from Edmonton in January, returned to Fort Saskatchewan last week, having completed the longest patrol ever made by a police detachment." He complained about the poor results of the patrol and found the situation very frustrating.

"Did they not see anything?" he wanted to know. He went on to question the effectiveness of the police in the face of widespread cattle rustling.[21]

During the 1880s, Canadian and U.S. authorities tended to work primarily on their own problems, as if the two frontiers were entirely separate, but the instances of cattle rustling showed little or no respect for political boundaries. Activities by Montana vigilantes such as "Stuart's Stranglers" were notorious. They either shot or hanged dozens of known or suspected rustlers, operating primarily along the Musselshell and Missouri rivers. Estimates put the number hanged in 1884 at twenty-one at the lowest.[22]

Somewhat later, it was reported in the papers that two men from southern Alberta—one of them a renegade constable of the NWMP—were arrested in Montana with stolen Canadian horses. In the process of being transported to Fort Benton for trial they were intercepted by a party of cowboys. After "very few preliminaries" they were escorted to the nearest tree and sent "on the hemp line route to the great hereafter." These activities had a dampening effect on rustling, which became less frequent because it was considered "too hot in Montana." As a result, many cattle thieves headed north.[23]

In the summer of 1878, rations had to be distributed among starving Indians, while sicknesses, including typhoid fever, carried off many whites and Indians alike around Fort Macleod and Fort Walsh during that wet summer. Many Canadian cattlemen were new at ranching and without experience of any kind. They seldom saw their cattle after turning them out on the open range. These ranchers, nervous about theft owing to the scarcity of meat, drove their herds south to Montana's rangelands. For many, it was temporary; they soon returned.

Almost all losses of cattle were routinely attributed to "the red men." At Fort Calgary, where Captain Denny was in command during the winters of 1879 and 1880, two cattlemen named Lynch and Emerson reported twenty head of their herd had been killed by Indians. The following spring, that same number bearing their brand were found lying together in Jumping Pond Creek, south of the Bow River, the same cattle whose loss had been charged against the Indians.[24]

By the mid-1890s, the Mounted Police, who took their campaign against cattle rustling seriously, were complaining openly of their inability to gain the upper hand. "This is an immense territory to watch," Commissioner Herchmer asserted in 1896, lamenting the amount of livestock theft going on. A year later, he noted that although the force had endeavored to patrol the country as usual, and had been successful in arresting many "cattle thieves and delinquents," advantage was being taken of their small numbers. The commissioner and his subordinates believed rustling was part of a growing trend toward crime in general. The detailed list submitted in an 1899 report was "rather long" and included many kinds of offenses.[25]

The frequency of cattle rustling induced extreme frustration among Canadian ranchers and instigated more than one lynching in Alberta. When rustling increased dramatically in Western Assiniboia, some of the ranchers there considered resorting to vigilante justice. "A great deal of stock has been stolen in this district during the last few years," a rancher wrote in a letter to a newspaper, "but up to the present time sufficient evidence has not been secured to convict or even to connect anyone with the thefts. In consequence of these thefts and the seeming inability of the "law" to cope with them, there . . . now are, I believe, steps being taken to form a 'Stockmen's Association,' which will . . . protect its members and punish thieves."[26]

In Montana, local ranchers made wider use of vigilance committees and summary executions, by hanging, in many instances. Their methods were criticized elsewhere as evidence of western barbarism, but in other circles they were considered real demonstrations of a capacity for local government. These actions were thought of as a condition of life on a raw frontier. Extralegal citizen action committees and their well-known use of the *posse comitatus* were seen as an established tradition in Montana Territory as it was being settled. When lawlessness got out of hand and legal forces were inadequate for the task, people were more inclined to resort to extralegal methods in order to send wrongdoers to "the boothill graveyard." Citizens banded together, as they did in Canada, to hunt down criminals and either execute them or banish them from the area. Where law and law officers were absent, the people felt justified in taking the administration of justice into their own hands as an expected first step.

Until recently, historians have found little evidence of Canadian ranchers taking the law into their own hands, and they maintain that vitriolic newspaper articles did not represent the attitude of the majority of ranchers for whom the newspapers professed to speak. But the same historians have had to admit that in certain instances, informal vigilance committees of ranchers would pay a visit to someone strongly suspected of putting his brand on other men's cattle. He would be escorted to the U.S. border and ordered never to return. Further research may unearth other examples of citizen action in law enforcement, more than have generally been acknowledged. In 1882, when a man named Bowles refused to help some Fort Macleod citizens fight a prairie fire, "after the boys got it out, they went to the creek where Bowles [was] camped, took him out and hanged him." There is evidence of violence and lynchings on the Canadian frontier, but this type of informal justice was rarely extended to Indians. Some ranchers actually seemed more concerned about white men's theft of horses, which required a sophistication with a branding iron that the Indians did not possess.[27]

In the late 1870s and 1880s, it was common knowledge in Montana that there was a problem with Canadian or "British" Indians crossing the border to make raids on American horses or livestock, then smuggling them back across the border where they were out of the reach of the American authorities. There were numerous incidents of cross-border horse theft. An 1889 newspaper reported "a gigantic horse theft industry at work along the Missouri River." Montana horses were stolen, taken north, and then sold "in the British country." Indian raiding parties crossed over from both sides of the line and returned with stolen horses. The animals were not only taken south from Canada and sold but were shipped by boat and disposed of in states farther to the east. The Mounties, at times, were made to look rather foolish when horses were stolen from pastures hard by their detachments.

A ring of horse thieves, including Charles and William Farrell and Jeff Pratt, were apprehended in Montana. They were caught red-handed with thirty-nine head marked with the brands of Alberta ranchers, only a part of the stolen horses brought south. The men were arrested by American lawmen and taken to Fort Benton to stand trial. When Indian raiding parties crossed the line from Canada and returned with horses stolen in Montana, their American owners usually followed up by reporting their losses at Fort Walsh, which became Alberta headquarters for the NWMP in 1878.

Scouting by Mounties ensued. Cecil Denny recounts that stolen property was almost invariably restored to the rightful owners. A great deal of police time was taken up by these American claimants, who were charged nothing for these services. They were treated the same as residents in Canadian territory. Unfortunately, there was no reciprocity in such matters. Rarely did American lawmen make any effort to return stolen horses to Canadian owners. States and territories along the border made their own laws and failed to provide one that would have allowed them to act in a similarly neighborly manner in cases where the circumstances were reversed and horses stolen in Canada were taken across the line into the United States.[28]

The possibility of American retaliation to cross-border raids, whether by whites or Indians, was taken very seriously in Canada. In a confidential letter to his commanding officer at Fort Macleod, NWMP Inspector W. W. Irving confided that he had just returned from Montana, where he had overheard stockmen say that "if the Canadians seized and sold U.S. stock which drifted or strayed across the line, they [the stockmen] would not go to the trouble of seizing Canadian stock drifting into their country and having it sold, but would either shoot the animals down or run them over a bank, and that the Canadians would be the heavier losers if a law of that kind [requiring reciprocity] went into effect."[29] But in the face of loud protests from stockmen on both sides of the line, a reciprocal arrangement was worked out in the 1890s.

If there was less racial violence on the Canadian frontier, as has often been claimed, it was owing to the fact that the NWMP did a reasonably effective job of settling Native bands on reserves and attempted to cement tolerable relations with them. Early efforts by officers of the force were designed to cultivate the trust and friendship of Native tribes by gaining the confidence and loyalty of the chiefs. Colonel Macleod believed that good relations with the Native peoples were crucial to establishing effective law enforcement, because in most cases it was impossible for policemen to arrest Indian suspects without the help of other Indians. Unfortunately, Macleod's efforts at fair dealing with the Indians was only transitory; they failed to establish any precedent, nor did they prevent the erosion in later years of successful control of the Canadian frontier.

It must also be recognized that European and Canadian settlers crowded in on lands reserved for the Indians less obtrusively than in the American West. But while perhaps less extreme than in Montana, racial violence did exist on the Canadian prairies. Warren Elofson cites the case of the Indian called Charcoal ("Almighty Voice") who was found by white buffalo hunters in a shallow grave with a ball of lead through his skull. More chilling was a vigilante killing at Blackfoot Crossing in retaliation for the murder of an issuer of rations to the Indian reserves. A posse of enraged, trigger-happy citizens, led by a few Mounties, hunted down the killer. The wounded Indian suspect fled into the bush, and the police ordered that he be taken alive. But when he reappeared, waving a knife and bleeding profusely, someone in the posse shot him dead.[30]

Such incidents and a continual barrage of letters to the NWMP and newspapers from irate ranchers, complaining about Indian depredations on white men's property, contradict the conventional wisdom about Canada's history of peaceful and enlightened Indian relations. Conduct of the more aggressive ranchers and settlers contains most of the same ingredients of friction and recipes for trouble that were found on a larger scale in the American West. At one time it was actually U.S. government policy to pay Indian tribes between $100 and $200 for each Indian murdered by a white man. This was done because no civilian court south of the border would convict a white man for killing an Indian.[31]

Both Canada and the United States resorted to negotiating treaties with various Indian tribes in their jurisdictions. Between 1857 and 1868, representatives of the Plains tribes in the United States assembled periodically at Fort Laramie in Wyoming Territory, where they were induced to agree to a series of treaties defining the boundaries of their lands and hunting grounds. Most of these lands were forfeited when each of the tribes ceded them to the government under pressure.

There was no further writing of treaties by the United States after 1872, when the old idea that the tribes were sovereignties was discarded. The change was made in part because the House of Representatives had long complained that the Senate played too big a role in Indian affairs. Under the U.S. Constitution, only the Senate can formulate and ratify treaties. After 1872, U.S. relations with Indian tribes had to be conducted by "agreements" that required approval by *both* houses of Congress. The practical results of this new arrangement were minimal.

The Canadian government signed a series of treaties with its Native peoples. For the territory under examination here, Treaty no. 7 has the greatest relevance. In June 1877, at Blackfoot Crossing in what is now Alberta, the assembled southwestern tribes (Peigan, Blood, Blackfoot, and Sarcee) agreed to "cede, release, surrender, and yield up to the Government of Canada for Her Majesty the Queen, and her successors forever," all their rights and privileges whatsoever to the lands, in return for "promises and assurances of support, if and when hard times should come."[32]

Although Canada's treaties were better considered and in many cases better honored than American treaties, both countries failed to honor these solemn agreements with the Native peoples, leaving in their wake displacement, a trail of tears, distrust, and a bitter legacy of broken promises, further demoralizing Indians and Métis. The failure to honor treaty promises made the whole business of law enforcement much more difficult, if not impossible, on both frontiers. Evidence will show that settlers in Western Canada were no more tolerant and understanding of the Native peoples than their American counterparts. In settled areas, such as Calgary, anti-Indian attitudes were at times more violent than in rural areas, but animosity toward Natives can also be discerned among members of the ranching community.

During the "starvation years," after the buffalo were decimated and before a workable system of distributing rations was put in place, the Peigan depredations in Alberta forced rancher E. H. Maunsell to return to Montana with the remnants of his cattle herd, half of which the Indians had stolen and killed to survive. Reportedly, Maunsell did not hold it against them, sympathizing with their plight. He returned to the Canadian range as soon as the Indians were settled on reserves and better provided for by the government. The Peigans even made him an honorary chief.[33]

The American frontier, settled earlier, was freer, more open, untamed, unprotected, and therefore more prone to violence. No force comparable to the Mounted Police existed to exert a moderating influence. Largely through their work, the Canadian frontier was more rigidly controlled. As a result, it is often depicted in literature as peaceful, orderly, and safe, but drab, dull, and lacking in colorful characters such as Wyatt Earp, hanging judges, the James Boys, and Annie Oakley. Canadians, too, had their share of colorful characters and events to light up their Western history, and many of them are now receiving unusual attention. They may not be as well known as American heroes of fact or fiction, but they are in many cases emerging from the mists of the past as vibrant personalities. Finally they are getting attention for a number of reasons, not the least of which is to help revise the long perpetuated mythology that the Canadian West was a peaceful, virtually crime-free frontier. Not for long will it likely be seen as a savory example of humanitarian concern for all its inhabitants, with scarcely a lethal shot fired or a stain of misdeed to sully its record. There were, to be sure, many more unruly white renegades and Indians along the path of white settlement in the territories south of the border at virtually every stage in the advance of the moving frontier. Lawless men were bound to turn up on both frontiers as they passed through periods of yeasty growth, but lawlessness was not tolerated for long, and means were eventually found to hasten its departure.

The novelist Wallace Stegner lived for long stretches on both sides of the international border and wrote extensively about his impressions of frontier experience. He wrote that in actual fact the boundary, sometimes called artificial and ridiculous, "was more potent in the lives of people like us than the natural divide of the Cypress Hills had ever been upon the tribes it held apart. . . . For the 49th parallel was an agreement, a rule, a limitation, a fiction perhaps, but a legal one, acknowledged by both sides, and the coming of law, even such limited law as this, was the beginning of a civilization in what had been a lawless wilderness. Civilization is built on a tripod of geography, history, and law, and it is made up largely of limitations."[34]

Editor's Note: The name of the North-West Mounted Police changed in 1904 to the Royal Northwest Mounted Police and again in 1920 to the Royal Canadian Mounted Police, which it remains today. The RCMP is a nationwide force with many duties, including investigations of federal offenses (similar to the FBI in the United States) and patrolling Canadian highways.

Notes

This paper is an expanded and updated version of a paper presented at the Comparative Frontiers Symposium, Norman OK, February 1993. The author thanks R. Douglas Francis for his helpful suggestions in preparing the expanded essay.

1. Cecil Denny, *The Law Marches West* (London: J. M. Dent & Sons, 1939), 1–2.
2. *Personal Recollections and Observations of General Nelson A. Miles* (Chicago: Werner, 1876), 345.
3. Paul F. Sharp, *Whoop-Up Country: The Canadian-American West, 1865–1885* (Helena: Historical Society of Montana, 1960), 38–39. On naming the fort, see Turner, *Across the Medicine Line*, 46.
4. Denny, *The Law Marches West*, 139–40.
5. S. W. Horrall, "The March West," in Hugh A. Dempsey, ed., *Men in Scarlet* (Calgary: Historical Society of Alberta, 1974), 15.
6. Beth LaDow, *The Medicine Line: Life and Death on a North American Borderland* (New York: Routledge, 2001), 38.
7. National Archives of Canada, February 23, 1870, John A. Macdonald Papers, v. 517, quoted in Rod C. Macleod, *The NWMP and Law Enforcement, 1873–1905* (Toronto: University of Toronto Press, 1976), 19.
8. Denny, *The Law Marches West*, 2–3; Horrall, "The March West," 16.
9. Horrall, "The March West," 16–17.
10. Robert M. Utley, *Frontier Regulars: The United States Army and the Indians, 1866–1891* (New York: Macmillan, 1973), 47.
11. Wallace Stegner, *Wolf Willow: A History, a Story, and a Memory of the Last Plains Frontier* (New York: Viking Books, 1962), 101.
12. National Archives of Canada (PAC), John A. Macdonald Papers, vol. 252, Morris to Macdonald, January 17, 1873.
13. Horral, "The March West," 19.
14. Horral, "The March West," 19–20.
15. Morris to A. A. Dorion, May 29, 1974, Morris Papers, Provincial Archives of Manitoba, quoted in Horrall, "The March West," 20.
16. Sharp, *Whoop-Up Country*, 86.
17. "Atchison's Plight," in *Missoulian*, July 1, 1887.
18. J. A. Crutchfield, *It Happened in Montana* (Helena: Felcox, 1992), 45–47.

19. For a fuller development of this subject, see F. R. Prassel, *The Western Peace Officer: A Legacy of Law and Order* (Norman: University of Oklahoma Press, 1972), 220–43.

20. *Fort Macleod Gazette*, May 14, 1883.

21. "Town and Country," *Regina Leader*, April 22, 1897.

22. *Yellowstone Journal*, October 30, 1884, quoted in Warren Elofson, "Frontier Cattle Rustling in the Land and Times of Charlie Russell," manuscript, 122.

23. "Lynched in Montana," *Fort Macleod Gazette*, April 11, 1885, quoted in Elofson, "Frontier Cattle Rustling," 122.

24. Denny, *The Law Marches West*, 136–38.

25. NWMP Annual Reports, 9, Report of the Commissioner, December 10, 1896; Report of the Commanding Officer of the Mossimin Subdivision, November 21, 1899.

26. "A Cattle Stealing Case," *Regina Leader*, March 12, 1896, quoted in Elofson, "Frontier Cattle Rustling," 120–21.

27. *Fort Macleod Gazette*, October 14, 1882; John Jennings, "Policemen and Poachers: Indian Relations on the Ranching Frontier," in Anthony W. Rasporich and Henry C. Klassen, eds., *Frontier Calgary: Town, City, and Region, 1875–1914* (Calgary: McClelland and Stewart, 1975), 92.

28. Denny, *The Law Marches West*, 133.

29. RCMP Papers, RG 18, A1, vol. 243, pt. 2, W. H. Irvine to P. C. H. Primrose, April 21, 1903, PAC, quoted in David Breen, "The Mounted Police and the Ranching Frontier," in *Men in Scarlet*, fn. 19, and 220.

30. Elofson, "Frontier Cattle Rustling," 108.

31. Francis P. Prucha, *American Indian Policy in the Formative Years* (Cambridge: Harvard University Press, 1962), 202.

32. Prucha, *American Indian Policy*, 10.

33. Jennings, "Policemen and Poachers," 89.

34. Stegner, *Wolf Willow*, 85.

6. Does the Border Matter?

Cattle Ranching and the Forty-ninth Parallel

Terry G. Jordan-Bychkov

International boundaries often influence spatial patterns of land use, society, culture, politics, and humanized landscapes. Geographers have long assumed that such borders can exert a shaping influence on human occupancy. As early as 1935, Derwent Whittlesey penned an article entitled "The Impress of Central Authority upon the Landscape," a sentiment more recently echoed by geographer David B. Knight, who wrote of "The Impress of Authority and Ideology on Landscape."[1] Canadian geographer Deryck W. Holdsworth found "Architectural Expressions of the Canadian National State."[2]

Yes, borders do matter to the cultural geography and history of any region they bisect. But does the particular border under consideration here matter—the Canadian–United States boundary west of the Lake of the Woods—and did it matter over a century ago when cattle ranchers established their enterprises on both sides of the line? After all, this particular boundary is so artificial in its perfect straightness and disregard for the lie of the land as to raise questions concerning its relevance to the cultural geography of North America. A thoughtful observer might even conclude that the Canadian and American Wests have more in common with each other than either does with its respective East. The presence of English-speaking peoples, on both sides of the line, who have always been at peace with each other, maintaining a demilitarized boundary, further undermines the notion that the forty-ninth parallel possesses much significance.

And yet this border does, demonstrably, make a difference. Canadi-

Table 2. Ten largest groups of immigrants to the borderlands

Canada—1991		United States—1990	
French	33.8%	German	23.3%
English	26.3%	English	18.4%
German	5.0%	Irish	17.8%
East Asian	4.8%	African	11.7%
Scottish	4.8%	Hispanic	9.0%
Italian	3.9%	Italian	5.9%
Irish	3.9%	French	5.3%
Ukrainian	2.3%	Scottish	4.4%
Native American	2.1%	Polish	3.8%
Jewish	1.4%	East Asian	2.9%

Source: Terry G. Jordan-Bychkov, Mona Domosh, and Lester Rowntree, *The Human Mosiac*, 7th ed., New York: Longman 1999, p. 348. The criteria are not identical in the respective national censuses, but the message is basically accurate.

ans are not like Americans in a variety of ways, perhaps most obviously in terms of the Old World national origins of the population (table 2). In particular, the proportions of French, German, Irish, African, and Hispanic ancestry differ markedly between the two countries. In the United States, persons of German and Irish origin account for fully 41 percent of the population, while in Canada these two groups account for less than 9 percent. Truly, we are not the same people.

View this contrast as a geographer does, by mapping it, and the forty-ninth parallel springs to life (figure 9). Along most of its course west of the Lake of the Woods, the border presents a fault line of national origin, mainly separating a huge zone of German dominance in the northern United States from English majorities in Canada.[3] Nor should we ignore the substantial Ukrainian presence on the Canadian side of the line. Along the entire length of the forty-ninth parallel, national origins match up in only three narrow corridors: a tiny German area in the Red River Valley, a miniscule Norwegian corridor connecting parts of North Dakota and Saskatchewan, and a narrow Pacific Coastal English belt. Elsewhere the boundary divides Germans from English, perhaps helping explain the American propensity for marching mindlessly off to war led by generals and admirals bearing surnames such as Schwarzkopf, Eisenhower, Pershing, Nimitz, and Custer. If any cultural continuity exists between the Old World and the New, then yes, the border should matter.

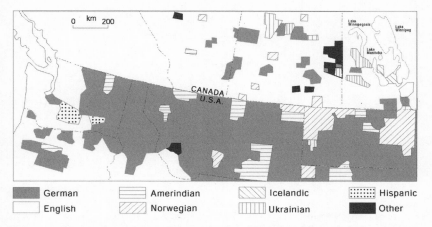

| German | Amerindian | Icelandic | Hispanic |
| English | Norwegian | Ukrainian | Other |

Figure 9. National origin groups in the borderlands. Adapted from Terry G. Jordan-Bychkov, "Does the Border Really Matter? Cattle Ranching and the 49th Parallel," in Simon Evans, Sarah Carter, and Bill Yeo, eds., *Cowboys, Ranchers, and the Cattle Business: Cross-Border Perspectives on Ranching History* (Calgary: University of Calgary Press, 2000), 3–4.

The forty-ninth parallel even seems to possess a behavioral aspect. Geographer John Hudson recently pointed out that the American side of the border seemed to attract assorted nut cases, loners, and anarchist groups.[4] Consider the activities of the Aryan Nation Nazis at Sand Point, Idaho; the dustup at Ruby Ridge in the same state; Ted Kaczynski busily building bombs in his isolated cabin; the Montana militia holed up in their ranch forts; and assorted survivalists playing at the "rape of the Sabine women." No comparable aberrant behavior seems to occur on the Canadian side of the line, as Hudson observed.

Closer to our topic of land use systems, Hendrik Reitsma considered the forty-ninth parallel from the perspective of agricultural geography some decades ago. He found a number of ways in which the border influenced farming. For example, the ratio between sheep and swine differed markedly from one side to the other. One might have expected sheep to be more numerous on the Canadian side, given the British fondness for mutton and lamb, but the pattern was reversed (figure 10). The explanation lay in a generous governmental wool subsidy in the United States. When that subsidy was subsequently repealed, the border contrast evaporated like a prairie morning fog.[5]

Evidence seems to be accumulating that the border does matter in di-

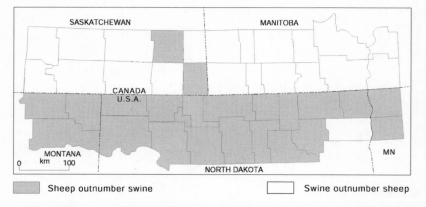

Sheep outnumber swine	Swine outnumber sheep

Figure 10. Sheep/swine ratio in the borderlands. Adapted from Terry G. Jordan-Bychkov, "Does the Border Really Matter?"

verse cultural and agricultural ways. Perhaps Canadian geographer Simon Evans was correct when he called the international boundary in the West an "institutional fault line." [6] Another Canadian geographer, Andrew Clark, assented, suggesting that the forty-ninth parallel, far from being an arbitrary and artificial border, divided two peoples and two separate westward thrusts. [7] As he pointed out, the boundary in the Prairies and Great Plains closely approximates the drainage divide between streams flowing to Hudson Bay and the Gulf of Mexico. The Missouri River, from the time of Lewis and Clark, served as an axis of United States expansion, while the Assiniboine-Qu'Appelle-Saskatchewan rivers, linked by a short portage, provided the way west for the fur traders from Montreal and later for the Hudson's Bay Company. These parallel flows later became cast in steel when transcontinental railroads were constructed, with terminals at Minneapolis and Winnipeg, Seattle, and Vancouver.

But let us not rush to judgment concerning the border. Contradictory evidence exists. Terrain, as contrasted with drainage systems, invited cross-boundary movements. The vast interior plains, a grassy corridor, beckoned Americans to come northward. Further west, in the mountains, elongated valleys are oriented north-south, as for example the Rocky Mountain Trench, the Kootenay, and the Okanagan valleys. These vales also directed human movement across the border, encouraging cultural blending (figure 11).

Evidence abounds that human patterns were influenced by cross-

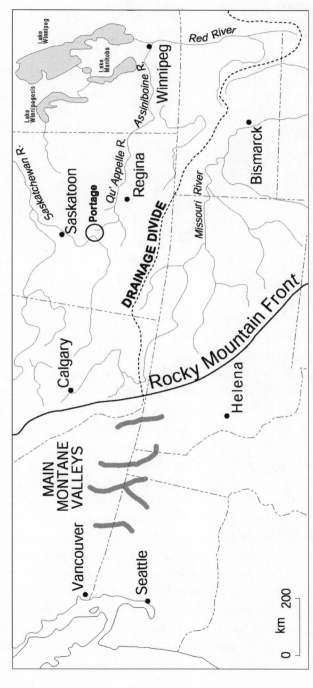

Figure 11. Selected terrain features and river systems. Adapted from Terry G. Jordan-Bychkov, "Does the Border Really Matter?"

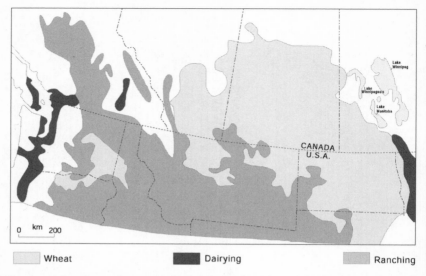

| Wheat | | Dairying | | Ranching |

Figure 12. Land use systems in the borderlands. Adapted from Terry G. Jordan-Bychkov, "Does the Border Really Matter?"

boundary migration and diffusion. No English dialect borders or even isoglosses respect the forty-ninth parallel.[8] A "moralistic" political ideology seems as deeply rooted in Manitoba and Saskatchewan as in Minnesota or the Dakotas.[9] And, more relevant to the issue of land use systems, virtually every classification of major agricultural types reveal distributions that seem completely free of the influence of the international boundary (figure 12).[10] In the East, dairying laps over the border, in several places, while in the prairies, plains, and mountains, wheat farming and livestock ranching straddle the forty-ninth parallel with impunity.

I would be the last person to propose that cattle ranching constitutes a monolithic type. In my synthesis of North American cattle ranching, I used the plural word "frontiers" in the very title of the book to convey the notion of very different systems with diverse roots.[11] In the North American West alone, I discerned three more or less independent types of cattle ranching. The relevant point is that none of the three seemed much affected by the international boundary. My analysis suggested that, insofar as cattle ranching was concerned, the border played no consequential role. The very use of the word "ranch" internationally implies as much.

A brief overview of my three types is in order. I labeled them the "Texas," "California," and "Midwestern" systems. The Texas system of cattle ranching arose as a blending of Hispanic and Anglo-American practices in the subtropical coastal plain of the American South. Characterized by an open-range system, it produced scrub cattle largely of Iberian origin and involved a profound neglect of the livestock, including no provision of winter feed. Its labor force, consisting of southern whites and blacks alike, managed the semiferal range cattle from horseback, using principally the hemp lasso. A distinctive vocabulary accompanied the Texas system, including words such as "cowboy," "lariat," "maverick," and "cavvyard." The Texas system surged northward up the Great Plains in a spectacular manner after 1865, during an unusually mild, wet period, but eventually this subtropical adaptive strategy proved unsuited to cold winter areas. The Texas system suffered collapse by 1890 in virtually all areas north of the Lone Star State. In any case, the Texans' diffusionary thrust had largely fallen short of the forty-ninth parallel. The Miles City area of eastern Montana and the Little Missouri River valley of adjacent Dakota Territory became the northernmost seats of major Texan influence.

A few Texans did cross the border. Simon Evans said that western Canadian prairies "were occupied briefly by the last survivors of a colorful company of men who had ridden the trails and followed the grass up from Texas."[12] By the late 1870s a few Texans were among the ranchers around Fort Macleod, and a couple even reached the Bow River valley. A famous African American cowhand of Texas origin, John Ware, made a reputation for himself in Alberta. Nevertheless, I maintain that the Texans largely fell short of the border, for climatic reasons unrelated to the presence of the forty-ninth parallel boundary.

Some say that Calgary today bears a Texan imprint. Personally, as a Texan myself, I cannot discern one iota of such influence in that lovely city, but if it does exist, then I would seek its origin in the oil industry rather than ranching.

The "California system" of cattle ranching developed as a Pacific coastal type with deep roots in the *charro* culture of the western Mexican highlands.[13] It bore much less Anglo-American influence, and its unique vocabulary consisted almost exclusively of corrupted Spanish words— "buckaroo," "hackamore," "oreanna," "major domo," "rancheria," and the like. Its material culture included such distinctive items as the single-cinched Visalia saddle (the Anglo-Texans used a double-cinched type), the rawhide lasso, and the "Spanish windlass," a device for pulling mired cattle out of tule marshes. Its Iberian breed of cattle was similar to those raised by Texans, but they lacked the spectacular horn span.

The California system had more of an impact on Canada than did the Texas system. Iberian cattle of Californian origin reached the Nootka Sound settlement on Vancouver Island as early as 1792, and others were brought to Fort Langley on the lower Fraser River by the 1830s. Anglo-Californians, who had adopted the system largely without modifications, marketed cattle in the British Columbia goldfields in the 1850s, and in the following decade some of them established ranches in the province, along the trails they had earlier used to reach the mining markets. In this manner, the Spanish windlass reached the interior plateau of British Columbia, as did the word "rancheria" to describe the Native American quarters on the periphery of towns and villages.

Still, the long-term Californian influence north of the border—or anywhere outside of California, for that matter—was negligible. The Californians, like the Texans, pursued a cattle-raising system born in and suited to the tropics or subtropics, to warm lotuslands. Both systems failed in harsher climates, and we cannot implicate the international boundary in these failures.

The third ranching system came out of the Appalachian Mountains and midwestern tallgrass prairies. Perfected in states such as Illinois and Iowa, it underwent a successful readaptation to the high valleys and plateaus of the Rocky Mountains in western Montana in the 1850s. This "Midwestern system" involved the provision of hay as winter feed, the raising of British-derived breeds, a careful tending of thoroughly tame stock, and the fencing of pastures at the earliest possible time.[14] Better suited to the northern climate, it displaced both the Texas and California systems and reigned supreme by 1900.

The midwestern system of cattle ranching crossed the border with ease, borne by the likes of Jerome and Thaddeus Harper, who were in British Columbia by 1859, Ben Snipes and John Jeffries of Yakima, "Spokane" Jackson, William Gates of The Dalles, and Dan Drumheller from Walla Walla. The genealogies and even life experiences of such men trace straight back to the American Midwest, as do the life histories of most cowhands who worked for them. As Thomas Weir, who wrote the definitive geographical work on ranching in the interior plateau, said, "Scratch a British Columbian rancher and you'll find an American expatriate."[15]

If you seek the visible evidence of the midwestern American ranching culture in Canada, you will find it in such items of material culture as the zigzagged log pasture fence, whose origins lie back in colonial Pennsylvania, the "Beaverslide" haystacker, perfected in the Big Hole, a Montana valley, and the imposing "mountain horse barn," built of notched logs and also apparently derived from the mountains of western Montana.[16]

In spite of the three American intrusions, and especially that of the midwesterners, was Canadian ranching not in some significant measure distinctive? If so, I cannot detect it, and I certainly did not approach the subject as some sort of chauvinistic American. As a geographer, I am sensitive to and delight in regional cultural differences.

Some have suggested that British influence was stronger among ranchers on the Canadian side of the line, as the national origins map also implies.[17] Even toponyms speak of such influence. Alberta, for example, is dotted with Scottish place-names, a nomenclature far more subdued in, say, Montana. One reads of a rancher from the North Country of England living in British Columbia and using collie dogs to help herd cattle. Inspecting the log structures at the Bar U Ranch south of Calgary, I discovered that their distinctive carpentry is unquestionably derived from Ontario rather than the American Midwest, as revealed in details such as end-only hewing and the dominant use of dovetailed notches.[18]

In the balance, though, toponyms, notch types, or other such details are largely inconsequential, as is the oddity of one Englishman's herder dogs. They do not describe the essential attributes of the ranching system north of the forty-ninth parallel. Instead, both on the Canadian prairies and in the mountains beyond, I discern the shaping influence of the American heartland. Western Canadians, seek your national identity elsewhere, for truly it does exist, and vibrantly. But as far as cattle ranching is concerned, the border does not matter.[19]

Notes

This essay originally was published in Simon Evans, Sarah Carter, and Bill Yeo, eds., *Cowboys, Ranchers, and the Cattle Business: Cross-Border Perspectives in Ranching History*

(Calgary: University of Calgary Press, 2000), 1–10, copyright 2000 by the University of Calgary Press, and is reprinted here with permission.

1. Derwent Whittlesey, "The Impress of Effective Central Authority upon the Landscape," *Annals of the Association of American Geographers* 25 (1935): 85–97; David B. Knight, "Identity and Territory: Geographical Perspectives on Nationalism and Regionalism," *Annals of the Association of American Geographers* 72 (1982): 514–31.

2. Deryck Holdsworth, "Architectural Expression of the Canadian National State," *Canadian Geographer* 30 (1986): 167–80.

3. Terry G. Jordan-Bychkov and Mona Domosh, *The Human Mosaic*, 8th ed. (New York: Longman, 1999), 340.

4. John C. Hudson, "Cross-Border Contrasts in the Rocky Mountains, United States, and Canada," *Abstracts, Association of American Geographers, 93rd Annual Meeting* (Washington DC: Association of American Geographers, 1997), 120.

5. Hendrik J. Reitsma, "Crop and Livestock Production in the Vicinity of the United States–Canada Border," *Professional Geographer* 23 (1971): 23–38, and his sequel, "Agricultural Changes in the American-Canadian Border Zone, 1954–1978," *Political Geography Quarterly* 7 (1988): 23–38.

6. Simon M. Evans, "The Origins of Ranching in Western Canada: American Diffusion or Victorian Transplant?" *Great Plains Quarterly* 3, no. 2 (1983): 79–91.

7. Andrew H. Clark, class lecture notes, University of Wisconsin, Madison, 1962.

8. Craig M. Carver, *American Regional Dialects: A Word Geography* (Ann Arbor: University of Michigan Press, 1986); Raven L. McDavid Jr., *Varieties of American English* (Stanford: Stanford University Press, 1980).

9. Daniel J. Elazar, *The American Mosaic: The Impact of Space, Time, and Culture on American Politics* (Boulder: Westview Press, 1994).

10. See, e.g., Edward B. Espenshade Jr. et al., eds., *Goode's World Atlas*, 19th ed. (Chicago: Rand McNally, 1995), 34, 77.

11. Terry G. Jordan, *North American Cattle Ranching Frontiers: Origins, Diffusion, and Differentiation* (Albuquerque: University of New Mexico Press, 1993).

12. Simon M. Evans, "American Cattlemen on the Canadian Range, 1874–1914," *Prairie Forum* 4 (1979): 121–35.

13. Jordan, *North American Cattle Ranching*, 159–69, 241–66.

14. Jordan, *North American Cattle Ranching*, 267–307.

15. Thomas R. Weir, *Ranching in the Southern Interior Plateau of British Columbia*, rev. ed. (Ottawa: Geographical Branch, Mines and Technical Surveys, 1964), 90–91.

16. Jon T. Kilpinen, "Traditional Fence Types of Western North America," *Pioneer American Society Transactions* 15 (1992): 15–22; Jon T. Kilpinen, "The Mountain Horse Barn," *Pioneer America Society Transactions* 17 (1994): 25–32.

17. Evans, "Origins of Ranching."

18. Terry G. Jordan, Jon T. Kilpinen, and Charles F. Gritzner, *The Mountain West: Interpreting the Folk Landscape* (Baltimore: Johns Hopkins University Press, 1977), 11, 61–62, 73.

19. As an antidote, the reader should consult Evans, "Origins of Ranching."

7. "Their Own Country"

Race, Gender, Landscape, and Colonization around the Forty-ninth Parallel, 1862–1900

Sheila McManus

In a September 1862 diary entry, Carolyn Abbott Tyler, a member of the 1862 Fisk expedition from Minnesota to Fort Benton, Montana, wrote that "every one [was] thankful the Blackfeet had gone [back] to their own country" after being in the region to hunt buffalo. A local Indian agent even warned the party not to winter in a certain valley because the Indian tribes used it as a neutral-ground shortcut to the buffalo hunt. The travelers were aware that the land was not designated as Blackfoot country, but it was not yet white man's country either. Other than isolated military or fur posts, the region did not yet "belong" to whites; it was not yet a country that they could call their own.[1]

Ruth Frankenberg has argued that the narratives of white women colonizers depict "landscape and the experience of it [as] racially structured—whether those narratives seemed to be marked predominantly by the presence or absence of people of colour." Furthermore, once a woman "is in a landscape structured by racism, a conceptual mapping of race, self, and others takes shape, following from and feeding the physical context."[2]

The diaries and reminiscences of white women who went to southern Alberta and northern Montana in the late nineteenth century illustrate a three-way dialect among race, gender, and white women's perceptions of land and landscape and the role these connections played in the establishment of white, English-speaking settler societies east of the Rockies. As white English-speaking women started arriving in the western edge of the plains, they and other newcomers, including black women and men and Chinese men, were greatly outnumbered by the aboriginal population. As a result, white women's diaries and reminiscences from the early years of colonization reveal their preoccupation with physical landscapes inhabited by aboriginal peoples and social landscapes complicated by racial diversity. By the end of the century, however, as white communities became firmly dominant in the physical and social landscapes, race faded into the background as a category of concern for these women, and gender came to the fore.

In political terms Montana and Alberta achieved independence from their federal governments in 1874 and 1905 after varying periods of territorial status. Although the language and categories of postcolonial analysis have only recently been applied to North America, it is appropriate to view the late-nineteenth-century North American West in a colonial context. Canadian historian Sarah Carter has argued that " 'colonialism' is a term that refers to a great variety of asymmetrical intersocial relationships and that colonial rule is highly varied in administration and impact." In their westward expansion, the American and Canadian federal states each endeavored to maintain "sharp social, economic, and spatial distinctions between the dominant and subordinate population. Colonial rule involved the domination, or attempted domination, of one group over another." Even after nominal political independence had been achieved in the region, a colonial "racial dimension and a dimension of inequality" remained because Montana and Alberta were still "run by whites for the prestige, power, and profit of whites."[3]

Although the North American West lacked the classically colonial landscapes of India or the tropics, white Canadian and American women alike still wrote about the beauty and majesty of the land that was so new to them. They were amazed by how far they could see in the clear dry air and how changeable the weather could be. They would note in that grand western tradition of claiming territory when they thought they were the first white woman, or the first person at all, to see a particular place. As in so many other colonial contexts, it was as if the land had not been "seen" until it was seen by white eyes. Ella Inderwick mentioned to her sister-in-law, for example, that she'd "found" a small pond while riding alone in southern Alberta, "a pond I must have been the discoverer of as no one knew of it and all wanted to see it." Even more blunt was the reminiscence of Margaret Harkness Woodman, who wrote in an 1892 letter that "I believe I can justly claim to be the first white woman" to see the Great Falls of the Missouri River in Montana, which she had visited in 1862.[4]

Embedded in Woodman's last comment, with its implicit awareness of both her racial and gender status, is the awareness that for many of these newly arrived colonizers the landscape, for all its beauty, was not always neutral and pastoral. Particularly in the American writings from the 1860s, 1870s, and 1880s, there is a sense that the landscape, though beautiful, was itself hostile because it did not yet completely belong to whites and was still in the hands of the supposedly hostile aboriginal population.

May Flanagan, for example, wrote in an 1890 letter to her cousin that when she and her mother came to Fort Benton in 1873, the "camping out and traveling through such a weird peculiar country would have been interesting and pleasant if it had not been for this constant dread of being popped over by an Indian shot any minute." That May herself was only an infant at the time reveals how powerfully her mother's impressions of vulnerability had shaped May's own "pioneer" narrative. Similarly, in her reminiscence of a trip to Fort Benton in 1882, Mary Douglas Gibson wrote, "The river was so low it was impossible to navigate at night, so we were anchored in midstream for greater safety from Indians as well as less danger from running aground." When her group decided to travel the last section overland, she remembered that they "were obliged to travel very slowly for the officers had to remain with their men who were walking, because of possible attacks from the Indians. . . . Everything seemed very strange and wild to me. I had never slept in a tent before, to say nothing of being in a country of Indians and wild animals."[5]

What is striking about this series of remarks and those of Tyler, which opened this essay, is that each links the aboriginal population to the physical landscape. Whether the terrain is perceived as possibly beneficial to the white observers, such as Tyler's valley, or a hindrance, like the low river, Indians are inextricably connected to that terrain. Significantly, aboriginal people were rarely seen by these writers, and yet they were fundamentally present in the landscape. The rivers and valleys were still thought to belong to the Indians, which compelled the incoming whites to deal with the people and the land simultaneously.

Similar reactions to southern Alberta's landscape and its connection with the indigenous "First Nations" peoples were recorded by an American family who had traveled to the area in 1893 to homestead but instead returned to the United States. Sadye Wolfe Drew remembered her mother's fears that a local native band that came to their camp was going to massacre her family, "but they were friendly." As their journey continued, the family's native guide would periodically "go onto a high place to look around and then wave for us to come. When he would do that mother was afraid he was giving a signal to the Indians to come and kill us. I don't think my mother slept much on that trip across the unsettled country." The area was not yet settled by whites, and so the land itself seemed unsettled, hostile, and remote. Drew, being less fearful than her mother, concluded, "It was a lovely country—lots of grass and water. We never saw a soul on the way except Indians and not many of them."[6]

There were other dissenting voices among the early American reminiscences from women who perceived neither the land nor its inhabitants to be a threat. Kate Hogan, a military wife whose husband was stationed near Fort Benton (today Montana) in 1867, wrote in a letter, "We have no trouble with Indians. See pleanty of them but they are peaceful but the Mosquitos are so bad that for a few days I couldn't sew." Alma Coffin Kirkpatrick wrote in her diary on July 19, 1878, "Now that there is no danger from Indians, ordinary travel is perfectly safe."[7]

There seem to have been fewer white women traveling to or through southern Alberta in the 1860s and 1870s than there were south of the border, likely due to smaller numbers of military and mining expeditions and outposts. By the 1880s Canada's First Nations peoples were still visible to white newcomers, but they were rarely represented as hostile and seemed to be less intimately connected to the landscape. After the Canadian government's treaty-making efforts in the 1870s, natives already seemed to be little more than the backdrop against which white activities took place. Ella Inderwick, for example, wrote in her diary upon her arrival in Calgary on October 29, 1883, "Think Calgary very nice but it is a village of tents and framed in Indians and squaws in plenty." Having lost the right to move freely, local Blackfeet were represented as a static component of the landscape.[8]

The closest the Canadian writers came to the sort of fear expressed in the American women's writings was during the Northwest Rebellion in 1885, when the resentment of Métis and aboriginal communities across the prairies at their poor treatment by the Canadian government seemed ready to burst out in violence. The land itself no longer seemed potentially dangerous, but its original inhabitants did. The rebellion was the main topic in twelve-year-old Julia Shortt's diary in late March and early April of that year. The diary does not mention any actual hostile activity on the part of the local Blackfeet, providing instead a picture of a white community fraught with tension. On March 31, Shortt wrote, "Mr. Spaulding says that the Indians are uprising and a whole settlement have been killed. Are afraid that they will rise near here too." There were rumors of the government giving whites guns and ammunition to defend themselves, and her community even briefly considered building a blockhouse. In her reminiscence she wrote that "for a few weeks the settlers all through the West lived in a state of terror. A big Indian Reserve lay to the east of us, two more Reserves were not far south, and there was the chance that at any time they, or scattered bands of unruly young Indian Braves from these tribes, might sweep through the country, spreading death and destruction." The Blackfoot wife of a white neighbor became the white community's "chief source of information," and she reported that the Canadian government was attempting to pacify local native communities by dramatically increasing the amount of food accorded to the reservations. Shortt noted, "This did much to calm and discourage any would-be aspirations to regain the territory given over to the white race."[9]

Only once did any of the writers, American or Canadian, actually have any sort of negative encounter with the aboriginal population. Lucy Stocking wrote in July 1874 that two men who had been drinking broke into her corral and then tried to enter the house. One of the white men in the house took the intruders' rifle away, and they fled. In the morning Stocking discovered that the men had been involved in a fight the night before, as the body of a native man had been left on the native camping ground. The next day she recorded that she had gone "to see the dead Indian."[10]

Many of the white women mentioned trying to use the local native women as domestic help in an attempt to co-opt them into what would have been considered a more "appropriate" or "useful" place in the racial and gender hierarchy. Inderwick wrote in an 1884 letter to her sister-in-law Alice, for example, "I have tried to make use of a squaw who is the nominal wife of a white man near us to do the washing but had to give it up. . . . the odds were too much for my courage and patience."[11]

The most common form of contact between the aboriginal and white communities was, of course, the marriage between native women and white men, which had begun during the fur trade. Although refusing to grant these relationships the status of "marriage," Carolyn Tyler wrote in her 1862 diary that the white men who worked for the fur company "all have Squas they all have children some of the Squas have several. . . . these Squas talk very well, they have lived for years with these white men. The Pegans are savages and wild if it was not for the squas who are living with these white men at this time 1862 every white man would have been killed The squas and halfbreed children is protection."[12]

Lillian Miller of Montana recalled that, thirty years later, many of the ranches in their area were owned by white men who had aboriginal wives. The white community referred to these men as "squawmen"; Miller, for example, noted that in the 1890s her family had bought their first and second ranches from squawmen. This word is striking because it suggests that the white husbands of native women had lost their racial status by choosing a nonwhite wife and that an old racial slur on native women had been passed on to the white men who were associated with them. Miller added that these men "and all the squaw men and families" eventually "sold their ranches and moved to the reservation where they could be with their friends. We often wondered about the white men who seemed to be content to live so, all their lives." Here again, the men's racial identity—their status as white men—was in question because surely no "real" white man would be content to live on an Indian reservation.[13]

The term "squawman" does not appear in any of the writings by the Canadian women, although Sarah Carter records the use of the word by North-West Mounted Police officers and in local newspapers in the late 1880s. She simply states that it was used "to denote men of the lowest social class," men who were blamed for a range of local crimes and for being troublemakers. These examples support the late-nineteenth-century view that "the races" were utterly distinct and distinguishable, which fed white fears of miscegenation, but a counternarrative also exists in some of the diaries and reminiscences being discussed here.[14]

Julia Shortt, for example, recalled that her family's nearest neighbor in southern Alberta in the late 1880s and 1890s had a Blackfoot wife "named Pokemi, and three small children. . . . Pokemi was very kind and liked us to come and visit and see the children, but she was shy and would not speak English." It was Pokemi who had acted as a liaison between the whites and her tribe during the 1885 Rebellion, and her husband's identity as a white man did not seem to be threatened in the eyes of the community as a result of his marriage to a Blackfoot woman. Instead, Canada's Indian Act had dictated that Pokemi lost her "official" native status when she married him, so they would not have been able to move to the reservation even if they had wanted to.[15]

Lillian Miller attributed the "rather surprising" friendliness of the natives in their region to the "fact that there had been many marriages between the early settlers and Indian girls. . . . The half breed children were our school mates." These aboriginal women and native-white marriages were visible but contained within white communities. In these instances, whiteness and white masculinity were not automatically or irreparably threatened by contact with native women. Furthermore, although the growing Métis population might have appeared threatening during such crises as the Northwest Rebellion of 1885, there was an often-explicit assumption that mixed marriages could create a buffer zone of safety for white communities.[16]

A recognition of the utility of intermarriage certainly never eliminated tension and confusion around racial differences. Rosanna Sturgis wrote in an 1867 letter that the steamboat she was on "took two more Familys on board at St. Joe for Ft. Benton. One is an old Indian trader his Wife is a squaw of the Blackfoot Nation, . . . his son was speaking of his Mother he said 'my *Father's Wife* is an *Indian* woman but she is a Lady.' " In Canada, due to an Indian Act that gave Indian status to any white woman who married a native man but removed status from native women who married white men, the categories of "Indian" and "white" were up to the bureaucrats to define. Drew wrote of her brief stay in Alberta in 1893:

"There was an Indian in the camp by the name of Andre Prudin who had a wife and two children. She and the children were blond with blue eyes, however they claimed to be Indians."[17]

On both sides of the border the number of references to local aboriginal and Métis populations decreased over time, particularly after such tragedies of the mid-1880s as the Northwest Rebellion in Canada and the Dawes Act that broke up many reservations and allowed the allotments to be sold to whites with the intent of speeding the assimilation of Indians into the dominant culture in the United States. Both federal governments were attempting to hone their containment and assimilation policies through these years, and the number of white colonizers was increasing steadily. White women continued to note the movement and presence of natives, but less often and with less detail. Mrs. Alfred Wyndham, for example, who ranched near one of the Blackfoot reservations in southern Alberta, mentioned Indians fewer than fifteen times between 1888 and 1891, mostly in connection to her son's position as a North-West Mounted Policeman.[18]

The aboriginal population was not the only group of visible "others" that the white women were seeing, although it was certainly the largest. Both Montana and Alberta had small communities of Chinese men, who had built the transcontinental railroads and thus preceded most of the other nonnatives to the region and growing communities of black people. While the white women always noticed and commented on their presence, their racialization was almost always simultaneously gendered and clearly divorced from the landscape. Although the whites, blacks, and Chinese were all equally new to the area, the terms of the federal states' colonial projects dictated that the latter two groups would have only a supporting role to play in the key spatial and social conquest of the region—that of white over native. Black and Chinese people were also more easily slotted into the preexisting racist hierarchies of the day, and their confinement to feminized service positions further reinforced their supposed inferiority to the small numbers of white newcomers. Unlike native women, who had to be taught how to be "useful" in white women's terms, the black and Chinese communities supposedly already "knew" how to fill service positions for the whites. Mary Gibson recalled, for example, that the boat she took up the Missouri in 1882 had a "colored steward," Ed Sims, who "served cold drinks and did everything in his power to make us more comfortable, or I should say, less miserable."[19]

Black women were mentioned more often than black men in white women's writing and were always patronizingly constructed in the servile, somewhat maternal role of "Auntie." May Flanagan remembered a black midwife in early Fort Benton, "old Aunt Leah, a big fat Negro mid-wife," whose presence and usefulness was linked to, and thus justified by, the birth of the first white baby. In an account of a trip down the Missouri from Montana to North Dakota in 1882, Flanagan noted approvingly that the riverboat had both "negro waiters" and a "negro laundress." Gibson wrote that on her ranch she "had a Missouri woman for a cook who only worked when 'the spirit moved her,' the balance of the time she sat, smoking a corn-cob pipe, near the kitchen stove, 'warmin' up,' but she was a good cook when sufficiently warm."[20]

These perceptions and representations of black women as essentially lazy service providers were by no means limited to Montana. Inderwick wrote in her 1884 letter that after giving up on teaching the local native woman to help with the laundry, she sent it "to a dignified coloured lady in Saint Frances who boasts that she and the Police Commissioner's wife were the first white ladies to arrive in the country—Time is nothing to her and if I were an ordinary woman and not a bride with a good trousseau I shiver to think what might happen [to] me—when weeks go by and no laundry can be cajoled from our aristocratic Aunties' dwelling." She does not comment further on the fact that her racialized representation of the laundress in Saint Francis does not match the representation the woman claims for herself. She says she is "white"; Inderwick says she is "coloured." The nature of her occupation probably would have been sufficient evidence for the rest of the town to agree with Inderwick.[21]

The presence of Chinese men was also deemed noteworthy by the authors of these texts, generally because the men seemed particularly "foreign" and because they were men who occupied feminized service positions. Gibson observed that "cooks, waiters, and 'chambermaids'" in the hotel in Fort Benton in 1882 were all Chinese, which made her fear for her life. She wrote, "As I had never before seen one of their race, I couldn't believe that it would be safe to eat food they prepared so I subsisted upon crackers, nuts and raisins which I bought at nearby stores, as long as we remained at the hotel." Ten years later Lillian Miller noted that the hotel in Chinook, Montana, also had a Chinese cook, but it had waitresses whose race she does not specify. There are no specific references in the pre-1900 Alberta diaries or reminiscences of Chinese men working as cooks in Alberta, although they seem to have been relatively common as cooks on the big ranches by that time. The Malcolm T. Millar ranch south of Calgary, for example, appears to have had anywhere from one to three Chinese men working in the house after 1900.[22]

Other than the perceived risks of food poisoning or withholding laundry, the black and Chinese populations were not viewed as threatening in the way that the aboriginal population had been, at least partly because the country was not "theirs" either and so they were automatically excluded from the spatial and territorial battles being fought. Furthermore, the racial and gendered "inferiority" of the nonwhite newcomers indicated that they already "knew" their place in the racist and sexist hierarchies of the day and thus would not create any major obstacles to the establishment of the young settler societies north or south of the border.

As white, English-speaking Americans and Canadians solidified their hold on the land and social structures around the forty-ninth parallel, the amount of attention the white writers paid to visible racial differences appears to have declined. Their gaze was increasingly preoccupied with other white women as their numbers increased and as the initial differences began to move into the realm of the taken-for-granted. Two of the sources used here, Ella Inderwick in Alberta in the 1880s and Lillian Miller in Montana in the 1890s, provide particularly rich descriptions of the white women in their areas.

Ella Inderwick wrote in her reminiscence that when her older brother had offered to pay her way to live with him in Alberta, he had told her that she had to "bring a girl with me who could cook—I could not be there alone" because there were "just rough men at the mill 'and cow men on the ranches.'" She went on to enjoy good relationships with the cowboys who worked her husband's ranch, who supported her various attempts to bring "civilization" to the ranch because she could ride very well: "I verily believe if I did not ride they would have nothing to do with me—as it is they are rather proud of me—and oh Alice—I do believe I could still take pleasure in riding if I were a deaf mute. . . . So when Jerry breaks my best cut glass dish I fly to the stables and have my Joy saddled and ride till I know that cut glass is nothing to make or mar one's good lovely day." [23]

Her love of riding and the amount of respect she got from the cowboys for being a good rider allowed her to overcome to some degree what she saw as the gendered liabilities put upon her. She is the only writer discussed here who expressed frustrations at the limitations placed on her as a woman. After her husband had refused to take her into town, she wrote in her diary on June 29, 1884, "I wish I was a boy. I could go where I chose by myself then." In the letter to her sister-in-law, after rhapsodizing about the "delights of this clear air," she added, "let the housekeeper in you think of the appetites [which] this air gives to men—and women—though we don't count much in this way here." [24]

She did wish that more white women lived near her. In an interesting aside, where the nonwhiteness of some of her female neighbors meant they were deleted from the category "women" altogether, she noted that she was the "only woman (white) on this river or the next for that matter as the next ranche is owned by a bachelor—so I am 22 miles from a woman—& though I like all the men and enjoy having them I simply long to talk to a woman—so about once a month I ride into Saint Francis with Charlie and stay a night with my dearest friend here Mrs. Borden. . . . She was the first white woman in Saint Francis and came by way of covered wagon from Montana—with her two children! What splendid pluck!" So eager was she for the company of other white women that Ella told her sister-in-law she had even "made all sorts of offers to a few of the men who are near us in the way of helping them get their shacks done up if only they will 'go east' and marry some really nice girls."

Not all of the white women who did live in her area met with her approval, however. Being a Canadian, she was particularly fond of criticizing the English women. She called the women of Fort Lorne, a North-West Mounted Police post, "a lot of cats—more or less—though since I have discovered two very sweet ones," and added that they "seem so gossipy and so different from the splendid great spirit of the west—and what the women ought to be." She told Alice that the few Englishwomen "who have come to these wilds are freaks!" One had brought all of her British traditions with her and made her brothers do the cooking and cleaning, another was "devoted to dogs," and the third was a very attractive woman who smoked and flirted with Ella's husband and did too much of the "hard work" around her and her husband's ranch.[25]

Lillian Miller's reminiscence of her life on a sheep ranch in Montana in the 1890s is also rich in detailed descriptions of the clothes, furniture, houses, and visiting patterns of the white women in her community. She wrote about visiting one new arrival with her mother and being "very impressed with the nice walnut furniture, and everything else that we saw. Mrs. Ross talked so glibly of storing the 'better' furniture, packing the 'better' china into barrels, and putting the silver in a bank vault, that when we returned home mother told father she was afraid they wouldn't stay long. How could Mrs. Ross adjust to the rugged life of a pioneer after being used to all that luxury?" Mrs. Ross was eventually able to demonstrate, however, that her privileged and almost excessive femininity, which seemed quite literally to be so out of place in the West, did not stop her from demonstrating "the stamina and fortitude, it takes to carry on."

Lillian's mother was not, apparently, threatened by the other woman's nicer things. Lillian wrote, "Of course, we had a better house, and mother did not have a jealous nature. She was content with what she had. Some of her better things were stored too in Iowa." Her mother could not have been completely content with what she had, however, as another local woman, Mrs. Sweet, made her "all hot and bothered" every time she came to visit. Lillian recalled that although their house "was always immaculate and ready for company," her mother saw it as "plain and unpretentious," and was worried about what she was "going to serve such a fine lady for lunch."[26]

By the end of the nineteenth century, then, as the white, English-speaking communities in southern Alberta and northern Montana became more firmly entrenched, gender seems to have replaced race as a dominant category of concern for white women. From a white viewpoint, decades of policies aimed at achieving spatial and social segregation and white domination appeared to be largely successful. As Sarah Carter has argued for Canada's Prairie West, the newcomers had erected "boundaries that defined them as members of a particular community," which "became increasingly segregated from the indigenous people as boundaries were defined and racial categories sharpened." The almost-complete disappearance of aboriginal people from the diaries and reminiscences of white settler women reflects their physical, social, and economic marginalization by white communities as much as their imaginary marginalization from the gaze of white women.[27]

Did the border make a difference in the relationship between race, gender, and landscape during the process of colonization? It does seem clear that white American women were initially much more afraid of the aboriginal population and of the new land as a result. And when any fears were raised, the Americans looked to the nearest army post for help while the Canadians generally looked to the federal government's Indian agents. But after the initial contact period between the incoming white population and the only-recently dispossessed aboriginal population, the Canadian and American settler societies, as portrayed in these writings by white women, seem to have come to similar accommodations with racial differences and the gender norms expected of other white women. It helped, no doubt, that they had placed themselves in the position of defining the racial and gender identity and status of the people with whom they still shared the land. The precise nature of the racial inflections and their coproductions with landscapes and gender on either side of the forty-ninth parallel await further comparative research, but once the colonizers had solidified their control over the colonized and their land, it appears to have mattered more to be unquestionably white than to be Canadian or American.

Notes

This essay originally was published in *Agricultural History* 73, no. 2 (Spring 1999): 168–82, © 1999 by the Agricultural History Society, and is reprinted here with permission of the University of California Press.

1. Carolyn Abbott Tyler, diary, September 10, 1862, SC 1430, Montana Historical Society (MHS), Helena.

2. Ruth Frankenberg, *White Women, Race Matters: The Social Construction of Whiteness* (Minneapolis: University of Minnesota Press, 1993), 69.

3. Sarah Carter, *Capturing Women: The Manipulation of Cultural Imagery in Canada's Prairie West* (Montreal: McGill-Queens University Press, 1997), 19.

4. M. Ella Lees Inderwick to sister-in-law Alice, 1884, M 559, archives, Glenbow-Alberta

Institute, Calgary AB; Margaret Harkness Woodman, San Francisco, to librarian of MHS, 1892, SC 988, MHS.

5. May G. Flanagan to cousin, ca. 1890, SC 1236, MHS; Mary Douglas Gibson, written reminiscence, n.d., SC 1476, MHS.

6. Sadye Wolfe Drew, written reminiscence, n.d., SC 1532, MHS.

7. Mrs. Kate Hogan letter, ca. 1867, SC 864, MHS; Alma Coffin Kirkpatrick, written reminiscence with some diary excerpts, July 19, 1878, SC 940, MHS.

8. Inderwick diary, October 29, 1883, archives, Glenbow-Alberta Institute.

9. Julia Shortt diary and reminiscence, M 1137, archives, Glenbow-Alberta Institute.

10. Lucy Stocking diary, July 4 and 5, 1874, SC 142, MHS.

11. Inderwick to Alice, 1884, archives, Glenbow-Alberta Institute.

12. Tyler diary, 1862, MHS.

13. Lillian M. Miller, "I Remember Montana," written reminiscence, SC 1404, MHS.

14. Carter, *Capturing Women*, 184–85.

15. Shortt reminiscence, archives, Glenbow-Alberta Institute.

16. Miller reminiscence, MHS.

17. Rosanna Sturgis, letter, 1867, SC 809, MHS, emphasis original to document; Drew reminiscence, MHS.

18. Mrs. Alfred Wyndham diary, 1888–91, A. C. Wyndham, archives, Glenbow-Alberta Institute.

19. Gibson reminiscence, MHS.

20. Flanagan memoirs, MHS; Gibson reminiscence, MHS.

21. Inderwick to Alice, archives, Glenbow-Alberta Institute.

22. Gibson reminiscence, MHS; Helen Millar, n.d., M 849, archives, Glenbow-Alberta Institute.

23. Inderwick reminiscence and letter to Alice, 1884.

24. Inderwick diary and letter to Alice, 1884.

25. Inderwick to Alice, 1884.

26. Miller reminiscences, MHS.

27. Carter, *Capturing Women*, xiii.

Part 3. Seeking Sanctuary on Both Sides of the Line

Over the past two and a half centuries, many have viewed the borderlands of the United States and Canada as a place of refuge from persecution. For example, at the time of America's War for Independence, despite "revolutionary" language about freedom of thought and ideas, thousands of loyalists to the Crown suffered persecution by other Americans who forced them to flee to Canada. Conversely, thousands of Acadian Roman Catholics, made equally unwelcome in Atlantic Canada, were forced to flee to the United States, settling in New England and eventually as "Cajuns" in Louisiana. And black slaves sought refuge in Canada, specifically in Chatham, Ontario—the end of the line on the "underground railroad."

This pattern of seeking sanctuary intensified with Anglo-European expansion into the American and Canadian Wests. American Indians, most notably groups of Sioux under the direction of the Hunkpapa leader Sitting Bull, fled across the border (often called "the medicine line" by American Indians) to "Grandmother's Land" to escape brutal U.S. military atrocities and the advent of the reservation system. Chief Joseph of the Nez Perce Nation almost succeeded in leading his people to Canada in 1877 when the U.S. cavalry cut him short near what is today the Montana/Saskatchewan border. Some Nez Perces had already fled across the border and lived among the Sioux.

But as Gerhard Ens and Michel Hogue show in their chapters here, Native and mixed race peoples (the Métis) of the Canadian prairies saw escaping to the U.S. borderlands as a safety valve for their survival against an equally hostile Canadian government. These authors and other historians are working to revise the outdated notion that there was somehow a more benevolent First Nations policy in Canada.

The wide open prairies and ranges of the American and Canadian Wests and the land policies that encouraged their settlement by European immigrants also attracted a variety of ethnic and religious groups seeking solace and freedom. Mennonites, Hutterites, and Doukhobors all established communities on both sides of the border. And as Peter Morris shows in chapter 10, Mormon settlers moved into southern Alberta seeking sanctuary from Americans opposed to their religion, specifically to polygamy. Morris frames his analysis of this history around a borderlands thesis, suggesting that interactions of people, regions, and borders represent a "special kind of comparative history" that provides a "fuller understanding of [a] shared continental context" between the United States and Canada. These patterns continued into the twentieth century, with other groups seeing the border as a line of refuge or escape (discussed in part 5).

Space constraints prevented more discussion of nineteenth-century dimensions of the borderlands as a sanctuary. However, listed below are a number of excellent works on the topic. Readers interested in the Sioux's cross-boundary history, for example, should consult the works of Black Elk (via John Neihardt), David McCrady, Beth LaDow, Robert Utley, and Paul Sharp. On the Nez Perce they should see books by Merrill Beal, Jerome Greene, Alvin Josephy, Linwood Laughy, and Merle Wells. Likewise listed are books regarding the establishment of religious communities in the borderlands. And for a unique study of how African Americans sought refuge from discrimination in the Canadian prairies, unfortunately to no avail, readers should consult Bruce Shepard's *Deemed Unsuitable*.

For Further Reading

On Native American/First Nation and Métis History in the Borderlands Region of the Plains and Rockies
On Migration to the Borderlands for Religious and Ethnic Refuge

On Native American/First Nation and Métis History in the Borderlands Region of the Plains and Rockies

Barkwell, Lawrence J., Leah Dorion, and Darren R. Prefonatine, eds. *Métis Legacy: A Métis Historiography and Annotated Bibliography*. Winnipeg: Pemmican, 2001.

Beal, Merrill D. "Flight toward Canada." Part 4 of *"I Will Fight No More Forever"*: *Chief Joseph and the Nez Perce War*. Seattle: University of Washington Press, 1963.

Burt, Larry. "In a Crooked Piece of Time: The Dilemma of the Montana Cree and the Metis." *Journal of American Culture* 9 (Spring 1986): 45–52.

————. "Nowhere Left to Go: Montana's Crees, Métis, and Chippewa and the Creation of the Rocky Boy Reservation." *Great Plains Quarterly* 7 (Summer 1987): 195–209.

Calf Robe, Ben, with Beverly Hungry Wolf. *Siksika: A Blackfoot Legacy*. Invermere BC: Good Medicine Books, 1979.

Camp, Gregory S. "The Dispossessed: The Ojibwa and Métis of Northwestern North Dakota." *North Dakota History* 69 (2002): 62–79.

Carpenter, Jock. *Fifty-Dollar Bride: Marie Rose Smith—A Chronicle of Métis Life in the Nineteenth Century*. Sidney BC: Gray's, 1977.

Dempsey, James. "Little Bear's Band: Canadian or American Indians?" *Alberta History* 46 (Winter 1993): 2–9.

Dusenberry, Verne. *The Montana Cree: A Study in Religious Persistence*. Norman: University of Oklahoma Press, 1998.

Ens, Gerhard. *Homeland to Hinterland: The Changing Worlds of the Red River Metis in the Nineteenth Century*. Toronto: University of Toronto Press, 1996.

Flores, Dan. "The Great Contradiction: Bison and Indians in Northern Plains Environmental History." In Charles E. Rankin, ed., *New Perspectives on the Battle of the Little Big Horn*. Helena: Montana Historical Society Press, 1996.

Foster, John E. "The Métis and the End of the Plains Buffalo in Alberta." In John E. Foster, Dick Harrison, and I. S. Madaren, eds., *Buffalo*. Edmonton: University of Alberta Press, 1992.

————. "The Plains Métis." In R. Bruce Morrison and C. Roderick Morrison, eds., *Native Peoples: The Canadian Experience*. Toronto: McClelland and Stewart, 1986.

Foster, Martha H. "A Montana Métis Community: The Evolution of an Ethnic Identity." PhD diss., UCLA, 2000.

Greene, Jerome A. *Nez Perce Summer, 1877: The U.S. Army and the Nee-Me-Poo Crisis*. Helena: Montana Historical Society Press, 2000.

Hogue, Michel. "Disputing the Medicine Line: The Plains Crees and the Canadian-American Border, 1876–1885." *Montana: The Magazine of Western History* 52 (Winter 2002): 2–16.

Josephy, Alvin. *The Nez Perce Indians and the Opening of the Northwest*. New Haven: Yale University Press, 1965.

LaDow, Beth. "Sanctuary," Chap. 3 of *The Medicine Line: Life and Death on a North American Borderland*. New York: Routledge, 2001.

Laughy, Linwood, ed. *In Pursuit of the Nez Perces: The Nez Perce War of 1877 as Reported by Gen. O. O. Howard, Duncan McDonald, and Chief Joseph*. Wrangell AK: Mountain Meadows Press, 1993.

McGrady, David G. "Living with Strangers: The Nineteenth-Century Sioux and the Canadian-American Borderlands." PhD diss., University of Manitoba, 1998.

————. "The Sioux, the Crows, and the Policies of Hunger, 1878–1881." Paper, conference of the Western History Association (WHA), Portland OR, October 1999.

————. "The 'Sioux,' the Surveyors, and the NWMP on the Canada–United States Boundary, 1872–1874." Paper, WHA, Denver, October 1995.

Morin, Jean-Pierre. "Empty Hills: Aboriginal Land Usage and the Cypress Hills Problem, 1874–1883." *Saskatchewan History* 35 (Spring 2003): 5–20.

Neihardt, John G. "Grandmother's Land." Chap. 12 of *Black Elk Speaks*. Lincoln: University of Nebraska Press, 1979.

Nicholls, Roger L. *Indians in the United States and Canada: A Comparative History*. Lincoln: University of Nebraska Press, 1998.

Peterson, Hans J. "Imasees and His Band: Canadian Refugees after the North-West Rebellion." *Western Canadian Journal of Anthropology* 8 (Spring 1978): 21–37.

Rosier, Paul. *Rebirth of the Blackfoot Nation, 1912–1954*. Lincoln: University of Nebraska Press, 2001.

Samek, Hana. "Evaluating Canadian Indian Policy: A Case for Comparative Historical Perspective." *American Review of Canadian Studies* 16 (autumn 1986): 293–99.

Sharp, Paul F. "Sitting Bull and the Queen." Chap. 12 of *Whoop-Up Country: The Canadian-American West, 1865–1885*. Minneapolis: University of Minnesota Press, 1955.

Sharrock, Floyd W., and Susan R. Sharrock. "History of the Cree Indian Territorial Expansion from the Hudson Bay Area to the Interior Saskatchewan and Missouri Plains." In David Agee Horr, ed., *Chippewa Indians*, vol. 6. New York: Garland, 1974.

Spry, Irene M. "Aboriginal Resource Use in the Nineteenth Century in the Great Plains of Modern Canada." In Chad Gaffield and Pam Gaffield, eds., *Consuming Canada: Readings in Environmental History*, 81–92. Toronto: Copp Clark, 1995.

St. Germain, Jill. *Indian Treaty-Making Policy in the United States and Canada, 1867–1877*. Lincoln: University of Nebraska Press, 2001.

Stegner, Wallace. "Half World: The Métis." Chap. II-4 of *Wolf Willow: A History, a Story, and a Memory of the Last Plains Frontier*. New York: Viking Books, 1955.

Taylor, Marian. *Chief Joseph: Nez Perce Leader*. New York: Chelsea House, 1993.

Utley, Robert M. *The Lance and the Shield: The Life and Times of Sitting Bull*. New York: Henry Holt, 1993.

Wells, Merle, ed. *Thunder in the Mountains: The Story of the Nez Perce War*. Couer d'Alene ID: Alpha Omega, 1992.

Woodcock, George, and Jim Miller, eds. *Gabriel Dumont: The Métis Chief and His Lost World*. Petersborough ON: Broadview Press, 2003.

On Migration to the Borderlands for Religious and Ethnic Refuge

Anderson, A. "Ethnic Identity in Saskatchewan Bloc Settlements: A Sociological Appraisal." In Howard Palmer, ed., *The Settlement of the West*. Calgary: University of Calgary Press, 1977.

Barry, Bill. *Ukrainian People Places: The Ukrainians, Germans, Mennonites, Hutterites, and Doukhobors and the Names They Brought to Saskatchewan*. Regina: People Places, 2001.

Boldt, Edward. "Conformity and Deviance: The Hutterites of Alberta." MA thesis, University of Alberta, 1966.

Brown, S. Kent, et al., eds., *Historical Atlas of Mormonism.* New York: Simon and Schuster, 1994.

Embry, Jessie L. "Two Legal Wives: Mormon Polygamy in Canada, the United States, and Mexico." In Brigham Y. Card et al., eds., *The Mormon Presence in Canada.* Edmonton: University of Alberta Press, 1990.

Erickson, Dan. "Alberta Polygamists? The Canadian Climate and Response to the Introduction of Mormonism's 'Peculiar Institution.' " *Pacific Northwest Quarterly* 86 (Fall 1995): 155–64.

Feldman, Anna. "Were Jewish Farmers Failures? The Case of Township 2–15-2nd." *Saskatchewan History* 55 (Spring 2003): 21–30.

Fox, Marilyn. "Jewish Agricultural Colonies in Saskatchewan with Special Reference to the Colonies of Sonnenfeld and Edenbridge." MA thesis, University of Saskatchewan, 1979.

Godfrey, Donald G., and Brigham Y. Card, eds. *The Diaries of Charles Ora Card: The Canadian Years, 1886–1903.* Salt Lake City: University of Utah Press, 1993.

Govia, Francine, and Helen Lewis. *Blacks in Canada: In Search of the Promise.* Edmonton: Harambee Centres Canada, 1988.

Hofer, Samuel. *The Hutterites: Lives and Images of a Communal People.* Saskatoon: Hofer, 1998.

Holt, Simma. *Terror in the Name of God: The Story of the Sons of Freedom Doukhobors.* Toronto: McClelland and Stewart, 1966.

Hostetler, John A. *Hutterite Society.* Baltimore: Johns Hopkins University Press, 1974.

Innis, David L., and H. Dale Lowry. *Lee's Creek, 1887: Logan, Cache Valley to Lee's Creek via the Fort Benton-Macleod Trail into Canada; Home at Last.* Privately published, 2002.

Katz, William Loren. *The Black West.* New York: Simon and Schuster, 1996.

Katz, Yossi, and John C. Lehr. "Jewish and Mormon Agricultural Settlement in Western Canada: A Comparative Analysis." *Canadian Geographer* 35 (Summer 1991): 128–42.

Knoll, Wilma Irene. "The History of the Hutterites of South Dakota." MA thesis, University of South Dakota, 1963.

Lalonde, Andre. "Colonization Companies in the 1880s." *Saskatchewan History* 24 (Fall 1971): 101–20.

Lee, Lawrence B. "The Canadian Irrigation Frontier." *Agricultural History* 40 (October 1966): 271–83.

———. "The Mormons Came to Canada, 1887–1902." *Pacific Northwest Quarterly* 59 (January 1968): 11–22.

Lehr, John C. "The Mormon Cultural Landscape in Alberta." In Roger Leigh, ed., *Malaspina Papers: Studies in Human and Physical Geographer,* 25–33. Vancouver: Tantalous Research, 1973.

Lehr, John C., and Yossi Katz. "Crown, Corporation, and Church: The Role of Institutions in the Stability of Pioneer Settlements in the Canadian West, 1870–1914." *Journal of Historical Geography* 21 (October 1995): 413–29.

Lewis, Wallace G. "Moxee—Another Promised Land: French-Canadian Resettlement in the

Yakima Valley, Washington." Paper, conference of the Western History Association (WHA), Colorado Springs, October 2002.

Lorenz, Gerhard. *The Mennonites of Western Canada: Their Origin and Background and Brief Story of Their Settling and Progress Here.* Steinbach MB: Derksen Printers, 1974.

Luebke, Frederick. *Ethnicity in the Great Plains.* Lincoln: University of Nebraska Press, 1980.

————. *European Immigrants in the American West: Community Histories.* Albuquerque: University of New Mexico Press, 1998.

Matheson, L. N. *The Doukhobors, the Hutterites, and Freedom of Religion.* Vancouver: University of British Columbia, 1967.

McLaren, John. "The Despicable Crime of Nudity: Law, the State, and Civic Protest among the Sons of Freedom Sect Doukhobors, 1899–1935." *Journal of the West* 38 (July 1999): 27–33.

Meinig, D. W. "The Mormon Culture Region: Strategies and Patterns in the Geography of the American West, 1847–1964." *Annals of the Association of American Geographers* 55 (June 1965): 197–201.

Quiring, Walter. *Mennonites in Canada.* Altona MB: D. W. Friesen, 1961.

Radtke, Hans D. *The Hutterites in Montana: An Economic Description.* Bozeman: Montana State University, 1971.

Rasporich, A. W. "Utopian Ideals and Community Settlements in Western Canada, 1880–1914." In R. Douglas Francis and Howard Palmer, eds., *The Prairie West: Historical Readings,* 338–61. Edmonton: Pica Pica Press, 1992.

Regehr, T. D. "Accommodation to a New Society: Mennonites in Canada." *Journal of the West* 38 (July 1999): 34–40.

————. *Mennonites in Canada, 1939–1970: A People Transformed.* Toronto: University of Toronto Press, 1996.

Shepard, R. Bruce. *Deemed Unsuitable: Blacks from Oklahoma Move to the Canadian Prairies in Search of Equality in the Early Twentieth Century Only to Find Racism in Their New Home.* Toronto: Umbrella Press, 1997.

————. "The Origins of the Oklahoma Black Migration to the Canadian Prairies." *Canadian Journal of History* 23 (April 1988): 1–30.

Smucker, Donovan E., ed. *The Sociology of the Canadian Mennonites, Hutterites, and Amish.* Waterloo ON: Wilfred Laurier University Press, 1977.

Szalasznyj, Kathlyn Rose Marie. "The Doukhobor Homestead Crisis, 1898–1907." MA thesis, University of Saskatchewan, 1977.

Tagg, Melvin S., et al. *A History of the Mormon Church in Canada.* Lethbridge, AB: Lethbridge Herald Co. for the Church of Jesus Christ of Latter-day Saints, Lethbridge Stake, 1968.

Taylor, Quintard. *The Forging of a Black Community: Seattle's Central District, from 1870 through the Civil Rights Era.* Seattle: University of Washington Press, 1994.

————. *In Search of the Racial Frontier: African Americans in the West, 1528–1990.* New York: W. W. Norton, 1999.

West, Karen. "Cardston: The Temple City of Canada." *Canadian Geographic* 71 (November 1965): 162–69.

Wilson, Laura. *Hutterites of Montana.* New Haven: Yale University Press, 2000.

Winks, Robin. *The Blacks in Canada*. New Haven: Yale University Press, 1971.

Woodcock, George, and Ivan Arakumovic. *The Doukhobors*. Toronto: Oxford University Press, 1968.

Youmans, Vance J. "Establishment of the Spokane Hutterian Brethren." *Pacific Northwest Forum* II-6 (Summer/Fall 1993): 15–32.

8. The Border, the Buffalo, and the Métis of Montana

Gerhard J. Ens

In the late 1860s and early 1870s, large numbers of Plains Métis began to move into Montana to exploit the last large herds of buffalo in North America. The Métis are those descendants of native women and European men who forged a new identity in the fur trade that was neither Indian nor white. These Métis communities arose in various geographic locations such as the Great Lakes, Upper Missouri, Red River, and the Canadian Northwest. The Plains Métis who could be found almost anywhere on the northern plains were a buffalo-hunting variant of this "New People." Most of these Métis had their origins further east, and many were Canadian or British by birth.[1] The temporary *hivernants* or wintering communities that the Métis established in Montana during this period became the basis of more permanent Métis communities in the 1880s when the United States/Canadian border became even more impermeable and the buffalo disappeared. They stayed in Montana even though the American government gave no recognition or rights to the Métis as a separate people. The questions this chapter addresses are why many of these Plains Métis, largely of Canadian or British origin, chose to stay on the American side of the border after the buffalo disappeared, and what role the border and national consciousness played in the choice of whether the Métis would become American or Canadian.

The Plains Métis had been borderland people for more than fifty years in the Canadian and American Wests before the 1870s, and to the extent that they recognized the border as a meaningful entity, it was a "white" or "English" construct to be manipulated. The Métis lived, worked, and hunted on both sides of the line, and they recognized its existence only when it was to their benefit. After 1870, however, the border began to play an ever-increasing role in their identity. As the buffalo began retreating both westward and southward, and as the American and Canadian governments began to police and patrol the border with increased vigilance, the Métis were drawn into what Richard Maxwell Brown has called the "Western Civil War of Incorporation."[2] This "civil war," which created an ordered capitalistic society in the West between 1850 and 1910, had a distinctly international aspect on the northern plains as this was the time when the international boundary was surveyed, patrolled, and defended. It was thus a war of incorporation that created two countries out of a single region and a war that involved the Canadian state as well as the United States. It is a process that can be profitably seen as the Americanization of the Plains Métis.

Before the 1870s the American/British border on the northern plains was of little consequence to the Métis who exploited the buffalo herds in this region. The Plains Métis who first came to prominence in the Red River/Pembina region began to spread westward in the 1840s and 1850s as the buffalo withdrew from the more easterly parts of the northwestern plains and as the number of the Red River Métis rapidly increased from 3,646 in 1835 to 12,000 in 1870. By the 1850s and 1860s their wintering villages could be found anywhere in the ecological zone where the buffalo wintered, irrespective of the international boundary (see figure 13).

The Convention of 1818, which had established the forty-ninth parallel as the boundary between the United States and the British possession, went largely unrecognized by the native peoples of the northern plains. For the Métis, the main repercussion was that the Hudson's Bay Company (HBC), realizing that their post along the border was now in American territory, moved the Pembina post to the Red River Settlement and put pressure on the Roman Catholic Church to relocate the Pembina mission to Red River, bringing the Métis with them. The HBC feared that if left at Pembina the Métis would take advantage of their new citizenship to flout the company's monopoly and go into the trade themselves. Even though the majority of the Pembina Métis did relocate to Red River in the British Territory, they lived and hunted where they wished and where it was safe to do so. Given that the Plains Métis' way of life was almost

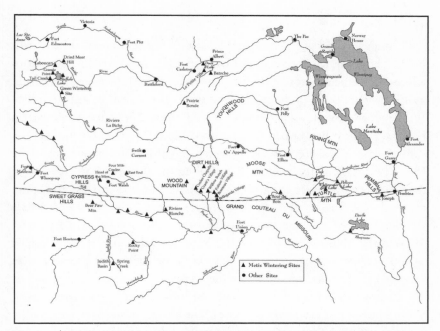

Figure 13. Métis wintering sites on the northern plains. Map by Gerhard Ens.

wholly dependent on the buffalo—they acted as provisioners for the fur trade and later became heavily involved in the buffalo robe trade—the Métis traveled as far as necessary to find the herds they needed.[3] In the 1830s, 1840s, and 1850s they hunted in Sioux territory as far south as Devils Lake and as far west as the Grand Coteau. They had permanent villages in the Red River Settlement, Pembina, and St. Joseph. By the 1850s and 1860s they were hunting as far west as Wood Mountain, Milk River, and the Cypress Hills, and the distance from their former villages necessitated the establishment of temporary wintering villages near the buffalo and where there was enough shelter and wood to allow them to survive a winter on the plains. From the 1850s onward these wintering villages stretched from the Souris (Mouse) River in the east to the Cypress Hills in the west and from Devils Lake in the south to the North Saskatchewan River in the north. They survived in these locations because of their kinship connections to surrounding Indian bands (Sioux, Ojibway, Cree, and Assiniboine) and their military prowess.

From the time the Métis began expanding southwestward in the 1840s there were almost yearly conflicts with Sioux. By 1858, however, the Chippewa (Ojibwa), Métis, and Dakota met in a Grand Council north of the Sheyenne River and west of Devils Lake to set tribal boundaries and establish peace among the three groups. The Métis were recognized as a legitimate band in the region and were represented by Jean-Baptiste Wilkie of St. Joseph (aka Norbexxa) and allowed to hunt in Sioux territories. [4] The other factor that reduced Sioux/Métis conflicts was the "Minnesota Massacre" of 1862, which put the Sioux at war with the U.S. Army. The Sioux needed allies among the British Métis, who were their main trade source for guns and ammunition, and in 1863 the Sioux traveled to St. Joseph to reaffirm the peace treaty. Although these treaties significantly reduced the hostilities between the Sioux and Métis and allowed the Métis access to buffalo hunting grounds north and south of the border, the expansionary nature of both the Métis and Sioux in these years led to sporadic conflicts into the 1870s.

Before the 1870s the border was no impediment to the Métis, who manipulated it for their own purposes. The history of the Métis' use of the international boundary is a study in itself, and so I will provide only one example. When the Red River Métis heard that the U.S. government was planning to negotiate a treaty with the Pembina and Red Lake Chippewa, many decided to relocate to the American side of the boundary to take advantage of the benefits of this treaty. During the negotiations, the Métis claimed that "it was they who possessed the country really, and who had long defended and maintained it against the encroachments of enemies." The treaty that was signed between the United States and the Pembina Chippewa on September 20, 1851, however, did not include the Métis as signatories, as the government believed it should not deal with people whom it regarded "as our *quasi* citizens." The government negotiator did stipulate that he would not object "to any just or reasonable arrangement or treaty stipulation the Indians might choose to make for their benefit." As a result the Chippewa inserted a clause into the treaty that $30,000 be given to their Métis relatives. [5] The treaty, however, was not ratified by Congress, and many of those who had claimed U.S. residence returned to the Red River Settlement in British Territory. The Métis' cavalier attitude toward the border was expressed more explicitly to Gen. Isaac Stevens, who was exploring a route for a railway from the Dakota plains in the summer of 1853. The first group he encountered was from Pembina, but the second group, led by a hunt chief named De L'orme (Delorme), had come from the Red River Settlement in British Territory. De L'orme told Stevens that they had a right to hunt in American territory, being residents of the territory on both sides of the boundary line. Stevens reported that "they claim the protection of both governments, and the doubt as to the position of the boundary makes them uncertain as to the government upon which they have the most claim. During the hunting season they carry with them their families and their property. Many children are born during these expeditions, and they consider that children born upon our soils during the transit possess the heritage of American citizens."[6]

By the 1860s, however, the boundary was becoming of increasing importance in Indian/white relations. Advancing American settlement, Sioux hostilities in Minnesota, and the Canadian government's interest in acquiring the British Northwest made the border a major factor in determining the responsibilities of the various governments in recognizing and protecting the rights of the various Indian groups in the region. As both the Métis and Indians were increasingly using the border to shield themselves from reprisals by the 1870s, it is not surprising that both governments would want better control of the border region. Within a few years the western boundary between the United States and Canada had been surveyed, and both the U.S. Army and the Canadian North-West Mounted Police were patrolling the border, significantly limiting cross-border traffic. These factors, combined with the southwestward retreat of the buffalo, would increasingly force the Plains Métis to choose a U.S. residence.

These developments brought the Plains Métis into Montana for the first time. Wintering villages had begun to appear in the 1840s at places like Turtle Mountain, Souris Basin, Riding Mountain, Wood Mountain, and along the Assiniboine, Qu'Appelle, and Saskatchewan rivers. They were a response to the westward retreat of the buffalo herds and the changing nature of the fur trade on the Upper Missouri River. Before 1840 the Plains Métis of Red River had secured most of the pemmican, dried meat, buffalo robes, and leather they required from the summer and fall buffalo hunts out of Red River and Pembina. Beginning in the 1840s, however, the buffalo retreated further and further west, and the Métis hunters had to travel hundreds of miles before even spotting a herd. Buffalo robes became increasingly important in the fur trade of the Missouri at this time. Beaver stocks had been depleted, and buffalo robes found lucrative markets in New York, Montreal, St. Paul, and St. Louis. These robes consisted of the skin of the buffalo with the hair left on and the hide tanned. Prime robes, those taken from November to February and in excellent shape, fetched good prices of ten to twelve dollars per robe by the 1870s. The Métis responded to this new market by smuggling their furs and robes across the border to American traders.

Beginning in the late 1840s and accelerating in the 1850s and 1860s, observers began to notice an increase in Métis' wintering communities west of Red River and Pembina in response to these new economic opportunities. While it was still possible to winter in St. Joseph in the 1850s and be close enough to the winter range of the buffalo to get winter robes, it was certainly no longer possible to do so wintering in the Red River Settlement or Pembina. As a result, more and more Plains Métis began spending their winters in small temporary communities west of Red River, where they could hunt the buffalo in winter. By the late 1860s and early 1870s, even the Métis of the settlement of St. Joseph were leaving en masse to winter on the plains. As time went on, these wintering villages moved in a southwesterly direction following the retreat of the northern herd, and by the 1870s, the orientation of most Plains Métis was south of the border. In 1878 prairie fires swept a wide area of grassland in the boundary region between Montana and what today is Alberta. The buffalo moved south, and what was left of the northern herd remained south of the border between the Milk River and the Judith Bain. The large herds never returned to Canada.[7] Not only were the last remnants of the northern herd concentrating in northern Montana, but increasing military vigilance along the international boundary by both the U.S. Army and the NWMP forced the Métis to choose an American residence. While the U.S. Army and the NWMP were primarily interested in stopping the arms and whiskey trade that was stirring up Indian hostilities, this increased border vigilance also ended the Métis' practice of taking their buffalo robes across the border to traders at Fort Benton. Given these factors, it became much more convenient for the Métis to claim American residency.

The Métis had began wintering in Montana in the 1860s, locating their communities on the Milk River where the Riviere Blanche (Frenchman's Creek or the Whitemud Creek) branches off into Canada. By the early 1870s, Métis settlements were springing up all over the Milk River country. Father Lestanc, who had built a mission at Wood Mountain for the Plains Métis, was forced to relocate to Montana because most of his group had left Wood Mountain. In 1871 he reported that there were sixty families wintering at Riviere Blanche, and by 1873 his camp alone had ninety families. He noted that no one knew precisely where the border was or if they were living in American or Canadian territory.[8] George M. Dawson, traveling with the British Boundary Commission in 1874, met numerous Métis groups between Wood Mountain and Montana, and noted that Wood Mountain had "seen its palmy days. Buffalo & Indians already too far west. Most of the families speak of wintering next at Cypress Hills." On July 19, 1874, he visited a Métis camp on the Milk River that numbered two hundred lodges and two thousand horses. This group of Plains Métis was wintering on Riviere Blanche well within the United States, and he noted they traded their goods via the Missouri River posts.[9]

The presence of these Canadian Métis in Montana worried the U.S. Army and Indian agents. Convinced that the Métis from Canada were trading whiskey and guns to the Sioux and using the border to shield themselves, the U.S. Army resolved to eliminate this traffic.[10] According to A. J. Simmons, the Indian agent of the Milk River Agency in Montana, the Métis had "urged Sitting Bull to resist the construction of the North Pacific Rail Road. So long as Sitting Bull's people remain hostile they have the exclusive trade and barter with them from which they derive large profits and so long as these Indians can procure ammunition from this source, it will be found a serious obstacle in the way of their effecting peace with the Government."[11]

On October 19, 1871, the Seventh Infantry stationed at Fort Shaw was ordered to proceed to the Milk River where this large group of "British" Métis had established their wintering villages. The Seventh Infantry was ordered to destroy all trade goods and drive the Métis out of the country. The army arrived at the Riviere Blanche on November 1, finding a camp of several hundred Métis (see figure 14). The settlement, consisting of houses and lodges scattered along four or five miles of the creek, was captured without any resistance. The houses of the two traders,

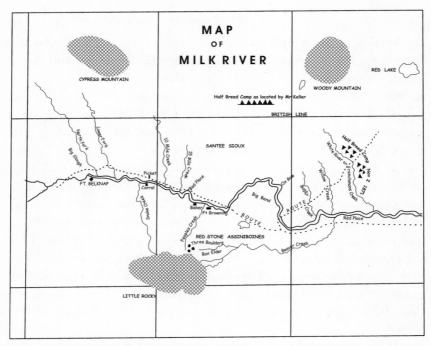

Figure 14. Sketch of the Milk River region, location of Métis wintering camps dispersed by the U.S. Army in 1871. Map in Provincial Archives of Manitoba, MG12, A1, Archibald Papers #697.

consisting of nine buildings, as well as the whiskey and trade goods valued at $10,000 were all burned, and John Kerley was arrested. The Métis were told that they were in violation of American law by selling liquor and ammunition to Indians, and they were thereby helping the Indians to make war on the United States. They were ordered to leave the country and not return. The Métis, for their part, argued that the whiskey and ammunition were the property of white traders who had only recently joined them, and they had lived on the plains (including the United States) all their lives. Besides, they argued, they could not move north because the plains were burnt. They begged to be allowed to remain, promising they would allow no traders among them. In consideration of their good conduct on this occasion, and because the destruction of the entire camp would have inflicted great hardship and suffering, the Métis were allowed to remain in their settlement if they obeyed American laws.[12]

This and other encounters with the U.S. Army convinced many Plains

Métis that American residence and citizenship were crucial not only to hunting the buffalo but also to being able to trade buffalo robes to American posts along the Missouri. When 140 Métis were stopped by the U.S. Army in Montana in 1879 and asked what nationality they were, all but 10 replied they were American. The 10 who declared they were British were escorted across the border, and the others were advised to go to the Judith Basin.[13]

By 1882 the buffalo herds had disappeared, even in Montana. This represented a real crisis for the Plains Métis, and they were faced with hard decisions as to what to do next. Those who had close kinship connections to tribal groups in Montana, such as the Blackfoot and Flathead, went into treaty. Some Métis who had come to Montana from Manitoba and North Dakota went back and reinvented themselves as the Turtle Mountain Chippewa and took treaty in 1892.[14] Others moved north to Canada and took scrip (a negotiable certificate entitling the holder to receive an allotment of public land) after 1885, but a large number, despite their British Canadian roots, remained in Montana and refused to leave.[15]

Those Plains Métis who remained in Montana after 1882 did so not only because there were employment opportunities but also because a significant number had come to see the United States as a homeland— something the Canadian Northwest no longer was. By the late 1870s and early 1880s, the border had become more than a line on a map; it had become something of a state of mind with its own mythology. This new way of looking at the border and the Canadian Northwest had begun shortly after the Riel Resistance in Red River and the transfer of the British Northwest to Canada in 1870, and it crystallized with the military suppression of the Riel Rebellion in the Northwest in 1885.

With the arrival of troops in Red River in the summer of 1870, the increasing pace of Canadian immigration to Manitoba, and the delays in fulfilling the land grants to the Métis promised in the Manitoba Act, many of the Plains Métis came to believe that they had been treated unjustly by the Canadian government. This feeling only increased as the government was slow to acknowledge Métis rights in the Northwest. By 1873 numerous reports were coming back to Alexander Morris, the lieutenant governor of Manitoba and the Northwest Territories, that the Indians and Métis of the Canadian Northwest were full of anxiety regarding the intentions of the Canadians toward them. Robert Bell, who wrote a report for Morris on the state of the West, noted that the notion that "the English have ceased to be their friends appears to be fostered . . . if not promoted by the half breeds." The Métis, he wrote, wanted nothing to do with surveys, treaties, railways, or settlement, and they considered the Canadians cowards. [16] When Pascal Breland was appointed by the Canadian government to investigate the presence of Sioux at Wood Mountain, he met with numerous Plains Métis who eventually would settle in Montana. He was informed that the state of affairs on the plains was critical and dangerous. In regard to the Métis, Edward McKay told him that the Métis, who lived and hunted on both sides of the border, had little respect for the Canadian government and were close to taking the law into their own hands. They were spreading rumors that the Canadian government wanted to exterminate the Indians and rob them of their country. The Métis, he said, "have so little public spirit that it is utter nonsense to depend on them for assistance." The talk of them being loyal, he said, "is outrageous as the majority don't know what it means and most of them scorn the idea. . . . Louis Riel is still their idol and should he or any smart fellow come out to lead them there will be a grand row. . . . They are becoming bolder every day under the inactive policy of the government and if the call be given a rebellion worse in every respect than the last will spread like a fire on the plains." [17] Many of the most troublesome Métis, he noted, were those who had left the British Territory several years earlier to live on the American side. They had recently returned to Wood Mountain to excite the Métis and Indians against the Canadian government and British rule. They promised assistance from the United States if the Métis and Indians could not prevent the Dominion from disposing of their lands. [18]

This discontent was evident as far north as St. Albert on the North Saskatchewan River. A large group of St. Albert Métis wintering at Buffalo Lake told Bishop Grandin in 1875 that "we know too well that we have nothing to hope from the Canadian Government except ill will and contempt. Rather than be ill treated (browbeaten) like our parents, we have decided to locate ourselves on the territories of the United States." Grandin refused this request, but noted the Métis were still planning to head south and cross the boundary when the time was right. [19]

These simmering hostilities continued throughout the 1870s, and when Louis Riel returned to the West in 1878, he quickly saw the potential for a new offensive against the Canadian state. From his base in Carroll, Montana (a settlement in the heart of the badlands or "breaks" of the Upper Missouri near the Judith Basin), Riel planned an invasion of Canada by the Métis allied to various Indian bands. This invasion would be the prelude to the establishment of a Confederacy of Métis and Indians in the Canadian Northwest. Riel sent for Ambroise Lepine, his former adjutant-general from Red River days, who agreed to meet Riel at Fort Assiniboine in late 1879 or early 1880. Archbishop Taché, aware that Lepine had gone west to meet Riel and aware of the potential trouble the two could create, contacted Lepine and warned him not to meet with Riel. Not wanting to offend the Catholic Church, and aware of the risk to his own safety if he got involved with Riel again, Lepine returned to Manitoba without meeting Riel. As he wrote Taché, it would not take a very large spark to light a fire in the West, as the Métis were very unhappy with how they were being treated by the Canadian government. To Riel he wrote that he was not prepared to sacrifice more for the Métis, as he had already seen the noose at close hand and was not prepared to risk all again.[20]

Riel was just as unsuccessful in persuading the Montana Métis and Indians to support his plan, and after a year or two he moved on to other projects.[21] Riel's plan to attack Canada and establish a Métis and Indian Confederacy, farfetched as it may have been, does indicate the Métis' discontent with the Canadian government and provides some explanation for why the Métis of Montana had no interest in returning to Canada after the buffalo disappeared.

These Montana Métis, the remnant of the buffalo-hunting Plains Métis, settled in railway towns along the line of the Great Northern Railway (Fort Buford, Poplar, Oswego, Wolf Point, Havre, Chinook, Harlem, Malta, Glasgow, Kipp, Box Elder). Given that the Great Northern ran parallel to the Milk River, some of these towns such as Malta, Havre, and Glasgow were, in fact, very close to old Métis wintering sites. As railway towns they offered the Métis jobs as construction workers, dirt movers, wood choppers, and buffalo bones collectors. Others settled away from railway centers where it was still possible to hunt small game and farm

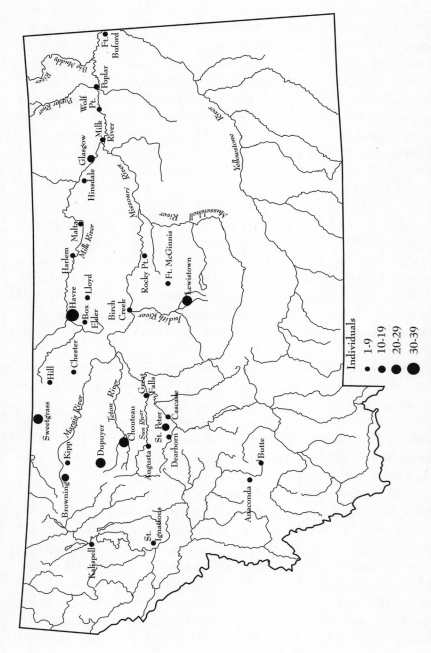

Figure 15. Métis settlement sites in Montana circa 1900. Map by Gerhard Ens.

(Dupuyer, Teton River, Sweetgrass, Choteau). Still others settled at Lewistown, Fort Benton, St. Peters, St. Ignatius, Augusta Hill, and Fort McGinnis, either homesteading, working as laborers on ranches and farms, or freighting. [22] Some indication of the distribution and concentration of former Canadian Métis living in Montana comes from scrip applications by the Canadian government between 1900 and 1904 from Métis living in the United States (see figure 15).

One of the larger Métis settlements in Montana was located in the Judith Basin at Spring Creek (now known as Lewistown). It was settled by Plains Métis buffalo hunters led by Pierre Berger. These families originated in the Red River/St. Joseph region of Manitoba and North Dakota. As the buffalo had retreated westward, this Métis band had relocated first to Wood Mountain and then to Milk River. By 1879 they were wintering on the Milk River between Harlem and Chinook, but with the herds growing smaller every year Pierre Berger began looking for a better location to winter and a location where his people might settle permanently. The larger wintering camps on the Milk were breaking up, and so Berger and twenty-five families decided to move to the Judith Basin where the last big herds were located and where there were other small game and lots of timber. Here they hunted the last buffalo. When these disappeared, they took up homesteads. Within a few years they were joined by other Plains Métis hunters from the Milk River, increasing the settlement to more than 150 families. This latter group had been told by the U.S. Army to leave the country or settle somewhere permanently. [23] These Métis raised stock or worked on area ranches after more settlers moved in.

The 1885 North-West Rebellion was the crystallizing event that changed a transborder people into the Montana Métis who regarded the border as protection from the Canadian government. After the Canadian military crushed Riel's forces at Batoche in the spring of 1885, hundreds of Indians and Métis fled south to escape persecution. These Métis, settling among the Métis who had been in Montana for at least a decade and a half, reinforced the mythology of the evils of the Canadian government. Approximately sixty Métis refugee families settled on Dupuyer Creek south of Blackfoot Reservation, and another group chose the south fork of the Teton River near Choteau. [24] Hiding in the canyons for fear of being sent back to Canada, these Métis lived off the land, hunting small game, "woodhawking," selling buffalo bones, and working on area ranches and farms.[25] Their anti-Canadianism and fear of deportation stayed with the Montana Métis for good reason. In 1896 the American government decided to solve the social problems created by these "indigent" Canadian-born Crees and Métis by forcibly shipping them back to Canada. In all, 537 persons were shipped by rail to Canada, but almost all returned, slipping back across the border over the next few weeks.[26]

Those Plains Métis who settled permanently in Montana had, over the course of a decade and a half, been transformed from a borderland people into American Métis. They willingly and deliberately chose an American residence and citizenship, at least in part, because of their belief that they had suffered an injustice at the hands of the Canadian government and that their rights and livelihood were better protected in the United States. They believed this despite the fact that the American government did not recognize the Métis as a separate group and accorded them no special political or economic rights. By 1885 the border had assumed almost mythical status as protection from persecutions by the Canadian state. This history of the Plains Métis should give pause to those historians who still hold the belief that the Canadian West was settled peaceably and that the Canadian government treated its native peoples more generously than the United States. For the Montana Métis, the demons of the "Western Civil War of Incorporation" were the Canadian state and military. They chose incorporation in the American body politic.

Notes

This essay is an expanded version of a paper presented at the conference of the Western History Association, Portland OR, October 1999.

1. See John E. Foster, "The Plains Métis," in R. Bruce Morrison and C. Roderick Morrison, eds., *Native Peoples: The Canadian Experience* (Toronto: McClelland and Stewart, 1986).
2. Richard Maxwell Brown, "Western Violence: Structure, Values, Myth," *Western Historical Quarterly* 24, no. 1 (February 1993): 5–20.
3. See Gerhard J. Ens, *Homeland to Hinterland: The Changing Worlds of the Red River Métis in the Nineteenth Century* (Toronto: University of Toronto Press, 1996), 28–56, 72–92.
4. "Affidavit of Michael Gladue locating the dividing line between the Sioux Indians and the Turtle Mountain Chippewa Country as settled between them, 9 February 1892."

Reprinted in "Turtle Mountain Band of Chippewa Indians," Sen. Ex. Docs. no. 444, 56th Cong., 1st sess., 1900, 151–52.

5. Report of the treaty made with the Pembina Indians, at Pembina, by Alex. Ramsey, November 7, 1851, included in "The Report of the Commissioner of Indian Affairs," House Ex. Docs., 32nd Cong., 1st sess., November 27, 1851, Serial Set #636, 285.

6. Report of Gen. Isaac J. Stevens in relation to the Indians on his route of exploration from the head of navigation of the Mississippi River to the Pacific Ocean, September 16, 1854, encl. no. 86 in the report of the commissioner of Indian affairs, November 25, 1854, House Ex. Docs. no. 1, 33rd Cong., 2nd sess., 1854–55, Serial Set #777, 401.

7. John C. Ewers, "Ethnological Report on the Chippewa Cree Tribe of the Rocky Boy Reservation and the Little Shell Band of Indians," in *Chippewa Indians*, vol. 6 (American Indian Ethnohistory: North Central and Northeastern Indians), report presented before the Indian Claims Commission, docket no. 221-B (New York: Garland, 1974), 72–74.

8. Jean-Marie Lestanc to Taché, May 3, 1872 (T10300–03), March 31, 1873 (T11789–92), Archives de l'Archevêche de Saint-Boniface.

9. Journal of George M. Dawson, June 22, 1874, reprinted in *Saskatchewan History* 21, no. 1 (Winter 1968), 19.

10. See "Report of Edward McKay on the State of Affairs in the Northwest," encl. to letter of Pascal Breland to Lieutenant Governor Morris, May 18, 1873, Provincial Archives of Manitoba, Lieutenant Governor Morris Papers, MG 12 B1, #164.

11. Letter of A. J. Simmons, U.S. Special Indian Agent, Milk River Agency, to Col. J. A. Viall, Superintendent of Indians for Montana, October 15, 1871, Fort Benton MT, NARA, M234, letters received by the Office of Indian Affairs, 1824–81, Montana Superintendency, 1864–80, reel 491.

12. J. A. Viall, Superintendent of Indians, for Montana to Gen. John Gibbon, October 18, 1871; H. B. Freeman, Capt., Seventh Infantry Report on Expedition against Half Breed Camp in Milk River District, November 6, 1871, Fort Browning; A. J. Simmons to J. A. Viall, November 6, 1871, Fort Browning; J. A. Viall to H. R. Clum, Acting Commissioner Indian Affairs, November 16, 1871, Helena MT, NARA, M234, Letters Received by the Office of Indian Affairs, 1824–81, Montana Superintendency; 1864–80, reel 491.

13. Canada Sessional Papers, no. 4 (43 Victoria, 1880), "Report of the Deputy Superintendent-General of Indian Affairs, 1879," 88.

14. See the interviews of some of these Métis in Historical Society of North Dakota Archives, WPA Historical Data Project, Rolette County. See also Gerhard J. Ens, "After the Buffalo: The Reformation of the Turtle Mountain Métis Community, 1879–1905," in Jo-Anne Fiske, Susan Sleeper Smith, and William Wicken, eds., *New Faces of the Fur Trade: Selected Papers of the Seventh North American Fur Trade Conference, Halifax, Nova Scotia, 1995* (East Lansing: Michigan State University Press, 1998), 139–51.

15. Both Verne Dusenberry and Joseph Kinsey Howard have described these Métis communities in relation to the buffalo economy, and Dusenberry has described the plight of these "dispossessed métis," but neither has attempted to explain why these Métis stayed in Montana after the buffalo disappeared. See Joseph Kinsey Howard, *Strange Empire: A Narrative of the Northwest* (New York: William Morrow, 1952); Verne

Dusenberry, "Waiting for a Day That Never Comes: The Dispossessed Métis of Montana," *Montana: The Magazine of Western History* 8, no. 2 (1958): 26–39.

16. Robert Bell to Morris, October 17, 1873, PAM, MG 12 B1, Lt. Gov. Morris Papers, #524.

17. "Report of Edward McKay on the State of Affairs in the Northwest," encl. with Letter of Pascal Breland to Alexander Morris, May 18, 1873, PAM, Morris Papers, #164.

18. "Memorandum of a Conversation with Mr. Edmund Mckay, formerly of the Hudson's Bay Company's service, and a man said, on good authority, to be thoroughly reliable and respectable," encl. to a letter of Wm. Thornton Urquhart to Judge McKegney, May 19, 1873, PAM, Morris Papers, #165.

19. Bishop Grandin to David Laird, Minister of the Interior, April 5, 1875, National Archives of Canada, RG 15, vol. 3622, file 4953.

20. Lepine to Taché, January 2, 1880 (T23082), Archives de l'Archevêche de Saint-Boniface; Lepine to Riel, January 1, 1880, PAM, MG 3 D2, file 14, Riel Papers.

21. Howard, *Strange Empire*, 338–53.

22. 1880 Census of Choteau County; Marriage Records of Fergus County, Valley County, and Sheridan County; *Teton Country: A History* (Choteau: Teton County Historical Committee, 1988); *Fred Nault: Montana Métis* (Rocky Boy School, 1977); Métis Cultural Recovery Inc., Interviews of Métis Descendants.

23. Mrs. Clemence Gourneau Berger, "Métis Come to Judith Basin," in *The Métis Centennial Publication, 1879–1979*, ed. Bill Thackeray (Lewistown, MT: Central Montana Publication Co., 1979), 13–16; Elizabeth Swan, "A Brief History of the First Catholic Pioneers of Lewistown," in Bobby Deal and Loretta McDonald, eds., *The Heritage Book of Central Montana* (Lewistown MT: Fergus County Bi-Centennial Heritage Committee, 1976).

24. John C. Ewers, "Ethnological Report on the Chippewa Tribe of the Rocky Boy Reservation and the Little Shell Band of Indians," 97; *Fred Nault*, 97.

25. *Teton County: A History* (Choteau: Teton County Historical Committee, 1988), 14–15; interviews of the descendants of the Teton and Dupuyer Métis Communities, Métis Cultural Recovery, Inc., Choteau MT.

26. Ewers, "Ethnological Report," 97; *Fred Nault*, 105–7.

9. Crossing the Line

Race, Nationality, and the Deportation of the "Canadian" Crees in the Canada–U.S. Borderlands, 1890–1900

Michel Hogue

On June 20, 1896, Montana District Court Judge C. H. Benton was handed a petition sworn by Buffalo Coat, a Cree man from Canada. Buffalo Coat claimed that forty soldiers from the Tenth U.S. Cavalry under the command of Lt. John J. Pershing had unlawfully and illegally detained him and thirty other Cree heads of family in a camp near Great Falls, Montana, in preparation for their deportation to Canada. In their petition, the men alleged they were residents of the United States, having been domiciled in the Montana Territory since 1885. They also noted that their group included about sixty children under the age of fifteen who were born on U.S. soil and others who had recently declared their intention to become U.S. citizens. They insisted that their confinement was done without due process of law, and they asked that Benton issue a writ of habeas corpus in order that they and their families could be set free. In response, Judge Benton ordered Pershing and Maj. J. M. J. Sanno to appear before him in the Cascade County Court House in Great Falls, along with those named in the petition.

Pershing had arrived in Great Falls a few days earlier armed with orders from his superiors to oversee the deportation of this group of Crees to the Canadian border. The group camped on the outskirts of Great Falls was one of the many Cree camps located throughout Montana in June 1896. After a protracted series of negotiations involving local and federal officials in the United States and Canada, the U.S. government sent the army to force the Crees back into Canada. Without waiting for his day in court, Pershing and his troops loaded the ninety-six Crees, along with their horses and possessions, onto a train bound for the Canadian border. The attempt by Buffalo Coat to block the deportation by filing a writ of habeas corpus was unsuccessful. Without addressing the questions of citizenship and nationality that the petition raised, Judge Benton agreed to the reply filed by Pershing and Sanno's attorney. He ruled that the deportation fell outside the court's jurisdiction, since army officers were acting under the authority of an Act of Congress. The judge dissolved the writ, and the deportation continued.[1]

In the 1890s, hundreds of "Canadian Crees" lived in camps scattered across the state of Montana. These bands had first appeared in the territory in the months following the suppression of the North-West Rebellion in Canada in 1885, a conflict that arose out of disagreements between the region's Métis population and the Canadian government over Métis land rights. Frustrated with government policy and local Indian Department officials, and facing desperate conditions after an especially severe winter, a large camp of Plains Crees became embroiled in the conflict when several Cree men from Big Bear's band killed nine inhabitants of the Frog Lake settlement (near Edmonton) on April 2, 1885, taking the remainder of the white settlers captive. While most of those associated with Big Bear's camp chose to surrender following subsequent clashes with Canadian troops, others followed Big Bear's second son, Little Bear, who sought asylum in the United States. Although U.S. State Department officials had granted the Cree refugees de facto asylum, without a reservation and with few means of support, their attempts to eke out an existence repeatedly brought them into conflict with white Montanans who demanded their expulsion.[2]

During the agitation to expel the Crees, Montana settlers and American and Canadian officials presented restrictive notions of citizenship, race, and nationality as a means to further their case for expulsion. The Crees, meanwhile, relied on similar notions to bolster their claims to remain in the United States. Whether by challenging the legal restrictions they faced in court, applying for citizenship, petitioning the government for land, blending in with reservation populations, or quietly seeking employment across the state, the Crees in Montana repeatedly sought to circumvent the physical and legal restrictions that the border marked. Their success in exploiting the differences that existed across it and in retaining a measure of their autonomy, however, was ultimately circumscribed by the fact that popular attitudes and policies governing Native peoples in both countries aimed to enforce such boundaries and confine them to the margins of North American society.

Much of the early agitation to deport the Crees centered on the bands of Crees who spent the winters of 1891 and 1892 in the valleys of western Montana. Their presence in the region and their use of state rangeland to graze their horses drew repeated criticism from area residents and officials. One of the most vociferous and persistent critics was Thomas O. Miles, a resident of Silver Bow County west of Butte. In the autumn of 1891, Miles complained to Montana's first governor, Joseph K. Toole, that fifteen lodges of Crees and their 120 horses had set up quarters on his winter range, appropriating the best pastures and forcing residents and taxpayers like him to graze their stock on inferior lands. Like the Crees, Miles had also migrated from Canada but had fared somewhat better. At twenty-one years of age, he reportedly left Canada with only ten dollars and a wagonload of provisions. He subsequently settled at Silver Bow Junction, fenced all available hay land, and achieved a measure of success as a rancher. Now he claimed that not only did the Crees monopolize state hay lands but every spring the residents of Silver Bow Junction lived in fear of Indian wars and "Messiah crazes" (the Ghost Dance of the 1880s and 1890s). He urged that they should be compelled either to go to their reservations or, if they were British or Canadian Indians, leave the country.[3]

Other residents voiced similar complaints about Cree depredations. State officials in Helena received letters protesting their slaughter of game and stock and the spread of infectious disease by their horses. Although sympathetic, Governor Toole stated that he could take no action without violating international law, since the Crees were not American wards. Instead, both he and U.S. District Attorney E. D. Weed petitioned Secretary of State James G. Blaine to remove the Crees. As foreign wards, they argued, the Crees had no right to remain within the state.[4]

Meanwhile, Blaine communicated the complaints of the Montana residents to the British ambassador at Washington, asking that he bring the situation to the attention of Canadian authorities in order that they might cooperate to remove the Crees from the region. After some consideration, the Canadian government agreed to receive at the border "any Indians belonging to Canada who have been guilty of marauding in the United States."[5] Although Blaine communicated the Canadian decision to Montana senator T. C. Power in April, months elapsed before authorities took any concrete steps to effect their removal. In September, Governor Toole wrote to the secretary of war asking for his assistance in removing the Canadian Indians. The commanding officer at Fort Assiniboine noted in response to an earlier query from the secretary of state that the majority of Crees in Montana were political refugees who had arrived in 1885. The army had allowed the refugees to remain but had attempted to prevent others from joining them. In response to Toole's request, the acting secretary of war reiterated the findings of its earlier investigation: that Cree men and women were employed in wood chopping, laundry, and other work and that "they are very useful, are well conducted, and would be greatly missed in the industries of the country were they now removed."[6]

Yet the tenor of the accusations against the Crees became increasingly shrill, especially in light of the army's refusal to assist in their removal. Their status as political refugees meant little to Weed, who maintained that the Crees were "trespassers pure and simple." He forwarded additional complaints from Miles to the secretary of war, alleging that the Crees wantonly destroyed the region's game "without regard to local laws or regulations," stole the stock of settlers, and subsisted by "larceny and plunder." Although there is little evidence to support this claim, press accounts pegged the number of deer killed by the Crees in 1891 at 3,000 during the previous year. More ominously, Weed and others threatened that if the government did not remove the Crees, serious difficulty would likely arise between them and white settlers.[7]

The Crees were not the only Native group in western Montana who were subject to charges that they were violating state game laws. In 1893, a resident of Marysville (near Helena) complained to the governor that Poker Jim, a Native from the Flathead Reservation, had made his annual trip to a small lake near the town to hunt elk and deer. Both Peter Ronan, the Indian agent, and Governor Toole's successor, J. E. Rickards, favored arresting and prosecuting Poker Jim for violating game laws, and they instructed the county attorney to attempt to secure sufficient proof to proceed with the prosecution.[8]

Unlike the complaints lodged against the Salish, Kutenai, or other tribes resident in Montana, those related to the Cree presence in the state hinged on the question of their foreign status. As foreigners, the argument went, the Crees had no right to remain within the state. Yet their "foreignness" also raised jurisdictional disputes that repeatedly undermined state officials' attempts to force the Crees out of Montana, since their federal counterparts were often less eager to address the issue. For example, Secretary of State W. Q. Gresham responded to further appeals to deport the Crees in 1893 by stating that since the Crees were not on any Indian reservation, they were not subject to the control of the commissioner of Indian affairs. The federal government, Gresham argued, had no control over the Crees in Montana and no power to deport them.[9]

The Crees responded by seeking to clarify their rights and secure a more permanent arrangement in the United States. In June 1893, Buffalo Coat, seven other Cree men, and their attorney appeared before William Cockrill, clerk of the Cascade County District Court, and signed Declarations of Intention to become citizens of the United States. Cockrill had previously refused to issue any such declarations and had referred the matter to the district attorney. Excluded from the provisions of the Fourteenth Amendment to the Constitution in 1868, Natives who lived on reservations and maintained tribal ties were not deemed citizens of the United States (unless governed by special laws passed by Congress). Although the 1887 Dawes Act conferred citizenship on those Natives who took up allotments and renounced their tribal ties, those who had not acquired private lands remained legal wards of the government.[10] Weed ruled, however, that there was no law preventing Natives from Canada from applying for U.S. citizenship. When attorney John Hoffman indicated that he had at least sixty more Cree clients who wished to become U.S. citizens, Cockrill again appealed to the district attorney. In response, Weed altered his earlier advice, telling the clerk that he should "decline to accept further declarations of intention from the Cree Indians and advise them that they have a right to institute proceedings in the proper court to compel you to issue papers to them."[11]

Although there is no indication that the Crees and their attorney challenged the matter in court, they continued to press the state government for a clarification of their status in Montana. In November 1893 they sent a petition to Governor Rickards, asking that the government grant them citizenship or establish a reservation for their use. In response, the governor claimed he had no authority in the matter and referred their request to Washington. The reply from the commissioner of the Bureau of Indian Affairs stated that he could not set aside a reservation, since the Crees also fell outside his jurisdiction. Instead, he suggested that the Crees be returned to Canada.[12]

Frustrated by the federal government's unwillingness to force the Crees out of the state or to set aside land for their use, Governor Rickards continued to agitate for their removal. In January 1896, he traveled to Washington to meet with federal authorities, and this time he met with greater success. Secretary of State Richard Olney took up Rickards's complaints, and as his predecessor, James G. Blaine, had done in 1892, he asked for the cooperation of the Canadian government in receiving the Crees. Once again, the Canadian government assented to the request, and the Committee on Foreign Relations approved the expenditure of five thousand dollars to effect the deportation.[13]

As the American and Canadian governments again expressed their unwillingness to cooperate to expel the Crees from Montana in the spring of 1896, it became clear that many of the Crees who had sought sanctuary in the United States after 1885 feared retribution for their part in the North-West Rebellion if they returned. In an attempt to clarify their situation, Little Bear and Buffalo Coat wrote to Canadian authorities (through a commissioner of the U.S. Circuit Court at Havre, Montana), stating their willingness to return to Canada, provided they receive a full amnesty from the government. Deputy Superintendent-General of Indian Affairs Hayter Reed's refusal to comment on the situation while international negotiations about their return were under way likely did little to allay their anxieties. Weeks later, Indian Commissioner Amédée Forget and North-West Mounted Police (NWMP) Superintendent R. Burton Deane traveled to Great Falls and detailed for the Crees assembled there the conditions of the Canadian amnesty. Deane reported, however, that most remained unconvinced and expected they would be prosecuted upon their return to Canada. In hopes of preventing the deportation, the Crees again turned to attorney John Hoffman, who petitioned Judge Benton for the writ of habeas corpus.[14]

Others who may have feared reprisals for their part in the Rebellion responded by breaking into small camps and scattering across the state, attempting to evade capture by U.S. troops. The Montana press reported that Cree camps in the West were preparing to leave for Idaho, while others were fleeing for more remote corners of the state. One man even committed suicide at Great Falls rather than return to Canada.[15] When Deane arrested Little Bear and Lucky Man (one of Big Bear's former headmen) for their participation in the Frog Lake massacre, it likely confirmed the fears of retribution that many of the Crees held. Both were exempt from the provisions of the amnesty, since the murders at Frog Lake had not occurred in battle. They were later tried at Regina, Saskatchewan, but were acquitted due to lack of evidence.[16] Métis settlers in Montana recalled the events of the 1896 deportation and feared that they too would be deported to Canada. Many apparently remained uneasy about the prospect of deportation well into the twentieth century.[17]

The deportations were carried out through June and July 1896, as U.S. Army troops fanned out across the state of Montana in search of Cree camps. While Lieutenant Pershing and the black regiment known as "Buffalo Soldiers," Company D, Tenth Cavalry, accompanied the first group of Crees from Great Falls north to the border, army commanders sent another detachment to capture Cree camps in Havre and Malta, Montana. Pershing later met bands of deportees at Custer, Montana, before overseeing the capture of Cree camps on the Flathead Reservation and near Missoula. By this time, the five thousand dollars appropriated by Congress for the deportation had run out. Forced to save on transportation, Pershing's force marched the final group from Missoula to the border.[18]

Canadian officials were determined to avoid repeating the mistakes they had made in 1887 when U.S. officials had attempted to deport 179 Crees who were not among the initial group of refugees to whom U.S. officials had granted asylum in the autumn of 1885. At the time the Mounted Police arrived at the border to receive a group of Crees deported by the U.S. Army—only to discover that the army escort had simply left the Crees at the border. They ensured, therefore, that members of the police met and escorted all returning groups of Crees. Although the initial groups of refugees arrived in Lethbridge by rail, the Canadian government sent Mounted Police officers to meet subsequent Cree parties at the border and to inform them of the conditions of their return. The police stated that they could choose the reserve to which they would travel and where they would receive the same assistance offered to Natives who had remained in Canada. They warned, however, that they would not be allowed to settle in the South or near the railway or be allowed to "run about the country." In total, the police reported that 532 Crees arrived in Canada, 7 of whom deserted before reaching their destinations.[19]

The Montana press closely followed the spectacle of the army rounding up camps of Crees. In late June, the *Fort Benton River Press* raised fears that many of the Crees were "skillfully dodging" the deportation by denying that they were Crees. In response, army officials informed Governor Rickards that a number of the individuals who had been captured had to be released because they were Ojibwas, Assiniboines, or Gros Ventres and had protested the fact that American Indians were being deported to Canada. The headmen of some of these small bands were apparently able to present some evidence that they were not Canadian, and army officials subsequently set them free.[20]

While the Montana press played up the purported attempts by the Native people captured by the army to avoid being sent to Canada, Superintendent Deane, who oversaw the reception of the Crees at the Canadian border, wrote to his superiors about the seemingly indiscriminate manner in which the U.S. Army carried out the deportation. On August 28, 1896, Deane recorded Joseph Lamear's declaration that American soldiers had taken him away by force from his home near St. Pierre's Mission on the Flathead Reservation. Lamear claimed that neither he nor his wife were Canadian Indians, since both had withdrawn from Treaty Four in 1885 and received scrip certificates from the Canadian government in extinguishments of their aboriginal title. Lamear had asked the soldiers that he be allowed to return to collect his property, which consisted of five horses and a box of household goods, but the soldiers refused. Deane issued rations to Lamear and his wife and suggested they take their case to the Indian commissioner at Regina.[21]

Joseph Lamear and his wife were not alone. In the process of collecting the various Cree camps from across the state, the army rounded up other individuals, mostly Métis, and delivered them to the international boundary. In other reports to his superiors, Deane told of a Métis man born in North Dakota who, while cutting cordwood at a sawmill near Fort Custer, was taken with his wife and some of his horses and shipped to Canada. A Métis man from Calgary who was visiting in Montana was captured and deposited at the border, destitute.[22]

While Deane wrote that these incidents demonstrated the "want of discretion" that characterized the deportation, the decision to deport Métis people demonstrates less a "want of discretion" and more a deliberate attempt to remove them from the state. In his communication to Governor Rickards in April 1896, Canadian Indian commissioner A. E. Forget stated that the Canadian government was willing to accept the Crees should they be brought to the boundary line but that, during their stay in the United States, the legal status of a number of the "Canadian Indians" and Métis in Montana had changed. Forget had calculated from the treaty annuity paylists that about 494 Treaty Indians had left their reserves in the Northwest Territories of Montana since 1885 (and an additional 263 had gone to the Dakotas). The majority of these were Crees from the Battleford and Onion Lake agencies, although Forget noted that many of these had since ceased to be considered "Indians" under the Canadian Indian Act. Either by virtue of their residence abroad for a period of greater than five years or through their formal discharge from Treaty and acceptance of scrip certificates in extinguishments of their aboriginal title, Forget argued that the government was no longer responsible for them. Forget told Rickards he presumed that the U.S. government would not disturb these people.[23]

That Governor Rickards did not feel bound by Canadian legal distinctions is clear from his insistence that all Crees, whether they held certificates or not, should be deported to Canada.[24] To some degree, this grouping of Métis with "Indian" peoples was also reflected in the practice in Montana of labeling all Métis or landless Indians, regardless of origins or the length of time they had lived in Montana before 1885, as Canadian Crees.[25] Since 1870, the Canadian government had recognized the Métis as a distinct people. In the United States, however, no special provisions or conceptual categories existed for individuals of mixed ancestry. Rickards's actions, therefore, also highlight the different conceptions of race that existed in the two countries. Whereas in Canada, the Indian Act barred the children of a white father and a Native mother from obtaining status as Indians under the law, in the United States, individuals of mixed white and Native blood were usually considered Indians.[26]

When Joseph Lamear or the other Métis people to whom Deane referred took their claims before the Canadian Department of Indian Affairs, they found that officials were not always receptive. With his characteristic compassion, Hayter Reed stated that the matter was beyond his department's jurisdiction.[27] For the remainder of the deportees, the Canadian government appears to have accepted all of the deportees regardless of their status, place of birth, and the statutory provisions that should have altered the legal status of many of the Montana Crees during their absence. After some deliberation, the Canadian government also decided to pay annuities to those who returned, although it refused to pay any arrears for the years they spent in the United States.[28]

The Montana press greeted with dismay reports that a group of about thirty deported Crees were near Shelby, Montana, in August 1896. The group, who apparently returned from Canada just weeks after Lieutenant Pershing had escorted the final group of Crees across the line, were not only among the first to return to Montana following their deportation. According to the complaints of an equally dismayed Thomas Miles, by the following year, bands of Crees had returned to Silver Bow County. In the spring of 1898, Buffalo Coat once again approached the governor asking for land and the opportunity to become self-sufficient on behalf of the nearly three hundred Crees who were in Montana.[29]

Despite initial attempts to discourage the return of groups of Crees, Canadian officials acknowledged their powerlessness to prevent their return to Montana. From the outset, NWMP and Department of Indian Affairs representatives voiced their concerns about the need to restrict the deportees' mobility. Before he met the second group of refugees at Coutts (in present-day Alberta), NWMP Inspector Williams received notice from Superintendent Deane to "keep them from leaving if possible, but take no step from which you have to recede."[30] As Deane's instructions indicate, there were legal limits to the ability of Canadian law enforcement agents to prevent their movement. During the 1885 North-West Rebellion, the Canadian government implemented a pass system requiring all Native people leaving their reserves to secure a pass from the Indian agent or farm instructor noting, among other things, the length of time they were allowed off their reserve. Although intended as a temporary measure, it remained in place after the cessation of hostilities. Never codified in law, the pass system contravened the promises contained within the treaties between the Canadian government and Native peoples. A legal opinion secured by the NWMP confirmed that its enforcement was illegal and indicated that, if challenged in court, the police would lose their right to enforce it.[31]

The actions of the police with regard to the movement of the deportees reflected this understanding of their limited capacity to act. In the summer of 1896, Indian Commissioner Forget suggested to the NWMP that, given the "restless disposition" of the newcomers, it would be particularly important to ensure that Indians in the Northwest were kept to their reserves and prevented from frequenting towns. While Forget was anxious that the police enforce the pass system, the commanding officer at Regina suggested instead that officers employ provisions of the Vagrant Act or sections of the Criminal Code regarding prostitution to restrict such movement, since they could not legally arrest anyone for being off their reserve without a pass. The police commissioner's circular issued to the police divisions across the Northwest adopted these suggestions but again instructed the police to "use all possible pressure to persuade [an Indian off-reserve] to return to his reserve, but not to exceed our legal powers.[32]

In September 1897, the commissioner again reminded police who came across parties of Crees camped in the borderlands "to use utmost endeavours to prevent Indians from leaving for [the] States." But later in the fall, Commissioner Forget admitted that, under the existing legislation, there was little either the Department of Indian Affairs or the NWMP could do if the Crees or others were determined to return to Montana. "There exists no means by which they can be prevented from roaming over the unoccupied lands of the Territory at will," Forget stated, "and having thus once reached the vicinity of the International Boundary they experience no difficulty in again re-entering U.S. Territory."[33] Indeed, the fact that so many of the Crees who were deported found their way back to Montana would appear to suggest that the effectiveness of such measures was rather limited. Nonetheless, the desire to confine the Crees and other Native peoples to reserves in Canada is perhaps more significant than the effects of this policy. The wish to segregate Native peoples from the rest of society that underlay policies like the pass system betrayed the visions members of the dominant society held about the place Native peoples should occupy in that society. South of the border, the agitation by Montana settlers about the violation of game laws stemmed from a similar desire to confine Native peoples to their reservations. All such attempts were premised on the desire to marginalize Native peoples physically and economically.

The return of the Crees to Montana, sometimes within weeks of their deportation to Canada, suggests that although the border may have been significant in terms of the racial and legal differences it marked, it was not impermeable. Indeed, the continued cross-border movement of the Crees until the turn of the century calls into question historians' assertions that the Canada–U.S. border solidified almost simultaneously during the late nineteenth century, or that, after 1885, crossing the border ceased to be an option for Native peoples in the borderlands. The experience of the Crees in Montana suggests that the solidification of the border or the attempts at confining Native peoples to reserves/reservations were neither absolute nor uncontested by those on the periphery.[34]

Moreover, the meaning of the border was different for the various groups who traveled across it and likely changed over time. Although the Cree men who filed into the Cascade County courthouse in June 1893 to declare their intention to become U.S. citizens were turned away, in the weeks before and after their appearance at Great Falls, other Canadian citizens made their way to the courthouse for the same purpose.[35] The flow of migrants across the border between Alberta, Saskatchewan, and Montana around the turn of the twentieth century suggests that the border held different meanings for non-Natives seeking a brighter economic future on either side of the line. Indeed, in her study of the Saskatchewan-Montana borderlands, Beth LaDow argues that, at this time, the presence of a "flotsam of seemingly nationless peoples" and a "transborder social ecology" comprised of similar populations, economics, and environment helped blur the lines between Canadians and Americans in this region.[36]

Yet the experience of the "refugee" Crees suggests that for individuals pushed to the margins of western Canadian or American society, their relationship with the border was rather more complicated. For the Crees who elected to follow Little Bear and flee to Montana after the 1885 North-West Rebellion, the existence of the border along the forty-ninth parallel was critical for the sanctuary that crossing it offered. Yet the Cree presence in Montana was not new. In seeking asylum in the United States, the refugee Crees traveled to territory they had inhabited intermittently throughout the 1870s and the early 1880s in search of the last remaining bison herds on the northwestern plains. Many of the individuals who followed Little Bear south in 1885 were born in Montana.[37] Moreover, as Buffalo Coat's petition highlights, the number of U.S–born Crees increased after 1885 when the Cree refugees and those who joined the group in the subsequent years remained in Montana and attempted to carve out an existence in the state.

Those who returned to Montana in the months following their deportation in 1896 no longer sought sanctuary. Some claimed they left because Canadian Indian agents refused to provide them with any rations or assistance, since they were non-Treaty Indians. Apparently dissatisfied with conditions on the former Bobtail Reserve in the Bear Hills (south of Edmonton), Little Bear returned to Montana with his family in 1898. Still others like "Horse Master," a Cree man interviewed by a NWMP constable while en route to Montana in 1897, likely returned to Montana in search of better paying and more secure employment.[38] The existence of better employment opportunities for the Crees in Montana was a result of the fact that, unlike most other Natives in Canada and the United States, they were not confined to a reservation. In turn, the visibility and relative freedom they experienced in Montana was, in part, what drew the attention of those settlers who agitated for their deportation.

As a result of the uncertainty surrounding their rights in the United States, the Cree position in the borderlands remained ambiguous. While those agitating to have them deported focused on their status as "foreign" wards, the Canadian government insisted that many of the so-called Canadian Crees had forfeited their claims to Indian status under Canadian law by virtue of their presence in the United States for a period greater than five years. The legal limbo they occupied also meant that, while in Montana, they fell outside the jurisdiction of the U.S. Bureau of Indian Affairs (BIA). Although this offered them a degree of freedom and autonomy perhaps not available to other Native groups on reservations in the state, it also meant they were ineligible for BIA support during the many difficult winters between 1885 and 1896. Moreover, their position as "Canadian Indians" continued to create legal and political obstacles as they sought to secure a permanent home in the United States in the years after the deportation.[39]

Although crossing the line into the United States continued to offer the Crees the possibility of greater autonomy through the end of the nineteenth century, the construction of boundaries between whites and nonwhites on both sides of the border ultimately circumscribed the range of movements available to them. Throughout the 1880s and 1890s, the Canadian and American governments sought to isolate tribal peoples while promoting programs aimed at encouraging their assimilation into the dominant society. At the same time, Canadian and American settler societies solidified their control over the region and enforced a greater physical separation between whites and Natives, thereby freeing up land and protecting white property rights. In this regard, the differences in the way settlers viewed the place of Natives in society on either side of the border eroded as white settlers shared similar views with regard to racial differences.[40]

Indeed, as Buffalo Coat and Joseph Lamear discovered, the exclusive notions of citizenship, race, and nationality held by the government officials who heard their claims often left little room for the Crees as they sought to secure a permanent place in the Canada–U.S. borderlands. For their part, representatives of both governments discovered as they attempted to assert their control over the borderlands that, although the forty-ninth parallel neatly divided the northwestern plains, the people whose territories the border bisected were not so easily classified. The Cree responses to the attempts to remove them from the United States illustrate the ways they challenged, circumvented, or sought to work within the restrictive categories imposed by governments, and their continued presence in Montana illustrates how the significance of the border was equally unstable and subject to negotiation. Yet, over time, the significance of the border for the sanctuary it offered and the differences in classifying races it marked subsided as efforts to confine Native populations on both sides of the border undermined the opportunities for escape that the border had offered. By the 1890s, the other boundaries or borders that the white settler societies constructed in the Canadian and American Wests were perhaps as meaningful as the forty-ninth parallel for the divisions they represented.

Notes

This essay is an expanded version of a paper presented at the conference of the American Historical Association–Pacific Coast Branch, Vancouver BC, August 2001.

1. Judgment Roll, Docket #2448, June 24, 1896, Montana District Court, 8th Judicial District, County of Cascade.
2. Blair Stonechild and Bill Waiser, *Loyal til Death: Indians and the North-West Rebellion* (Calgary: Fifth House, 1997), 180–88; U.S. Congress, House, *Cree Indians, Montana,* 49th Cong., 1st sess., 1886, Exec. Doc. no. 231, 2–3.
3. Thos. O. Miles to J. K. Tool[e], November 22, 1891, Montana Historical Society (MHS), MC35a, Montana Governors Papers, Joseph K. Toole administration, box 2, file 15; Raymond Gray, "History of the Cree Nation," 1942, WPA Federal Writers' Project, manuscript held at MHS, 16.
4. E. D. Weed to Secretary of State, January 18, 1892, MHS, Thomas O. Miles, Reminiscence SC 475; Correspondence re: Cree Indian Removal; R. P. Stout, ed., *Official Correspondence Relating to the Admission of Montana as a State into the Union and Other Official Papers Comprising Correspondence with State and War Departments at Washington, and Including Proclamations and Official Addresses of Jos. K. Toole* (Helena: C. K. Wells, 1892), 83–85.
5. James G. Blaine to Sir Julian Pauncefote, January 26, 1892; Order in Council (OIC) #1004, March 29, 1892, National Archives of Canada (NAC), Department of Indian Affairs RG 10, vol. 3863, file 84138, part 1.
6. Stout, *Official Correspondence,* 81, 89–90; James G. Blaine to Thomas C. Power, April 20, 1892, MHS, SC 475, 20; J. Bates to Asst. Adjutant General, February 18 and 21, 1892, MHS, MC 46, Fort Assiniboine Papers, Misc. Copy Book, vol. 5.
7. E. D. Weed to Thomas Miles, December 2, 1892; E. D. Weed to Secretary of War, December 2, 1892; J. K. Toole to Thomas Miles, December 3, 1892, MHS, SC 475; *Chinook Opinion,* October 13, 1892; Gray, "A History of the Cree," 17, 38.
8. John V. Cole to Governor Rickards, June 29, 1893; Peter Ronan to Alex C. Bodkin, June 30, 1893; and C. B. Nolan to Governor Rickards, July 26, 1893; all in MHS, MC 35a, J. E. Rickards administration, box 17, file 3. See also Louis F. Warren, *The Hunter's Game: Poachers and Conservationists in Twentieth-Century America* (New Haven: Yale University Press, 1997), chaps. 5 and 6.
9. *Fort Benton River Press,* July 5, 1893, August 30, 1893.
10. Declaration of Intent Books, vol. 3, 272–78, Cascade County Historical Society Archives, Great Falls MT; Francis Paul Prucha, *The Great Father: The United States*

Government and the American Indians (Lincoln: University of Nebraska Press, 1984), 2:681–86.

11. *Great Falls Leader*, July 20 and 27, 1893.

12. *Helena Independent*, October 13, 1893; *Fort Benton River Press*, November 15, 1893.

13. *Great Falls Daily Tribune*, January 1, 1896; *Senate Reports*, vol. 4, no. 821, 54th Cong., 1896, 1–3.

14. Geo. Sweet to Commissioner, Indian Affairs, May 1, 1896; Hayter Reed to Geo. Sweet, May 6, 1896, NAC, RG 10, vol. 3863, file 84138, part 1; R. Burton Deane to Commissioner, June 9, 1896, NAC, Royal Canadian Mounted Police RG 18, vol. 1353, file 76–1897, part 2.

15. *Great Falls Daily Tribune*, May 17, 1896; *Great Falls Leader*, June 22, 1896. Some apparently got a jump on the deportation by returning to Canada in advance of the troops. Thomas W. Aspdin to Indian Commissioner, June 1, 1896, NAC, RG 18, vol. 1353, file 76–1897, part 2.

16. James Dempsey, "Little Bear's Band: Canadian or American Indians?" *Alberta History* 41, no. 4 (Autumn 1993): 4–5.

17. See, e.g., MHS, Oral History Collection (OH) 1878, Luke Salmond interview, March 4, 1996; OH 1877, Jim Brewster interview, November 17, 1995; OH 1871 Alice Gleason interview, March 17, 1995.

18. "Record of Events," June, July, August 1896, National Archives and Records Administration (NARA), Records of the Adjutant General's Office (RG 94), Returns from U.S. Military Posts, Fort Assiniboine, 1892–1903, M617, roll 42; Frank E. Vandiver, *Black Jack: The Life and Times of John J. Pershing* (College Station: Texas A&M University Press, 1977), 1:144–49.

19. [R. Burton Deane to Cree refugees], July 23, 1896, NAC, RG 18, vol. 1353, file 76, part 2; "Appendix C—Annual Report of Superintendent R. B. Deane, Commanding 'K' Division, 1896," *Sessional Papers*, no. 15, 1897, 95.

20. *Helena Independent*, June 26, 1896.

21. R. Burton Deane to Commissioner, NWMP, September 10, 1896, NAC, RG 18, vol. 1353, file 76, part 2.

22. Appendix C, *Sessional Papers*, 1897, 94–95; R. Burton Deane to Commissioner, NWMP, June 26, 1896, NAC RG 10, vol. 3863, file 84138, part 1.

23. A. E. Forget to Deputy Superintendent-General of Indian Affairs, February 25, 1896; A. E. Forget to Governor, State of Montana, April 1, 1896, NAC RG 10, vol. 3863, file 84138, part 1. Under the provisions of the Indian Act, "Any Indian, having for five years continuously resided in a foreign country without the consent of the Superintendent-General or his agent, shall cease to be a member of the band of which he or she formerly was a member." Indian Act, RSC 1880, sec. 11.

24. *Great Falls Daily Tribune*, June 11, 1896.

25. Verne Dusenberry, "Waiting for a Day That Never Comes," *Montana: The Magazine of Western History* 8, no. 2 (1958): 32.

26. Jean Barman, "What a Difference a Border Makes: Aboriginal Racial Intermixture in the Pacific Northwest," *Journal of the West* 38, no. 3 (July 1999): 18–19.

27. Hayter Reed to A. E. Forget, August 25, 1896, NAC RG 10, vol. 3863, file 84138, part 1.

28. A. E. Forget to Deputy Superintendent-General of Indian Affairs, September 30, 1896;

[Hayter Reed] to A. E. Forget, October 12, 1896, NAC, RG 10, vol. 3863, file 84138, part 1.

29. Thos. O. Miles to Governor R. B. Smith, May 30, 1897, January 9, 1898, MHS, MC 35a, R. B. Smith administration, box 28, file 9; *Lethbridge News*, March 16, 1898.

30. R. Burton Deane to Inspector Williams, June 21, 1896, NAC, RG 18, vol. 129, file 507–97.

31. Sarah Carter, *Lost Harvests: Prairie Indian Reserve Farmers and Government Policy* (Montreal: McGill-Queen's University Press, 1990), 150–54.

32. F. H. Paget to Commissioner, NWMP, July 3, 1896; A. Bowen Perry to Commissioner, NWMP, July 8, 1896; Circular Memorandum no. [186], July 9, 1896; NAC, RG 18, vol. 1354, file 76, part 3.

33. Const. H. A. Still to Officer Commanding, Maple Creek, September 6, 1897, RG 18, vol. 129, file 69–97; A. E. Forget to Secretary, Department of Indian Affairs, November 8, 1897, RG 10, vol. 3863, file 84138, part 1.

34. Jeremy Adelman and Stephen Aron contend that the solidification of the border during this period reduced the "freedom exit" of aboriginal peoples. See "From Borderlands to Borders: Empires, Nation-States, and the Peoples in Between in North American History," *American Historical Review* 104, no. 3 (1999): 840.

35. Declaration of Intent Books, vol. 3—see applications January–December 1896, Cascade County Historical Archives.

36. Beth LaDow, *The Medicine Line: Life and Death on a North American Borderland* (New York: Routledge, 2001), 99, 116–17.

37. Dempsey, "Little Bear's Band," 8.

38. Dempsey, "Little Bear's Band," 6; John Richards to Officer Commanding, Maple Creek, June 6, 1897; H. A. Still to Commissioner, NWMP, September 2, 1897, NAC RG 18, vol. 1382, file 76–1887.

39. Verne Dusenberry, *The Montana Cree: A Study in Religious Persistence* (1962; reprint, Norman: University of Oklahoma Press, 1998), 40, 46.

40. Roger L. Nichols, *Indians in the United States and Canada: A Comparative History* (Lincoln: University of Nebraska Press, 1998), 207; Sheila McManus, "The Line Which Separates: Race, Gender, and the Alberta-Montana Borderlands, 1862–1892" (PhD diss., York University, 2001), 219–22, 254; Sarah Carter, *Capturing Women: The Manipulation of Cultural Imagery in Canada's Prairie West* (Montreal: McGill-Queen's University Press, 1997), xiii.

10. Charles Ora Card and Mormon Settlement on the Northwestern Plains Borderlands

Peter S. Morris

On a late September morning in 1886, Charles Ora Card of Logan, Utah, crossed the international boundary into Canada for only the second time in his life. His first visit to Canada fourteen years earlier had been a rather forgettable event—a nighttime trip across southern Ontario on his way from Buffalo to Detroit. But such was not the case this time, and upon passing the stone monument marking the boundary between Washington Territory and British Columbia, Card reportedly took off his hat, "swung it around and shouted *in Collumbia We are free.*"[1]

Card's excitement at passing into Canadian territory—or more precisely, *out* of U.S. territory—is understandable. Accompanied on foot by two fellow members of the Church of Jesus Christ of Latter-day Saints, Card was on an expedition to find a suitable location north of the border for a new Mormon colony—one that would be safe from the interference of U.S. officials. Card, like a number of other Mormon leaders at the time, was a practicing polygamist. Illegal in U.S. territories since 1862, Mormon polygamy came under increasing attack after the passage of the Edmunds Act in March 1882, which made plural marriage a federal felony. Card was stripped of his post as county selectman at that time, and during the following four years, he lived a transient existence in and out of hiding from U.S. officials. In fact, less than two months before leaving on his reconnaissance trip to Canada, Card had been captured at his home by a federal marshal, only to flee from that marshal's custody in dramatic fashion while aboard a train departing from Logan. Shortly after this narrow escape, Card requested permission from church leaders to join the new Mormon settlements in northern Mexico, but he was directed to explore the possibilities of settlement in the North instead.[2]

Viewed in this context, Card's exclamation of freedom is a classic example of seeing and using the border as a place of personal refuge. As it was for others both before and since—most famously Sitting Bull—the forty-ninth parallel for Card appeared to be a "medicine line," a line of safety almost magical in its apparent simplicity.[3] Like home base in a children's game of tag, Card would be safe north of the border from American law officers. More important, Card hoped that it would not be just he who found liberty in Canada but rather a whole community of fellow Mormons who would be free to honor both their religion and their family commitments via the open practices of polygamy.

As had been true for Sitting Bull, however, the medicine line offered only partial refuge to Card and his brethren. Although the Mormon settlements in southern Alberta became an unqualified success as stable farming communities in a challenging semiarid environment, plural marriage was no more welcomed north of the border than it was to the south. In fact, even before Mormon Church president Wilford Woodruff formally urged his fellow Saints in the fall of 1890 to "refrain from contracting any marriage forbidden by the law of the land"—effectively ending polygamy as an official component of Mormon religious practice—the small community of Mormons in Alberta lived what historian Jessie Embry has called a "de facto monogamy." Specifically it appears that only a handful of early male immigrants to the Cardston district brought more than one wife. Most, instead, came with only their first or second wife, leaving the other(s) behind in the States.[4]

The story of Charles Card's emigration to the North is but one example of the interconnected and interwoven experiences of the U.S. and Canadian Wests. Rather than two parallel worlds divided more or less completely by a sharp, distinct boundary, the United States and Canada are more like conjoined twins, each possessive of its own identity but also very much tied together as parts of the same continental entity. Moreover, the tangled web of connections that cross the forty-ninth parallel, such as the wives, children, and other family members left behind by Mormon emigrants in the 1880s, should not lead us to conclude that this border has been an insignificant or invisible presence. While its visibility and its impacts may wax and wane with changing laws and conditions on either side, the border nonetheless is there, and it has been a significant presence shaping the region's history and geography.

The significance of these observations lies in their implications for conventional approaches to transnational study of the North American West. Such efforts to understand the United States' northern borderlands have typically followed a comparative approach.[5] Here, after all, are two countries just begging for comparison. They are neighbor nations who have grown from similar cultural and colonial roots and have faced many of the same environmental and human challenges, especially in regard to their western interiors. Yet they have maintained distinctive national identities, and their histories appear to be as different as Gary Cooper's Texas Ranger and Preston Foster's Canadian Mountie in the 1940 Cecil B. DeMille film *North West Mounted Police*.[6] A comparative study involving the United States and Canada, then, would appear to be an ideal way to isolate and examine the impact of national laws and policies and of national cultures on the development of a region such as the Great Plains of North America.

As interesting and productive as the many comparative efforts made to date have been, there is reason to question their cumulative impact. Specifically, it seems that the basic idea of a comparative study offers us relatively little toward producing a transnational, synthetic understanding of the North American West, an understanding in which the Canadian and American Wests are viewed together, as part of the same continental or hemispheric story. Historian Paul Sharp, after all, reminded us in 1950 that "the settlement of the Canadian West is actually the final chapter in the Anglo-American conquest of the Great Plains," echoing similar comments made in 1940 by Marcus Hansen and John Brebner that the histories of the United States and Canada are "not parallel but integral."[7] Despite these observations, we continue to understand western Canada and the western United States through predominately nationalistic lenses, and we tend to link them together, if at all, as parallel counterpoints. [8] Furthermore, because the border's function in a comparative study is primarily to serve as an independent variable—a given condition used to explain some other phenomenon—the comparative tendency of previous

Canadian-American studies has reinforced the notion that the forty-ninth parallel is a simple straight line. In fact, little has changed since political geographer Stephen Jones made the following observation sixty years ago: "Few international boundaries are better known and few are less understood than the forty-ninth parallel separating western Canada and the United States. Its striking simplicity, apparent artificiality, and long tranquillity have made it notable, yet this very simplicity in form and function has discouraged closer study." [9]

U.S. history does not end at the forty-ninth parallel, nor does Canadian history. The boundary between these two countries does matter, however. Well over a century old, the border predates most of the peoples and places that now inhabit the region, and it has played a role in shaping individual and group identities—not to mention its legal, geopolitical influence. To provide us with the fullest understanding of the forty-ninth parallel's presence in North America's western interior, we need to develop some sort of hybrid approach. We need to combine the comparative approach's ability to isolate and examine national-level differences with the integrated-borderland approach's ability to synthesize the U.S. and Canadian experiences into a single, coherent story.

The establishment of a Mormon settlement in southern Alberta at the end of the nineteenth century illustrates these ideas. Despite their dominant local presence in a number of communities around the St. Mary's River southwest of Lethbridge and the highly significant role they played in bringing irrigation to the region, the Latter-day Saints of the Cardston district do not figure prominently in the historiography of the Canadian West. To a large extent, this is understandable; they represent only about 2 percent of the citizens of Alberta, where roughly half of all Canadian Mormons continue to live. [10] Moreover, the story of the Mormons' south-to-north migration fits uneasily with the dominant east-to-west orientation of the historiographies of both Canada and the United States. Consequently, if mentioned at all, the Mormons of southern Alberta appear in histories of western Canada as just one of many examples of "group settlement" in the multicultural prairies. [11]

As the editors of a recent multidisciplinary collection of essays have suggested, one particularly promising line of research concerning the Mormons in Canada would involve the comparative approach. How, for example, did the experiences of Mormon settlers in Canada differ from the experiences of Mormons in Mexico or in other satellite communities throughout the interior West? Likewise, did the Cardston district really become, as sociologist Brigham Young Card has suggested, a "distinctive western Canadian Mormon country" that was "more than a reproduction of Utah Mormon culture"?[12] These clearly are questions worth pursuing. But to view the Mormons' emigration to Canada in purely comparative terms would miss a number of questions regarding the geographic integration of North America and the significance of the U.S.–Canadian border.

It was a complicated array of international forces, after all, that brought the Mormons to southern Alberta and then fostered their development. The initial force pushing the Mormons northward was the need to find a place of refuge for Saints practicing plural marriage. But recall that Charles Ora Card's first request had been to seek refuge in northern Mexico, where Mormon settlements already had been established. By redirecting Card to British Columbia and then Alberta, church leaders appear to have been motivated by a variety of factors, personal, political, and theological. For example, the church's president during the turbulent 1880s, John Taylor, was a native of England who emigrated with his parents to Canada at the age of twenty-four. After converting to Mormonism and moving to the States, Taylor became a close associate of the church's founder, Joseph Smith, and led its mission in England. Not surprisingly, Taylor, who as early as the 1840s had actively promoted relocating the Mormons to Vancouver Island, saw Card's request for refuge abroad as a chance finally to establish a Mormon colony on British soil.[13]

In addition to the church president's personal attachment to the British Empire, the decision to send Card to Canada was influenced by Mormon theology. According to Joseph Smith's millennial vision, England as the most powerful country on earth would be the final terrestrial kingdom to fall in the face of Armageddon. More important, Joseph Smith had prophesied that the Mormon people would find benevolent shelter on British soil, where the Saints could safely await their ultimate ascension into the new kingdom of God.[14] Charles Ora Card himself did not learn of Joseph Smith's prophecy until January 1887, when he was awaiting his resettlement of Canada while spending the winter in hiding in Utah. But his diary entry for January 21, 1887, suggests that news of this prophecy left a significant impression:

> Bro. Samuel Smith of Brigham City told me he was present in a priesthood meeting in the basement of the Temple in Nauvoo in the year 1843 and heard the prophet Joseph Smith state that England or the nation of Great Brittain [*sic*] would be the last nation to go to peaces [*sic*]. She would be instrumental in aiding to crush other nations even this nation of the United States & she would only be over thrown by the 10 tribes from the North. She would never persecute the saints as a nation. She would gather together great treasures of Gold & yet we should seek refuge in her dominion.[15]

The Cardston colony's Canadian location served the church on a more earthly level as well. Card believed that his Canadian settlement would be temporary and that he would return to the States once the polygamy issue had been settled. But church leaders denied his request to return to his home in Utah after the Woodruff Manifesto, and in 1890 he was assigned to head up the new Canadian branch of the church. As the new church president, George Q. Cannon, another English native, noted in 1900, the Alberta colony's location was too valuable to the church to let it fade away. In addition to giving the Mormons a formal presence on British soil, the church's cooperative work with the Canadian government toward developing irrigated agriculture in southern Alberta gave it a significant foreign ally whose support Mormon leaders found helpful in dealing with the U.S. government, with whom their relationship continued to be tenuous.[16] In addition, Mormon Utah faced a shortage of both land and capital in the 1890s, and it found a wonderful opportunity for a symbiotic exchange with government and business leaders in southwest Canada. Specifically, the church finalized a deal in 1894 with Alexander and Elliott Galt and their Lethbridge-based Northwest Coal and Navigation Company. Under this agreement, the Mormons provided the labor, while the Galts and their British interests provided the land and capital, in order to build an irrigation canal diverting water from the St. Mary's River to Lethbridge, facilitating the settlement of the company's 20,000-acre land grant.[17]

The presence of the international boundary and the fact that it represented both the end of the United States and the beginning of the British Empire drew the Mormons north. Although this expansive church likely would have found its way north of the forty-ninth parallel regardless of the international boundary, it is unlikely that today there would be a concentrated "Mormon Country" in southern Alberta if not for the border's presence.[18]

Although it is impossible to understand fully the genesis and development of the Cardston district without accounting for the great significance of the border, in other ways the presence of the forty-ninth parallel seems meaningless to the Mormons of this area. Like Mormons throughout the West, the Mormons of southern Alberta remain part of what geographer Donald Meinig called the "Mormon Culture Region," an oblong territory flanking the western slope of the Rocky Mountains with a core that remains cemented near the Great Salt Lake.[19] In addition to family ties in the States, many Canadian Saints make a pilgrimage once or twice a year to the church's semiannual General Conference in Salt Lake City. Likewise, Cardston's top students are likely to attend college at Brigham Young University or at Utah State University, rather than at more proximately located Canadian schools. Even the church's organizational geography seems to deny the international boundary's presence. The Cardston district has had its own "stake"—roughly equivalent to a Catholic diocese— since 1895, but it remains grouped with stakes in the United States as part of the church's North American West "area." More symbolically, the official mailing address of the Mormon temple in Cardston is a post office box in Babb, Montana, a tiny crossroads located adjacent to the eastern edge of Glacier National Park.[20]

Finally, the border's ambiguous presence in the Cardston district is further seen when one considers the question of national identity. That the first Mormon settlers in southern Alberta would have a rather confused attachment to their new home nation should be no surprise. Most had been born in the States and had ties to people and places south of the forty-ninth parallel. Yet Canada was providing them with shelter from the persecution they had faced in the United States. And as Charles Ora Card had done on his reconnaissance trip a year earlier, when the first group of settlers crossed the border into Canada, they "halted and gave *three cheers* for our liberty as exiles for our religion."[21] Reflecting both their practical motivations and a good-neighbor ethic, the Mormons were urged by church leaders to embrace their new country. In order to qualify for government homesteads, many became naturalized Canadian citizens. Likewise, within two months of arriving at their new settlement along Lee's Creek, the Mormons invited their Gentile (non-Mormon) neighbors from local ranches and the Mounted Police to join them for a daylong picnic celebration of Canada's July 1 Dominion Day. This celebration— which consisted of speeches, songs, games, and horse races and, according to Card, "passed off pleasantly & without the use of stimulants"— undoubtedly eased some of the local Canadians' fears regarding their new neighbors' loyalty to queen and country, even if the lack of "stimulants" may have left the Mormons appearing somewhat foreign to them.[22] In contrast, no mention whatsoever is made in Card's diaries of any sort of Independence Day celebration on July 4.

Still, despite their genuine appreciation of their new country and their desire to be good neighbors, the Mormon colonists retained strong emotional ties to their mother country south of the forty-ninth parallel. As one Cardston native later recalled in an oral history interview, "We never spoke of 'Utah'; it was always 'down home.'" Nobody better demonstrates that continuing attachment to the south than Card himself. Alberta was really only a seasonal residence for him, as he spent at least a part of most winters in Utah to conduct business with church officials and spend valuable time with his wives, children, and other family members left behind in the States. Indeed, he returned to Utah permanently in 1902, once it was decided that his mission in Canada was complete.[23] Thus, much as Beth LaDow found in her study of the Montana-Saskatchewan border region, it appears that the Mormons of southern Alberta settled into a complicated set of overlapping local, regional, national, and religious identities—a mix of identities perhaps best captured by the cycle of holidays that are celebrated "with equal enthusiasm" in Cardston every July: Canadian Dominion Day on the first, the founding of Cardston on the third, U.S. Independence Day on the fourth, and Brigham Young's 1847 arrival in the Salt Lake Valley on the twenty-fourth.[24]

The history of Mormon settlers in southern Alberta illustrates how scholars will need to develop new metaphors to understand fully North

America's western past, ones that can accommodate the ever-shifting, ever-changing nature of the forty-ninth parallel's presence on the Canadian-American grasslands. This famous linear boundary between the western United States and Canada is anything but a straight line; its tangled web of transborder connections and its waxing and waning significance in the political, economic, and emotional lives of border residents belies its cartographic simplicity. Such a project will involve more than simply examining the two countries' Wests as parallel, comparative counterpoints. In addition to the demographic "mingling" of their peoples, Canada and the United States have pursued public policies that were heavily influenced by the presence of the other country. What is needed is not simply a proliferation of comparative studies that attempt to assess the two countries' Wests as if they were neatly and unproblematically divisible. Indeed, what we need is a special kind of comparative history, one that recognizes the dialectical relationship between these two neighbor nations and gives us a fuller understanding of their shared continental context.

Notes

1. Card diary entry for September 29, 1886, in Donald G. Godfrey and Brigham Y. Card, eds., *The Diaries of Charles Ora Card: The Canadian Years, 1886–1903* (Salt Lake City: University of Utah Press, 1993), 12 (hereafter Card diaries). Both the emphasis and Card's double-consonant spelling are from the original.
2. Card diaries, biographical note, xxxv–xxxviii. For a brief overview of Mormon polygamy and U.S. efforts to eliminate it, see Jessie L. Embry, "Two Legal Wives: Mormon Polygamy in Canada, the United States, and Mexico," in Brigham Y. Card et al., eds., *The Mormon Presence in Canada* (Logan: Utah State University Press, 1990), 170–71.
3. Beth LaDow, *The Medicine Line: Life and Death on a North American Borderland* (New York: Routledge, 2001).
4. Davis Bitton, *Historical Dictionary of Mormonism* (Metuchen NJ: Scarecrow Press, 1994), 179–80; Embry, "Two Legal Wives," 177–78. Details of the Canadians' cool reception of Mormon polygamy are provided in Dan Erickson, "Alberta Polygamists? The Canadian Climate and Response to the Introduction of Mormonism's 'Peculiar Institution,'" *Pacific Northwest Quarterly* 86 (Fall 1995): 155–64.
5. For a sampling of studies from the past half century by geographers and historians who compare some aspect of the American and Canadian Wests, see Paul F. Sharp, "Three Frontiers: Some Comparative Studies of Canadian, American, and Australian Settlement," *Pacific Historical Review* 24 (1955): 369–77; Dick Harrison, "Fictions of the American and Canadian Wests," *Prairie Forum* 8 (1983): 89–97; Paul W. Gates and Lillian F. Gates, "Canadian and American Land Policy Decisions, 1930," *Western Historical Quarterly* 15 (1984): 389–406; Hana Samek, "Evaluating Canadian Indian

Policy: A Case for Comparative Historical Perspective," *American Review of Canadian Studies* 16 (Autumn 1986): 293–99; Norbert MacDonald, *Distant Neighbors: A Comparative History of Seattle and Vancouver* (Lincoln: University of Nebraska, 1987); H. A. Reitsma, "Agricultural Changes in the American-Canadian Border Zone, 1954–1978," *Political Geography Quarterly* 7 (January 1988): 23–38; Howard R. Lamar, "Comparing Depressions: The Great Plains and Canadian Prairie Experiences, 1929–1941," in Gerald D. Nash and Richard W. Etulain, eds., *The Twentieth-Century West: Historical Interpretations* (Albuquerque: University of New Mexico Press, 1989), 175–206; Max Gerhart Geier, "A Comparative History of Rural Community on the Northwest Plains: Lincoln County, Washington, and the Wheatland Region, Alberta, 1880–1930," PhD diss., Washington State University, 1990; Frances W. Kaye, "Canadian-American Prairie-Plains Literature in English," in Robert Lecker, *Borderlands: Essays in Canadian-American Relations* (Toronto: ECW Press, 1991), 222–42; and Walter Nugent, "Comparing Wests and Frontiers," in Clyde Milner, Carol O'Connor, and Martha Sandweiss, eds., *Oxford History of the American West* (New York: Oxford University Press, 1994), 803–33.

6. Released by Paramount Pictures, November 6, 1940.

7. Paul F. Sharp, "When Our West Moved North," *American Historical Review* 55 (January 1950): 287; Marcus Lee Hansen and John Bartlett Brebner, *The Mingling of the Canadian and American Peoples* (New Haven: Yale University Press, 1940), 2.

8. My thinking here follows similar arguments recently made by geographer Victor Konrad and historian Ian Tyrell, who urge scholars to explore transborder interaction and transnational integration rather than simply accept the present-day nation-state as the de facto unit of analysis in an exploration of comparative differences. See Victor Konrad, "The Borderlands of the United States and Canada in the Context of North American Development," *International Journal of Canadian Studies/Revue Internationale d'études Canadiennes* 4 (Fall 1991): 77–95; Ian Tyrell, "American Exceptionalism in an Age of International History," *American Historical Review* 96 (October 1991): 1031–55.

9. Stephen B. Jones, "The Cordilleran Section of the Canadian–United States Borderland," *Geographical Journal* 89 (May 1937): 439.

10. According to the 1981 Canadian Census, there were 82,090 Mormons in all of Canada, including 42,185 in Alberta. The latter figure represented 1.9 percent of the province's total population. For these and other Canadian Mormon census counts, see Dean R. Louder, "Canadian Mormon Identity and the French Fact," in Card et al., *The Mormon Presence in Canada*, 305–11.

11. C. A. Dawson, *Group Settlement: Ethnic Communities in Western Canada* (Toronto: Macmillan, 1936).

12. Introduction in Card et al., *The Mormon Presence in Canada*, xvii–xviii; Brigham Y. Card, "Charles Ora Card and the Founding of the Mormon Settlements in Southwestern Alberta, North-West Territories," in Card et al., *The Mormon Presence in Canada*, 78.

13. Bitton, *Historical Dictionary of Mormonism*, 239–40; Melvin S. Tagg et al., *A History of the Mormon Church in Canada* (Lethbridge: Lethbridge Herald Co. for the Church of Jesus Christ of Latter-day Saints, Lethbridge Stake, 1968), 16.

14. This millennial vision as a motivation to settle Canada is mentioned by Yossi Katz and John C. Lehr, "Jewish and Mormon Agricultural Settlement in Western Canada: A Comparative Analysis," *Canadian Geographer* 35 (Summer 1991): 134.

15. Card diaries, 30–31.

16. Lawrence B. Lee, "The Canadian-American Irrigation Frontier," *Agricultural History* 40 (October 1966): 275.

17. Lawrence B. Lee, "The Mormons Come to Canada, 1887–1902," *Pacific Northwest Quarterly* 59 (January 1968): 18–19; Tagg et al., *A History of the Mormon Church in Canada*, 63–64.

18. A general description of Canada's "Mormon Country" is provided by Karen West, "Cardston: The Temple City of Canada," *Canadian Geographic* 71 (November 1965): 162–69.

19. Donald W. Meinig, "The Mormon Culture Region: Strategies and Patterns in the Geography of the American West, 1847–1964," *Annals of the Association of American Geographers* 55 (June 1965): 197–201.

20. Dean R. Louder, "Canadian Mormon Identity," 313.

21. Card diaries, June 1, 1887, 57 (emphasis in original).

22. Card diaries, July 1, 1887, 59.

23. Card was married four times. He divorced his first wife, Sarah Jane Birdneau, in 1884 after seventeen years of marriage—and eight years after marrying his second wife, Sarah Jane Painter. He married his third wife, Zina Presindia Young Williams, in 1884; one of Brigham Young's daughters, she accompanied Charles to Canada and, as "Aunt Zina," is remembered fondly as Cardston's leading pioneer. Like Charles, Zina returned to Utah after fulfilling her northern mission. She died in her native Salt Lake City in 1931, after serving for many years as matron of Latter-day Saints College. Charles died in 1906, spending his final years with his fourth wife, Lavinia Clark Rigby, whom he had married in 1885. Beryl Bechtell, ed., *Chief Mountain Country: A History of Cardston and District* (Cardston AB: Cardston and District Historical Society, 1987), 8–11; Card diaries, 2 n. 3.

24. Louder, "Canadian Mormon Identity," 311, 312; LaDow, *The Medicine Line*.

Part 4. Farming, Industry, and Labor Interactions in the Borderlands

During the late nineteenth and early twentieth centuries interactions between the American West and western Canada increased. There was especially an increase in agricultural relations in the borderlands as American farmers migrated into western Canada responding to the ideology of the region being the "Last Best West." There have been some excellent studies on the topic of these migration patterns (see especially the works by Paul Sharp, Bruce Shepard, and Randy Widdis listed below). But as I argue in chapter 11, the agricultural history of the region needs to be seen in its continental context—how farmers on both sides of the border in the Great Plains became dependent on an agricultural commodity from Mexico.

Many grain farmers in the region also became dependent on itinerant harvesting and threshing crews. In chapter 12, Evelyne Stitt Pickett shows how the work of hoboes, harvest Wobblies, and other laborers was a transboundary phenomenon. Significantly, she writes, these workers "became a floating army that changed the face of the American and Canadian Wests."

And further into the Inland Empire and Pacific Northwest, farmers discovered "nature's garden and a possible utopia" for the production of fruit. Here, as Jason Bennett writes in chapter 13, the orchard developers were "industrious men" working in a "feminized landscape" to create their visions of a "blossoming empire." Bennett examines the agricultural, environmental, and gender implications inherent in the terms and ideology of the region's fruit industry, and argues that the forty-ninth parallel "served as a mirror and a window" to reflect both familiar and foreign concepts.

Interested readers will find other works on these topics under For

Further Reading. Especially important for an understanding of the region's labor history are the books and articles on timber and harvest Wobblies (works by Tim Hamson, Greg Hall, Robert Tyler, and Patrick Renshaw), on worker-controlled timber initiatives (by Richard Rajala), on labor radicalism in the Northwest (by Carlos Schwantes, Paul Phillips, Mark Leier, and David Bercuson), on First Nations and Asian labor (by John Lutz, Paige Raibmon, and Chris Friday), and on transboundary gold mining in the region (by Robert Ficken).

For Further Reading

On Agricultural and Industrial Interactions in the Borderlands
On Transboundary Agricultural Migration and Settlement Patterns
On Labor History in the Borderlands

On Agricultural and Industrial Interactions in the Borderlands

Bicha, Karel Denis. *The American Farmer and the Canadian West, 1896–1914.* Lawrence: Coronado Press, 1968.

———. "The North Dakota Farmer and the Canadian West, 1896–1914." *North Dakota History* 29 (1962): 297–301.

Broadway, Michael. "Where's the Beef? The Integration of the Canadian and American Beef-Packing Industries." *Prairie Forum* 23 (spring 1998): 19–30.

Cox, Thomas R. *Mills and Markets: A History of the Pacific Northwest Lumber Industry to 1900.* Seattle: University of Washington Press, 1974.

Danysk, Cecilia. *Hired Hands: Labour and the Development of Prairie Agriculture, 1880–1930.* Toronto: McClelland and Stewart, 1995.

Evans, Sterling. *Bound in Twine: Transnational History and Environmental Change in the Henequen-Wheat Complex for Yucatán and the American and Canadian Plains, 1890–1950.* College Station: Texas A&M University Press, forthcoming.

———. "Prison-Made Binder Twine: North Dakota's Connection with Mexico in the Early Twentieth Century." *North Dakota History: Journal of the Northern Plains* 68 (2001): 20–36.

Everitt, John C. "The Borderlands and the Early Canadian Grain Trade." In Lecker, ed., *Borderlands,* 146–72.

Ficken, Robert E. *Unsettled Boundaries: Fraser Gold and the British-American Northwest.* Pullman: Washington State University Press, 2003.

Foran, Max. "The Impact of the Depression on Grazing Lease Policy." In Simon M. Evans, Sarah Carter, and Bill Yeo, eds., *Cowboys, Ranchers, and the Cattle Business: Cross-Border Perspectives on Ranching History,* 123–38. Calgary: University of Calgary Press, 2000.

Francis, James M. "Montana Business and Canadian Regionalism in the 1870s and 1880s." *Western Historical Quarterly* 12 (July 1981): 291–304.

Geier, Max Gerhart. "A Comparative History of Rural Community on the Northwest Plains: Lincoln County, Washington, and the Wheatland Region, Alberta, 1880–1930." PhD diss., Washington State University, 1990.

Isern, Thomas D. "The Adoption of the Combine on the Northern Plains." *South Dakota History* 10, no. 2 (Spring 1980).

———. *Bull Threshers and Bindlestiffs on the North American Plains.* Lawrence: University Press of Kansas, 1990.

———. "Harvest Hands across the Border." Chap. 8 of *Custom Combiners on the Great Plains.* Norman: University of Oklahoma Press, 1981.

———. *Of Land and Sky: Essays in the History of Western Canadian Agriculture.* Calgary: University of Calgary Press, forthcoming.

———. " 'Your Word Is Your Bond': Recollections of a Custom Combiner, Vernon A. Wildfong." *Saskatchewan History* 49 (Spring 1997): 15–21.

Jones, David C., ed. *"We'll All Be Buried Down Here": The Prairie Dryland Disaster, 1917–26.* Edmonton: Alberta Records Publication Board, 1986.

Lamar, Howard R. "Comparing Depressions: The Great Plains and Canadian Prairie Experiences, 1929–1941." In Gerald D. Nash and Richard W. Etulain, eds., *The Twentieth-Century West: Historical Interpretations,* 175–206. Albuquerque: University of New Mexico Press, 1989.

Lecker, Robert, ed. *Borderlands: Essays in Canadian-American Relations.* Toronto: ECW Press, 1991.

Lee, Lawrence B. "The Canadian-American Irrigation Frontier." *Agricultural History* 40 (October 1966): 271–83.

Marchildon, Gregory P., ed. *Agriculture at the Border: Canada–U.S. Trade Relations in the Global Food Regime.* Regina: Canadian Plains Research Centre, 2000.

McGregor, Alexander Campbell. *Counting Sheep: From Open Range to Agribusiness in the Columbia Plateau.* Seattle: University of Washington Press, 1982.

Reitsma, Hendrik J. "Agricultural Changes in the American-Canadian Border Zone, 1954–1978." *Political Geography Quarterly* 7 (1988): 23–38.

———. "Crop and Livestock Production in the Vicinity of the United States-Canada Border." *Professional Geographer* 23 (1971).

Schwartz, Mildred A. "Political Protest in the Western Borderlands: Can Farmers Be Socialists?" In Lecker, ed. *Borderlands,* 28–53.

Sharp, Paul F. *The Agrarian Revolt in Western Canada: A Survey of American Parallels.* Minneapolis: University of Minnesota Press, 1948.

Thompson, John Herd. *Family, Farm, and Community: The Rural Northern Plains, 1860–1960,* forthcoming.

Voisey, Paul. *Vulcan: The Making of a Prairie Community.* Toronto: University of Toronto Press, 1988.

On Transboundary Agricultural Migration and Settlement Patterns

Bishop, Erin I. "Dry Farming in the Judith Basin of Montana: Promotional Activities Luring Settlers West." *Pacific Northwest Forum* II-3 (Fall 1990): 25–40.

Gold, Norman Leon. "American Migrations to the Prairie Provinces of Canada, 1890–1933." PhD diss., University of California, 1933.

Hall, D. J. "Clifford Sifton: Immigration and Settlement Policy, 1896–1905." In R. Douglas Francis and Howard Palmer, eds., *The Prairie West: Historical Readings*, 281–308. Edmonton: Pica Pica Press, 1992.

Hansen, Marcus Lee. *The Mingling of Canadian and American Peoples.* New Haven: Yale University Press, 1940.

Harvey, David D. *Americans in Canada: Migration and Settlement since 1840.* Lewiston NY: Edwin Mellen Press, 1991.

Hudson, John C. "Migration to an American Frontier." *Annals of the Association of American Geographers* 66 (June 1976): 242–65.

Laut, Agnes. "The Last Trek to the Last Frontier: The American Settler in the Canadian Northwest." *Century Magazine* 78 (May 1909): 99–111.

Lewis, Wallace G. "Moxee—Another Promised Land: French-Canadian Resettlement in the Yakima Valley, Washington." Paper, conference of the Western History Association (WHA), Colorado Springs CO, October 2002.

Meldrum, Ronald. "West to Eden: Inland Settlement in the Northwest." *Pacific Northwest Forum* 5 (Fall/Winter 1980–81): 39–48.

Norrie, Kenneth H. "The Rate of Settlement of the Canadian West, 1870–1911." *Journal of Economic History* 35 (June 1975): 410–27.

Riis, Nelson. "The Wallachin Myth: A Study in Settlement Abandonment." *BC Studies* 17 (Spring 1973): 3–25.

Sharp, Paul F. "The American Farmer and the 'Last Best West.'" *Agricultural History* 21 (April 1947): 65–75.

———. "When Our West Moved North." *American Historical Review* 55 (January 1950): 286–300.

Shepard, R. Bruce. "American Influence on the Settlement and Development of the Canadian Plains." PhD diss., University of Regina, 1994.

———. *Deemed Unsuitable: Blacks from Oklahoma Move to the Canadian Prairies in Search of Equality in the Early Twentieth Century Only to Find Racism in Their New Home.* Toronto: Umbrella Press, 1997.

———. "The Origins of the Oklahoma Black Migration to the Canadian Prairies." *Canadian Journal of History* 23 (April 1988): 1–30.

Widdis, Randy W. "American-Resident Migration to Western Canada at the Turn of the Twentieth Century." *Prairie Forum* 22 (Fall 1997): 237–62.

———. "Saskatchewan-Bound: Migration to a New Canadian Frontier." *Great Plains Quarterly* 12 (Fall 1992): 254–68.

———. *With Scarcely a Ripple: Anglo-Canadian Migration into the United States and Western Canada, 1880–1920.* Montreal: McGill-Queen's University Press, 1998.

On Labor History in the Borderlands

Avery, Donald. *Dangerous Foreigners: European Immigrant Workers and Labour Radicalism in Canada.* Toronto: McClelland and Stewart, 1979.

Bercuson, David Jay. *Confrontation at Winnipeg: Labour, Industrial Relations, and the General Strike.* Kingston: McGill-Queen's University PRess, 1974.

————. "Labour Radicalism and the Industrial Western Frontier, 1897–1919." *Canadian Historical Review* 58 (June 1977): 154–75.

————. "The One Big Union in Washington." *Pacific Northwest Quarterly* 169 (July 1989): 127–34.

Bradwin, Edmund S. *The Bunkhouse Man: A Study of Work and Pay in the Camps of Canada, 1903–1914.* Toronto: University of Toronto Press, 1984.

Butler, Anne. *Daughters of Mercy, Sisters of Joy: Prostitutes in the American West.* Urbana: University of Illinois Press, 1987.

Calvert, Jerry W. *The Gibraltar: Socialism and Labor in Butte, Montana, 1895–1920.* Helena: Montana Historical Society Press, 1988.

Daniel, Cletus E. "Wobblies on the Farm: The iww in the Yakima Valley." *Pacific Northwest Quarterly* 65 (October 1974): 66–75.

Findlay, John M., and Ken S. Coates, eds. *Parallel Destinies: Canadian-American Relations West of the Rockies.* Seattle: University of Washington Press, 2002.

Friday, Chris. *Organizing Asian American Labor: The Pacific Coast Canned Salmon Industry, 1870–1942.* Philadelphia: Temple University Press, 1994.

Gray, James H. *Red Lights on the Prairies.* Toronto: Macmillan of Canada, 1971.

Graybill, Andrew. "Texas Rangers, Canadian Mounties, and the Policing of the Transnational Industrial Frontier, 1885–1910." *Western Historical Quarterly* 35 (Summer 2004): 167–92.

Hak, Gordon. "Red Wages: Communists and the 1934 Vancouver Island Loggers Strike." *Pacific Northwest Quarterly* 69 (July 1989): 82–90.

Hall, Greg. *Harvest Wobblies: The Industrial Workers of the World and Agricultural Laborers in the American West.* Corvallis: Oregon State University Press, 2001.

Hamson, Tim. "Wobblies in the Woods: The 1917 Lumber Strike in the Inland Empire." *Pacific Northwest Forum* II-4 (Summer/Fall 1991): 69–80.

Heron, Craig, ed. *The Workers' Revolt in Canada, 1917–1925.* Toronto: University of Toronto Press, 1998.

Isern, Thomas D. *Bull Threshers and Bindlestiffs on the North American Plains.* Lawrence: University Press of Kansas, 1990.

————. *Custom Combining on the Great Plains.* Norman: University of Oklahoma Press, 1981.

Jordan, Teresa. *Cowgirls: Women of the American West.* 1982; reprint, Lincoln: University of Nebraska Press, 1992.

Leier, Mark. *Where the Fraser River Flows: The Industrial Workers of the World in British Columbia.* Vancouver: New Star Books, 1990.

Lutz, John. "Border Crossings: Canadian Indians as American Laborers." Paper, wha, Denver co, October 1995.

————. "Work, Sex, and Death on the Great Thoroughfare: Annual Migrations of 'Canadian Indians' to the American Pacific Northwest." In Findlay and Coates, eds., *Parallel Destinies*, 80–103.

Marshall, Daniel P. "American Miner-Soldiers at War with the Nlaka'pamux of the Canadian West." In Findlay and Coates, eds., *Parallel Destinies*, 31–79.

Mitchell, James L. "A Hobo on the CPR." *Alberta History* 33 (Winter 1985): 14–27.

Mitchell, Tom, and James Naylor. "The Prairies: In the Eye of the Storm." In Craig Heron, ed., *The Workers' Revolt in Canada, 1917–1925*. Toronto: University of Toronto Press, 1998. 176–230.

Mount, Jeremy. "The Genesis of Western Exceptionalism: British Columbia's Hard Rock Miners, 1895–1903." *Canadian Historical Review* 71 (September 1990): 317–45.

Phillips, Paul A. *No Power Greater: A Century of Labour in British Columbia*. Vancouver: BC Federation of Labour, 1967.

Raibmon, Paige. "Border Hopping: Native American Labor and Culture in the Hop Fields of Puget Sound." Paper, WHA, Portland OR, October 1999.

———. "Meanings of Mobility: Migration, Labor, and Civilization in the Late Nineteenth-Century Northwest Coast." Paper, WHA, Colorado Springs CO, October 2002.

Rajala, Richard A. "The Forest as Factory: Technological Change and Worker Control in the West Coast Logging Industry." *Labour/leTravail* 32 (Fall 1993): 73–104.

Ramirez, Bruno. *Crossing the Forty-ninth Parallel: Migration from Canada to the United States, 1900–1930*. Ithaca: Cornell University Press, 2001.

Renshaw, Patrick. *The Wobblies: The Story of Syndicalism in the United States*. Garden City NY: Doubleday, 1967.

Savage, Candace. *Cowgirls: Real Cowboy Girls*. Vancouver: Greystone Books, 1996.

Schwantes, Carlos A. *Hard Traveling: A Portrait of Work Life in the New Northwest*. Lincoln: University of Nebraska Press, 1994.

———. *Radical Heritage: Labor, Socialism, and Reform in Washington and British Columbia, 1885–1917*. Seattle: University of Washington Press, 1979.

Smith, Charleen. " 'Crossing the Line': American Prostitutes in Western Canada, 1895–1910." In Elizabeth Jameson and Sheila McManus, eds., *One Step over the Line: Toward a History of Women in the North American Wests,* forthcoming.

Taylor, Quintard. " 'There Was No Better Place to Go'—The Transformation Thesis Revisited: African American Migration to the Pacific Northwest, 1940–1950." In Paul W. Hirt, ed., *Terra Pacifica: People and Place in the Northwest States and Western Canada*, 205–19. Pullman: Washington State University Press, 1998.

Toy, Eckard V., Jr. "The Oxford Group and the Strike of the Seattle Longshoremen in 1934." *Pacific Northwest Quarterly* 69 (October 1978): 174–84.

Tyler, Robert L. *Rebels of the Woods: The IWW in the Pacific Northwest*. Eugene: University of Oregon Books, 1967.

Van der Linden, Marcel. "Transnationalizing American Labour History." *Journal of American History* 86 (December 1999): 1078–92.

11. The Twine Line

Mexican Henequen, U.S.–Canadian Relations, and Binder Twine in the Northern Plains and Prairie Provinces, 1890–1950

Sterling Evans

Farmers, historians, economists, geographers, and other scholars rarely think of Mexico when talking or writing about grain farming in the American and Canadian plains in the late nineteenth and early twentieth centuries. Yet a unique Mexican–U.S.–Canadian relationship developed from 1890 to 1950 that centered around the production of henequen (*Agave fourcroydes*). Also called sisal, although that is a different but related plant (*Agave sisalana*), and often mistakenly called "hemp," henequen was used for the manufacture of binder twine. Twine was an essential component for harvesting grain crops on North American farms as it was used in reaper-binders to tie bundles that would then be hand-gathered into shocks to await threshing (before the widespread use of combines). American and Canadian grain producers became dependent upon henequen production in Yucatán, Mexico—a dependency that created a noteworthy economic and political relationship between the three nations. As the current sociological, geopolitical, economic, and environmental dimensions of the North American Free Trade Agreement (NAFTA) become known today, the history of binder twine offers instructive parallels and conclusions connecting Mexico, the United States, and Canada early in the twentieth century.

Henequen fiber was not manufactured into binder twine in Mexico. That process belonged to North American companies like Cyrus McCormick's International Harvester of Chicago (which dominated the market and controlled pricing for many years), Peabody Cordage of Boston, and other manufacturers. To compete and to assist local farmers, several midwestern states developed their own twine mills at state penitentiaries using inmate labor. Minnesota pioneered the idea and opened its prison twine mill in the mid-1880s. Other states and provinces followed suit: North Dakota, Kansas, and Ontario (the Toronto Central Prison) in the 1890s, and Wisconsin, South Dakota, Missouri, Michigan, Indiana, and Oklahoma early in the twentieth century.[1] The government of Canada established a prison twine plant at its federal penitentiary in Kingston, Ontario, in 1894.

Several points of this angle of the history of twine have yet to be discussed in the literature. Canadians became dependent on the henequen fiber. The Canadian government solicited the cooperation of American prison officials (in Minnesota) in establishing its Kingston twine mill. What transpired was an example of transboundary cooperation seldom seen in competing business interests. But that competition became problematic when contraband twine from prisons in the northern United States flooded the market in Canada's prairie provinces. The flow of fiber from Yucatán was interrupted in 1915 during the Mexican Revolution when revolutionary forces blockaded Yucatán's port of Progreso. North American farmers and cordage manufacturers feared that the year's bumper crop would not be harvested due to the blockaded henequen and urged governmental intervention. Both Washington's and Ottawa's responses to this "crisis" cast light on the degree to which the United States and Canada had become dependent upon the Mexican commodity. The reactions resulted in a twist in the relations between the two countries—a twist along the "twine line" of the U.S.–Canadian border that reached deep into Mexico.

The story begins with the transformation of the Great Plains (on both sides of the forty-ninth parallel) from a land of buffalo and later cattle grazing to a region of cereal grain production. Farm implement companies hastened agricultural expansion all across North America by rallying to invent and mass-produce machinery that could increase and quicken the harvest of grain. One such creation was the mechanical twine knotting device for the power reaper-binder that implement manufacturers perfected in the 1870s. Previous to twine, implement manufacturers produced wire

Figure 16. Early twentieth-century John Deere twine binder. Photo taken by author in Kenmare, North Dakota, July 1999.

binders that were cumbersome and caused problems when livestock ingested the wire with the discarded straw left over from threshing. Wire binders ceased production in 1883.

Twine binders (figure 16) were readily accepted by farmers on the American and Canadian plains. One Canadian farmer-writer, for example, argued that "of the factors which contributed most to the expansion of the western grain fields, none had more far-reaching influence than the invention of the mechanical knotter which permitted the use of twine." He recalled that a man with a team of horses and a binder could do in a day what previously took six men to do.[2] The McCormick Harvesting Machine Co. sold an average of 152,000 binders a year between 1897 and 1902, and after it merged with other implement manufacturers in 1902 to form International Harvester (IH), it averaged sales of 91,000 binders a year for the next decade.[3] In the United States, binders were used across most of the northern and midwestern grain growing regions. In Canada, as historian Tony Ward has written, there was a "rapid adoption of the twine binder" as wheat production expanded across the prairie provinces. The first binders started trickling into Manitoba in 1881 and into Alberta one year later. Their drop in price from the original $260 (Cdn.) in the

1890s to $155 (Cdn.) from 1900 to 1910 further popularized the implement. But while "the early binders gave a good deal of trouble," as Grant MacEwan acknowledged, "they were accepted at once and for nearly fifty years nobody considered an alternative."[4]

The Canadian government, however, imposed a tariff on U.S.-made farm implements. The duties followed technological advancements. They rose from 17.5 percent in the 1850s (primarily for early reapers used in Ontario before the wheat boom in the prairie provinces) to 25 percent in the 1870s (wire binders) to 37.5 percent by 1880s (twine binders and other implements). Cyrus McCormick was clearly annoyed at such policies and petitioned the U.S. State Department to intercede on such matters, although that proved unsuccessful. He also commissioned twenty-five agents to Canada to help market his implements there. But they had a tough time convincing farmers that the more expensive U.S. implements were better than the Canadian-made counterparts (primarily Massey-Harris). One agent wrote to company headquarters that "Canadians are clannish and strongly prejudicial." Frustrated, but unwilling to build manufacturing plants in Canada (in order to maintain central control in the United States), McCormick instructed agents to sell out their stock and to urge customers to buy the Canadian implements. Selling no more than one thousand binders in Canada in his lifetime, McCormick was greatly undersold by Massey-Harris, Deering, and other competitors. Even his son Cyrus II (who ran IH) missed the mark when he thought the wheat boom in Manitoba would never last because it "was too dependent on one crop."[5]

Despite McCormick's lethargic trade in Canada, many farmers in the prairie provinces came to rely on binders and other implements from the United States. By 1893 the demand was so great that 40,000 members of the Order of the Patrons of Industry (a farmers' organization) signed petitions to lobby Ottawa to lift or reduce the tariffs on foreign-made implements. Many of the tens of thousands of Americans who immigrated to the region (especially to Saskatchewan) in the first two decades of the twentieth century brought their implements with them. And according to one historian, Russian Mennonites and other European immigrants who moved to the Canadian prairies from the United States "depended upon binders of Yankee invention to harvest their grain."[6]

The improved harvesting technology, coupled with a soaring world demand for grain (especially during World War I) greatly accelerated the wheat belt across the North American plains. The number of acres of harvested wheat in the United States jumped from nearly 36.7 million in 1890 to 69.2 million by 1938 (harvested bushels of wheat climbed from 449 million to 920 million). The rate of increase in Canada was even more dramatic—from 42.2 million bushels in 1891 to over 540 million bushels by 1940. Ninety-five percent of the output in 1940 came from the three prairie provinces. Wheat acreage there increased from almost nil to 27.7 million acres in the same period.[7] Saskatchewan led the region and became Canada's wheat province (symbolized yet today by wheat on the license plates and a shock of wheat on the provincial highway markers). The number of farms in Saskatchewan rose from 13,445 in 1901 to 125,500 only twenty-five years later. As one report noted, "The climate of the province is ideal for the production of wheat. . . . Natural conditions fit Saskatchewan for producing the world's best wheat." Canada's amazing wheat boom is further reflected in the fact that it went from supplying 5 percent of the world's total exported wheat in 1911 to 40 percent by the end of the 1920s.[8]

It is hardly surprising, then, that the binder-dependent grain expansion on the Great Plains created what historians have called a "nearly limitless demand" for sisal fiber and "expanded the demand for . . . twine geometrically." Six pounds of twine were needed to harvest every acre of wheat. Accordingly, IH came to dominate the trade of Yucatecan henequen and built its own twine manufacturing plants to supply the harvest demands. By 1914 the conglomerate consumed nearly half as much imported henequen fiber—584,000 tons—as the other significant twine producers (cordage companies and penitentiaries) combined.[9]

The binder therefore transformed not only grain production in the United States and Canada but also the agricultural and economic landscape of Yucatán. As early as the 1890s, henequen had become Mexico's leading export crop. Production rose from 42,000 bales in 1876 to 1.5 million bales by 1915 (a bale equals 400 pounds of fiber).[10] According to a U.S. Senate report, by 1919 "practically all" of Yucatán's henequen was produced for the U.S. market and 90 percent of binder twine was made of Yucatán sisal. For the same year in Canada's seven cordage plants (in Ontario, Quebec, and Manitoba), the production of binder twine accounted for nearly 90 percent of all cordage products manufactured, although slightly under half the amount was made of Mexican henequen. The rest was made of abaca (Manila "hemp") from the Philippines, a somewhat better fiber for twine but one that was more expensive partly because of the distance to import it. The amount of Canadian-produced twine more than doubled from 1919 to 1920 (from 16.3 million pounds to 34.7 million pounds).[11]

Like they did on implements, however, Canadian tariffs extended to cordage and kept much of the henequen twine out of the country. As early as 1898 there were calls for an end to the duties on imported twine. One pamphlet complained of the government "combines" that controlled the manufacture and sale of twine and pointed to members of Parliament by name who were reaping unfair benefits from the government's involvement. The author of an anonymous letter to the editor of a farmers' journal, however, argued that Canadian twine was "of good quality," supplied jobs to at least one thousand people, and prevented unfair competition from the U.S. manufacturers. Nonetheless, by the end of the century the Order of Patrons of Industry lobbied hard for an end to the duties on U.S. twine. The Order sent petitions with over 25,000 signatures to Ottawa requesting that the tariffs be lifted. The price of binder twine was more than halved, however, when it fell from eighteen cents a pound in the 1880s to seven cents a pound in 1910.[12]

The price reduction was due in part to Canada's efforts to increase production of twine at home. But while officials kept a tariff on U.S.-made twine, they welcomed input on how to develop a twine mill at the Kingston Penitentiary. Minnesota prison officials were quick to offer advice and services, despite how Canada's efforts could cut into a potential market for Minnesota twine across the forty-ninth parallel.[13] During and after World War I, however, there were shortages of twine in Canada and in Europe. This caused many Canadian farmers to demand American twine, via legal or black market routes. Canadian manufacturers tried to stem this tide by arguing that U.S. prison–made twine was of inferior quality ("irregular and unreliable") due to the "class of labour" in those penitentiaries ("free labour factories"). They even asserted that the twine bore labels "intended to mislead the public" of its origin, which would lead to "grave injustices to [the] farmers" of Canada. Thus Canadian cordage companies lobbied strongly for increased border inspections of twine. But although the government cooperated and did increase inspections, by 1925 over half of the binder twine used in Canada came from the United States, especially when large quantities of twine were rushed into the prairie provinces at the end of the season when supplies were running thin and the demand for twine was intense. Much of the twine came in from the Michigan penitentiary, which aggressively marketed its product in other states.[14]

Finally, one particular year during the wheat boom of World War I is noteworthy for our discussion of how the U.S.–Canadian twine line reached into Mexico. The climate of 1915 had graced the Great Plains with the best harvest yields to date and for years to come. In the United States, over one billion bushels of wheat would be harvested that year—the only time the production level hit the billion-bushel mark between 1866 and 1943. North Dakota farmers led the way, harvesting nearly 160 million bushels of wheat that year—50 million more than their nearest competitors in Kansas. Yields in Canada were similarly productive. What Vernon Fowke referred to as "the fabulously bountiful crops of 1915" and John Herd Thompson called the "spectacular crop in 1915" was Canada's nearly 400 million-bushel production—nearly double its previous production high. Canada's agriculture commissioner, C. C. James, was quoted in the *Toronto World* as saying that "the farm production of all Canada in 1915 exceeded in value the farm productions of any previous year by at least $300,000,000."[15]

Missing in any of the reports is mention of the twine needs that kind of bumper crop would require. Indeed it was massive, yet coincidentally it was the same year during the Mexican Revolution that ousted dictator Porfirio Díaz from his thirty-five-year reign, when Venustiano Carranza and his constitutionalist forces marched on Yucatán with sights on the lucrative henequen industry. Henequen growers had benefited greatly from Díaz's policies, which included removing the last group of un-"assimilated" Indians, the Yaquis, from Sonora to work as slave laborers in Yucatán.[16] So to secure the peninsula and to prevent any potential arms shipments to counterrevolutionaries, Carranza imposed a blockade of the port of Progreso that restricted thousands of bales of fiber from being exported to the North. The port was closed for a month. News of this action, referred to in the U.S. media as the "Sisal Situation," spread quickly through the implement, cordage, farming, and prison twine industries. [17] With summer looming, a bumper crop across the region to harvest, and a depletion of twine supplies, an imminent disaster was lurking.

The "Sisal Situation" came to test the Woodrow Wilson administration in how far it would go to defend fiber, implement, and farm interests. Twine manufacturers deluged the office of Secretary of State William Jennings Bryan (a Nebraskan) with letters and telegrams urging the United States to take action. Messages came in from congressmen from agricultural states, prison wardens who were worried about acquiring fiber for their twine mills, implement dealers, and cordage company representatives. Several telegrams urged that Yucatán be declared a neutral zone during the Mexican Revolution so that nothing would stand in the way of getting binder twine to North American farmers. Cyrus McCormick II even "called on" Secretary Bryan in person to urge action. McCormick and his company had contributed $66,000 to Wilson's election, and he was keenly interested in the 200,000 bales of sisal tied up at Progreso—119,000 of which belonged to IH. [18]

Secretary Bryan replied to the industry correspondents with the message that "the Department [of State] was continuing its efforts to relieve the condition" and that a special emissary had been commissioned to Mexico to deal with Carranza. Meanwhile Bryan and President Wilson conferred on what course of action would be appropriate. They made the decision to send the USS cruiser *Des Moines* to Progreso to monitor the situation and later to send the USS collier *Brutus* and the gunboat *Olympia* as backups. With those moves, on March 14 Bryan sent a stiff warning to Carranza—an ultimatum, really—saying that the U.S. naval officers on board these ships were "to prevent any interference with commerce to and from the port" if Carranza did not lift the blockade. [19] The threat seemed to work and the situation was defused when Carranza bowed to U.S. demands and ordered his blockading ships away from Progreso. The last thing the Mexican revolutionaries needed was trouble, or a naval attack, from the United States. This type of "gunboat diplomacy" was typical of the early 1900s U.S. foreign policy—actually something that Wilson and

Bryan had opposed during previous administrations—that was based on the legal concept of "no duty to retreat."[20]

Although fiber was once again moving out from the port of Progreso, it seemed to be moving very slowly (not in "adequate quantities," as the *New York Sun* reported on March 26), and worse, rumors of other dangers of the Revolution and how they could affect henequen production were making their way back to the United States and Canada. Now, it was thought, revolutionaries were burning plantations and storehouses of fiber in Yucatán. Letters and telegrams again poured into Secretary Bryan's office, urging the United States to monitor these new threats which would impede the grain harvests. The rumors turned out to be unfounded, but Bryan did monitor the situation.[21]

What was Ottawa's response to this "Sisal Situation"? As that *New York Sun* article pointed out, "Canadian farmers [were] just as vitally concerned" about the possibility of not being able to bind their harvests. Thus the Canadian government monitored the crisis very closely but via the British ambassador to the United States in Washington; it did not send a special emissary to the States or to Mexico. The British ambassador, Sir Cecil Spring-Rice, kept in close touch with both Secretary of State Bryan and the governor general of Canada about what he called the "deplorable situation in Mexico." But the British and Canadians were quick to defer any action to the United States. Spring-Rice wrote that "the only Power who can do anything to remedy [the situation] is the United States Government . . . and it must not be forgotten that they have a large force within striking distance." With that in mind, in a letter to Secretary Bryan, Spring-Rice underscored his commonwealth's agricultural and financial interests in the matter:

> I am delighted to see in the press reports that serious steps are being taken to secure the export from Yucatan of Sisal Grass for twine. As I ventured to point out to you, Canada is deeply interested in the export for the use of Canadian farmers, and many British houses . . . have invested large sums in the production and distribution of Sisal for the use of both Canadian and United States consumers. I am confident therefore that your Government in the common interest of the agricultural

population of this continent will be ready to co-operate in every possible manner, in the preservation of this most important industry.[22]

He also kept the governor general of Canada updated, reporting that "about 15,000 tons of sisal twine is [sic] exported annually to Canada for use as binding material. . . . The manufacturers [growers] in Yucatan are at present in some anxiety as to the possibility of making exports by the port of Progreso, as trade of the port has recently been interfered with by an armed vessel employed by the Carrancista authorities. I understand however the United States Government are fully alive to the importance of keeping open this source of supply of twine." And in a report attached to the letter, Spring-Rice outlined the implications of a fiber shortage: "The Sisal from Yucatan must come forward quickly because any delay in its arrival could easily occasion a world-wide disaster. Unless they can count on a supply of twine, the Agricultural machinery factories would have to suspend manufacturing because the binder cannot work without twine. . . . On account of the European war, the agriculturalists generally are planting enormous acreage of grains in order to take advantage of the high prices so that more twine will be needed this year than in the past."[23]

The *Toronto Globe* fueled worries about the destruction of henequen fields when it headlined the story "Canada's Hemp Supply Endangered at Yucatan." It reported how Ambassador Spring-Rice was conferring with American officials in the interests of Canadians. It also assured Canadian readers that "steps [would] be taken to prevent any interference with the shipment of the much-needed product" and how the United States "gave notice" that gunboats "would be used if necessary to keep the port open." Other Canadian newspapers followed the story, too, but perhaps not as closely as their American counterparts. None of the major wheat belt newspapers in the prairie provinces (*Manitoba Free Press*, *Saskatoon Phoenix*, *Regina Leader*, *Calgary Albertan*, *Calgary Daily Herald*, or *Edmonton Bulletin*) carried stories about the potential crisis, although the *Calgary Daily Herald* did mention in an article on March 15 of that year that "the United States was determined to raise the blockade and, if necessary, use the cruiser *Des Moines* to do so.[24]

Instead, on the very day of Bryan's ultimatum to Carranza (March 15, 1915), the prairie newspapers covered the story of a new twine manufacturing plant planned for Calgary. Winnipeg's *Manitoba Free Press* reported that the Western Canada Cordage Co. Ltd. would employ 375 workers, produce twenty-seven tons of binder twine a day, and cater to markets in Alberta and Saskatchewan. The plant was being built, the article said, due to the $4,027,309 worth of twine that was imported into western Canada from the United States in 1914—an amount that could be better spent at home. To avoid the potential problems in the flow of henequen from revolutionary Mexico, all of the raw material to be used in this new plant would come from the Philippines (Manila "hemp"), New Zealand, the Hawaiian Islands, and the west coast of Mexico, which produced other kinds of fibers, albeit in far less quantity than Yucatán's henequen. On the same day, the *Saskatoon Phoenix* reported how a flax mill would be started in Saskatoon by a company out of Great Falls, Montana. Flax had been called on for many years as a possible locally grown fiber that could be used to make twine. IH had experimented with a flax mill in St. Paul, Minnesota, and the Canadian government had done the same with twine plants in Ontario from Saskatchewan-grown flax. None of the efforts paid off, unfortunately for flax supporters, because the flax fiber never created a strong enough twine to tie bundles, and it often broke in the binder's mechanical knotter.[25]

Other fibrous plants were considered for twine in the early part of the twentieth century. Experiments with wire grass and industrial hemp (true hemp, *Cannibis sativa*) were performed, especially by IH, which developed large tracts of hemp in North Dakota, and by independent growers in Kansas. Wire grass proved ineffectual, and hemp quickly exhausted the soil. Hemp was also at the center of a smear campaign engineered by William Randolph Hearst, who argued that all hemp was narcotic, even though industrial hemp did not carry THC (tetrahydracannibinol), the psychoactive ingredient that was bred into nonindustrial strains of *C. sativa*, which produces marijuana. Hearst worried that hemp could replace wood pulp—of which he had huge land holdings and investments—that was used for paper products.[26]

Thus it was primarily henequen twine that continued to be used for grain harvests until the late 1940s and 1950s when most farmers switched to using combines—the harvester that both cuts and threshes grain with no need to bind the stalks into bundles.

Between 1890 and 1950, farmers on the Great Plains of the United States and Canada depended on this seemingly minor commodity. Along with that dependence came a variety of twists and turns on the "twine line": a hurried rush to produce the twine needed; demands that grew due to war, immigration to the prairie provinces, and a desire to feed the world; competition between industrial and state sectors to produce twine; competition and cooperation between the U.S. and Canadian officials, especially in the prison sector; development of trade restrictions between the two countries, and ways around them in the borderlands of the northern plains and prairies provinces; and relations that evolved over the impact of a halt in the flow of fiber from Yucatán during Mexico's revolution. But the "Sisal Situation" perhaps best illustrates the North's dependence on a Mexican commodity and to what degree the United States would go to protect the flow of fiber. While Canada did not enter this show of force, it certainly supported, and indeed lobbied for, whatever the United States could do to prevent any interference with commerce. Part of this thinking was to support the war effort in Europe, but it is noteworthy to recall that none of the parties involved in the North considered the importance of what Carranza and the constitutionalist revolutionaries were fighting for in Mexico—including their disgust at the slave labor practices in the very henequen plantations on which the northern wheat belt depended. And that lack of interest extended to when the combine-induced decline of the henequen market hit Yucatán. Like so many other times and places in Latin America, the boom/bust cycle occurred with no support of the exploiting nations/corporations to help create alternative economies. And for that, perhaps there are important lessons to consider from the binder twine experience as Canada and the United States continue to work to expand NAFTA and are now working to develop a Free Trade of the Americas (FTA).

Notes

This essay was originally a paper presented at the conference of the American Historical Association–Pacific Coast Branch, Vancouver BC, August 2001.

1. See Sterling Evans, "Prison-Made Binder Twine: North Dakota's Connection with Mexico in the Early Twentieth Century," *North Dakota History: Journal of the Northern*

Plains 68, no. 1 (2001); Evans, "From Kanasín to Kansas: Mexican Sisal, Binder Twine, and the State Prison Twine Factory, 1890–1840," *Kansas History: Journal of the Central Plains* 24, no. 4 (2001); and Evans, "Entwined in Conflict: The South Dakota State Prison Twine Factory and the Controversy of 1919," *South Dakota History* 35 (Summer 2005): 95–124.

2. Grant McEwan, *Between the Red and the Rockies* (Toronto: University of Toronto Press, 1952), 206.

3. Barbara Marsh, *A Corporate Tragedy: The Agony of International Harvester Company* (Garden City NY: Doubleday, 1985), 42.

4. Tony Ward, "Farming Technology and Crop Area on Early Prairie Farms," *Prairie Forum* 20, no. 1 (1995): 24; MacEwan, *Between the Red and the Rockies*, 207. See also Lewis H. Thomas, "A History of Agriculture on the Prairies to 1914," *Prairie Forum* 1, no. 1 (1976): 44–45.

5. William T. Hutchison, *Cyrus Hall McCormick, 1856–1884* (New York: Appleton-Century, 1935), 647–51, 685.

6. Hutchison, *Cyrus Hall McCormick*, 651; Vernon C. Fowke, *Canadian Agricultural Policy: The Historical Pattern* (Toronto: University of Toronto Press, 1946), 261.

7. U.S. Department of Agriculture, Agricultural Marketing Service, *Wheat: Acreage Yield Production by States, 1866–1943* (Washington: Government Printing Office, 1955), 2; Dominion Bureau of Statistics, *Wheat Review* (1956), as reprinted in Vernon C. Fowke, *The National Policy and the Wheat Economy* (Toronto: University of Toronto Press, 1957), 75.

8. University of Saskatchewan, College of Agriculture, "Farm Business in Saskatchewan," *Agriculture Extension Bulletin*, no. 37 (June 1927): 11–12; U.S. Department of Agriculture, *Wheat*, 51; Gerald Friesen, *The Canadian Prairies: A History* (Toronto: University of Toronto Press, 1987), 329. For more on how prairie province farmers were "eager to take advantage" of the international market during and after World War I, see John Herd Thompson, *The Harvests of War: The Prairie West, 1914–1918* (Toronto: McClelland and Stewart, 1978), 23–70.

9. Gilbert Joseph, "Revolution from Without: The Mexican Revolution in Yucatán, 1915–1924," PhD diss., Yale University, 1978, 27, 101; Gilbert Joseph and Allen Wells, "Corporate Control of a Monocrop Economy: International Harvester and Yucatán's Henequen Industry during the Porfiriato," *Latin American Research Review* 17, no. 1 (1982): 73; Ward, "Farming Technology," 33.

10. Joseph, "Revolution from Without," 56; Joseph and Wells, "Corporate Control," 71.

11. Statement of Eliseo Arredondo (henequen growers' representative in New York), *Investigation of Mexican Affairs: Preliminary Report and Hearings of the Committee on Foreign Relations, U.S. Senate* (Washington: Government Printing Office, 1920), 891; Dominion Bureau of Statistics, *Report on the Cordage, Rope, and Twine Industry in Canada, 1919 and 1920* (Ottawa: Ministry of Trade and Commerce, 1922), 1–5.

12. Anonymous pamphlet, *The Binder Twine Steal* (Ottawa, 1899), 1–5; *Farmer's Sun*, February 3, 1898, 3; Ward, "Farming Technology," 24.

13. National Archives of Canada, RG 13, series D-1, vol. 1027, file 39, "Binder Twine, Kingston Penitentiary," parts 1 and 2.

14. Letters, Brantford Cordage Co. (of Ontario) to G. H. Clarke of the Department of

Agriculture in Ottawa from early 1925, National Archives of Canada, RG 17, vol. 3088, file 47–2, "Inspection and Sale Act."

15. U.S. Department of Agriculture, *Wheat*, 2, 10–11; Fowke, *National Policy*, 78; Thompson, *Harvests of War*, 68. Crop figures are from Statistics Canada as reprinted in Charles F. Wilson, *Century of Canadian Grain: Government Policy to 1951* (Saskatoon: Western Producer Prairie Books, 1978), 182; James in *Toronto World*, February 3, 1916, 1.

16. Henequen growers had used Yaquis as slaves on their plantations until this pivotal year, 1915, when Carranza's forces liberated them. News of the buying, selling, and trading of Yaquis, and the horrendous conditions in which they lived and worked, reached the American press in 1910 via the muckraking journalism of John Kenneth Turner, who published a series of articles entitled "Barbarous Mexico" in the *American Review*, now in book form. See Turner, *Barbarous Mexico* (Austin: University of Texas Press, 1969). For further analysis on what happened to the Yaquis and their land in Sonora when they were removed to work on the henequen plantations, see Sterling Evans, "Yaquis vs. Yanquis: An Environmental and Historical Comparison of Coping with Aridity in Southern Sonora," *Journal of the Southwest* 40, no. 3 (Autumn 1998): 363–96.

17. See *New York Times*, March 16–21, 1915. Coverage was often front-page news.

18. U.S. State Department, Relations with Mexico, microfilm roll 206, 812.61326/12–216. Campaign contribution information is from Arthur Link, *Wilson: The Road to the White House* (Princeton: Princeton University Press, 1947), 403.

19. U.S. State Department, Relations with Mexico, microfilm roll 206, 812.6326/128. See also Kendrick Clements, " 'A Kindness to Carranza': William Jennings Bryan, International Harvester, and Intervention in Yucatan," *Nebraska History* 57, no. 4 (1976): 478–90.

20. See chapter 4 of Richard Maxwell Brown, *No Duty to Retreat: Violence and Values in American History* (New York: Oxford University Press, 1991).

21. *New York Sun*, March 26, 1915, 1.

22. Spring-Rice to Right Honourable Sir Edward Gray, April 1, 1915, and March 24, 1915, National Archives of Canada, RG 25, vol. 1161, file 572.

23. Spring-Rice to Governor General, March 23, 1915, National Archives of Canada, RG 25, vol. 1161, file 572.

24. *Toronto Globe*, March 23, 1915, 13; *Calgary Daily Herald*, March 15, 1915, 1.

25. *Manitoba Free Press*, March 15, 1915, 10; *Saskatoon Phoenix*, March 15, 1915, 1.

26. See Jack Herer, *The Emperor Wears No Clothes: The Authoritative Historical Record of Cannibis and the Conspiracy against Marijuana* (White River Junction VT: Chelsea Green, 1998); and the section on *cannibis* in Michael Pollan, *Botany of Desire: A Plant's Eye View of the World* (New York: Random House, 2001).

12. Hoboes across the Border

Itinerant Cross-Border Laborers between Montana and Western Canada

Evelyne Stitt Pickett

Between 1870 and 1920 a vast army of floating workers roamed the American and Canadian Wests servicing the natural resource industries of mining, lumbering, and grain and livestock production. They worked in the fisheries, in railroad construction, and on irrigation projects. Such industries provided work for hundreds of thousands of people who, lured west by gold, adventure, or the possibility of land, became enmeshed in the industries' transitory hire-and-fire cycle. The literature on these itinerant laborers—their contributions and exploitation—has been steadily growing in the past few years.[1]

To this transient labor force, the international boundary meant little. To be sure, the forty-ninth parallel has in many ways represented a division of the two countries' ideas and events, but similarities abound. Montana, which shares an extended border with British Columbia, Alberta, and Saskatchewan, has a long history of resource extraction. Its mountain ranges, extending into British Columbia and Alberta, initiated mining and logging industries, and its eastern plains invited hay-hands to follow the grain harvest north into Saskatchewan and Manitoba. Livestock production developed concurrently on both sides of what Indians called the Medicine Line, and the extension of railroads—the Northern Pacific across Montana in the 1880s, the Great Northern Railway's expansion to Seattle by 1893, and the Canadian Pacific's reach westward to Vancouver by 1885—all stimulated regional development north and south of the international boundary.

The experience of the casual labor force was much the same on both sides of the international border. Whether north or south of the boundary, itinerant workers in the West encountered great distances between places of employment. In this, the western casual laborer differed from his eastern counterpart. Set like islands in a vast ocean of land, western resource industries in Canada, Montana, and elsewhere required geographic mobility. Workers who came west tended to stay, but they moved freely across the boundary because the industries that employed itinerant workers were the same whether north or south of the border. Just as Montanans and other Americans sought wage work in Canadian natural resource industries, Canadians ventured to Montana for the same reason. To be sure, Canada tried to stop the influx, but with little consistent success. Although they provided significant services for casual laborers in both countries, women seldom traveled with the wandering men.

Romantic myths evolved about the free lifestyle of hoboes, but in reality their lives were harsh, and they were usually exploited. Poor working conditions, corrupt employment agencies, low wages, and union turmoil were the rule, not the exception, and workers tended to blame people of color for the inequities. While government committees investigated their plight, workers gravitated to Canadian skid rows in Edmonton and elsewhere as readily as they did to such havens in Billings, Montana, and other American cities. Loneliness, death, and dismemberment threatened them, whether they rode the Canadian Pacific or the Northern Pacific. In cities and towns, they might simply be used. Charging them with vagrancy, civil authorities in both countries frequently put itinerants to work without pay. To express their dissatisfaction, thousands of casual laborers, drawn to the ideas of radical syndicalism, helped swell the membership of the Industrial Workers of the World (iww) and Canada's One Big Union.

Work in most resource industries was cyclical: grain was harvested, timber was cut, bridges and railroads were completed, and mining bonanzas turned to bust. When work finished at a particular place, and often before, workers moved to another locale. Carleton Parker, executive secretary of the California State Immigration and Housing Commission, submitted figures to show that in 1912 some 3.5 million casual laborers moved from one job to another in the American West. Lumber camp workers, he said, stayed fifteen to thirty days on average; they remained in construction ten days; in harvesting, seven days; and in mining, sixty days. Many, he said, crossed the international border in search of comparable work. As one Canadian historian put it, "What was casual about a casual laborer was the terms of employment. It was sporadic, unreliable, and they were usually poorly paid."[2]

The rapid expansion of an itinerant labor force in Montana and Canada's western provinces occurred between the California gold rush and World War I, a time when telegraph and railroad lines tied West to East and integrated extractive industries into the world market. There had been few wandering laborers among the fur traders and mountain men, but when the California gold rush hearkened to individuals all over the world at midcentury, labor patterns changed. Thousands who headed west dreaming of wealth became wageworkers for mining companies. When the gold seams played out, unemployed miners grabbed their few belongings and dashed to the next locality hoping to find another bonanza. For many workers, this pattern of mobility eventually spread to the construction and natural resource industries.

The lure of western settlement also drew laborers west. To encourage settlement, railroad companies sent agents to the eastern United States, Canada, and Europe, where they distributed brochures in several languages. As feeder lines spread like webs to the extractive industries, Canadian railroads advertised for workers from Britain and the United States. Immigrants responded. When George Isaac traveled to British Columbia in 1862 by way of the Isthmus of Panama, he recalled being packed into a ship like a herring in a barrel. Pursuing the dream of striking it rich, he found wage work instead at Montana and Alberta mines and logging camps. Finnish emigrant Otto Kola headed to Montana with other Finns to work in the mines, but in the summer he traveled to the British Columbia Coast to work on fishing boats. Such men became part of a "wageworkers' frontier." Dependent upon others for pay, they created a huge community of itinerant manual laborers ever on the move in the sparsely settled Rocky Mountain and Pacific regions.[3]

Where towns sprang up, they spurred building booms that required laborers. Even as Canadian workers headed south across the border, others from the United States headed north. Canadian Ernest Allcock said that for years all he seemed to do "was go from one irrigation project to another in Montana" and meet other men who drifted around. In the American West, 51 percent of the transients were white, male, and American born. Between the ages of sixteen and forty, only 10 percent had ever married. They were joined by immigrants from abroad, half of whom had left wives behind in their countries of origin.[4]

Itinerant laborers who roamed the country looking for work after 1870 were known as "hoboes," and among them the term was respectable. Turn-of-the-century magazines romanticized their wandering lives, and songs and poetry evolved, much of it written by the roaming laborers themselves. What may have appeared outwardly as egalitarian nonetheless had a hierarchy. Dean Stiff, a hobo for decades, defined hoboes as those who drifted about looking for work or traveled to and from work areas. By contrast, he said, "tramps, below hoboes, were dreamers who wandered but did not look for work seriously." Below the tramps were "bums" and "yeggs," whom Stiff considered parasitic. "Bums will beg the bread and butter from a child on the street, but yeggs will take it." Alan Pinkerton, a late-nineteenth-century railroad detective, concurred, although his sympathies lay with the railroad companies.[5]

The term has lost its status, especially since the Great Depression, although Webster's 1947 dictionary identified hobo as simply "a migratory worker." More recently, hobo has come to mean "a wanderer or vagrant, usually homeless or poor." Instead of men dressed in their one suit of clothes going from one workplace to the next, the term now invokes images of people dressed in rags hopping trains.

Whatever the image, trains were prominent in the lives of itinerant laborers. As the national network of rails expanded, hundreds of men came to regard the railroad as their special form of free transportation. They clambered onto the trusses beneath the cars or rode atop or inside freight cars. When riding the trusses they turned both their shirts and suit jackets inside out. Thus keeping the grease and cinders from being ground into the material, they arrived at the next destination with a modicum of cleanliness, especially if they went directly to a job site.[6]

In the early years, trainmen made little effort to keep such men off their trains. In the 1870s, free riders were simply an unavoidable nuisance, but as trains came to carry a hundred men or more, rail companies hired detectives (hoboes called them bulls or shacks) to keep them off the trains.

In Canada, the North-West Mounted Police collaborated with railroad detectives to monitor hoboes. Mounties seem to have been kinder than American lawmen, escorting hoboes from trains rather than throwing them off.[7]

Still the men rode, trying to stay out of sight of the bulls. Once in a while a "brakey" (brakeman) helped conceal a rider, but more often he would either throw the freeloader from the train or exact a fee, which he slipped into his pocket. Simon Johnson recalled a brakeman collecting one dollar for his ride from Logan, Utah, to Butte, Montana. William O. Douglas, later to become a U.S. Supreme Court justice, recalled paying several such fees as his train lumbered across Montana heading east. John Jennings, who considered hoboing a privilege of the itinerant "blanketstiff," resented being charged.[8] Fred T. Barrett related being charged when riding the Canadian Pacific, but John Thompson remembered the kindness of a trainman with a warm heart on an extremely cold night. He and forty other hoboes were hanging on and under Canadian Pacific boxcars in the switchyard when this trainman put on an extra closed boxcar and hustled them all into it, admonishing them to be quiet so he would not get into trouble.[9]

Despite such kindnesses, hoboes flirted with danger when they rode the rods. Countless numbers were killed falling from trains, and even more were maimed for life. Sixteen hoboes were killed and eighteen injured along a short section of rail in Livingston, Montana, between October 1903 and October 1904.[10] Hoboes continued riding the rails nonetheless, particularly the Turkey Track from Great Falls, which connected with the Canadian Pacific at Lethbridge, Alberta.[11] Whether hoboes rode the rods, blinds, bumpers, or train decks, trains constituted the easiest and quickest form of transportation as itinerant laborers wandered from one resource job site to another.

When hoboes were not working, many headed for hobo jungles—usually located within a mile or so of a division—where they rested, ate, and washed their clothes, usually in a large can filled with soap and water. The last hobo to leave the clearing became responsible for the only law of the jungle: wash the grub cans (leaving them bottom up) and put out the fire. Such campsites were common along the Canadian railroads as well as the Great Northern, Northern Pacific, and connecting rails.[12]

Hobo jungles seldom catered to women. Floating workers between 1870 and 1920 rarely worked alongside women because geographic mobility and the strenuous labor involved did not suit most women at that time. Still women were present in the resources industries. They did not hold jobs side by side with casual laborers in mining, logging, or construction, but they worked as cooks for the crews who migrated to their farms, or nearby farms, to harvest grain. Women lived at or near the farms where the crews were doing the threshing, and they put in as many hours a day as the men, rising at 3:00 a.m. to serve breakfast before dawn so the men could be in the fields at daybreak.[13]

Men did the cooking in the lumber and construction camps in the late nineteenth and early twentieth centuries. James Mastin recounted the story of traveling as a cook with logging and construction crews in Montana and Saskatchewan. A woman stopped at the cook car, looked at the dough around Mastin's fingernails, and commented, "I always clean my nails after I bake," whereupon Mastin answered: "I always clean mine before I start." Men cooked for the logging camps through World War I, after which larger camps began hiring women, usually the wives of loggers, as cooks. Exceptions were rare. One of them was Montanan Minnie Christensen, who worked with her husband's threshing rig for eight years. All the men he hired were single, so she slept in the cook car. Sadye Wolf Drew not only cooked for the various threshing crews but worked in the field as well, running the steam engine and binder.[14]

Women throughout the resource sector performed one service for itinerants for which they have received little credit: they supplied the traveling mendicants with food when they came begging at the back door. Hoboes usually offered to do work when forced to seek handouts. Not all women were generous with foodstuffs, but it was commonly recognized that the best place to go for a handout was the red-light district.[15]

Labor historians have seldom considered prostitutes as part of the casual labor force, despite their mobility. Their role, though peripheral, was real, and they moved from one town to another when bonanza turned to bust or as logging sites shifted. Indeed, although Canadian historian James Henry Gray contended that prostitution was confined to the cities and settlements in late-nineteenth-century Canada, he noted that the girls worked the passenger trains between Winnipeg and the Pacific Coast.[16]

Before World War I, few women "rode the rods," according to Box-Car
Bertha, who hoboed in the 1920s. Hurdy-gurdy girls, who moved from
mining camp to cattle camp, were usually not prostitutes. The "gurdies"
were a fluctuating, floating population who drank and danced with the
miners, but like the prostitutes, they have not been counted among the
floating army of casual laborers.[17]

For most itinerants, it was a predatory world. Andrew Roddan, director of a Canadian skid row mission, perceived the hobo as an indispensable factor in building Canada's infrastructure, yet noted that hoboes
were much maligned. "As a rule they are a good class of men," he said,
"rough and uncouth on the outside, but when you come to know them
they are very human, generous, and responsive to a touch of kindness.
The irregularity of their work has a very serious reaction on their outlook
on society and life." Exploitation imprisoned them in itinerancy, for they
never made enough money or had enough steady work to escape their
condition.[18]

In the early years, industries in neither Montana nor Canada gave
much consideration to the living conditions of itinerants. Instead, casual
laborers were viewed as human machines who performed muscle services.
Employers provided few amenities, such as adequate sleeping accommodations and toilet facilities. Bunkhouses in the lumber industries, hastily
built on skids so they could be easily moved, had planks or metal crescent
slabs as bunks. Charles Kennedy recalled one place where a hole in the
floor served as a fireplace. Earle Marsh said one logging camp had cracks
in the walls so wide "you could throw a suitcase through them."[19]

Heading north to Canada did not improve things. Loggers in British
Columbia complained of wretched conditions. Archibald S. Kerr, who
went north to work as a scaler at a logging camp at Swift Creek, said
when he stepped into the bunkhouse with its three tiers of narrow bunks
filled with loose straw, he discovered the bunk assigned to him was already
occupied. When he asked the bull cook where else he could sleep, he was
told there was room; two to a bed was common. On both sides of the
border itinerants recalled men having to sleep two to a bunk on boards
three feet wide with no blankets, no sheets, and few bathrooms.[20]

When Governor Samuel V. Stewart of Montana appointed a commission to investigate lumber camp conditions, the panel reported unsanitary

situations in the living quarters, toilets, and dining rooms in a majority of the camps. Canadian government documentation revealed similarly poor conditions in lumber, coal, and mining camps. Stinking outhouses, cold, damp bunkhouses, and outbreaks of typhoid fever were common. Faced with wretched conditions and poor pay, workers just quit and moved on. Howard Henderson, a retired Canadian high-rigger, said leaving a job became his declaration of independence: "If I didn't like it, I just quit." He recalled that the men he knew in the camps seldom stayed more than three or four weeks before they drifted to another camp in search of something better. [21]

Workers in railroad camps fared little better, according to a study of mobile railroad camps by Canadian sociologist Edmund W. Bradwin. Bradwin noted that although these "bunkhouse men" doubled the railway mileage of Canada, their rewards were meager. Leaky buildings, crowded conditions, dirty bedding and water, no lights in the bunkhouses, and no vermin control denied many men much-needed rest after a long day. Such conditions, he believed, became the impetus for Canada's radical unionism. [22]

Harvest hands were not exempt from forlorn living conditions. Sources described how workers slept in haystacks and stables before a long day's haying. Born in 1887 in England, Ernest Allcock, who had headed to Saskatchewan to work in the hay fields, said he encountered "lousy meals" and had to drink "sour water" from a lake polluted with horse and cattle droppings. Electing to forgo two weeks' wages, he left. But there were exceptions. Earle Marsh said most farms provided better accommodations for their permanent "hired hands," and he noted that the Campbell Corporation in Montana paid him five dollars a day and provided good bunkhouses. Still, many itinerant workers who went from hay field to hay field had to sleep in the haystacks because they had no special housing. C. D. Taylor described the bunkhouses on the Canadian and American ranches where he worked in the 1890s as being overcrowded and miserable. Itinerant laborers had to make do to earn a dollar a day. [23]

Most itinerants were unprepared for the poor conditions and unhappiness that entered their lives. Young John Smith, who came to the West to claim its promise, found bitter disappointment. He went from one job to another until one day, homesick, he entered a Montana saloon just to talk to someone. It then became easier to go into saloons, and when he was not walking, working, or riding the brake beams, he would go to the saloon, where "Charlie" would talk about making enough money to go to the Klondike or "Ed" would talk about taking up land in Alberta. He found that many men in the bars had the same ambitions he did, yet they went from ambition to hopelessness and many, with the onset of alcoholism, to unemployable.[24]

Josiah Flynt Willard, a policeman who traveled undercover with itinerants, believed the love of liquor lured men into "vagabondage" (a term he used to cover hoboes, tramps, and bums). Montana deputy sheriff John McKinley recalled that "the lumberjacks came down on Saturday nights, got drunk, and fought until they were landed in the mud holes along in front of the saloons." Fred Barrett, who worked with hay crews on both sides of the border, said many itinerants crossed the border because gaming houses in Montana were "wide open and open all night for their pleasure." He recalled one sheepherder who trailed his 2,100 sheep into Canada so he would not be tempted to gamble away all his money. The sheepherder said he could resist drink but not Montana's numerous gambling dens, which others found so tempting. Some itinerants, like Walter E. Bodington, came south from British Columbia to gamble. "Montana Territory was a rough place for a young man to land into," Bodington recalled. "Wide open all night . . . gambling. The game was the old French game of Faro with no limit whatever."[25]

Montana cowboys, heading to work on Alberta cattle ranches, had to shed their six-shooters at the border "as trees shed their leaves in the fall," and could pick them up when they returned to Montana. Realizing that Americans would not favor an armed military force along the border, the Canadian government in 1873 created the North-West Mounted Police, a federal force that supplemented provincial police. Although small in number, the Mounties brought much order in their efforts to control the relative lawlessness and gun-fighting prevalent in the American West.[26]

However successful they were at stopping the flow of firearms, the North-West Mounted Police seldom stopped the flow of itinerant laborers moving back and forth across the border. Early settler Bella Blackburn recalled laborers crossing the border with "no bother at all with customs."

Hoboes waved to the Mounties as they rode along the Turkey Track from Shelby, Montana, to Lethbridge, Alberta. Frederick Stewart and others testified to untrammeled commuting across the boundary. Harold Hollenbeck recalled crossing the border easily when he worked as a logger in Alberta and as a thresher in Saskatchewan and Montana until about 1915.[27]

Cross-border hiring was common. Andrew Onderdonk, an American contractor on the CP, could not meet the demand for labor in British Columbia in the 1880s and solicited 6,500 Chinese and 2,500 American workers from American employment agencies. He encountered no problems at the border. Canadian Federal Royal Commission reports cited an instance involving Frank A. Wood and W. W. Wright, representatives from the Silver Lead Mines Association, who procured workers for that Canadian mine in 1899. When Bernard MacDonald, president at the LeRoi Mining Company, attempted to hire American citizens in 1899, he observed: "It is well understood that the only source of supply is the United States. Eastern Canada cannot furnish them because of the distance." He added that "the alien labor laws try to make it impossible to bring in men, and yet as a matter of fact most of them here drifted in from the U.S." Records from the War Eagle mine indicated that in 1899, 48 percent of workers were British subjects and 52 percent were from other countries. Of the 283 non-British workers, 251 were Americans.[28]

These were not isolated incidences. Rossland Miners' Union files reveal numerous letters showing how the LeRoi Mining Company advertised for American labor at its Canadian mine. A letter dated January 16, 1901, signed by Americans Joseph Parent, William Baslow, and John Barton, employees of LeRoi, and sworn to before a Canadian notary public, declared they had been solicited to come to British Columbia to work. Rossland Miners' Union 38 decried the hiring of "cheap foreign labor" and initiated procedures to curtail cross-border hiring.[29]

At the same time the president of the War Eagle attested to the need for American labor, W. L. Hagler, secretary of the Sandon Miners' Union in British Columbia, sent a telegram to Sir Wilfrid Laurier complaining that one thousand Canadian miners were forced to work across the border in U.S. mines because of the importation of American miners into Canada.[30] The union made such a scrap about hiring American workers that by 1911 legislation curbing employment of foreigners reduced the number of American miners to 10 percent.

The union's activism did not affect cross-border threshing crews, however, which continued to move north as the harvests ripened. Signs, erected by Canadian railroads across Minnesota, North Dakota, and Montana, urged American workers to ride the trains to Saskatchewan and Manitoba at reduced rates: "40,000 American Citizens needed to harvest the 400,000,000 bushel crop in Western Canada." Despite stronger Canadian legislation against it, cross-border soliciting for employment recurred during World War I when the Canadian government added fifty-two immigration agents with specific instructions to recruit 9,000 border-state workers to help with provincial labor shortages.[31]

Getting employers in touch with employees was often a problem, and at one point the Great Northern Railway considered doing something about it. In a letter dated July 24, 1923, railroad executive E. F. Flynn suggested establishing employment agencies in railroad station waiting rooms. "It is the natural place for the office," he wrote, "and I think [it] would promote considerable good feeling between the Company and the farmers." Rejecting Flynn's suggestion, however, a Mr. Budd contended that such a facility would add to congestion at the stations, and Flynn demurred.[32]

For their part, itinerants consulted a network of employment agencies to find work. Hastily set up on both sides of the border, hoboes called such agencies "slave markets." In most instances it was up to the itinerant to get to the job site by walking or "riding the rods." When he arrived at the job site chosen by an agency, he would often find the position filled and be out his two dollar employment fee, or he might be fired within a week to make room for newer arrivals who had paid similar fees to the same agency.[33]

Employment agencies also might charge exorbitant fees and send men to places where jobs did not exist. J. R. Mitchell recalled paying two employment agencies in Vancouver a dollar each. Neither found him a job on either side of the border. Another itinerant said he paid his two dollars to an employment agent, reported to the job, and worked for two days before being fired along with thirty other workers. The grade boss had collected fifty cents for every worker the agency sent; the higher the turnover, the more money both made. Thus workers arriving at a job would meet others walking away who had just been fired.[34]

Men complained of ill treatment from shyster employment agencies on both sides of the border. In 1913 and 1914, the Montana Commission on Labor urged that such agencies be put under state regulation, "or better still they should be abolished entirely." Responding to protests, the Canadian federal government began coordinating statistics on harvest labor requirements in 1920, but not until 1929 did government agencies replace less scrupulous bureaus.[35]

Saloons ran an informal kind of employment agency. Workers could check handwritten bulletins on barroom walls, and if such a notice brought employment, the saloon keeper asked that the recipient drink up part of his pay. Barroom employment notices were common along skid row in Billings and Edmonton.

When out of work, transient laborers sought refuge in cities and towns in a number of ways, and one of the most accommodating places was skid row. Such areas provided a plethora of saloons, free or inexpensive accommodations, cheap food, employment agencies, prostitutes, and anonymity. Dress and physical appearance were of secondary importance, and deviant behavior was tolerated. Adopted from the Pacific Northwest, the term "skid row" originally described the trail down which logs were skidded to the sawmill and along which loggers lived in a community of flophouses, saloons, gambling houses, and other institutions common to the lives of homeless men. Like the term, such areas became common throughout the United States and Canada, and by the late nineteenth century most cities had them. Itinerants appreciated skid row because they provided cheap shelter in the winter as well as cheap newspapers like the *People's World* that commiserated with them about their plight.

Elsewhere, itinerants slept free on the floor at flophouses or paid ten cents for bare wooden bunks. Salvation Army hotels and other missions offered accommodation if boarders listened to a gospel message. The county jail (or "the boodle," as itinerants called it) offered another option to the homeless, especially in smaller towns. Jail at least afforded them refuge and a free bunk. Alfred N. Richards, jailor at Helena's Lewis and Clark County jail, listed many such "boarders" between September 1, 1889, and August 15, 1891, and Canadian sources revealed comparative listings. The practice peaked in the 1890s, but rose or fell with the increase or decline in area employment between the Civil War and the 1920s.[36]

As utilitarian tolerance waned and labor demands changed, however, communities grew less tolerant. Housing hoboes in the local jail came to seem old-fashioned. After the turn of the century, Montana police tended to arrest hoboes. They did so under a vagrancy law passed in 1881 to include "persons who lodged in any barn, shed, outhouse, or other place without the permission of the owner." When vagrants could not pay their fines, deputies put them to work on civil projects. The Hamilton city marshal had them clean streets, and Glasgow police put them to work pulling weeds. At times harsher treatment was used, such as the Dillon police magistrate who put men on the rock pile for twenty-five days.[37]

Leniency also diminished as city residents grew to fear transients. Claiming that drifters brought crime and disorder, newspapers warned citizens to watch their property. Cold weather would bring an influx of hoboes, and newspapers noted that with these "weary Willies" came crime.[38]

Still, depending on the law officer, the custom of "letting beds" at the local jail continued on both sides of the border. Between 1916 and 1918, Bozeman officers "let" 471 beds to homeless men. Dillon police gave them a blanket and directed them to the basement floor of city hall. Canadian jails were often made available for overnight sleeping, but to curtail vagrancy, Canadian authorities created industrial farms not only for vagrants but also for political prisoners, petty thieves, and strikers. Inmates were expected to work for no pay.[39]

Confronted with low wages and wretched working conditions, shunned and patronized by traditional institutions, increasingly unwanted and under pressure from civil authorities, the casual labor force eventually turned to radical ideology, and unions began distributing pamphlets to them, some free of charge and others for nominal prices.

Interest in radicalism was a cross-border phenomenon even before the Industrial Workers of the World was formed. While a member of the Western Federation of Miners in 1901, "Big Bill" Haywood wrote to F. E. Woodside of the Rossland Miners' Union in British Columbia to urge that Woodside encourage workers in their plight. Said Haywood: "There is no 49th parallel of latitude in Unionism—the Canadian and American workingmen have joined hands across the boundary line for a common cause against a common enemy."[40]

With formation of the IWW four years later in 1905, unionists recruited new members in logging camps and among threshing crews. Some in the casual labor force distrusted such efforts; others embraced the union eagerly. Itinerant laborer Joe Opalka said IWW members made life miserable for workers until they joined, but fellow itinerants Joe Holland and Ted Olsen claimed they were not threatened. Others thanked the IWW. Former IWW members in Montana credited the union with making positive changes, such as providing better bunks, clean sheets, blankets, and better toilet facilities in the lumber camps. After World War I, many logging camps upgraded housing and toilet facilities for workers.[41]

That the casual labor force wanted better wages and living conditions more than to overthrow the system was borne out by author and journalist Frederick R. Wedge, who, having heard that the IWW was trying to overthrow the U.S. government, secured a union card and masqueraded as an IWW member. Working in lumber and railroad camps, hoboing, and even going to jail for possession of the IWW card and the "Little Red Songbook," Wedge concluded that workers cared more about improved living conditions and wages than revolution.[42]

As the union gained strength, however, authorities at all levels feared IWW radicalism. As in Montana, IWW strategy in Canada was to effect fundamental social change through confrontation. The IWW, first chartered in Canada in 1906 as the Vancouver Industrial Mixed Union no. 322, soon spread throughout the western provinces. Between 1901 and 1911, the Department of Labor attributed 1,300 strikes to IWW activity. By 1911 the IWW had 47,183 members in western Canada, and by 1912 the union had become a force of consequence in the western provinces with locals as far east as Winnipeg.[43] Canadian prairie farm workers also attracted IWW organizers.

When the IWW exploited a strike of railroad workers on the Grand Trunk Pacific and the Canadian Northern Railroad in the summer of 1912, however, union activities quickly incurred the hatred of politicians and the Canadian press. The official response was stern and swift. U.S. immigration officials began working closely with dominion and provincial police to prevent entry of IWW agitators into Canada, and immigration inspectors worked with Montana officials equally anxious to halt their activities. Officials on both sides of the border arrested anyone who carried the IWW card. Canadians formed One Big Union in 1918, but it lost power in the 1920s, as did the IWW.

By the 1920s, the world of the itinerant laborer was changing as well. Just as technological advances created a world for casual labor in the late nineteenth century, technology transformed that world again in the 1920s and 1930s. After 1870, mechanical threshing machines that brought larger harvests required more laborers. In the timber industry, steam donkeys and steam engines entered the forests, escalating the speed and extent of logging, which in turn required more workers.

By the early twentieth century, however, the idea of superabundance, which had paved the way for rapacious exploitation of natural resources, began giving way to notions of science-based production processes. Faster and more efficient ways of tearing down forests and digging up land were developed, but higher efficiency led to replacing "muscle power" with machine power. The Fordson tractor, introduced in 1917, became the harbinger of modern agribusiness, and by 1919 farmers in the United States owned 158,000 tractors. One tractor replaced several men and horses, and women soon proved they could handle a tractor, too. Similarly, the spread of labor-saving machinery numbered the days of the huge itinerant hay crews. Alexander Campbell McGregor reported that 1929 was the last time his company used large crews of traveling harvest hands and that soliciting laborers from across the Canadian border was no longer necessary. Payroll records showed that within a period of four seasons 529 fewer men (71.7 percent) were hired.[44]

Meanwhile, the automobile changed the nature of travel itself. Migrant workers could buy a jalopy on a share system. Automobiles not only carried workers from place to place but also brought the markets closer to the farm, helping to put an end to rural isolation. During harvest several men were required to pack the wheat into sacks and tie them, but when trucks began carrying wheat in bulk, the need for extra hands at harvest on the bonanza grain ranches declined markedly. In addition, World War I siphoned off the itinerant labor surplus. Men enlisted in the armed forces or pursued better-paying employment in defense industries.[45]

The transition continued after the war. As men of the prewar casual labor force grew older, they began to shun the itinerant life and settle down. Immigrants brought their wives to the states and provinces, and men who had once viewed hoboing as adventurous turned their thoughts to marriage and family.

With steady employment, itinerant workers propelled themselves into better lifestyles, and as the populations of western states and provinces increased, "home guards," willing to take odd jobs but stay at home, manned the mines, fields, and orchards. The wageworkers' frontier receded, and the attraction of radical unionism waned. Stricter immigration laws and customs control restricted the freedom to cross and recross the border. Migratory workers did not disappear, but after the 1920s they were confined increasingly to agriculture.

Despite their modern reputation, hoboes between 1870 and 1910 were seldom ignorant misfits or begging bums who stole for subsistence, but rather working men caught in an endless round of cyclical employment. Many were intelligent, and their writings indicate that when they started on their journeys, they experienced the buoyancy of youth with its hope for adventure and achievement. But for some, dreams were soon shattered by painful exploitation, bitterness, and distrust. Roaming ever and always to look for work, they became a floating army that changed the face of the American and Canadian Wests. Unsung, they nevertheless provided the muscle for the natural resource industries and modern development of the twentieth century.

Notes

This essay is extracted from an article that originally appeared in *Montana: The Magazine of Western History* 49 (Spring 1999): 19–31, and is reprinted here with permission.

1. See, e.g., Mark Wyman, *Hard Rock Epic: Western Miners and the Industrial Revolution, 1860–1910* (Berkeley: University of California Press, 1979); Melvyn Dubofsky, *We Shall Be All: A History of the Industrial Workers of the World* (Chicago: Quadrangle Books, 1969); Carlos A. Schwantes, *Radical Heritage: Labor, Socialism, and Reform in Washington and British Columbia, 1885–1917* (Seattle: University of Washington Press, 1979); Paul A. Phillips, *No Power Greater: A Century of Labour in British Columbia* (Vancouver: BC Federation of Labour, 1967); Cecilia Danysk, *Hired Hands: Labour and Development of Prairie Agriculture, 1880–1930* (Toronto: McClelland and Stewart, 1995); and Greg Hall, *Harvest Wobblies: The Industrial Workers of the World and Agricultural Laborers in the American West, 1905–1930* (Corvallis: Oregon State University Press, 2001).

2. Carleton Parker, *The Casual Laborer and Other Essays* (1920; reprint, New York: Russell and Russell, 1967), 17, 74–79; State of Washington, Bureau of Labor, *Eleventh Annual Report, 1917–1918* (Olympia: State of Washington, 1918), 74; Rolf Knight, *Indians at Work: An Informal History of Native Indian Labour in British Columbia, 1858–1930* (Vancouver: New Star Books, 1978).

3. George Alvin Isaac, "Sourdough and Side Bacon," ms, 3, 20–28, W/Is/I, British Columbia Provincial Archives, Vancouver (BCPA); Otto Kola, interview with David L. Myers, December 4, 1975, p. 11, PAC 75–28dm, Oral/Aural History Program, Washington State Archives, Olympia.

4. Ernest Hubert Allcock, reminiscence, pp. 20–28, Add. Mss 723, BCPA; Parker, *Casual Laborer*, 113.

5. Dean Stiff, *The Milk and Honey Route: A Handbook for Hoboes* (New York: Vanguard Press, 1931), 32; Andrew Roddan, *Canada's Untouchables: The Story of a Man without a Home* (Vancouver: Clark and Stewart, 1932), 15–25; Robert A. Burns, *Knights of the Road: A Hobo History* (New York: Methuen, 1980), 100; Max Wilson interview with David L. Myers, January 26, 1975, PAC 76–32dm, Washington State Archives, Olympia; Alan Pinkerton, *Strikers, Communists, Tramps, and Detectives* (New York: G. W. Carleton, 1878), 140–80; Donald Duke, "The Railroad Tramp," *American Railroad Journal* 1 (1967–68): 33–45.

6. Bill Fisher, former employee, Southern Pacific Railroad, interview with author, August 1992.

7. F. W. Godsal, reminiscence, p. 1, SC 748, Montana Historical Association, Helena (MHA); Basil Oswin Robinson, reminiscence, Add. Mss 197, BCPA.

8. Simon "Sam" Johnson, interview with Penelope Lucas, OH 527, MHA; John Jennings letters, SC 23, MHA; William O. Douglas, *Go East Young Man: The Early Years* (New York: Random House, 1974), 76–78.

9. Fred T. Barrett Diary, 1900–1919, pp. 10–20, MG8B13, Manitoba Historical Archives, Winnipeg; John Thompson, letter, pp. 5–6, mss. 2659, BCPA.

10. Clark C. Spence, "Knights of the Tie and Rail," *American Heritage* 27 (August 1965): 10; Northern Pacific Railroad records, boxes 138H.8.7(F) and (B), and 137H.17.9(B), Minnesota Historical Society, St. Paul.

11. Alvin Pearson reminiscences, pp. 10–52, Special Collections, Nebraska State Historical Society, Lincoln; James L. Mitchell, "A Hobo on the CPR," *Alberta History* 33 (Winter 1985): 14–27; Archibald S. Kerr, autobiography, BCPA.

12. Edward Hula, p. 14, OH 722, MHA; Nels Anderson, *The Hobo: The Sociology of the Homeless Man* (Chicago: University of Chicago Press, 1923), 17–21; Stiff, *Milk and Honey*, 21.

13. Carlos A. Schwantes, "Concept of the Wageworkers' Frontier: A Framework for Further Study," *Western Historical Quarterly* 18 (January 1987): 45; Abigail Mitton, OH 678, and Bert Wilke, OH 662, MHA; Winnifred J. Burt, "My Pioneer Days in Saskatchewan," and Clara Hughes, "My Pioneer Days in Saskatchewan," essays file, R-E 514, Zonta Club of Regina Papers, Saskatchewan Archives Board, Regina; Edna Patterson, interview with author, July 1986, Elko NV.

14. James Mastin, R-E687, p. 3, accession #R80–552, Saskatchewan Archives Board, Regina;

Mary Kanduch, OH 415, Pauline Harmon, OH 166, Minnie Sampson Christensen, OH 407, MHA; Sadye Wolfe Drew reminiscence, pp. 6–32, SC 1532, MHA.

15. Thompson letter, 8; Roddan, *Canada's Untouchables,* 15–25; Stiff, *Milk and Honey,* 161.

16. C. L. Hansen-Bret, "Ladies in Scarlet: An Historical Overview of Prostitution in Victoria, British Columbia, 1870–1939," pp. 15–21, mss collection, BCPA; James H. Gray, *Red Lights on the Prairies* (Toronto: Macmillan of Canada, 1971), 10–17; Anne Butler, *Daughters of Joy, Sisters of Mercy: Prostitutes in the American West* (Urbana: University of Illinois Press, 1987).

17. Ethel Lynn, *The Adventures of a Woman Hobo* (New York: George H. Doran, 1917), 2; Ben L. Reitman, *Sisters of the Road: The Autobiography of Box-Car Bertha* (1937; reprint, New York: Harper and Row, 1975), 13–15; Glenda Riley, *A Place to Grow: Women in the American West* (Arlington Heights IL: Harlan Davidson, 1992), 173; Gray, *Red Lights on the Prairies,* 173.

18. Roddan, *Canada's Untouchables,* 15–25, 27.

19. Charles Kennedy, p. 11, OH 266, and Earle Marsh, OH 344, MHA.

20. Kerr autobiography, 12–49, BCPA.

21. State of Montana, Third Biennial Report of the Department of Labor and Industry, 1917–18 (Helena: State of Montana, 1918), 46–58; Labour records ephemera, BCPA; Allcock reminiscence, 7–8; "Report of Alberta Coal Mining Industry Commission, December 23, 1910," United Mine Workers of America, District 18 Papers, Glenbow-Alberta Institute, Calgary; Richard A. Rajala, "Bill and the Box: Labor Protest, Technological Change, and the Transformation of the West Coast Logging Camp," *Journal of Forest History* 33 (October 1989): 170; Howard Henderson, retired high-rigger, interview with author, July 1991, Port Alberni, BC.

22. Edmund S. Bradwin, *The Bunkhouse Man: A Study of Work and Pay in the Camps of Canada, 1903–1914* (Toronto: University of Toronto Press, 1984), 29–58.

23. Allcock reminiscence, 21; Marsh interview; C. D. N. Taylor, "Nothing Down," ms., pp. 1–31, manuscript archives, BCPA.

24. Will Irwin, "The Floating Laborer," *Saturday Evening Post,* May 9, 1914, 4–5, 43–49.

25. Josiah Flynt Willard, "How Men Became Tramps: Conclusions from Personal Experience as an Amateur Tramp," *Century* 50 (October 1895): 945; John W. McKinley, SC 34, MHA; Barrett Diary, 10–20; Bodington reminiscence, 24.

26. Godsal reminiscence, 1.

27. Bella Blackburn, interview with Gerald Panting, 1953, p. 1, Farm Methods File, Manitoba Historical Archives, Winnipeg; Frederick W. Stewart Diaries, 1892–1902, Add. Mss 137, BCPA; Hollenbeck interview.

28. Phillips, *No Power Greater,* 40–49; Canadian Federal Royal Commission reports, p. 104, Add. Mss 1899, BCPA. Editor's note: Canada's Alien Labor Act of 1879 was geared toward preventing the hiring of contract and scab labor outside of Canada.

29. Rossland Miners' Union #38 Papers, BCPA.

30. W. L. Hagler to Sir Wilfrid Laurier, November 11, 1899, BCPA.

31. David Jay Bercuson, "Labour Radicalism and the Industrial Western Frontier: 1897–1919," *Canadian Historical Review* 58 (June 1977): 154–75; Donald Avery, *Dan-*

gerous Foreigners: European Immigrant Workers and Labour Radicalism in Canada (Toronto: McClelland and Stewart, 1979), 11.

32. E. F. Flynn to Mr. Budd, July 24, 1923, and Budd to Flynn, n.d., 19E114F, Great Northern Railway files, Minnesota Historical Society, St. Paul.

33. Eustace Smith, Add. Mss 331, BCPA; Kola interview, 11–15.

34. J. R. Mitchell, p. 17, SC 30, MHA; Irwin, "The Floating Laborer," 5.

35. State of Montana, *First Biennial Report of the Department of Labor and Industry, 1913* (Helena: State of Montana, 1913), 14–22.

36. Alfred N. Richards, Lewis and Clark County Sheriff Records, August 3, 1899–August 12, 1891, SC 1185, MHA; Bill Bowser Papers, North-West Mounted Police mss., BCPA.

37. Legislative Assembly of the Territory of Montana, *Laws of the Territory of Montana, 1881* (Helena: State of Montana, 1881), 81; Jeff Kolnick, interview with author, July 1991, St. Paul, MN; Larry V. Bishop, "Law, Order, and Reform in the Gallatin, 1893–1918," *Montana: The Magazine of Western History* 30 (Spring 1980): 19.

38. Kalispell Bee, October 31, 1902; Whitefish Pilot, November 19, 1904.

39. Magistrate Records, Bozeman Police Department Daily Log, 1916–18, Bozeman MT; Manitoba Industrial Prison Farm Records, F4901 #1, Manitoba Legislative Library, Winnipeg.

40. In David Jay Bercuson, "The One Big Union in Washington," *Pacific Northwest Quarterly* 169 (July 1987): 127.

41. Joe Opalka, OH 724, J. R. Rambo, OH 438, Joe Holland and Ted Olsen, OH 257, MHA; Rajala, "Bill and the Box," 168–79.

42. Frederick R. Wedge, *Inside the IWW* (Berkeley: F. R. Wedge, 1924), 10.

43. Marianne Morris, Add. Mss 971, BCPA; Allcock reminiscence, 36–40; Bercuson, "Labour Radicalism," 154–75; Industrial Workers of the World, *The History of the IWW in Canada*, pamphlet (Chicago: IWW, n.d.), 1.

44. Alexander Campbell McGregor, *Counting Sheep: From Open Range to Agribusiness in the Columbia Plateau* (Seattle: University of Washington Press, 1982), appendix.

45. Thomas D. Isern, *Bull Threshers and Bindlestiffs: Harvesting and Threshing on the North American Plains* (Lawrence: University Press of Kansas, 1990), 10–22.

13. "Nature's Garden and a Possible Utopia"

Farming for Fruit and Industrious Men in the Transboundary Pacific Northwest, 1895–1914

Jason Patrick Bennett

Amid historical images of prairie homesteaders, West Coast bushwhackers, and inland hard-rock miners, the dawn of the twentieth century bore witness to a lesser-known but equally dramatic alteration of social and natural landscapes in the North American West. Within numerous arid valleys that dotted the region, diverted streams and harnessed rivers nourished blossoming fruit farms and the dreams that brought thousands of settlers to tend them. Framed by enchanting images of comfort and plenty, glowing brochures and pamphlets extolled the wondrous wealth and cultured virtues of horticulture in Oregon, Washington, and British Columbia. By 1900 the area was in the grips of a fruit fever as government, land developers, and railway companies conducted a boisterous promotion that found parallels on both sides of the border. In a real sense, "the Boundary" separating the American republic and the British colony served as a mirror and a window in shaping reflections that were both familiar and alien.

Invested with overtones of a biblical paradise, the feminized landscape of the Pacific Northwest organized an agricultural utopia that was extolled as the rightful domain of industrious "white" men defined by the qualities of intelligence and refinement. Central to the character of this blossoming empire was the belief that purity of race and the absence of labor strife were assured by the ascendancy of nature and science in peaceful union, carefully managed by progressive farmers. As a principal actor in this vision, the farmer was nonetheless affected by the region's natural environment as it both impressed upon and was modified by boosters and settlers, forging in its wake a new "genteel man" that embodied a sensitivity to the sublime beauty of nature in balance with an abiding faith in scientific knowledge. Although it provided industrial society with powerful tools to exploit the natural world, fruit farmers believed science could also be used to further nature's "intended design." In this way, horticulture represented both a rejection of industrial excess and an affirmation of scientific values, just as settlers embraced the natural environment as the key to salvation while celebrating their ability to manage it.

Long plagued by the specter of a crude frontier determinism, western history has benefited from an increasingly influential group of scholars championing a new environmental awareness in our collective histories.[1] While it is true that the stock image of an egalitarian West has been long dismantled by historians attentive to the role of conflict and inequality under the rubric of New Western History, environmental historians such as Richard White have argued persuasively for the need to fashion a history that recognizes "the reciprocal influences of a changing nature and a changing society."[2] Nevertheless, debates over "place" and "process" confirm Donald Worster's assertion that despite banishing "frontier" from our historical lexicon, Frederick Jackson Turner still "presides over western history like a Holy Ghost."[3] Critical as we may be within recent historiography, it is my assertion that, contrary to our stock image of Turner's West, contemporaries of the late nineteenth century were intensely aware of inequality and conflict as evidenced in their concerted drive to transform both nature and society. In other words, the "innocent" West emerged precisely because colonizers encountered resistance and conflict, whether social, economic, or environmental.

By conducting a comparative examination, I hope to expand our frame of reference and gain insight into how these promoters and settlers imagined themselves and their relations to their natural surroundings both locally and across "the boundary." The 1846 agreement between Britain and the United States to extend the border along the forty-ninth parallel and through the disputed Oregon Country not only ignored the territorial realities of several First Nations, including the Okanagans, but subsequently fostered an isolationist tendency in American and Canadian historiography. In other words, the convenience of the border in framing national stories has occluded cross-border influences and linked histories. The establishment of fruit farming communities throughout the region in the late nineteenth century is one such "linked history" that demands further attention.

Within the Anglo-American world of this period, technological change and social dislocation fostered comparable middle-class insecurities about working-class militancy and the decline of Christian civilization. Similarly, the growth of capital investment, transportation technologies, and territorial governments in the Pacific Northwest facilitated a booster ethos that found a receptive audience among men and women longing for escape into a realm ruled by "Dame Nature." Among the orchards, financial prosperity would be secured alongside cultural and physical rejuvenation. This was particularly important for "white" men, since it was believed that isolation from the natural world was threatening to undermine his civilizing control and moral fortitude. By fusing the benefits of nature with the advances of scientific knowledge, a new society would be cultivated in the Pacific Northwest. [4] While previous writings tend to emphasize the role of shrewd and calculating boosters who capitalized on a middle-class longing for country living, I argue that other cultural constructs must be reexamined to appreciate fully the attraction and belief in fruit farming as a settlement process and vocation. Critical to our understanding is how the environment was marshaled and altered to sustain the ideal of a natural empire home to "industrious men, beautiful women, and merry children." [5] Indeed, the utopian vision of nature and society fostered by boosters and settlers fueled this transformative process, only to erode in the face of ecological and social challenges, often with unintended consequences.

In the context of forging competing identities, this corner of North America is unique, since both British Columbia and the American Pacific Northwest enjoyed simultaneous population growth by promoting and establishing the same agricultural practice on a large scale. The settlements that were forged in its wake continued to marginalize First Nations, which began with the transition from a fur-trade economy in the 1840s, followed by the successive gold rushes that migrated from California to the Yukon. By the end of this period, the move to promote a settler society began in earnest. While the colonization of British Columbia remained relatively uneven until the early 1900s, the growth of communities in the Pacific Northwest was already thirty years in the making, accounting for the earlier formation of commercial fruit farming. Despite these differences, both sides of the boundary engaged in an aggressive promotional campaign during a period that Canadian geographer Cole Harris characterized as "fruit-mad days" for the middle class.[6] A significant tool in achieving population growth was the production of promotional literature by government agencies, local boards of trade, and private developers. The principal aim of these materials was to make the new venture of commercial fruit farming appear familiar by framing it in a language and cultural framework that celebrated rural values and rural living. While promises of fantastic wealth from the cultivation and sale of fruit resonated powerfully, the cultural attributes of fruit farming undoubtedly played a pivotal role in encouraging people to identify with fruit farming not only as a vocation but also as a lifestyle.

Despite their location in different political projects, the rural imagination in British Columbia and the American Pacific Northwest share a surprising affinity. Born of a general period marked by rapid industrial expansion and urbanization, social commentators began a public dialogue about the potential pitfalls of unbridled progress. The linking of industry with overcrowded cities, class strife, and social instability gained increasing currency, as did the association of the city with moral failings and temptations.[7] Against this backdrop of middle-class fear, a renewed interest in the countryside began to take shape. In the realm of education, Ernest Thompson Seton helped form a legacy of outdoor instruction for young boys with his establishment of the Woodcraft Indians, soon followed by the founding of the Boy Scouts of America with Robert Baden-Powell and William Boyce in 1910.[8] Concurrently, the utility of outdoor recreation in maintaining a vibrant manhood found more adherents with the promotion of sport throughout America and the British Empire.[9]

While making campfires and playing rugby had their utility, the urban environment remained unaltered. To be truly successful in revitalizing society, commentators and planners reexamined urban space and planning. Notions of incorporating nature and the city helped spur the extension of green space, allowing Frederick Law Olmsted to refashion urban design with creations such as New York's Central Park and Montreal's Mount Royal.[10] More radical plans, such as those penned by Sir Ebenezer Howard, called for the creation of garden cities where curved lanes and trimmed hedges would infuse a peaceable existence so that class antagonisms between labor and the bourgeoisie would "naturally" dissipate. For at least twenty years Howard's ideas continued to resonate among middle-class reformers and government officials, prompting elected officials in U.S. Senate and the Canadian House of Commons to examine the potential success and impact of Howard's ideas in the New World.[11] Interest in reformulating the relationship between nature and society can also be linked to the burgeoning conservation movement in the United States and Canada. In both countries, support for more parks and protected areas was buttressed by a growing popular belief in the regenerative powers of wilderness for its human visitors, echoing John Muir's view that parks were useful "not only as fountains of timber . . . but as fountains of life."[12]

On this axis between progress and nostalgia, the lure and promise of fruit farming held sway over countless minds convinced of the need for the bracing influences of nature in human life. Rather than tinkering with the aesthetics of urban space with parks and boulevards, fruit farming was planted squarely in a rural experience that combined the lifestyle of rustic living with the wholesome, progressive occupation of farming. Infused with divine providence, the natural purity of the countryside would ensure that the errors of human society would be corrected thanks to one's close association with the natural environment. The intimate relationship between social harmony and nature found widespread currency, prompting one contemporary observer to admonish "The farther we wander from the guidance of Dame Nature, the farther we are from perfection; the more we deviate from *her* ways, the more precarious our progress."[13] Although in this guise fruit farming appears categorically anti-modern— that is, a rejection of industrialism and capitalism—reflections of paradise were traded and sold in an imperial world and market system that was firmly grounded in the modern project. In many arid locales, the process of establishing fruit farms was only made possible with the tools of modern technology, such as the creation of integrated irrigation systems, not to mention the steam and rail that made these far-flung settlements accessible to the outside world. In this way, the image of fruit farming negotiated these tensions to produce a new vision of modernism—a vision that combined promises of fantastic profits and dreams of nature's harmonious bounty.

At the same time, raising fruit presented men with an alternative masculine archetype that has been neglected in our examination of a gendered West. At the risk of simplification, historians have explicitly or implicitly contrasted a masculine "violence" with a feminine "domesticity." In her book *The Land Before Her*, Annette Kolodny contrasts men's violent fantasies in conquering virgin wilderness with women's dream of home and community in a cultivated garden. More recently, Glenda Riley echoes a similar theme, arguing in *Women and Nature* that women "created a docile West that could, and should, be gentled" because of a European heritage that "encouraged women to save and protect their families, cultures, and surroundings" in contrast to men's conditioning to "exploit western lands." [14] Of course, from an environmental and social perspective, domestication can be just as disruptive and violent as a more overt process of conquering, but my current concern is to argue that men were also architects and proponents of a "gentled" West through the vocation of fruit farming. Alongside images of rugged cowboys and manly sportsmen, visions of patient farmers tending their blossoming gardens found enthusiastic adherents who transformed the landscape of the transboundary Pacific Northwest.

Dreams of Eden are a recurring motif in the history of North America. From the earliest period of European colonization, comparisons with the garden described in the book of Genesis appeared in the accounts of government officials, missionaries, settlers, and entrepreneurs. In the early twentieth century, these allusions found dramatic expression with the idea and promotion of fruit farming in British Columbia, Oregon, and Washington. In many instances, the myth of Eden is often introduced informally, with extensive references to making the land into a "continuous garden." More directly, an Okanagan brochure claimed that "instead of the 'Lost Garden of Eden,' as [British Columbia] has been termed, it is a newly-found earthly paradise. Nature's offering to the man who wants to really know life." Similarly, an American writer penned that fruit farming "is a pleasant occupation, in a sense carrying one back to Eden."[15] Describing the appeal of fruit farming in the Pacific Northwest, another author traces its divine antecedents for his audience, reciting how the Creator had "laid out the Garden of Eden and planted trees for ornament as well as for fruit." In a fortuitous parallel with current fruit promotion efforts, the author reveals how God placed "the first couple [within the Garden] and intended them to be horticulturalists." With clear implications for contemporary society, we learn that Adam and Eve "were happy as long as they remained in their country home. But in an evil hour, they left it, and ever since man has striven to place those who were given him to love and care for in a similar Garden of Eden."[16] Whether invoked directly or indirectly, allusions to Eden not only suggest divine approval of fruit farming but also illustrate how horticulture could find appeal among Christians inclined to commune with God and nature through their very vocation. Naturally, it also served as a convenient method of elevating the potentially corruptive practice of selling land to a realm less crudely economic and profit oriented.

On a broader level, Edenic images of nature spoke to personal health, whether spiritual or physical. The preoccupation with health also revealed middle-class fears of the declining moral fabric of society that threatened to undermine the maintenance of the Dominion and the Republic, respectively. Whether considering a move to British Columbia's Okanagan Valley or Oregon's Hood River Valley, concern with health found equally creative expression. Extolling the benefits of pure air and the absence of climatic extremes such as heat and cold, "and the consequent freedom from malaria," a Canadian booster proclaimed British Columbia "a vast sanitarium" where settlers "invariably improve your health" while "insomnia and nervous afflictions find alleviation, the old and infirm are granted a renewed lease of life, and children thrive as in few other parts of the world."[17] Without a doubt, the relationship between a benevolent natural world and physical health are prominent themes of the rural imagination on both sides of the boundary. During an age when sudden and fatal illnesses were commonplace, a preoccupation with health is clearly understandable. Middle-class views were consequently very receptive to arguments promoting the healing virtues of rural life in both countries.

The wondrous effects of a healthful climate compelled a Washington writer to argue "a more equable climate than Wenatchee does not exist. Its invigorating qualities impart a glow to the blood and a springiness to the step. There are no sudden changes with the revolving seasons."[18] Pleasant climes invariably found easy association with good health for boosters and settlers alike. And a healthy social harmony was never too far in the background, such as when a Summerland, British Columbia, promoter bragged that "to our balmy climate are added skies of Italian blue, woodlands of Arcadian beauty, mountains and canyons of mighty grandeur, valleys and benches of chanting contour, ripping and placid waters, myriad Orchards of luscious fruits, while crowing all are the happy homes of industrious men, beautiful women and merry children."[19]

The industrious man at the center of the happy home was following in the footsteps of Adam toward a possible Utopia. Guided by both art and reason, the fruit farmer embodied the principles of modern scientific progress with sensitivity to the sublime beauty of creation. An Oregon writer proffered that "there is an inseparable companionship between trees and man not readily accounted for, and there are few men who lack the desire to plant and surround themselves with trees." Another promoter gave credit to the "gentle orchardists" of Wenatchee for transforming the arid land into an "ideal haven of peace, plenty, and prosperity— the highest example of modern civilization."[20] Among Canadians, the remarks of Lord Grey enjoyed further popularity when he observed that with fruit farming "qualities of mind are necessary . . . which are not so essential to success in wheat growing or ordinary mixed farming."[21] Lord Grey's careful distinctions would not have gone unnoticed among practitioners of that higher art, since wheat farming was held in contempt by many British Canadians for its association with Ukrainians and Poles settling on the Canadian prairies. Although eastern Europeans might succeed where earlier British settlers failed, the traits of masculine refinement and intelligence demanded by horticulture ensure that Anglo-Canadians would be the sole inheritors of this ancient vocation.

The argument that fruit farming provided an ideal environment for the cultivation of a healthy people invariably elicited ideas of order and racial purity. With little doubt, the invitation to build strong, healthy communities among the orchards suggested that fruit farming should be reserved for "superior" men to the exclusion of all others. Environmental ramifications extended well beyond a healthy glow to affect the nature of society itself. In addition to local boosters, state politicians such as Colorado governor Alva Adams mused, "The climate and conditions that are best for apples are best for man. Anarchy never gathered fruit from its own apple tree."[22] Historical agrarian revolts notwithstanding, Governor Adams's sociological assessment emerged north of the border as well. In the Canadian context, aristocratic enthusiasm reached a new crescendo with the widely published views of Lord Grey, who remarked that fruit farming was "a most beautiful art" cultivated by "a refined and cultured class of people—the finest class on earth."[23] Fruit farmers were not violent brutes steeped in ignorance but men practicing an art that required intelligence and careful discipline.

As much as they were rooted in rebirth and new beginnings, visions of the natural environment buttressed rather than undermined Anglo-American fears and prejudices. Elaborating on the relationship between environment and human development, one booster suggested that the climatic similarities between British Columbia and "the cradle of the greatest nations of the world" provided irrefutable proof that, like Europe, the province possessed "the climate best adapted to the development of the human race."[24] In this manner, the rural imagination rationalized a racial superiority that excluded all of those deemed unworthy, whether First Nations, Chinese, or African American. In British Columbia, these concerns assumed explicit form, such as when a Kelowna author rejoiced that the local population was "chiefly English and Canadians of British descent." Similarly a Medford, Oregon, author assured the reader that the Rogue River Valley "is distinctly an American settlement . . . of the best class. There are no colonies of Japanese, Chinese, Hindoos, or Negroes to lower the standard of labor and of American civilization."[25] Thus the sense of social stability that Governor Adams and Lord Grey perceived in horticulture justified the exclusion of nonwhite settlers, since its basis lay in the "natural law" of the nonhuman environment. At once prejudice was elevated from the realm of ignorance to the will of the Creator as expressed in men's rational husbandry of the land.

In a departure from their northern counterparts, however, American settlers and promoters nurtured the politics of Progressivism upon a foundation of agrarian Republicanism. Evoking the spirit of Thomas Jefferson, one Oregon writer warned that "America would degenerate as soon as it ceased to be an agricultural and horticultural nation" due to the coming of "greed and money," casting the fruit farmer as a progressive guarantor of American democracy.[26] Others still found purpose in echoing the general themes of spiritual and moral regeneration stemming from the Progressive movement. A Wenatchee brochure trumpeted that fruit farming was "a good illustration of the fact that legitimate commercial enterprise is the handmaid of the social and moral uplift of the people. Within the ranks of the United States Reclamation Service, statistician C. J. Blanchard remarked, "May not our [Yakima] desert develop new systems of ethics and morals to lead us back from the material and spiritual into ways of gentleness and simple living?"[27]

Simple living in orchard communities in British Columbia often translated into regal living, complete with morning fox hunts, afternoon polo matches, and evenings at the opera. Unlike communities to the south, fruit farming in British Columbia attracted a significant influx of middle-class Britons from the British Isles and eastern Canada in addition to native-born Canadians. The result saw many communities bear the distinctive imprint of their British patrons, compete with familiar pastimes and associations from the Old Country.[28] While their conceptions of nature had roots in the Romantic visions of Wordsworth and Shelley, settlers were keenly aware of fruit farming's aristocratic heritage thanks to figures such as Lord Aberdeen and Lord Grey. During their appointment as governors-general of Canada, both men established orchards in British Columbia, a fact oft-repeated in print and speech. Dreams of imperial privilege and cultured status rather than yeoman-style democracy found ample expression within the discourse of fruit farming and rural living in British Columbia.

Nevertheless, a similar belief in the importance of fruit farming for the future of humanity was echoed among government officials, promoters, and farmers in the Dominion. Maxwell Smith, editor of *Fruit Magazine* in Vancouver, British Columbia, railed against public education in Canada and the United States claiming that the curricula were to blame for "the deserting of the land, the spoiling of good farmers, and the creation of poor preachers, lawyers, and doctors." According to Smith, the future of upright young boys was at stake, since skewed school programs meant that a young man would "not get a fair idea of the desirability and the joys of the beauty of the study of Nature as he ought." The result was an army of unemployed men who drifted from city to city, divorced from the land and the purifying benefits of agriculture as the backbone of the nation-state. The association between horticulture and the ideal male citizen came easily to fruit farmers, and few opportunities were passed up to reiterate this relationship. There is little doubt that Smith would have endorsed one such epigram that circulated among members of the Oregon State Horticultural Society that read, "Apple orchards are better nurseries of citizenship than the deck of battleships or military camps."[29]

If apple orchards were nurseries, then annual horticultural fairs and exhibitions were finishing schools, bringing together communities in friendly competition where ornate displays served to reinforce a sense of masculine sophistication and feminine bounty. The organization of exhibits was an exhaustive process, requiring an enormous amount of effort from farmers to pay, organize, transport, and set up their entries, often at great expense. In a moment of common cause that transcended borders, communities throughout the Pacific Northwest rallied to participate in regional, national, and international competitions to display the bounty of their natural environments. It was in these venues that farmers and officials judged not only the quality of fruit and its presentation but also its reflection upon the men behind each community exhibit. Those who prospered at these competitions served as valuable examples to entrants that fell short of the mark. As one fruit exhibitor remarked, "The man who has not been able to put his stuff just right is able to see wherein he has failed."[30] Displaying fruit was never just about arranging produce, but stood as a testament to the "artistic manner" of men who were not afraid of tying colorful bows to their displays and arranging delicately hundreds of crimson apples to achieve just the right shine. Good apples and good men went together.

According to promoters and orchardists in Canada and the United States, it would not be enough to bask in the warm glow of a summer's sunset of Arcadia. Ever aware of the modern world and modern civilization, writers and settlers emphasized the importance of progressive science in cultivating a new man among the valleys of the Pacific Northwest. For many, the technological embodiment of this practical intelligence was the miracle of irrigation that unlocked arid inland interiors and transformed them into lush gardens and fertile valleys. No longer would men find themselves the hapless victims of a nature they did not understand. According to the father of the irrigation movement, William Smythe, irrigation "is a religious rite. Such a prayer for rain is intelligent, scientific, and worthy of man's divinity." To put knowledge in the place of superstition is the first step which men take in entering into partnership with God." [31] The perceived gift of irrigation was freeing people from dependence upon the weather by providing farmers with the ability to water their crops with techniques rooted in the latest advances of farm management. Equally important to transforming deserts was Smythe's argument that irrigation fostered a cooperative spirit and close association between men as they came together out of environmental necessity. The American West would finally blossom into a long series of beautiful villages, making it difficult "for the beholder to say where the town ends and the country begins."[32] In this manner, the power of irrigation not only held out the promise of rationalizing the natural environment through enlightened management, but it also spoke to the celebration of educated men intent on forging communities in connection with their natural surroundings, rather than against it.

The progressive air surrounding Smythe's vision of scientific irrigation translated easily into the language and vision of horticulturalists, especially since many fruit districts were the product of extensive irrigation systems. Whether early family farmers in Washington's Yakima Valley or hopeful settlers in British Columbia's Okanagan Valley, the quest for good water and good men went hand-in-hand. Throughout the region settlers and boosters organized irrigation schemes supported by cooperative organizations or private corporations. In both countries settlers agitated for an expanded role of local and federal governments in the construction and maintenance of irrigation projects due to prohibitive costs, engineering difficulties, and labor shortages. South of the border, both Democrats and Republicans fashioned pro-irrigation planks in their party platforms by 1900. This political consensus ushered the passage of the National Reclamation Act of 1902 and the creation of the Reclamation Service charged with "reclaiming" arid lands for human use, a mission that dovetailed with dreams of fruited valleys. Across the border, provincial government officials became increasingly responsive to agitating farmers who were chafing under poorly managed irrigation works operated by private business, leading to a revised Water Act in 1914 and direct involvement in irrigation schemes by 1920. [33] These venues provided further reinforcement that irrigation was more than a method of delivering water but a technique to transform the environment and social relations as well. In British Columbia, the Western Canadian Irrigation Association proudly bore the motto on its 1912 program, "Intelligent men no longer pray for rain—they pay for it." Evoking the time of the Pharaohs, the Wenatchee Commercial Club predicted, "As the Valley of the Nile under irrigation became the seat of the highest type of ancient civilization, so will the Valley of the Columbia under irrigation become . . . the most advanced modern civilization." [34]

Critical to the maintenance of this industrious man was an extensive infrastructure of institutions and associations that provided opportunities for social discourse and the exchange of technical expertise. Local community newspapers served such a purpose with their daily discussion of fruit-related issues, whether economic conditions in overseas markets or the prospects for a generous harvest. A vibrant publishing industry also arose around the subject of fruit farming, offering an assortment of texts ranging from guides for prospective settlers to manuals illustrating the successful sorting and packing of fruit. [35] To contend with changing practices and challenges, agricultural colleges in Britain and Canada eagerly established programs to educate farmers on the issues ranging from careful pruning to the selection of appropriate stock. In Washington and Oregon, the creation of colleges in rural districts was motivated by the desire to ensure agricultural programs were available to newly arrived farmers in the expanding fruit districts. Other venues such as the YMCA provided evening instruction to young men on the demands and requirements of prosperous orchardists. [36] In addition, local boards of trade and farmer organizations were vital institutional forums for the reaffirmation of fruit farming's primacy as a social and ecological reality. State and provincial governments on both sides of the boundary established and funded agricultural experiment stations with resident experts who identified and catalogued ideal soil compositions for various fruits that might be grown in the Pacific Northwest. When examining fruit stocks, researchers tested the suitability of particular fruit species for regional climatic conditions as well as resistance to various ecological dangers such as vulnerability to pests and blight. The findings of these experiment stations in places such as Summerland, British Columbia, and Pullman, Washington, were followed closely by horticultural associations and chambers of commerce and quickly disseminated among fruit farmers. In keeping with the industrious man, these stations personified the unification of science in the service of "perfecting" nature or, in the words of William Smythe, "finishing nature's work."

The work of these experiment stations appears to have accelerated the trend toward monoculture in the Pacific Northwest, with apples as the main preference. However, a move toward a monocultural model left farmers vulnerable to potentially devastating infestations that could spread through hundreds of acres with alarming speed. Areas that were originally heralded as "pest-free," such as the Okanagan Valley, were soon home to new organisms like the coddling moth, thanks to the movement of rail cars from infested regions.[37] Not to be defeated, horticulturalists turned to these same experiment stations for the latest advice on applying arsenic to eradicate these organisms. However, the persistence of such organisms remained an uncomfortable reminder that the progressive farmer could not always "finish" nature to his desired end.

Economic competition and the enormous expenses faced by growers in getting their fruit to market fueled the establishment of local cooperatives responsible for the packing and transportation of crops. Through these mediums and situations, farmers were once again instilled with their particular sense of masculine identity in spite of economic and environmental difficulties that challenged the ideals of cooperation and brotherly harmony.

Although irrigation was a network for both agricultural and human growth, the business of constructing water systems and nourishing orchards threatened to accomplish the opposite. In many areas, such as British Columbia's Okanagan Valley, labor shortages plagued the establishment and expansion of fruit farming districts. As early as 1890, the Aberdeens turned to the local Indians as a source of labor. Although Lady Aberdeen initially observed that Indians performed agricultural work "far better than the white people or Chinese," racist attitudes continued to construct an image of the Indian as lazy, drunk, and unreliable.[38] Consequently, as "white" labor began to increase during the settlement period, settlers increasingly turned against their early laborers. But in a familiar scene twenty years later, the *Kelowna Daily Courier and Okanagan Orchardist* pronounced, "Labouring men are in great demand, owing to the commencement of work on so many large irrigation projects this spring." Despite the promise of growth such work promised, "so far, the supply [of labor] is entirely insufficient, and the companies are at a loss what to do, as they are loathe to import Orientals."[39] Once young orchards began to produce fruit in five to seven years, the need for labor to pick and sort fruit became even more acute. In scenes repeated throughout the region, orchardists met at the local Farmers' Exchange to learn that "fruit packers are badly needed . . . and a young man is allowing a golden opportunity to slip by."[40] Fear of the dreaded "Asiatic" made the need for "good" labor a constant refrain throughout the Pacific Northwest. While such prejudices were common throughout both countries, the dream of reclaiming paradise made the objective of excluding "undesirables" particularly urgent.

Intimately related to issues of race and labor was the theme of sexuality. With little doubt, appeals to Eden's first family and allusions to "beautiful women" demonstrated the appropriateness of fruit farming for married men. Allusions to wholesome communities of upstanding citizens also prefigured the family as the fundamental building block of these rural societies. While men were certainly the primary audience of these promotional appeals, the vocation of fruit farming betrays a feminine landscape that allowed men to imagine the land as both mother and seductress. In one Oregon brochure, the author speculates that as men approach their later years, "they feel a strong, overmastering desire to spend [their] later years and die in the country, on the bosom of the great mother of us all, generous, teeming earth."[41] As outlined earlier, the earth was also a great mother in sustaining the family through nourishment and a pleasant environment. The feminized land is further illustrated with numerous photographs depicting young girls and women donning white summer dresses among the neatly rowed trees of the orchard. More than the markers of family or blissful escape, the young girls personify the womanly blossoming of the land. These depictions are plentiful and find equal expression in both Canadian and American settings.

Men's sexualized relationship with the land was also expressed in prose, poetry, and song. However, these displays are more prevalent with the Pacific Northwest, which may be partly related to the region's earlier experience with fruit farming. One particularly revealing example is the comments of Henry Dosch, secretary of the Oregon State Horticultural Commission. Waxing on the noble pursuit of horticulture, Dosch confesses, "The poet who watched and raved over the development of a beautiful girl baby into maiden and ultimate womanhood, will find its counterpart in an Oregon orchard. To stand and watch in early Spring the quickening of the tree, the gradual development of leaf and bud, and the gentle, timid opening of its bewitching blossoms, filling the air with intoxicating fragrance, and finally the fruitage of the magnificent apples and pears for which Oregon has become famous is a poem in itself."[42] In another instance, poet Sam Simpson characterized his relationship with the orchard in the language of courtship:

> And I think, when the trees display a crown
> Like the gleam of a resting dove,
> Of a face that was framed in tresses brown
> And aglow with a mother's love;
> At the end of the orchard path she stands,
> And I laugh at my manhood's doom,
> As my spirit flies with lifted hands
> To the feast of apple bloom.
> She was more than fair in the wreath she wore
> Of the creamy buds and blows,
> And she comes to me from the speechless shore
> When the flowering orchard glows.[43]

It is important to stress that displays such as these were not simply a random arrangement of sexual metaphors, but rather served to dramatize explicitly the virtues of the industrious farmer attuned to his perceived responsibilities as cultivator and caretaker of the feminized landscape—a labor of love.

While the growth of urban centers within a resource-based economy is a common theme in the history of the Pacific Northwest, the contours of its rural past is often less familiar. A particularly fascinating aspect of this rural identity was forged with the promotion and establishment of fruit farming at the turn of the century. During this time, British Columbia in conjunction with Washington and Oregon bore witness to a "fruit fever" that transformed the region's environment and social milieu as governments, land developers, and railway companies conducted a boisterous promotion that found parallels on both sides of the border.

During a period of social and economic change, horticulture presented men with a vocation that confounded easy distinction between the "exploitation" of men and the "gentling" of women. As portrayed in period literature and brochures, life under the blossoming orchard not only represented the possibility for personal riches but encompassed personal health, racial purity, social stability, and moral soundness. The architects and beneficiaries of this possible utopia were "industrious men" who balanced art and science through their daily work in horticulture, much like their rural ideal that blended progress with nostalgia. Although it was a product of contrasting national identities, this masculine archetype bridged the republican and imperial divide with an array of similar ideas and images. Indeed, the utopian vision of a blossoming empire fostered by boosters and settlers fueled this transformative process, only to erode in the face of ecological and social realities, often with unintended consequences.

Notes

This essay is an expanded version of a paper presented at the conference of the American Historical Association–Pacific Coast Branch, Vancouver BC, August 2001. Research for this project was supported by a fellowship from the Social Sciences Research Council of Canada.
 1. For an introduction to western-themed work, a good starting point is Donald Worster, *Under Western Skies: Nature and History in the American West* (New York: Oxford University Press, 1992); William Cronon, George Miles, and Jay Gitlin, *Under an Open Sky: Rethinking America's Western Past* (New York: W. W. Norton, 1992); Richard White and John Findlay, eds., *Power and Place in the North American West* (Seattle: University of Washington Press, 1999).
 2. Richard White, "American Environmental History: The Development of a New Historical Field," *Pacific Historical Review* 54, no. 3 (1985): 335.
 3. Donald Worster, quoted in T. R. Reid, "Shootout in Academia over History of U.S. West," *Washington Post*, October 10, 1989.
 4. John Fahey, "Selling the Watered West: Arcadia Orchards," *Pacific Historical Review* 62,

no. 3 (1993): 455–74; Paul Koroscil, "Boosterism and the Settlement Process in the Okanagan Valley, British Columbia, 1890–1914," *Canadian Papers in Rural History* 5 (1986): 73–105.

5. British Columbia Archives and Record Service (BCARS), Victoria BC, Summerland Board of Trade, "Home of the Big Red Apple."

6. R. Cole Harris and Elizabeth Phillips, eds., *Letters from Windermere, 1912–1914* (Vancouver: University of British Columbia Press, 1984), x.

7. See George Altmeyer, "Three Ideas of Nature in Canada, 1893–1914," *Journal of Canadian Studies* 11 (August 1976): 24.

8. See H. Allen Anderson, *The Chief: Ernest Thompson Seton and the Changing West* (College Station: Texas A&M University Press, 1986); John Henry Wadland, *Ernest Thompson Seton: Man in Nature and the Progressive Era* (New York: Arno Press, 1978).

9. See J. A. Mangan, ed., *The Cultural Bond: Sport, Empire, and Society* (London: Cass, 1993); J. A. Mangan, ed., *Making European Masculinities: Sport, Europe, Gender* (London: Cass, 2000); Varda Burstyn, *The Rites of Men: Manhood, Politics, and the Culture of Sport* (Toronto: University of Toronto Press, 1999).

10. See Witold Rybczynski, *A Clearing in the Distance: Frederick Law Olmsted and America in the Nineteenth Century* (New York: Scribner, 1999); Irving D. Fisher, *Frederick Law Olmsted and the City Planning Movement in the United States* (Ann Arbor: UMI Research Press, 1986).

11. Sir Ebenezer Howard, *Tomorrow: A Peaceful Path to Real Reform* (London, 1898), 46; Thomas Adams, *Rural Planning and Development: A Study of Rural Conditions and Problems in Canada* (Ottawa: Commission of Conservation, 1917), 246.

12. John Muir, *Our National Parks* (Boston: Houghton Mifflin, 1901), 1.

13. A. R. Sennett, *Garden Cities in Theory and Practice*, vol. 1 (London: Bemrose, 1905), 2.

14. Annette Kolodny, *The Land before Her: Fantasy and Experience of the American Frontiers, 1630–1860* (Chapel Hill: University of North Carolina Press, 1984); Glenda Riley, *Women and Nature: Saving the "Wild" West* (Lincoln: University of Nebraska, 1999), xiii, 191.

15. Kelowna Centennial Museum (KCM), Central Okanagan Land, (1911?), 7; Library of Congress [LC], Medford Commercial Club, "Medford Oregon, Rogue River Valley" (Medford, 1909), 50.

16. LC, Henry Dosch, "Horticulture in Oregon" (Lewis and Clark Centennial Exposition Commission, 1906), 2.

17. KCM, Grand Pacific Land Company (1911), 3.

18. LC, Wenatchee Commercial Club, "Wenatchee, the Gateway to the Land of the Perfect Apples" (1910), 7.

19. BCARS, Summerland Board of Trade, "Home of the Big Red Apple."

20. LC, Dosch, "Horticulture in Oregon," 9.

21. KCM, Central Okanagan Land (1911), 3.

22. LC, Proceedings and Papers of the Oregon State Horticultural Society (1910), 89.

23. KCM, "The Okanagan Valley Booklet" (1905), 5.

24. KCM, Grand Pacific Land Company, "Kelowna, British Columbia" (1911), 3.

25. KCM, Kelowna Board of Trade (1918), 14; LC, Medford Commercial Club, "Medford, Oregon, Rogue River Valley" (1910), 41.

26. LC, Dosch, "Horticulture in Oregon," 9.

27. LC, Wenatchee Board of Trade, "Wenatchee" (1910), 31; C. J. Blanchard, "Manless Land for Landless Man," *Irrigation Age* 24 (1909): 231, quoted from W. Thomas White, "Main Street on the Irrigation Frontier: Sub-urban Community Building in the Yakima Valley, 1900–1910," *Pacific Northwest Quarterly* 77 (1986): 99.

28. See Patrick Dunae, *Gentlemen Emigrants: From the British Public Schools to the Canadian Frontier* (Vancouver: Douglas and McIntyre, 1981); Jean Barman, *Growing Up British in British Columbia: Boys in Private School* (Vancouver: UBC Press, 1984); Paul Koroscil, "Resettlement in Canada's British Garden of Eden," in C. Kerrigan, ed., *The Immigrant Experience* (Guelph: University of Guelph Press, 1992): 129–64; Jason Patrick Bennett, "Apple of the Empire: Landscape and Imperial Identity in Turn-of-the-Century British Columbia," *Journal of the Canadian Historical Association* 9 (1998): 63–92.

29. LC, Proceedings and Papers of the Oregon State Horticultural Society (1910), 65, 89.

30. LC, Proceedings and Papers (1910), 62.

31. William Smythe, *The Conquest of Arid America* (New York: Macmillan, 1907), 331. In contrast to Smythe's idealism, the history of irrigation produced by contemporary scholars often highlights its destructive environmental toll and its abuse by powerful elites. A key text is Donald Worster, *Rivers of Empire*. The transformation of irrigation from a progressive and cooperative enterprise to a tool of agribusiness is documented in Donald J. Pisani, *From the Family Farm to Agribusiness: The Irrigation Crusade in California and the West, 1850–1931* (Berkeley: University of California Press, 1984). See also Mark Fiege, *Irrigated Eden: The Making of an Agricultural Landscape in the American West* (Seattle: University of Washington Press, 2000).

32. Smythe, *The Conquest of Arid America*, 46.

33. Kenneth Wayne Wilson, "Irrigating the Okanagan: 1860–1920," MA thesis, University of British Columbia, 1989, chap. 5.

34. BCARS, Western Canada Irrigation Association, Kelowna, 1912; LC, Wenatchee Commercial Club, "Wenatchee, the Gateway," 31.

35. Edwin Dickerson, ed., *The Little Packer* (Yakima WA: Quickprint, 1920); J. T. Bealby, *Fruit Ranching in British Columbia* (London, 1911); J. S. Redmayne, *Fruit Farming on the "Dry Belt" of British Columbia: The Why and Wherefore* (London: Times Book Club, 1910).

36. Young Men's Christian Association, *Apple Growing in the Pacific Northwest* (Portland OR: YMCA, 1911).

37. David Dendy, "A Worm in the Apple," in *Beyond the City Limits: Rural History in British Columbia* (Vancouver: UBC Press, 1999), 14.

38. J. T. Saywell, ed., *The Canadian Journal of Lady Aberdeen, 1893–1898* (Toronto: Champlain Society, 1960), October 30, 1894.

39. *Daily Courier and Okanagan Orchardist*, April 7, 1910, 5.

40. *Daily Courier and Okanagan Orchardist*, December 28, 1911, 4.

41. LC, Dosch, 8.

42. LC, Medford Commercial Club, 1909, 50.

43. LC, Proceedings and Papers of the Oregon State Horticultural Society, 1910.

Part 5: Crossing the Medicine Line in the Twentieth Century

The essays in part 3 examined various aspects of how the border, or medicine line, was crossed for purposes of sanctuary in the nineteenth century. The borderlands continued to be a refuge in the twentieth century, but as the three essays and one addendum here show, it was now characterized by more of a United States–Canada flow of people fleeing from policies or laws with which they disagreed. One such policy was the Volstead Act, which from 1919 to 1933 became the Eighteenth Amendment to the U.S. Constitution prohibiting the "manufacture, sale, or transportation" of alcoholic beverages. Prohibition stimulated the alcoholic beverage, smuggling, and tourist economies along both U.S. borders, although most of what has been written on the subject deals with the Mexican side, especially its impact on the development of Tijuana. In chapter 14, however, historian Stephen Moore analyzes how Prohibition became a boon for tourism in southern British Columbia, as Americans in the Pacific Northwest sought freedom to drink across the border, becoming "refugees from Volstead."

The 1920s also witnessed the transboundary development of white supremacy groups in western Canada. It was during that decade that the Ku Klux Klan enjoyed a significant resurgence in the United States, with new local Klan groups sprouting in the Pacific Northwest. Some Klan leaders sought refuge in western Canada to export and practice their beliefs safely there. In chapter 15 Eckard Toy traces the history of this phenomenon and provides comparative analysis of the Klan and other racist Far Right groups in the American and Canadian Wests.

Taking refuge in Canada became even more popular during America's war in Vietnam. An estimated 125,000 Americans—first draft dodgers (estimated at 60,000 individuals, sometimes called "Skeedaddlers") and later war deserters, and often with their wives, girlfriends, or other friends—fled across the border in the 1960s and 1970s to create the largest political exodus in U.S. history. Canada, especially during the Pierre Trudeau government (1968–1979), was generally receptive to these Americans. Prime Minister Trudeau gave the war resisters his "complete sympathy" and stated that Canada in those years should be a "refuge from militarism." And when President Jimmy Carter granted amnesty to the draft dodgers in 1977, roughly half of those who fled the United States chose to remain in Canada.

Although there has been a wealth of literature generated on the topic of fleeing to Canada during the war, little has specifically addressed the question of war resisters who fled to the Canadian West. Renée Kasinsky, however, conducted research on draft dodgers and deserters in British Columbia in the late 1960s and early 1970s, and her essay here offers an illustrative snapshot from that period. She examined, among other things, the class and social background of the resisters, how being a refugee affected their lives in Canada, the kind of material and psychological support they received from British Columbians, and if the resisters were able to assimilate successfully into Canadian life. Readers interested in this topic should also be aware of the film *Northwest Passages* (created by the Center for Northwest Studies and Micromedia Productions out of Bellingham, Washington), which investigates the underground railroad that helped American draft dodgers get into Canada during the Vietnam War.

Finally, I have added a brief addendum at the end of this section that addresses early twenty-first-century patterns of seeking refuge across the medicine line—in a more literal sense of its meaning—in western Canada. It addresses how medical marijuana users from the United States have fled to British Columbia at a time when laws against such practices were stiffened in the United States but relaxed in Canada.

For Further Reading

On Prohibition in the Borderlands

On Far Right Extremist Groups in the Borderlands Region

On American Draft Dodgers and Deserters in Canada during the Vietnam War

On Prohibition in the Borderlands

Campbell, Robert A. *"Sit Down and Drink Your Beer": Regulating Vancouver's Beer Parlours, 1925–1954.* Toronto: University of Toronto Press, 2001.

Clark, Norman. "The 'Hell-Soaked Institution' and the Washington Prohibition Initiative of 1914." *Pacific Northwest Quarterly* 56 (January 1965): 1–16.

Gilman, Hyde Odell. "A Comparison of the Repeal Movements in Washington, Oregon, and Idaho." MA thesis, University of Washington, 1963.

Heibert, Albert John. *Prohibition in British Columbia: Bibliography* [microform]. Ottawa: National Library, 1969.

Moore, Stephen T. "Defining the 'Undefended': Canadians, Americans, and the Multiple Meanings of Border during Prohibition." *American Review of Canadian Studies* 34 (Spring 2004): 3–36.

————. *Of Bootleggers and Borders: Canadians, Americans, and the Prohibition-Era Northwest.* Forthcoming.

————. "Prohibition and Popular Culture in the Pacific Northwest." Paper, conference of the Pacific Northwest American Studies Association, Coeur d'Alene ID, April 1998.

————. "Tourists, Bootleggers, and Temperance Unions: Culture and Canadian-American Relations during Prohibition." Paper, conference of the Society for Historians of American Foreign Relations, College Park MD, June 1998.

Thompson, John Herd. "The Prohibition Question in Manitoba, 1892–1928." MA thesis, University of Manitoba, 1969.

On Far Right Extremist Groups in the Borderlands Region

Aho, James A. *The Politics of Righteousness: Idaho Christian Patriotism.* Seattle: University of Washington Press, 1990.

Barrett, Stanley R. *Is God a Racist? The Right Wing in Canada.* Toronto: University of Toronto Press, 1987.

Calderwood, William. "Religious Reactions to the Ku Klux Klan in Saskatchewan." *Saskatchewan History* 26 (Autumn 1973): 103–12.

Fawkes, Tom. *Conspiracy of Hate.* Vancouver: BC Labour News, 1980.

Franklin, Joe. "The Ku Klux Klan in the City of Spokane, 1921–1924." *Pacific Northwest Forum* 9 (Winter 1986): 18–23.

Harwood, William. "The KKK in Grand Forks, North Dakota." *South Dakota History* 1, no. 4 (Fall 1971): 301–35.

Henson, Tom M. "Ku Klux Klan in Western Canada." *Alberta History* 25 (Autumn 1975): 1–8.

Horowitz, David, and La Grande (OR) Klan no. 14, *Inside the Klavern: The Secret History of the Ku Klux Klan of the 1920s.* Carbondale: Southern Illinois University Press, 1999.

Lay, Shawn, ed. *The Invisible Empire in the West: Toward a New Historical Appraisal of the Ku Klux Klan of the 1920s.* Urbana: University of Illinois Press, 1992.

Peterson, Joe. "The Great Ku Klux Klan Rally in Issaquah, Washington." *Pacific Northwest Forum* 2 (Fall 1977): 23–24.

Rambow, Charles. "The KKK in the 1920s: A Concentration in the Black Hills." *South Dakota History* 4 (Winter 1973): 63–81.

Robin, Martin. *Shades of Right: Nativist and Fascist Politics in Canada.* Toronto: University of Toronto Press, 1992.

Sher, Julian. *White Hoods: Canada's Ku Klux Klan.* Vancouver: New Star Books, 1983.

Toy, Eckard V., Jr. "The Far Right in the Far West since the 1930s." Paper, conference of the Western History Association, Los Angeles, October 1987.

————. "The Ku Klux in Oregon." In G. Thomas Edwards and Carlos A. Schwantes, eds., *Experiences in a Promised Land: Essays in Pacific Northwest History,* 269–86. Seattle: University of Washington Press, 1986.

————. "Right-Wing Extremism from the Ku Klux Klan to the Order, 1915–1988." In Ted Robert Gurr, ed., *Violence in America,* vol. 2: *Protest, Rebellion, and Reform,* 131–52. Newbury Park, CA: Sage, 1989.

United States Commission on Civil Rights, Montana Advisory Committee. *White Supremacist Activity in Montana* [microform]. Denver: U.S. Commission on Civil Rights, Rocky Mountain Regional Office, 1994.

Ward, Peter. *White Canada Forever: Popular Attitudes and Public Policy toward Orientals in British Columbia.* Montreal: McGill-Queen's University Press, 1978.

On American Draft Dodgers and Deserters
in Canada during the Vietnam War

Cramer, David. "O Canada: It Was Painful to Be Accused of Treason by My Own Parents." *Boston Globe,* April 30, 2000, M11.

Dickerson, James. *North to Canada: Men and Women against the Vietnam War.* Westport CT: Praeger, 1999.

Emigration to Canada: Legal Notes for Draft-Age Men. Nashville: Southern Student Organizing Committee, 1967.

Emrick, Kenneth Fred, ed. *War Resisters, Canada: The World of the American Military-Political Refugees.* Knox PA: Pennsylvania Free Press, 1972.

Gottlieb, Sherry Gershon. *Hell No, We Won't Go! Resisting the Draft during the Vietnam War.* New York: Viking Books, 1991.

Hagan, John. *Northern Passage: American Vietnam War Resisters in Canada.* Cambridge: Harvard University Press, 2001.

————. "Their Road Not Taken Went Back Home: American Draft Resisters Fled Vietnam through Canada; A Generation Later They Are a Unique Breed of Citizen." *Boston Globe,* June 17, 2001,

Haig-Brown, Alan. *Hell No, We Won't Go: Vietnam Draft Resisters in Canada.* Vancouver: Raincoast Books, 1996.

Immigration to Canada as an Alternative to the Draft. Nashville: Southern Student Organizing Committee, 1967.

Kasinsky, Renée G. *Refugees from Militarism: Draft-Age Americans in Canada.* New Brunswick NJ: Transaction Books, 1976.

Kusch, Frank. *All American Boys: Draft Dodgers in Canada from the Vietnam War*. Westport CT: Praeger, 2001.

Perrin, Dick. GI *Resisters: The Story of How One American Soldier and His Family Fought the War in Vietnam*. Victoria: Trafford, 2001.

Peterson, Carl. *Avoidance and Evasion of Military Service: An American History, 1626–1973*. San Francisco: International Scholars, 1997.

Satin, Mark. *Manual for Draft Age Immigrants to Canada*. Toronto: House of Anansi Press, 1968.

Sotiron, Minko. "Draft Dodgers and the Canadian Imagination: Impact and Consequences." Paper, conference of the Association for Canadian Studies in the United States, Portland OR, November 2003.

Surrey, David. *Choice of Conscience: Vietnam Era Military and Draft Evaders in Canada*. Westport CT: Praeger, 1982.

Todd, Jack. *Desertion: In the Time of Vietnam*. Boston: Houghton Mifflin, 2001.

———. *The Taste of Metal: A Deserter's Story*. Toronto: Harper Flamingo Canada, 2001.

Williams, Roger N. *The New Exiles: American War Resisters in Canada*. New York: Liveright, 1971.

14. Refugees from Volstead

Cross-Boundary Tourism
in the Northwest during Prohibition

Stephen T. Moore

C. D. Smith, a columnist for the *Victoria Daily Colonist*, called them "refugees from Volstead." He likened the American tourist during Prohibition to the refugees of Belgium during World War I and to the Israelites in their exodus from Egypt. But none of these, he writes, "exceed in sympathetic interest the refugees from Volstead, driven forth by the Eighteenth Amendment." He continued: "Their appearance does not at all suggest privation in the sense of their being starved, hollow-eyed, with haggard faces, torn feet and bleeding hands caused by the dangers and privations of the journey. Neither are they attired in conventional garb of harassed wanderers. . . . They are mostly clothed in plus-fours and their one look is of assured triumph and anticipation. They have 'got there.' Nothing else matters." [1] Though written tongue-in-cheek and with some exaggeration, Smith's commentary was not far from the mark. With the failure of world Prohibition, drys in the United States determined that if they could not protect Prohibition elsewhere, at least they would protect it at home. While drys clung determinedly to their new isolationism, however, wets adopted a more internationalist perspective. As wartime Prohibition in British Columbia gave way to government control, Americans suffering under the Eighteenth Amendment headed north in droves. For thirsty Americans, just beyond the border lay a wet refuge, a sanctuary from the restrictive shackles of Volstead.

The Evergreen Playground

During Prohibition, the concept of Canadian-American "relations" invariably brought to the American mind the vague reminder that Canada was sort of a northern extension of the United States, a "delightfully wet place for a vacation." [2] It was the one country into which American tourists could drive their own motor cars and, save for a brief examination at a customs station, barely know that a border had been crossed. The American tourist could continue to drive on the same side of the road, speak in English, use American money, buy American magazines, and as an article in the *Literary Digest* pointed out, down "drinks that were his own once but are no longer." It asserted that "the American may well have [had] more trouble getting back into his own country, if . . . he [did] not carry his Americanism on his face." [3]

Nowhere was this more true than in the Pacific Northwest where Americans had long viewed British Columbia as a sort of northern playground. Travel pamphlets, newspapers, and other periodicals routinely described the region encompassed by Washington and British Columbia as the "Evergreen Playground." "International Circuit Tours" routinely ferried the tourists between Seattle, the San Juan Islands, the Olympic Peninsula, Victoria, and Vancouver. It was rare to find an American tour company that did not include the Puget Sound region in its circuit. In almost any Sunday edition of the local newspapers, one could find suggestions for border travel routes, such as the scenic Bee Line Highway that stretched between Banff and Spokane, or the Pacific Highway between Seattle and Vancouver.

That Americans viewed British Columbia as a sort of northern extension was no accident. It was the product of a conscious effort by business and government officials to facilitate travel across the border. Local travel agents and travel pamphlets routinely advertised the lack of "red tape" at the international border. Local boards of trade distributed literature about local cities to tourists arriving in Canada by rail. Agents in British Columbia prominently offered information on attractions in Seattle, confident that once there, tourists would naturally find their way to British Columbia. Provincial and state authorities routinely met to discuss uniform motor vehicle traffic laws and enforcement measures, while auto clubs offered reciprocal towing and emergency services. So closely linked were American and British Columbian efforts to promote tourism that, early in the decade, chambers of commerce in Washington and Oregon united with their counterparts in British Columbia to form the Pacific Northwest Tourists Association.

The most obvious symbol of the region's cross-border outlook was British Columbia's adoption of driving on the right side of the road in 1922. Brought about mainly through the efforts of local automobile clubs and chambers of commerce, the decision to begin driving on the right was not uniformly popular. As Stewart Holbrook observed, numerous letters to the province's dailies denounced the change as a "traitorous adoption of 'Yankee notions,' " and predicted a profusion of collisions and wrecks. Other Canadians, however, knowing that the flood of American tourists was inevitable, decided that it would be safer to accommodate the notoriously reckless, and now inebriate, American driver than it would be to confuse him or her with the traditional British practice of driving on the left.[4]

Before the 1920s, tourism remained the pastime of the relatively wealthy who could afford to travel by rail. The automobile made it possible for those of more moderate means to enjoy travel as well. Businessmen in the western states and provinces recognized the profit to be made in attracting tourists of all social classes and launched vigorous campaigns for road construction. They reasoned that in developing auto travel between the provinces and the states, they would promote closer social and economic ties as well.

As the *Spokane Daily Chronicle* noted in 1929, "The international boundary at 49 [degrees] separates communities under different flags, but with many mutual interests and eager for more frequent association. Sections of poor highways on both sides of the boundary are the real barrier, not the international line." Responding to these concerns, British Columbia added over 250 miles of new trails and over 500 miles of paved roads in 1925 alone and similar improvements occurred in Washington. The most important north-south connection between British Columbia and the States was the newly completed Pacific Highway, which stretched from California to Vancouver. As the final section was completed between

Seattle and New Westminster in 1923, one observer noted simply that the highway was "magnificent."[5]

Government and private business collaborated to offer a range of tourist facilities, from rest areas and automobile campgrounds to bungalow camps (the predecessor of motels) and upscale hotels that would appeal to a broad spectrum of society. By mid-decade, it was not uncommon to see long processions of American automobiles inexpensively touring Vancouver and lower British Columbia from Central Park Auto Camp at Burnaby or Hastings Park in Vancouver. For British Columbians touring in Washington, Seattle's Woodland Park offered space for over six hundred cars at a mere fifty cents per day. For the more wealthy American tourist, Victoria offered the palatial Empress Hotel for two dollars per night.[6]

A Wet Oasis

Once British Columbia became a wet oasis in an otherwise dry North America, thirsty Americans intensified their efforts to seek recreation and relaxation there. To be sure, the spread of the automobile most certainly would have sent American tourists across the border, if only for the " 'foreign' touch which is part of the joy of travel."[7] Nevertheless, the Eighteenth Amendment certainly hastened the invasion.

Ardent drinkers who lived near the Canadian border knew exactly what to do. They followed the advice of a popular refrain, "Forty miles from whiskey / And sixty miles from gin, / I'm leaving this damn country / For to live a life of sin."[8] No sooner had Prohibition taken effect in the United States than the *Seattle Post-Intelligencer* began to joke about the northward migration: "One thing about prohibition, you don't need surveyors to find the boundary line of Canada." The trail left by migrating tourists clearly marked the way. Soon many who did not live near the border, and who may never have visited Canada before, found the trek to Canada irresistible. Americans sought Canada because of the freedom it afforded them, not only to drink but to drink without worrying about spies or "stool pigeons." Tourism and the comforts of tourism—the garages, filling stations, roadhouses, and snack bars—created a new method of escape from American temperance run amok.[9]

Historically, Canada has always been a sanctuary of sorts for refugees fleeing some sort of ill-treatment in the United States. British loyalists fled to eastern Canada during and after the American War for Independence. In Harriet Beecher Stowe's *Uncle Tom's Cabin*, Canada was "these shores of refuge" for escaping slaves. Likewise, bands of persecuted Native Americans routinely fled across the border, ahead of pursuing American troops. As Wallace Stegner describes in *Wolf Willow*, "The medicine of the line of cairns was very strong. Once it had been necessary to outrun your pursuing enemy until you were well within your own country where he did not dare to follow. Now all you had to do was outrun him to the Line, and from across that magical invisible barrier you could watch him pull to a halt, balked, helpless, and furious.[10] And much later Vietnam-era draft dodgers saw Canada as a relief valve for social unrests. Tourists during Prohibition were merely another example (albeit, a less-persecuted example) of Americans who found that by crossing the border they might avoid, or at least alleviate, the more uncomfortable aspects of being American.

In 1930, the *Literary Digest* reported that more people crossed the Canadian-American border every year than passed across any other international border. Ottawa calculated that some thirteen million Americans visited Canada in 1929, a figure that represented approximately one-tenth of the total American population. One historian has suggested that the number of Americans visiting Canada was even greater. During the Depression year 1931–32, John Bartlet Brebner estimates the figure to be closer to twenty million. In 1929, some 181,798 cars reported at British Columbia ports of entry alone.[11] While this figure cannot account for the number that crossed the border without reporting, it was a number sufficient to require United States Customs to issue instructions to its officers to discontinue the practice of counting the number of automobiles that crossed into Canada. Their energies were more desperately needed for inspecting incoming traffic. For similar reasons, Canadian officers soon gave up trying to record the license plate number of every American car entering the Dominion.[12]

American entrepreneurs eagerly packed up and moved north to serve their fellow citizens on Canadian soil. As with the earlier gold rushes, these entrepreneurs recognized that the real profits lay not necessarily in liquor sales but in providing comfortable places for Americans to drink. Hotels, roadhouses, and personal residences owned by Americans or financed with American money sprang up all along the international border. H. L. Sawyer was the proprietor of the International Hotel and Bar located just ten feet north of the border and 100 feet north of the American customs house at Eastport, Idaho. As one Treasury agent reported, "Eastport is not a city or town, and can scarcely be called a village. It is simply a point where the railroad crosses the international boundary line. [13] Just as blatant an attempt to circumvent Prohibition was the St. Leonard Hotel located just across the border from Blaine, Washington. Senator Wesley Jones of Washington complained that the hotel was nothing more than a "grog-shop," for no other businesses were located within miles. [14]

Canadian entrepreneurs, hotel proprietors, brewers, distillers, railway officials, boards of trade, mayors, and premiers were likewise eager to pamper the American tourist. As Simon Fraser Tolmie, a member of Parliament from British Columbia, noted to his colleagues, "I come from a province where we cater to the tourist trade, and we have tens of thousands of visitors to that part of the country. They leave a lot of money there every year, and we are beginning to think that the work of inducing tourists to come to British Columbia and enjoy themselves is becoming quite an industry." [15] When one dry legislator, hoping to minimize drunkenness, introduced an amendment restricting liquor purchase permits to nonresidents, it was quickly dismissed. When, three months later, the legislature passed a law making liquor permits easier for Americans to obtain, it was wildly cheered. Although American tourists needed to secure a permit before purchasing liquor in British Columbia, the permit cost a mere $2.00, after which they could buy whatever quantity they desired. The Minister of Customs at Ottawa even issued instructions to customs officers to assist visitors in making out their tourist permits and to do so free of charge. Before this, enterprising individuals had made it a practice to open offices near border points where, for a fee of fifty cents, they offered to fill out the necessary paperwork. [16]

Finding liquor once north of the border was not particularly difficult to do. The first thing that greeted Americans as they crossed the border on the Pacific Highway at Blaine were large signs advertising the virtue of a particular brand of whiskey or beer. Not coincidentally, pictures of these advertisements that lined the Pacific Highway were widely circulated in the American press, one with a caption that read, "A bit of BC scenery that helps one to forget the bad roads." [17] Even the provincial government made sure that it was not too difficult for American tourists to find government liquor stores. One Conservative member of Parliament from New Westminster, William Garland McQuarrie, reflected frustration about this when he noted,

> The first idea that motorists from the other side of the line get is, naturally, that he can buy whiskey, beer and other liquors in British Columbia. . . . He does not have to go very far before he finds a liquor store. We had one at New Westminster, but that was about 18 miles from the border; it was not near enough. Although New Westminster is the first place of any consequence on the road from the border to Vancouver, the government, in order to help the poor individuals from the other side who might feel the necessity for liquor, put in another vendor's place on the south side of the New Westminster Bridge, where there is no population at all. [18]

There were many reasons that Canadians so eagerly facilitated the tourist trade. Most, of course, related to economics. First, American tourism in Canada favorably affected Canada's balance of trade with the United States. While Canadian tourists continued to travel to the United States during the Prohibition years, their numbers nowhere approached the number of American tourists traveling north, for obvious reasons. Many British Columbians looked upon a journey to the United States with, in the words of the American consul in Vancouver, "about the same enthusiasm as a camel regards a trek across the Sahara Desert. The oases are few and far between—and then the thirst destroyer is mostly ice water." [19]

Between 1922 and 1928, for example, Canada's trade deficit with the United States hovered between $100 million and $300 million annually. But these figures did not include American tourist expenditures, which estimates placed at $140 million to $275 million. Thus tourism was a valuable "invisible export." If Americans spent $150 million in Canada, it was like Canada sending to the United States goods of an equal value. At its high point in 1929, Commerce Department statistics suggest that American tourists spent $300 million in Canada, and Canadian Department of Trade and Commerce figures place that value at an even higher $309 million. By the late 1920s, the American tourist trade was so important that it ranked among the top three largest industries in the Dominion.[20] To put these values in relative terms, American tourist receipts were more than twice the value of Canada's wheat exports to the entire world.

Naturally, the Great Depression had a chilling effect on tourism. By 1932 the figure had shrunk to a relatively meager $183 million and, by 1933, to an even smaller $117 million. Still, because Canadian tourists continued to spend lesser amounts in the United States than Americans spent in Canada, tourism continued to affect Canada's balance of trade favorably.[21]

The economic value of this "industry" was not lost on British Columbia, where tourism was considered a "renewable resource." When the province sold $20 million worth of lumber one year, the province finished the year with $20 million less timber. On the other hand, after American tourists spent $20 million in the province, the province still had the same scenic resources that had attracted the tourists in the first place. In 1924, Vancouver authorities estimated that tourists spent an astounding $40 million in their city alone. Indeed, some of the chief advocates for government control in British Columbia had argued against Prohibition on the basis of the "drawing card" that regulated sale would be for promoting tourism.[22] Provincial legislation that made liquor more difficult for American tourists to obtain usually faced stiff opposition from local businesses in British Columbia. No tourist resort would ever vote to dry up its means of attracting patrons. The British Columbia Hotelman's Association long remained one of the chief advocates for the right to sell beer by the glass in their province. It rightly argued that without the ability to sell beer in hotels, Americans simply would choose to stay in auto camps outside towns, where they could buy their liquor from conveniently located liquor stores.[23]

Thus when the United States began to plead with Canada to assist in the enforcement against bootleggers and rumrunners, it came as no surprise that those most sympathetic were Canadian businesses that profited from American tourism. Many British Columbians were concerned that the province's reputation as the center of bootlegging to the United States would so tarnish its reputation that tourists would no longer come, even for a drink.[24] Others were concerned that bootlegging made it unnecessary for Americans to come to the province at all. One Canadian commented, "Even our more mercenary citizens had far rather see an American come up here to get [liquor], spending fifty dollars in hotel bills, ten in souvenirs, a hundred in furs, and whatever may be left in diamonds—than to have night-riders with silent trucks convey it to the American victim in his home town. Then we only get the money for the liquor." In early 1929, the president of the Canadian National Railways echoed this sentiment when he petitioned the prime minister. "I think our policy should be to assist the Government of the United States in every way to make that country bone dry," he wrote, "the dryer it is the better it will be for us."[25]

Yet aside from economics, there was one other reason why Canadians actively courted the American tourist. Travel had a secondary influence that was more subtle but perhaps more far-reaching in its effects. As one member of the House of Commons noted in 1925, it "builds up the good-will and understanding and opens the eyes of the visitor to the possibilities of the country." Anything that made Americans more conscious of their neighbors to the north was seen as important by Canadians who had long felt neglected or overlooked by the Americans. This was one of the reasons why the Prohibition era was so important for Canadian-American relations generally; it gave Americans a view of Canadians that they would not otherwise have had. If Americans left with a greater infinity for things Canadian, so much the better. King George V of England, an outspoken critic of American Prohibition, was apparently delighted by the contemporary rhyme:

> *Four and twenty Yankees,*
> *Feeling mighty dry,*
> *Took a trip to Canada*
> *And bought a case of rye.*
> *When the case was opened*
> *The Yanks began to sing—*
> *'To hell with the President!*
> *God save the King!'*[26]

Cognizant of the opportunity to make a good first impression, the Customs Department ordered inspectors to be on their best behavior. A 1928 circular warned that the officer "who allows his temper to show itself, and acts in a discourteous manner . . . will be sent to the freight yards or manifest room where his peculiar temperament will not offend others." In 1929, the department further directed: "When a tourist drives up to a Customs office on the frontier, it is the duty of the examining officer to go outside and interview the visitor. The Department has been advised that at certain offices the Customs officer sits at his desk and waits for the caller to come to him. It need hardly be stated that this treatment savors of discourtesy and must be abandoned forthwith."[27]

The Limits of Hospitality

American perceptions, such as those of many American tourists, that depict Canada as a sanctuary or refuge are one of the few ways that the American view of Canada corresponds with the Canadian one. As Russell Brown points out, however, this apparent similarity actually arises from an important cultural difference. For Americans, border has always represented a place across which one may escape when pressures in the United States become too great. For the Canadian, on the other hand, the border is what makes Canada a sanctuary from American cultural excess. Northrop Frye has noted that Canada's national identity is characterized by a "garrison state" mentality. While this may seem extreme, the underlying sentiment, that Canada is somehow a shelter from the United States, has always been an important component of Canadianism. For Canadians, the Dominion has always served as a refuge from American cultural debauchery, whether it be crime, American magazines, movies, television, or, in the case of Prohibition, the political tendency to legislate morality.[28] During the American experiment with national Prohibition, American tourists who saw British Columbia as a wet refuge were seen by British Columbians with a certain amount of ambivalence. While most British Columbians remained enamored by the profits to be made, many were also wary about the negative effects tourists had on the Canadian social and cultural fabric.

The fact that Americans had to head north for liquor naturally led British Columbians to question the farce that prevented Americans from buying the same liquor at home. Most found it mildly amusing that while British Columbians spent their leisure time hiking, playing cricket, or enjoying an afternoon tea, the American tourist was usually at a local hotel "guzzling" Scotch. British Columbians, unlike their American counterparts, did not have to waste time hunting for liquor or waste brain power thinking of ways to cheat the government. It certainly reaffirmed the belief that the British Columbian approach to liquor control was manifestly better.

Still, if all American tourist behavior had been so benign, few Canadians would have given it much thought. Unfortunately, not all Americans who came north in search of drink were congenial to Canadians of the steadier sort. In one case, the *Vancouver Province* reported that sailors from American halibut vessels at port in Prince Rupert were regularly seen "intoxicated" or "semi-intoxicated," and that one had maliciously broken several hundred dollars' worth of store-front glass with a chair. Sir Charles P. Piers, a contemporary observer, added, "Our American friends coming from a dry country, are perhaps a trifle too much out on the spree, and the nights are in consequence somewhat hectic with their jazz songs, while the water in the early morning resembles a battlefield, so strewn is it with the corpses of dead bottles, all of which have undoubtedly done their duty."[29] Naturally, the *Province* disregarded the fact that sailors on leave, whether Canadian or American, were usually anything but sedate. For his part, Piers failed to allow that many British Columbians quite appreciated American jazz and many other aspects of American culture. Nevertheless, British Columbians viewed evidence of American misbehavior as a challenge to the "peace, order, good government" mantra that Canadians held so dear.

At times, even the economic argument proved less than convincing. Thirsty Americans often made short day-trips across the border, purchased liquor, and returned across the border without otherwise contributing to the Canadian economy. Doing so confirmed in the minds of many British Columbians the long-standing belief that Americans were "cheap." Apparently, after one too many admonitions to treat American tourists with deference, one customs officer made up a ditty to describe the typical American:

A machine rolls in from the U.S.A.—a family on the trail;
They carry a tent to save on rent, they have extra gas by the
    pail,
They carry their food, they carry their oil, they have blankets
    and pots;
They are rarin' to go and will spend their dough on the gratis
    parking lots.
You open the door, they put up a roar, you hand them a free
    permit,
They whine of red tape and call you an ape but you mustn't
    mind a bit;
You dig up their gats from under the mats and insist they check
    the rods;
If your temper they try, you mustn't reply, they are tourists
    and therefore gods. [30]

Between Americans being cheap and mischievous, some British Columbians began to regret the invitation they had extended to the baser elements of the American population.

British Columbians also resented the commonly held assumption that
Americans came to British Columbia only for the liquor. Most would
have preferred to believe the naïve pronouncement made by Assistant
Secretary of the Treasury Lowman that "it's not the supposed American
thirst but the lure of Canada's beautiful scenery, fine hospitality, and
good roads" that led Americans to cross the border. [31] British Columbians
facilitated tourism because they believed that, in doing so, they were
helping Americans to learn more about Canada. In an interesting bit
of irony, however, because provincial authorities located liquor stores
so close to the border, American tourists sometimes did not need to
learn anything about British Columbia at all. One of the more thoughtful
observers noted, "The Americans come with plenty of money, and stay
at the much-advertised hotels, gulping down the Rockies in predigested
doses, then race through in a Pullman car to the next big hotel on the
coast. And how can they know anything of the province?" [32]

No more pleased about the migration of American tourists were drys
on both sides of the border. The British Columbia chapter of the Women's

Christian Temperance Union (WCTU) constantly railed against the provincial government that, the temperance organization believed, was in the liquor business only to make money even if it debauched American tourists in the process. Likewise, the WCTU chapter at Blaine, Washington, angrily protested to the American consul in Vancouver that roadhouses located close to the international border received little attention from provincial authorities. [33] Spokane's two dailies, the *Spokesman-Review* and the *Daily Chronicle*, made informing their readers about the supposedly detrimental effect of British Columbia's liquor system on tourism a regular part of their coverage. In an article titled "Another Angle on Canadian Booze," the *Chronicle* endorsed the sentiments of one reader who wrote, "I'm not going up to British Columbia for any of the holidays this year. I know many others who will not go because the roads are filled with drunken drivers as the result of the spree over the line. I don't like to go up there because on all the holidays the streets of the 'beer cities' are filled with drunken men." The *Vancouver Daily Province* promptly responded, chastising the Spokane paper for drawing "what is essentially a false picture of government liquor control in this province." It went on to comment: "The *Chronicle* is either a fanatical Dry, or it has some other obscure motive for discouraging people in Washington from visiting us here in British Columbia."[34] Indeed, both Spokane papers were fanatically dry.

Short of revoking the passports of Americans seen drinking in Canada—a policy William Jennings Bryan actually advocated—there was little that committed drys or American authorities could do to discourage the flow of tourists northward. As Andrew Sinclair points out, it was "such suggestions of petty coercion" that ultimately ensured the Eighteenth Amendment's demise. [35] In the meantime, Americans continued to head north of the border. Perhaps most important for the path Prohibition would eventually take in the United States, American tourists who traveled to British Columbia witnessed the workings of government control. When the failures of American Prohibition became more apparent later in the decade, this experience proved an important factor in the effort to repeal national Prohibition in the United States. The Canadian system offered a legitimate and realistic approach to temperance.

Notes

This essay is extracted from a chapter in the author's PhD dissertation, "Bootlegging and the Borderlands: Canadians, Americans, and the Prohibition-Era Northwest," College of William and Mary, 2000.

1. *Victoria Daily Colonist*, August 30, 1925, 14.
2. R., "Neighbors: A Canadian View," *Foreign Affairs* 10, no. 3 (1932): 417.
3. *Literary Digest*, September 6, 1924, 19.
4. *New York Times*, January 1, 1922, sec. 2, 15; Stewart Hall Holbrook, *Far Corner: A Personal View of the Pacific Northwest* (New York: Macmillan, 1952), 29–30; Sir Charles P. Piers, *Sport and Life in British Columbia* (London: H. Cranton, 1923), 112–13.
5. *Spokane Daily Chronicle*, October 27, 1929, 4; Piers, *Sport and Life*, 116.
6. *Seattle Post Intelligencer*, August 21, 1924, editorial page; *Vancouver Sun*, July 8, 1925, 1; Victoria and Island Development Association, *Tourists' Map and Guide to Victoria*, 1918, British Columbia Archives, Victoria.
7. *New York Times*, February 24, 1930, 20.
8. Quoted in Andrew Sinclair, *Prohibition: The Era of Excess* (Boston: Little, Brown, 1962), 335.
9. *Seattle Post-Intelligencer*, December 6, 1920, 6; December 13, 1920, 6; *New York Times*, April 6, 1930, sec. 10, 4, 7; Sinclair, *The Era of Excess*, 317.
10. Stowe and Stegner quoted in Russell Brown, "The Written Line," in Robert Lecker, ed., *Borderlands: Essays in Canadian-American Relations* (Toronto: ECW Press, 1991), 8.
11. *Literary Digest*, February 15, 1930, 60–61; *New York Times*, February 24, 1930, 20; *New York Times*, February 23, 1930, 23.
12. *Annual Report of the Secretary of the Treasury* (1927), 115, (1928), 82; Dave McIntosh, *The Collectors: A History of Canadian Customs and Excise* (Toronto: NC Press, 1984), 338.
13. *Vancouver Sun*, April 4, 1925, 1; Assistant Secretary of the Treasury to Secretary of State, August 4, 1927, 842.114/14, RG 59, National Archives and Records Administration (NARA), hereafter State Department consular files cited by decimal number only (e.g. 842.114/14).
14. Wesley Jones to Secretary of State, September 1, 1913, 842.114/7.
15. House of Commons, *Debates*, June 3, 1921, 4495.
16. *Victoria Daily Times*, March 17, 1921, 1, 3; American Consul (Prince Rupert) to Secretary of State, August 26, 1930, 811.114Canada/4349; *New York Times*, July 13, 1928, 2.
17. *Seattle Post-Intelligencer*, October 3, 1920, sec. 5, 1.
18. House of Commons, *Debates*, May 2, 1923, 2415.
19. *Seattle Post-Intelligencer*, July 15, 1923, D1; American Consul (Vancouver) to Secretary of State, September 30, 1927, 842.114/290.
20. *New York Times*, September 9, 1928, sec. 3, 1, 5; March 27, 1931, 24; December 21, 1932, 18; June 24, 1929, 38; Canada, Senate, *Debates*, May 23, 1934, 401; Charles W. Stokes, "Prohibition's Decline and Fall in Canada," *American Review of Reviews* 77, no. 2 (February 1928): 174.

21. *New York Times*, March 15, 1933, 13. For further prohibition period tourism statistics that corroborate these general trends, see *New York Times*, April 14, 1932, 38; March 15, 1933, 13; September 23, 1934, sec. 4, 4.

22. *Victoria Daily Times* quoted in House of Commons, *Debates*, April 16, 1925, 2096; *New York Times*, February 15, 1925, sec. 8, 18; *British Columbia Legislative Assembly Clipping Books*, February 17, 1920, British Columbia Archives, Victoria.

23. *Vancouver Daily Province*, December 15, 1928, 1; *Victoria Daily Times*, November 8, 1930, 4.

24. *Vancouver Daily Province*, November 17, 1924, 6.

25. *Literary Digest*, September 23, 1922, 21; H. W. Thornton to Minister of Railways and Canals, January 7, 1929, RG 25, DI, vol. 742, reel T1758, frames 514–16.

26. Canada, House of Commons, *Debates*, April 16, 1925, 2094; rhyme quoted in Sinclair, *Prohibition*, 335.

27. McIntosh, *The Collectors*, 336–37.

28. See Northrop Frye, ed., *The Bush Garden: Essays on the Canadian Imagination* (Toronto: Anansi, 1971), 213–51.

29. American Consul (Prince Rupert) to Secretary of State, December 3, 1929, 842.114 Liquor/73; Piers, *Sport and Life*, 63.

30. Quoted in McIntosh, *The Collectors*, 337.

31. American Consul (Prince Rupert) to Secretary of State, August 26, 1930, 811.114Canada/4349.

32. Hilda Glynn-Ward, *The Glamour of British Columbia* (New York: Macmillan, 1926), vii–viii.

33. *Victoria Daily Times*, September 29, 1929; American Consul (Vancouver) to Secretary of State, February 26, 1925, 811.114Canada/181.

34. *Spokane Daily Chronicle*, May 29, 1928, 4; *Vancouver Daily Province*, June 4, 1928, 6.

35. Sinclair, *The Era of Excess*, 336.

15. Hoods across the Border

The Ku Klux Klan and the Far Right in the American and Canadian Wests

Eckard V. Toy Jr.

When Canadian immigration authorities arrested American Ku Klux Klan leader David Duke in Vancouver, British Columbia, in April 1980, Duke explained that he was visiting Canada for "white powder," not "white power."[1] Canadian officials let him go skiing and then expelled Duke on the grounds that he had been convicted of inciting a riot in the United States. But a more probable cause was that during previous visits to Toronto and Vancouver in 1979, Duke had inflamed racial animosities and stimulated the growth of the Klan in Canada.

This was not the first time Canadian authorities had deported an American Klan leader from Vancouver. Fifty-five years earlier, in 1925, they expelled Luther I. Powell, who was one of the principal Kleagles (organizers) of the Invisible Empire in the American West. Powell, a King Kleagle, was a principal Klan organizer in Texas, California, the Pacific Northwest, and Alaska and was instrumental in organizing the Kanadian Knights of the Ku Klux Klan in British Columbia. The ambitious and inventive leaders of the Klan in Oregon in the 1920s created a number of Klan auxiliaries and allied groups, including the colorful Royal Riders of the Red Robe. Dr. Martin W. Rose, a Portland physician and naturalized citizen from Canada, worked closely with Grand Dragon Fred L. Gifford and Luther Powell in establishing this organization for foreign-born citizens, and it was no coincidence that Rose exported the Royal Riders to Canada. David Duke was simply following a well-traveled two-way ideological road to western Canada.[2]

As this chapter will illustrate, there were other examples of trans-boundary transfer of Far Right ideology and racist thought, much of which was readily accepted in western Canada. Questions to consider include to what extent the Ku Klux Klan and the Far Right evolved into different forms in the United States and Canada. Did a reform movement or reactionary populism shape the KKK and the Far Right in Canada and the United States? Are cultural values and social factors similar? One thing is clear: This two-way migration of people, ideas, and institutions shaped a cultural network that spanned generations and transcended geographical boundaries.

Maj. Luther Ivan Powell, originally of Shreveport, Louisiana, belonged to the second Ku Klux Klan, which William Joseph Simmons founded in Atlanta, Georgia, in 1915. That Klan moved into the American West in the early 1920s, and fragments of it survived in most states into the 1930s. Klan Kleagles followed rails and roads throughout the West in pursuit of members and dollars. The first wave of Kleagles moved westward from the Deep South through Arkansas to Texas, Kansas, Oklahoma, and California, followed by a second wave of organizers moving westward from Indiana and Illinois. In early 1921, Kleagles from Texas and California continued their clockwise movement, entering Oregon and then recruiting members in Washington, Idaho, and Alaska. As they circled the West, Klan Kleagles made periodic and sometimes delayed forays into the Rocky Mountain and Great Plains states. Generally, Klan strength in the American West peaked and declined between 1921 and 1926. Klans in states on the southern and coastal fringes of the region typically began to weaken by 1924, just as Klans in the heartland of the West were reaching peaks in membership and political activity.

Although it was a national organization founded on racial and religious bigotry and tainted by a vicious strain of violence, local issues and local leaders often dominated the Klan agenda. Opportunistic Klansmen exploited political realignment and merged moral and educational issues with racism, nativism, anti-Semitism, and anti-Asian and anti-Catholic sentiments. Men, by the tens of thousands, rallied to the Klan banner, and thousands of women joined the Ladies of the Invisible Empire and the Women of the Klan.[3] Although western states had only an estimated 7 percent of total Klan membership, Klansmen and their allies constituted

a significant proportion of the population in some states. Klan membership in Oregon, for example, exceeded 35,000 in a population just over
700,000. And Western Klans achieved significant political successes in
Texas, Oklahoma, and Oregon.[4]

In Canada, Kleagles had their greatest successes in Ontario and the
Canadian West. They approached in a pincer movement, with Hoosiers
working westward into Saskatchewan from Ontario, former Oregon
Klansmen eastward from British Columbia, and Nebraskans northward
into Alberta. The Canadian Klan thrived in smaller communities, but had
significant strength and its headquarters in urban areas. It began later than
the American Klan, usually the mid- to late 1920s, and maintained its
strength longer into the 1930s.[5] Between 1927 and 1930, writes William
Calderwood, "Saskatchewan was the scene of the Klan's greatest impact
in Canada."[6]

The first Kleagles and leaders were from the United States, and the
structure and ideology of the Canadian Klans were based on the U.S.
model. Initially, Canadians used the same printed forms and literature,
and some early members even repeated an oath swearing allegiance to
the Constitution of the United States. Although there were variations
in later literature and sometimes in Klan hoods and gowns, Canadian
doctrines, oaths, and rituals resembled those in the United States. Canadians also burned crosses. Organizational viability required adjustment to
Canadian social and cultural factors, so Canadian leaders and issues were
important. Considering the size of the population, the Klan in western
Canada was fairly large.[7] We must allow for exaggeration, but the British
Columbia Klan claimed 13,000 members in 1927, there were several
thousand in Alberta, and estimates for Saskatchewan range from 10,000
to 50,000 members, resembling Oregon.[8]

Kleagles in both countries followed a similar recruiting strategy. They
made initial contacts among Masons, Odd Fellows, Elks, and American
Legionnaires in the United States, and found a reservoir of recruits among
the Masons, veterans groups, nativist organizations, and especially the
Orange lodges in Canada. Both Klans found support in the Protestant
churches, since Canadians and Americans inherited strong English cultural traditions of anti-Catholicism and nativism. Anti-Catholic hostility
in Canada was more pronounced and more often directed at specific

targets like Quebec, the Roman Catholic Church, parochial schools, and the French language. Canadians did not have to confront the issue of Prohibition, but many embarked on moral crusades against prostitution and "dope" resembling those conducted by their compatriots in several western states. Klans on the Pacific Slope, above and below the forty-ninth parallel, also shared anti-Asian and anti-radical sentiments and traditions of violence against those groups. If American Klansmen in California and the Southwest expressed anti-Hispanic sentiments, Canadians, especially in British Columbia, earned a reputation for "Paki-bashing."

Since they developed after the fragmentation of the U.S. Klan, there were competing Klans in Canada: Kanadian Knights of the KKK; Canadian Knights of the KKK; and Invisible Empire, Ku Klux Klan of Kanada. While these competing organizations exploited the social and political characteristics of each province, they also promoted a unifying theme of loyalty to empire, a Canadian version of "100 percent Americanism." Canadians also displayed a maple leaf emblem on the right breast of their robes opposite the traditional Klan symbol.

The Ku Klux Klan withered in wartime, but it revived briefly and barely in parts of the American West after World War II and during the civil rights era in the 1960s. Klansmen also penetrated the western states and Canada during the 1970s and 1980s, most visibly with David Duke's Knights of the Ku Klux Klan, Tom Metzger's California Klan, and Texas Klansmen protesting Vietnamese fishermen. [9] Once again, Americans recruited in Canada, especially in Ontario and British Columbia, from the mid-1970s into the 1980s. Several Canadian leaders received training in recruiting and paramilitary techniques in the United States, and four Canadian Klansmen and neo-Nazis, including a woman, were among the persons convicted of plotting with their American counterparts to overthrow the government of the island of Dominica in the Caribbean in 1981. [10] Today a Pacific Northwest branch of the Knights of the Ku Klux Klan has its headquarters in Tacoma, Washington.

With the Klan in disarray by the 1980s, groups like the Aryan Nations and its Christian Identity faith filled the Far Right vacuum. The British-Israel (or Anglo-Israel) movement added another dimension to the transnational cultural exchange. The idea that the British were the lost tribes of Israel "but never Jews" had existed for many years before Englishman John Wilson shaped it into the British-Israel movement between 1815 and the 1840s.[11] This new religious movement emerged during the nineteenth century and coincided with popular notions of Anglo-Saxonism and Manifest Destiny. British-Israelites even identified the United States as Manasseh, the thirteenth tribe. Wilson believed that England descended from the tribe of Ephraim. Manasseh was Joseph's less blessed son.[12]

British-Israelism found fertile soil in Canada and the United States during the Gilded Age, and in the United States it was initially strongest in the Northeast, until Pentecostalists in southern California absorbed some British-Israel themes early in the twentieth century.[13] The movement took other directions in the West when the Rev. Reuben H. Sawyer of the East Side Christian Church in Portland, Oregon, emerged as a lecturer for British-Israelism throughout the Pacific Northwest and western Canada, especially in Vancouver. Sawyer was also one of the founders of the British-Israel World Federation in London in 1919–20. He was philo-Semitic and published many articles favorable to British-Israel beliefs and lectured for the movement in the Pacific Northwest, Canada, and England. In late 1921, Sawyer began working as a lecturer for the fledgling Ku Klux Klan in the Pacific Northwest and was blatantly anti-Semitic. He made the first major public appeal for the Klan to an audience of nearly six thousand at the Portland Municipal Auditorium on December 22, 1921.[14]

Other forms of this movement emerged. Howard B. Rand, a lawyer from Massachusetts, led the British-Israel movement in the United States from the 1920s until World War II, and Herbert Armstrong's Worldwide Church of God, which he founded in Eugene, Oregon, during the 1930s, retained the essential theological characteristics of British Israelism. In 1930, as the American representative of the London-based British-Israel World Federation, Rand established the Anglo-Saxon Federation of America with headquarters in Detroit. By 1932, the new federation had a Pacific Coast district with members in all Pacific Slope states, "book-rooms in Los Angeles and Oakland, and a weekly radio program in Los Angeles."[15]

From the late 1930s through the 1940s, Canadians from Vancouver and Victoria provided a second source of inspiration and ideas for Rand's movement. Establishing a network extending from Vancouver through the Pacific Northwest to Los Angeles, they added a virulent Canadian strain of anti-Semitism to Rand's federation. These new ideas led to the founding of the Christian Identity movement shortly after World War II and reflected a timely convergence of post-Holocaust anti-Semitism with "right wing political causes during the Cold War decades."[16]

"A cadre of West Coast preachers," primarily from southern California, reshaped British-Israelism into Christian Identity. Their doctrine emphasized three beliefs: (1) white "Aryans" were the true descendants of Israel on a mission from God; (2) Jews were not Israelites but were literally children of the Devil; and (3) the world was on the verge of Apocalypse, Aryans needed to battle the Jewish conspiracy and its allies in order to save the world, and nonwhites were pre-Adamic "Mud People."[17] During the 1950s and 1960s, the Rev. Wesley Swift (1913–70), an associate of Smith, a former Methodist, and an organizer of the Ku Klux Klan in 1946, was the principal figure in the Christian Identity movement. "More than anyone else," political scientist Michael Barkun emphasizes, Swift "was responsible for popularizing Christian Identity in right-wing circles by combining British-Israelism, a demonic anti-Semitism, and political extremism."[18]

After Swift's death in 1970, William Potter Gale, a retired U.S. Army officer, James K. Warner, a former aide to George Lincoln Rockwell, and Richard Girnt Butler, a Lockheed engineer, each claimed to be his theological heir. Gale, a founder of the Posse Comitatus in the late 1960s, maintained a Christian Identity church in California, Warner moved his New Christian Crusade Church near David Duke in Louisiana, and Butler moved to Idaho, where he established the Aryan Nations in the mid-1970s.

Born in the American West, Christian Identity has reversed the flow of the British-Israel movement. It has spread throughout the United States, into western Canada, and overseas. Aryan Nations groups in Canada demand the inclusion of parts of British Columbia, Alberta, and Saskatchewan in the "Northwest Imperative" of a separate racial nation for whites. Terry Long, who was born in Canada and lived in the United States for ten years before graduating from the University of Alberta, was appointed Canada's "Aryan Warrior Priest" by Butler of the Aryan

Nations. Long prepared his Alberta farm as a Canadian version of the Aryan Nations compound at Hayden Lake, Idaho. The Vancouver British-Israel group changed its name to the Association of Covenant People in 1968 and maintained offices in British Columbia and Washington state.

These examples of the cross-border transfer of individuals, families, fraternal organizations, political ideology, and religious ideas in the American and Canadian Wests reinforce the convergence and continuity of cultural themes. But there is another factor. While many Canadians blame racism and nativism on an "American virus," it is obvious that Canada has a weak social immune system.[19]

This chapter has only begun to explore that issue. More research is needed for us to have a better understanding of how economic factors, demographic patterns, and cultural identity contributed to the growth of the Klan in both countries. We need to know more about the organizers of the Canadian Klan. Many of them arrived directly from the United States; others were homegrown products. We also need to know more about the social sources of Klan membership. To what extent did the Klan have a heightened appeal to first- or second-generation immigrants from the United States, especially in the prairie provinces? Membership records and demographic studies could help answer this question.

Although Canada has stricter laws about political activities and the distribution of hate literature, geographical proximity to the United States, the smuggling of printed and visual materials, and new sources of information technology have effectively nullified them. Most Canadians have access to American radio and television and newspapers, magazines, and books. Cheap printing techniques, audiotapes and videotapes, FAX machines, and computer transfer of data, information, and photographs allow widespread dissemination of hate literature. And there continues to be an unlimited potential for comparative studies of racism and the Far Right in the American West and Canada.[20]

Notes

This essay was originally presented at the conference of the Western History Association, Denver, October 1995.

1. *New Westminster Columbian*, April 2, 1980; *Portland Oregonian*, January 24, 1926.
2. For additional background on Powell, see Eckard V. Toy, "The Ku Klux Klan in Oregon,"

in G. Thomas Edwards and Carlos A. Schwantes, eds., *Experiences in a Promised Land: Essays in Pacific Northwest History* (Seattle: University of Washington Press, 1986), 271, 273, and 283.

3. See Kathleen M. Blee, *Women of the Klan: Racism and Gender in the 1920s* (Berkeley: University of California Press, 1991), 60–65, and Eckard V. Toy Jr., "The Ku Klux Klan in Oregon; Its Program and Character" (MA thesis, University of Oregon, 1959), 126–28.

4. David M. Chalmers, *Hooded Americanism: The History of the Ku Klux Klan*, 3d ed. (Durham: Duke University Press, 1987).

5. Newspapers in Montreal and Victoria reported Klan Kleagles in Canada in 1921 and 1922. Cited in Julian Sher, *White Hoods: Canada's Ku Klux Klan* (Vancouver: New Star Books, 1983), 25, and Martin Robin, *Shades of Right: Nativist and Fascist Politics in Canada, 1920–1940* (Toronto: University of Toronto Press, 1992), 1, 11, 17–18.

6. William Calderwood, "Religious Reactions to the Ku Klux Klan in Saskatchewan," *Saskatchewan History* 26 (Autumn 1973): 103.

7. See Sher, *White Hoods*, 19–59; Tom M. Henson, "Ku Klux Klan in Western Canada," *Alberta History* 25 (Autumn 1977): 1–8.

8. Sher, *White Hoods*, 32, 42, 49–50.

9. Sher, *White Hoods*, 86–112; Stanley R. Barrett, *Is God a Racist? The Right Wing in Canada* (Toronto: University of Toronto Press, 1987), 120–55.

10. In *White Hoods*, 165–79, Sher described it as "a Canadian caper."

11. Michael Barkun, *Religion and the Racist Right: The Origins of the Christian Identity Movement* (Chapel Hill: University of North Carolina Press, 1994), 6, 11.

12. Barkun, *Religion*, 11, 13

13. Barkun, *Religion*, 21.

14. Barkun, *Religion*, 22–26, 29, 49–50; Eckard V. Toy, "Robe and Gown: The Ku Klux Klan in Eugene, Oregon, during the 1920s," in Shawn Lay, ed., *The Invisible Empire in the West: Toward a New Historical Appraisal of the Ku Klux Klan of the 1920s* (Urbana: University of Illinois Press, 1992), 153–54.

15. Barkun, *Religion*, 30. For more on the Worldwide Church of God, see Roger R. Chambers, *The Plain Truth about Armstrongism* (Grand Rapids MI: Baker Book House, 1972).

16. Barkun, *Religion*, 44–51.

17. Barkun, *Religion*, viii–ix.

18. Barkun, *Religion*, 60–61.

19. Karen J. Winkler, "Scholars Call for New Focus in Studies of U.S. Culture That Emphasize Differences among American Nations," *Chronicle of Higher Education*, November 15, 1989, A5–7; Barrett, *Is God a Racist?* 299. Related studies are W. Peter Ward, *White Canada Forever* (Montreal: McGill-Queen's University Press, 1978) and Robin, *Shades of Right*.

20. Eckard V. Toy Jr., "The Far Right in the Far West since the 1930s," paper presented at the Western History Association meeting in Los Angeles, October 9, 1987.

16. Fugitives from Injustice

Vietnam War Draft Dodgers and Deserters in British Columbia

Renée G. Kasinsky

It was a typically wet January day in Vancouver, British Columbia, when three American deserters set out together to hitchhike to parts of eastern Canada in early 1970. They had heard from the rumor mill that there it was easier to get jobs in order to qualify for permanent residence status. Little did they suspect that they would find themselves that very evening in the custody of Royal Canadian Mounted Police (RCMP) officers, who would deliver them across the American border at the Sumas crossing into the hands of the United States Shore Patrol. In short order their world had been turned upside down again. They were very far from their original destinations and no longer in the free zone north of the forty-ninth parallel. In the course of forty-eight hours they had been illegally deported from Canada, placed in a Navy patrol van, and sent to the military stockade at Fort Ord, California.

Of all the allegations of deserters being "shanghaied" across the border by Canadian officials cooperating with their American counterparts, this case alone has been publicly documented. It resulted in a federal judicial inquiry in Canada.

The three protagonists in this case were Army deserters who had enlisted under the pressure of the draft. None had completed high school, and no one was over twenty-two years old. In almost all ways they were

This chapter was originally published in *Refugees from Militarism: Draft-Age Americans in Canada* (New Brunswick NJ: Transaction Publishers, 1976). Reprinted by permission of Transaction Publishers. Copyright © 1976 by Transaction Publishers.

typical of the backgrounds of most deserters in Canada. John Kreeger came from Chico, California, an affluent community, although his family lived on welfare allotments. "My mother's a poor person living in a rich person's world," John said. In high school John's teachers and counselors made it clear to him that he was "wasting their time and that he could be serving his time in the Army and saving the taxpayers' money." Despite his protests, he was dropped from the school rolls and subsequently channeled into the military. He did not enlist, however, until he received his notice of induction. Upon enlisting in the Army, he made it clear that he would do "anything but the infantry." From the outset John never wanted to be a soldier, hoping he would receive a discharge for being excessively AWOL. During the time he was AWOL, he traveled in underground circles where he met many other AWOL GIs who were also trying to get out of the service. He survived by getting odd jobs and living off charity. John eventually met some people from the resistance in the San Francisco area and obtained access to the *Manual for Draft-Age Immigrants to Canada*. His attitude regarding desertion began to undergo a change. The first times he went AWOL he was told by those around him that it was a crime to desert from the Army; then he was being commended for his actions. John said of the resistance people: "They were strong leftists, and they felt that you were doing your part for the country when you go AWOL and desert. . . . It began to occur to me that it's really a crime to kill people in Vietnam. The government's been committing a crime in Vietnam."

Since John had been AWOL so long, he was convinced he would go to Leavenworth Federal Penitentiary if he returned to the Army. So he made the decision to "split" to Canada. He made use of the contacts of the underground railroad, staying in various homes of sympathizers along the western seaboard. He crossed the Canadian border illegally as a visitor on January 16, 1970.

In Vancouver, John received immigration counseling at the Vancouver Committee to Aid American War Objectors and was referred to the hostel run by the American Deserters Committee. There he met two other deserters, also from California, who had been AWOL only a couple of weeks. He had been in Canada only three days when they made plans to leave Vancouver together.

Before the actual deportation occurred, John Kreeger, while still in custody, contacted a Unitarian minister, who contacted a lawyer, and together they made public their knowledge of the illegal deportation on CBC's *Weekend* national show. David Lewis, leader of the New Democratic Party (NDP, Canada's labor party) in 1970, raised the issue in Parliament. The public pressure by the NDP as well as citizens' groups like the British Columbia Civil Liberties Association resulted in a government judicial inquiry into the incident. Meanwhile, the deserters escaped from military custody. Two were recaptured, and Kreeger managed to evade law enforcement authorities in the United States with support from friends and the underground. A month later he was helped to return to Canada legally in order to testify at the inquiry.

Judge Stewart, who conducted the inquiry, came to the conclusion that the three deserters had been unlawfully returned to the United States by RCMP constables in the presence of an immigration officer. He argued that misunderstanding, confusion, and coincidence were the reasons for the deportation and that it "was an isolated and unplanned incident."

The outcome of the inquiry made a "special case" of John Kreeger. Although he was not given landed immigrant status because he did not qualify under the immigration point system, which favored the educated, skilled immigrant, he received a special work permit unlike other deserters at the time. He became known to a number of professional people, including his lawyer, who helped him with legal problems, housing, and references when he needed them. Most deserters did not have these kinds of contacts. Yet this did not help John to find a job and live an easy life. He was still a transient, unskilled youth, and he had a difficult time securing employment. It took six months of hard times before John located his first job at Vancouver warehouse, beginning at the bottom of the pay scale with no union benefits.

In the fall of 1973 John began to feel more secure in Canada. A multi-colored information center bus rolled up to John's corner in Vancouver, a working-class section where many immigrants lived. It brought word of a sixty-day amnesty for all those illegal immigrants and visitors who would be given the opportunity to become landed immigrants, regardless of their poor education and training. The glut of deportation appeals facing the appeals board made it impossible to obtain an appeal hearing for as long as a decade, necessitating a more lenient approach toward those illegal immigrants and visitors who came to Canada before November 30, 1972. John had read an advertisement concerning this Adjustment of Status Program. However, his prior experience made him mistrustful of the Department of Manpower and Immigration's intentions. It was only when the word came from the Canadian Coalition of War Resisters' information bus, sponsored as part of Immigration's $1.4 million advertising campaign, that John went down to the Vancouver immigration office to register and obtain landed immigrant status.[1]

Three years had passed since John was welcomed into Canada by the Vancouver Committee to Aid American War Objectors, only to be illegally deported. The activity of the aid groups had come full circle. They had begun as an informal assistance network for American war objectors and were officially regarded by Ottawa officials as antiestablishment protest groups. The aid groups had become so effective in their immigration counseling that the Canadian Immigration Department was forced to solicit their assistance and fund them for uncovering the thousands of illegal immigrants to whom the Canadian government offered amnesty. Thus within a seven-year period an oppositional movement had become part of established Canadian life.

The Vietnam War and Exile

The Vietnam War may well have been the most unpopular war in American history. In order to conduct it, it became necessary for the government to appeal to law and order and apply illegal measures to stifle evergrowing dissent and resistance.

The government found it necessary to end the draft, to offer conditional clemency for war resisters in order to placate hostile public opinion, and eventually to extricate itself entirely from a direct military role in the conflict in Southeast Asia. The unpopularity of the war toppled two presidents from their high office: Lyndon Johnson by his refusal to run for another term and Richard Nixon by resignation upon exposure of his involvement in the Watergate scandal. Resistance to it was expressed by the opposition of young draft-age American men like John Kreeger who personally suffered the consequences of the war and its unpopularity. The resistance movement in the United States estimated that by 1974 approximately 200,000 men in America were fugitives from the draft or the military, were awaiting trial, or were in prison.[2]

Official government statistics from August 4, 1964, the date of the Tonkin Gulf Resolution in the Senate, to December 29, 1972, the last day on which a registrant entered involuntarily into the armed forces, indicate that approximately 1.8 million men had been inducted.[3] By June 1973 the draft was nonexistent and in its place was a volunteer army. Approximately 8,000 men had been convicted for refusal to accept induction. Half of them had received probationary sentences, and the other half served jail time. As of January 1, 1974, official figures cited 4,400 fugitives from the Selective Service System, of which an estimated 3,000 were in Canada.[4]

The number of desertions during the Vietnam War was even more indicative of the unpopularity of the war. Approximately half a million men deserted from all services for varying lengths of time. The high number of long-term AWOLs far exceeded that of the Korean War and rose with the increasing public dissatisfaction of the Vietnam War. At the end of 1973, official statistics reported almost 29,000 deserters at large, with some 2,000 believed to be in foreign areas.[5]

In summary, the government estimated in 1974 that between 5,000 and 6,000 Americans, both dodgers and deserters, were in exile in Canada. My own estimated figures of American refugees from both the Selective Service System and the military are at variance with the official government figures cited above. Using Canadian immigration statistics of draft-age American males during the Vietnam War years, I estimate that there were between 30,000 and 40,000 American exiles in Canada alone. The official statistics for those men who had been fugitives from the draft and the military have been greatly deflated and do not properly present the widespread nature of dissent to the Vietnam War that existed among draft-age American youth during this period.

American war refugees in Canada fall into two distinct groups: draft dodgers and deserters. These were the descriptive terms used by Canadians to refer to these men, with no pejorative meaning intended. Between 1964 and 1974, they fled the United States and immigrated to Canada as an expression of their opposition to the Vietnam War.

How did these Americans view themselves in relation to the United

States government, and how did their refugee status affect their lives in Canada? To what extent did class and social background factors affect America's treatment of resisters and influence their careers in Canada? What sustained the successful refugee in exile in psychological and material terms, and what kinds of aid did he receive? What impact have these men made on Canadian life? Did these political refugees successfully assimilate into Canadian life, or did they return to the United States?

These men perceived themselves as having to choose between obeying their consciences or obeying the rules of the state. The sons of the middle class who had a college education became draft dodgers when they were no longer favored by the deferrals of the Selective Service System. The sons of the lower-income and working classes were inducted into the armed service directly from high school, or else they volunteered in the hope of obtaining a skill and traveling beyond their narrow life circumstances, and they became deserters. For the dodger this occurred when the Selective Service System interfered with his life and career aspirations; for the deserter, the break came when he was incorporated into the Vietnam War machine. Their personal confrontation with the draft and the Vietnam War helped these young men to define their beliefs and forced them into bold, assertive action in which they sought refuge in the "North Country Fair."

Once in Canada, however, these men had to apply for landed immigrant status and permanent residence. The draft dodgers were successful for the most part in obtaining such status, whereas the door was closed to the majority of deserters. These men began to realize that the channeling of the Selective Service System, which in the words of one study had "succeeded in drawing ever more sharply the lines of class in the United States," was being continued in Canada via the Canadian Immigration Act.[6] The immigration system, heavily biased toward an individual's education, occupational training, and skills, discriminated in favor of the educated, skilled draft dodger and against the working-class, unskilled, uneducated deserter.

The Canadian groups that helped these Americans resettle in Canada were initially organized as apolitical charitable organizations whose major objective was to obtain landed immigrant status (permanent residence) for all refugees seeking their help. However, when a large number of deserters who sought their aid were unsuccessful in obtaining immigrant status, these organizations were forced to become political pressure groups struggling against the continental channeling of draft dodgers and deserters.

The draft dodgers, then, for the most part, were able to start their new lives where they had left off, continuing their education, finding skilled and professional work, or maintaining themselves as small entrepreneurs in the counterculture. The deserters continued to be fugitives, without landed immigrant status, with its consequences of living underground, unemployed and without roots, until an amendment of the Immigration Appeal Board Act in 1973 permitted all illegal visitors to obtain such status under relaxed criteria.

These American refugees became disillusioned and increasingly estranged from the mainstream of American society. As new pioneers they attempted to transplant the American dream onto their Canadian lives. Although most of the draft dodgers were successful in beginning their lives anew, most of the deserters were not able to get a foothold in Canada. Thus the question of amnesty and returning to the United States, for most of these refugees, was seen as a political question. They resisted any conditional amnesty, including President Gerald Ford's terms for 1975. Most draft dodgers indicated that they would not return to America to live, as they had already transplanted their lives. Only deserters who had not assimilated into Canadian life were tempted to return, although most did not because the terms did not accept the justice of their position in opposition to the Vietnam War. Those politically articulate refugees like Roger Williams, who wrote *The New Exiles* and who eventually succeeded in returning to the United States, explained that repatriation rather than amnesty was the issue at hand. "The question, really, is not whether or not anyone, or any government, has the right to prevent them from returning when they have done nothing in light of the Vietnam War which can remotely be called a crime. They have the inalienable right to return." [7]

These young men stood at a unique moment in history. To comprehend their reasons for going into exile is to understand one of the major sociopolitical forces that shaped the lives of all draft-age American males in the Vietnam War period: the continental youth channeling system of North American capitalism. This system had a political, social, and economic component. It was a system designed by the state (political) that manipulated the career patterns and life chances of draft-age youths (social) in order to integrate them into North American capitalism and to maximize its productive capacity (economic).

The channeling began with the Selective Service System exerting control over the career patterns and life chances of all draft-age American youth. It was designed to subordinate these youth to the interests of the American economy, an economy dominated by multinational corporations.[8] It then guided the dissidents of the Selective Service System into exile, creating both the middle-class draft dodger and the working-class deserter. It favored the dodger because his education and skills were the most useful to the economy. This selection process based upon distinctions of class (education and occupation skills) was continued in Canada vis-à-vis the Immigration Act and Canada's branch plant economy. United States–based multinational corporations were able to channel dissident youth from the motherland and reintegrate the middle-class dodger into the branch plant economy of Canada, which was under their economic control. Thus the story of America's refugees from militarism represents the intersection of personal biography with social history. The experiences of these Americans stand witness to one of the central conflicts of our time in the West: the struggle between individual conscience and the political aspirations of the state.

An Observer's View

I spent six years in Canada as a participant observer, from the summer of 1969 through 1975, interviewing and meeting with American refugees. Research on those who were fugitives was a very sensitive area; trust and rapport were critical in obtaining personal information. Due to their suspicion of outsiders, survey techniques proved to be an ill-suited method of obtaining information about political refugees. Many could not afford to reveal information about themselves to a researcher whose motives were not expressed. Therefore, an important aspect of my observation method was to establish a trusting relationship with individuals and groups over a sustained period so that I could observe representative and uncensored behavior. For this study, being a woman was a distinct advantage in establishing the necessary rapport with these American refugees. I was not subjected to as much questioning, especially with regard to the possibility of my being an undercover FBI agent or spy for the American government, as were male observers. It was also less embarrassing to those men who felt uncertain or ashamed of their actions to disclose their feelings to a woman. I was not perceived as a competitor or as someone who would pass judgment on their choice because I might have acted differently with regard to my own military status.

My home base was Vancouver, British Columbia, the major port city in western Canada, where American refugees flocked by the thousands due to the relatively mild climate and the spectacular countryside. More than two-thirds of my direct observation was done in Vancouver, although I spent much time during these years in the major cities of Toronto, Ottawa and Montreal, where the major American refugee aid groups were located. Since I was an American citizen who had immigrated to Canada around the same time as the start of my study, I experienced many of the same problems these young Americans faced in getting settled. I had to find a place to live, obtain landed immigrant status, get a job, begin making new friends, and reorient myself to a different country. But since I was not a fugitive from justice, I did not have to use underground contacts in coming to Canada as some of these Americans did. Neither was my choice in coming to Canada forced on me by the lack of any viable alternatives in the United States other than jail or the military. I was not cut off from my friends and relatives and could easily cross the border and return freely to the States—a simple act that most of these men could not do without risking arrest.

My methodology consisted of observing the total process whereby these Americans first became political refugees to their eventual assimilation in varying degrees into Canadian life. To observe the first part of this process, I became a volunteer worker at the Vancouver Committee to Aid American War Objectors, doing a variety of routine tasks such as sending out replies to incoming correspondence from Americans inquiring about Canada and answering phone calls. This gave me the opportunity to chat casually with newcomers, observe their interaction with the aid of counselors, and generally learn about the functioning of the aid group. The aid group helped place these newcomers in private homes or refugee hostels for the first few weeks. In addition to direct observation, I used a historical approach to describe the refugee aid organizations in Canada since their inception in 1966.

During 1969 and 1970, at the height of the emigration, I systematically spent time at some of the refugee hostels in Vancouver, chatting with the occupants and observing some of their activities. I regularly attended gatherings where Americans congregated. I also attended special meetings and conferences for American refugees and their supporters. As a sympathetic party, I had a number of American refugees living in my home for their first few weeks in Canada during the duration of my research. I formed close relationships with some of these individuals. Some of them have been key informants, discussing with me the implications of my findings and suggesting new issues I had overlooked. Still other major discoveries were made accidentally as I was hitchhiking or traveling through Canada while on holidays from my work.

Although the direct observation method offered me a large range of detailed interaction data on American refugees, there were some things it could not answer. It did not allow me to contact a large sample of individuals and none that was as representative as possible. Thus, in order to obtain more systematic information, I supplemented my observation methods with a detailed eight-page questionnaire. It was organized according to experiences and crucial episodes that had structured the lives of American refugees while they were involved with the draft, the military, and Canadian activities. This I gave as an interview schedule to 123 American refugees from the four major Canadian cities in 1970. It consisted of one-half draft resisters and one-half deserters. An attempt was made to include a diverse group, taking into consideration the length of time an individual had been in Canada, regional differences, and men who settled in different areas in Canada. These persons were obtained by the "snowballing technique" in which the first few refugees who participated often volunteered their friends and suggested other refugees whose experience was different from their own.

To obtain a somewhat larger sample I also cross-checked some of my information with another questionnaire that was administered by the counselors of the Vancouver Committee to all those men who sought their aid over a two-month period in the summer of 1970. I tallied approximately 425 questionnaires from this source to compare with my own sample.

In addition to the questionnaires, I taped thirty in-depth interviews across Canada with refugees whom I determined to be representative of diverse social types. The interviews probed complex questions on identity and labeling which I was not able to explore fully through field observations or questionnaires. In total, I contacted over 1,200 American refugees across Canada through these three research approaches. The methods of direct observation and the historical approach, when combined with the analysis of questionnaires and in-depth interviews, permitted a systematic study with considerable cross-checking of data and conclusions.

Social Backgrounds of American Refugees

Who were the young men who fled to Canada, either to dodge the draft or to desert from the American armed forces? To understand them we must look at the individual and social biographies of these young refugees from militarism. The picture we have in our minds based on newspaper and magazine accounts is that most of these young men were radicals of the New Left or hippies who had given up their belief in the American dream. Such a view has not been substantiated. These new immigrants to Canada represented a diverse section of the American youth population as a whole. The first pamphlet of the Canadian aid groups entitled "Escape from Freedom" summed up this diversity of American draft dodgers and commented upon their distinctly American origins: "This is the first group of immigrants from the States who can't be stamped with a specific political, social, or religious stripe. They are as diverse as Americans themselves; a composite portrait simply cannot be drawn. But certain outlines do emerge. They are the best educated group of immigrants Canada has ever had. . . . But the most striking thing is how 'American' draft resisters are in most respects. Perhaps what some would call their weakness is that they believe in all the things America is supposed to stand for."[9]

In my questionnaire sample, one-third of these men had grown up in the western part of the United States. This bias toward westerners was due in part to my sampling technique, as the bulk of the interviews were held in British Columbia. Almost another third of these men came from the northwestern part of the United States. The South and the Midwest were each represented in about 20 percent of the cases. Almost two-thirds of these men came from urban areas. Their average age was twenty-two, with the deserters being a few years younger than the draft dodgers. Most of the refugees had American citizenship, but there were some Canadian refugees returning home to Canada who had been living in the United States. These Canadians were called by the Selective Service System; they failed to report and were classified as fugitives. Not all the Canadians who found themselves in the clutches of Uncle Sam's army decided to leave the country. At least eight of them took up American citizenship after having fought in Vietnam. A number of them died on the battlegrounds in Vietnam. There were also seven young men who were aliens living in America and who also had been drafted. An additional seven men were former American citizens who had renounced their citizenship and were also classified as aliens by the Selective Service System.

Almost all of the refugees were white; black Americans accounted for only 3 percent of my sample. From participant observation and my interviews with counselors and other refugees, it is clear that this number of black refugees was representative of the low percentage of blacks who had sought emigration as a solution to their draft or military problems. Those blacks who did come to Canada were from middle-class families, and almost all had attended one or two years of college. Fifty percent of my sample were of Anglo-Saxon descent, and 15 percent were of Eastern European descent. The remaining refugees had German, Italian, Scandinavian, American Indian, Irish, and Latino backgrounds.

About two-thirds of the refugees claimed to have no formal religious affiliation. Of those who did, the descending order of preference was Protestant, Catholic, and Jewish in the ratio of 4:2:1. Other religions represented included Buddhist, Quaker, and Unitarian. Significantly, how-ever, almost half of the refugees felt that religion was important to them, even though only one-third professed formal religious ties. The great majority of the parents of the refugees professed some form of formal religious affiliation in the same ratio as their sons, with only 15 percent claiming to have no religious affiliation. This suggested that the religious young men had not departed from the religions of their parents, though there seemed to be an increasing profession of nonattachment to formal religions with succeeded generations. Those men who grew up in religious homes assumed their religious nonconformism as a reflection of their own thinking and development.

Thus it would seem that the refugee's value orientations and beliefs were more crucial than such personal and social characteristics as his geographical location, ethnicity, and class in distinguishing him from his parents' generation and his American peers.

Both draft dodgers and deserters had certain common experiences and values that distinguished them from their parents and their peers. They rebelled against their upbringing for the most part and adopted different values and lifestyles from their parents.

I asked the men to indicate their lifestyle in a few words and to indicate their parents' lifestyle. The responses to these questions indicated strong contrasting value systems. Some of the most vivid responses were found in the following list of expressions, the first one referring to the refugee's lifestyle and the second referring to that of his parents:

> drifter/stable middle class
> moving to farm/moved from farm to city
> casual/uptight
> moving/stagnant
> transient/settled

These terms all related to a type of motion or movement. The active, unbound, exploratory movements of the refugee contrasted sharply with the restrained, "stagnant" lifestyle that described his parents. The second list of expressions related to the differences in values between the refugees and his parents:

> freethinking/conformist
> freaky/straight
> free/comfortably limited
> radical/moderate
> nonconformist/traditionalist
> communal/capitalistic

The "inner-directed," freethinking man, personifying the refugee, contrasted sharply with the man who derived his values from the consumer-oriented marketplace.

Many of these Americans dissented in their opinions from those of their peers within their communities. These young refugees indicated in their personal histories and decisions that they should be characterized as nonconformists within their peer group. In relation to their colleagues in the universities or in the military, they were either singled out or felt themselves to behave and think differently from those persons around them. Often their opinions against the war in Vietnam served to articulate distinctive values, especially in those areas of the South and Midwest where there was relatively little dissent against the war in the early years. Some of them were cut off from their families and hometowns because of their nonconformist ideas and behavior. Others were subjected to strong pressures from their friends when these friends learned of their decision to come to Canada. For example, a black draft dodger reported that his friends accused him of coming to Canada because he was trying to become like "Whitey."

Statistical data supported the theory that these refugees were independent nonconformists. The majority of Americans stated that they were little influenced by what others thought of their decision to leave the country. This demonstrated that their decisions to a large extent reflected their own thought and determination of action. Comparing dodgers to deserters reflected that a higher percentage of the deserters, 39 percent compared with 24 percent of the dodgers, were influenced in their decision to leave the country. This was indicative of the greater degree of pressure on men in the military to conform. In contrast, dodgers were usually students, and conformity was not the valued norm for them, at least in philosophical terms.

In addition to having a common background of nonconformist views and actions, both the draft dodger and deserter in Canada shared another important characteristic, namely, that their flight to Canada was in most cases the first political act of significance in their lives. These men could not be branded as political activists for the most part. Although almost all of them were opposed to the Vietnam War, most of them were not leaders in the resistance movement or antiwar activities either on or off the campus. Most of them participated in one or two large peace demonstrations, but for the most of them, this was the first time they had to make a major decision of a political nature. The chief exceptions to this generalization were those draft dodgers who came to Canada between 1968 and 1970.

Half of the refugees defined themselves as "radical," including a few as socialists, anarchists, and communists. Another quarter described themselves as "apolitical." These latter individuals favored a radical life-style but claimed that they were "beyond politics" or explained that everything in their lives was political. The remaining quarter was pre-dominantly "liberal," with only a few persons describing themselves as "conservative." This political grouping was the opposite of the parents' political orientation, as seen through the eyes of their sons. Half of the parents were characterized as political conservatives, among them John Birchers and [Ronald] Reagan and [George] Wallace supporters. One-quarter of these men described their parents as liberal, and the remaining quarter divided between "apolitical" and "no reply" with only 4 percent of the parents referred to as "political radicals."

Another major area in which dodgers and deserters were similar was that they had neither a criminal background nor an extensive record of previous convictions. The Vancouver Committee sample, together with my sample, indicated that out of a total of four hundred refugees who were asked if they had ever been convicted, only forty-four men or five percent indicated convictions other than parking tickets. The largest ma-jority of these convictions were for petty theft or misdemeanor charges. Approximately twenty were arrested for drug-related charges, mainly the possession of marijuana. Two deserters had been convicted of grand larceny; however, in some states possession of marijuana was considered a felony. The number of convictions among these men did not appear to be overly high for their age range, considering that most of the laws they had violated discriminated against youth as a group.

American refugees, therefore, were similar in most ways to their youthful counterparts in the United States with the exception that they were for the most part nonconformists with strong views against the war. More important, however, there were striking differences between the draft dodgers and the deserters in terms of their social background and their career routes to Canada. The deserters were more recent arrivals in Canada. Although the draft dodgers had sought refuge in Canada since 1965, deserters only began coming to Canada in larger numbers since 1968. Fifty-nine percent of the draft dodgers in my sample had been in Canada from one to three years, whereas only 21 percent of the deserters had been in Canada that long.

A number of factors explain why deserters came to Canada later than the draft dodgers. In the United States, newspapers carried stories daily about war atrocities until the public began to see through the maze of propaganda and generally became more favorable toward the antiwar position. The year 1968 saw the development of resistance groups against the draft and, concurrently, the beginnings of a GI movement against the war. Resistance in the Army (RITA) began an underground press whose primary circulation was directed to GIS. RITA made its presence felt on all major military bases in the form of informal coffeehouses. In Canada, more information about emigration as an alternative to the draft was making its way into resistance circles in the United States from those first resisters who had organized refugee aid organizations. The media carried stories on these men and their organizations, letting other men know there was a way out.

Generally, the deserters who came to Canada between 1966 and 1970 were younger than those draft dodgers who emigrated during this period. When I compared my sample taken in the winter of 1969 with the Vancouver Committee sample taken in the summer of 1970, a striking difference could be seen in the younger age group of men ages seventeen to twenty. In my sample only 17 percent of the dodgers and deserters fell within this age group, whereas in the Vancouver Committee sample 43 percent of the men were between the ages of seventeen and twenty. In their sample were 127 draft dodgers; none were in this age group in my sample. Here was a strong indication of the effect of the new draft lottery system, initiated in January 1970, in which the burden of the draft was designed to weigh most heavily on the younger men. It was also noteworthy that 10 percent of individuals over twenty-six used the Vancouver Committee to aid them in immigrating to Canada.[10] Among this group were families with young sons, veterans, a number of whom had already served in Vietnam, all receiving honorable discharges. Fifty-three women, almost all of whom were single, also filled out questionnaires at the Vancouver Committee during these months. During the Vietnam War era, American women ages fifteen to twenty-nine who received landed immigrant status in Canada exceeded that of draft-age American men.[11] All of these diverse groups together represented the broadening of the spectrum of political refugees seeking aid from the Canadian groups in Canada in the early 1970s.

The most important difference between the dodgers and the deserters was in the social class of these men. Since education has traditionally been an important index of relative class position in our society, the educational background of their parents reveals this difference. The data indicate that the parents of dodgers had considerably more college education than the parents of deserters. Two-thirds of the parents had some college experience or had obtained their college degrees, the latter group accounting for about half the total sample. By way of contrast, only one-third of deserters had parents with college experience or college degrees. The bulk of such families, about two-thirds, had only some high school experience or a high school diploma.

A comparison of the occupational levels of parents of American refugees yielded similar findings. The bulk of the dodger families, about two-thirds, were skilled tradesmen, professionals, or managers, whereas these categories encompassed only half of the deserters' families. The other half of the latter group were in the unskilled or semiskilled category, as compared with only about one-third of the dodgers' parents.

Thus we can conclude generally that on the basis of their socioeconomic level of education and occupation, dodgers' parents tended to be middle and upper class, and deserters' families tended to come from the working class.

What other observers had not sufficiently characterized, however, and what showed up clearly in my data was the size of the minority in the sample. I noted that about one-third of the deserters' families had some college experience and were in the skilled or professional category. The class distinction between the dodgers and the deserters became more apparent when we considered the educational and occupational levels of the dodgers and deserters themselves. As we might expect, these tended to correlate fairly closely with those of their parents.

The results of my questionnaire regarding the educational and occupational status of the refugees substantiated the claim made by the refugee aid groups that these men were quite educated. My data also verified that there was a strong class distinction between the dodgers and the deserters. While 90 percent of the dodgers had some college experience, 64 percent having acquired bachelors of arts or professional degrees, only half of the deserters had college experience, with most of them having only one or two years in a junior or technical college. As one's educational level closely correlated with one's occupational level in an urban technological society, the occupational data closely paralleled the educational portraits of these men. My data showed that whereas only 5 percent of the dodgers had full-time unskilled or semiskilled work, almost half of the deserters had such unskilled or semiskilled work. Almost all of the dodgers were full-time students or engaged as skilled tradesmen or professional workers.

The Vancouver Committee data on both the educational and occupational levels of these men substantiated the overall conclusions of my data. Since it was approximately three times the size of my sample and represented more of a random sample of refugees collected over a two-month period, it was probably more representative of the larger community of American refugees in Canada.

Another major difference between the draft dodger and the deserter stemmed from his relation to American law and his experience with jail. A total of thirty men out of my sample of 123 indicated that they had spent time either in jail or in a military stockade or had received an indictment for their arrest by the FBI for desertion or dodging the draft. Of these men, twenty, or two-thirds of them, were deserters. The actual proportion of deserters was probably even higher; many of them indicated that they did not know if they had been indicted, since they had been "on the lam" in the United States and had been living "underground." The use of underground contacts in coming to Canada was also more frequent among deserters than among dodgers. Almost three times the number of deserters than dodgers made use of underground contacts in coming to Canada. Two major factors seemed to be involved here. Because a higher number of deserters had been indicted and were being sought by the FBI, they were forced to take more precautions and to be more secretive in their relations and not to rely upon their known friends and acquaintances. There also seemed to be a more concerted effort in the various movement and GI counseling groups to direct GIs to Canada and supply them with a list of underground stops and contacts. Resisters or dodgers, especially those who had not already resisted or refused induction, were discouraged from coming to Canada by these movement groups.

It is clear that the deserters were relative newcomers to Canada, coming in larger numbers only since 1968. They tended to rely, more than the dodgers, upon underground contacts in making their way to Canada. They were generally a couple of years younger than the dodgers, although this began to alter as younger men were drafted by the lottery system in 1970. The middle-class background of the dodger and the working-class background of the deserter were the most crucial factors, however, for the individual's relationship to the Selective Service System.

> Editor's note: In September 2004, various residents of the borderlands town of Nelson, British Columbia (just north of the Idaho and Washington lines), engineered the idea to host a weekend commemorative forum honoring the American draft-dodgers from the Vietnam War, and to build a permanent memorial for them. According to the *New York Times*, Nelson and the Slocan Valley of British Columbia are considered to have the highest concentration of U.S. draft resisters in Canada, and many of the leaders of this event were Americans who fled the United States during the war in Vietnam and who relocated in this region. Organizer Isaac Romano, director of the July 2006 commemoration that is called the Our Way Home Reunion Weekend, stated that the celebration would "mark the courageous legacy of Vietnam War resisters and the Canadians who helped them resettle in this country during that tumultuous era." The festival includes a long list of both Americans and Canadians who were instrumental in the peace movement of the 1960s and who supported the war resisters. News in the United States of the event and the possible memorial, however, so enraged members of such organizations as the Veterans of Foreign Wars that a boycott was planned against the town of Nelson and the province of British Columbia. Romano and other Our Way Home leaders, worried about the economic impact a boycott would have on their small community and not wanting ill feelings toward the United States as a whole, at point scrapped plans for a permanent memorial but retained plans to host the weekend reunion.[12]

Notes

1. *Vancouver Sun*, October 1, 1973.
2. Hearings before the Subcommittee on Courts, Civil Liberties, and the Administration of Justice of the Committee on the Judiciary, House of Representatives, 93rd Cong. (Washington DC: U.S. Government Printing Office, 1974), 794.
3. "Vietnam War Draft Evaders and Deserters: An Official Count," *Congressional Digest* (October 1974), 230.
4. Administrative Office of the United States Courts, Washington DC; *Congressional Digest*, 230.
5. Jack Calhoun, "AWOLS: What They're Like," *AMEX* 3 (January/February 1973): 48; hearings before the Subcommittee on Courts, Civil Liberties, and the Administration of Justice, testimony of Walter H. Morse, General Counsel, U.S. Selective Service System.
6. Paul Lauter and Florence Howe, *The Conspiracy of the Young* (New York: World, 1970), 193.
7. Roger N. Williams, *The New Exiles* (New York: Liveright, 1971), 401.
8. Irving Louis Horowitz, "Capitalism, Communism, and Multinationalism," *Society* (January/February 1974): 32–43.
9. *Escape from Freedom; or, I Didn't Raise My Boy to Be a Canadian*, published by SUPA, Toronto, 1967.
10. See J. McRee Elrod, "The Over–Draft Age War Objector in Canada," in Kenneth P. Emerick, *War Resisters Canada* (Knox PA: Free Press, 1972).
11. See *Canadian Immigration Statistics, 1960–75* (Ottawa: Queen's Printer, 1975).
12. *New York Times*, November 21, 2004, sec. 9, p. 1. The Romano quotation is from Joe Kovacs, "Draft-dodger Memorial Ignites Rage among Vets," *WorldNetDaily*, September 26, 2004 (posted at *www.WorldNetDaily.com/news/article.asp?article_id=4036*. For further information regarding the celebration: *www.ourwayhomereunion.com*.

Addendum

Sterling Evans

Seeking Refuge for
Medical Marijuana Use in the Early Twenty-first Century

While compiling this book in 2002–2004 it was reported that three new patterns of American emigration to Canada for purposes of refuge were developing. One was for medical users of marijuana (*Cannabis sativa*) who were primarily leaving California for British Columbia. The second involved Americans moving to Canada to escape the conservative Bush administration's post-9/11 policies (stressing opposition to the Patriot Act and the wars in Afghanistan and Iraq of 2001–2005). And the third was for gay men and women who began to move across the border when Ontario and British Columbia legalized same-sex marriages in the summer of 2003. These last two areas, especially since the Canadian government legalized same-sex marriage for the entire country in 2005, will require future research when more demographic data and analysis are available, but this brief addendum on the first area is meant to begin discussion of these newer refugee topics.

On July 30, 2002, Canada instituted new regulations that permitted the growing and smoking of specified amounts of medical marijuana ("medipot") by patients who could demonstrate its medicinal necessity. Smoking cannabis has been proven to assuage the symptoms of cancer and other fatal diseases and can ease the pain caused by serious injuries. Many "compassion clubs" for medipot users have sprung up throughout British Columbia, especially in Vancouver, to support American and Canadian patients in need of the drug. Some Americans have moved legally and have applied for landed immigrant status. Others have requested political asylum or refugee status as fugitives from drug charges in the United States. Still others are living an underground existence with support from marijuana activists, including members of the BC Marijuana Party, which provides legal aid to medipot patients.

Many of these refugees had previously used marijuana in California pot clubs, made legal by the passage of Proposition 215 in 1996, which sanctioned medipot to treat some illnesses. In 2001, however, Attorney General John Ashcroft and Drug Enforcement Administration Director Asa Hutchinson in the new Bush presidency applied federal laws to crack down on California's clubs and to press charges against many medipot users, hundreds of whom have now fled to Canada.

One such American refugee in British Columbia is Steve Kubby, the 1998 Libertarian Party candidate for governor of California, who suffers from a rare form of adrenal cancer and who had been brought up on drug possession charges. He was later acquitted, but he and his wife moved to Sechelt, British Columbia, a small town on the Sunshine Coast that is home to several compassion clubs, where they run an Internet news program on marijuana issues and where they received permission to grow their own cannabis plants. He explained, "For many of us, this is a matter of life and death. I know I would be dead without marijuana." Physicians in California and British Columbia have confirmed that Kubby's twenty-five years of pot smoking since his cancer diagnosis in the late 1970s has been "the only reason he is alive." He continued, "If I don't smoke pot my blood pressure goes through the roof and would either burst a blood vessel or cause a heart attack."

Similarly, Steve Tuck, whose pot club in Humboldt County, California, was raided and closed, fled to British Columbia. Tuck, a disabled Army veteran who survived a 1987 parachuting accident that caused spinal and brain injuries, told a reporter, "I have to have marijuana to stay alive." He stated that if he were returned to the United States to face charges, he would die "choking on my vomit in jail."

The heightened demand for medipot has increased the output of British Columbia's already robust marijuana production. Ironically, according to Clifford Krauss, some British Columbia growers are former Americans who were draft dodgers fleeing the Vietnam War in the 1960s, a point not lost on California medipot refugee Renee Boje. She told Krauss, "It's an exodus. Canada has a history of protecting American people from its own government, like during the Vietnam War and the Underground Railroad that protected American runaway slaves." And heartened at Canada's tolerance, Steve Kubby stated, "It's threatening to the whole ideology of prohibition which says any marijuana use is criminal."[1]

Many thousands more of these refugees will continue to cross into Canada if the U.S. laws against medipot are not relaxed, perhaps giving new meaning to Brewer and Shipley's 1971 hit single, "One Toke over the Line." More research will be needed on this and other refugee issues to continue our understanding of the borderlands as a sanctuary.

Note

1. Thomas D. Elias, "Medical Marijuana Users Take Refuge in Canada," *Newsday*, May 28, 2002, 15; Clifford Krauss, "Ill Americans Seek Marijuana's Relief in Canada," *New York Times*, September 8, 2002, 4, 15.

Part 6. Natural Resources, Conservation, and Environmental Issues in the Borderlands

As this book began in part 1, discussing bioregions and a sense of place within the borderlands' natural environments, so it ends by examining other aspects of the region's natural resources, conservation, and environmental issues. One of the most important natural resources in the borderlands of the Pacific Northwest has always been salmon. In chapter 17, Lissa Wadewitz frames salmon fishing in the late nineteenth and early twentieth centuries around a borderlands thesis—the interaction of fish, Native Americans/First Nations, the salmon industry, and comparative policies on both sides of the international line. She concludes that for many involved in salmon fishing the border itself became more of a target of opportunity than a barrier, and that it increased the level of competition in the industry.

But what role has the boundary played in conservation initiatives in the region? By tracing the history of Alberta's Waterton Lakes National Park, and how the border divides it from, or connects it to, Glacier National Park in Montana, Cate Mortimer-Sandilands shows that there are important cultural, political, and ecological implications to the cleared border swath that runs between the two parks.

Other transboundary environmental issues abound in a region characterized by the stunning scenery of Pacific Northwest forests, the Rocky Mountains, and the wide-open spaces of the Great Plains grasslands—regions that are also endowed with some of the world's best timber and deposits of coal, oil, natural gas, and minerals. Thus a clear clash of values exists between proponents of increased economic development and advocates of conservation, the preservation of biodiversity, and tourism. Todd Wilkinson unpacks these contrasts in chapter 19, and via his research, analysis, and interviews with environmental activists in the borderlands of Montana and Alberta, he compares environmental issues and policies of the American and Canadian Wests.

For Further Reading

On Salmon in the Pacific Northwest Borderlands
On Forestry and Conservation in the Borderlands
On Other Transboundary Environmental and Energy Issues

On Salmon in the Pacific Northwest Borderlands

Arnold, David. "The 'Original Conservationists' and Salmon Management on the Northwest Coast, 1880s-1940s." Paper, conference of the American Historical Association–Pacific Coast Branch (AHA-PCB), Vancouver BC, August 2001.

Barcott, Bruce. "Aquaculture's Troubled Harvest." *Mother Jones*, November/December 2001, 38–45.

Boxberger, Daniel. *To Fish in Common: The Ethnohistory of Lummi Indian Salmon Fishing.* Lincoln: University of Nebraska Press, 1989.

Burke, Adam. "River of Dreams: The 30-Year Struggle to Resurrect Washington's Elwha River and One of Its Spectacular Salmon Runs." *High Country News* 33 (September 24, 2001): 1, 8–12.

Busch, Robert H. *Salmon Country: A History of the Pacific Salmon.* Toronto: Key Porter Books, 2000.

Clarren, Rebecca. "Bracing against the Tide: On the Rugged Coast of British Columbia, Tribes, Fishermen, and Environmentalists Fight a 'Salmon Apocalypse.'" *High Country News* 35 (March 17, 2003): 1, 8–11.

———. "Hatching Reform." *High Country News* 34 (June 10, 2002): 1, 8–12.

Cone, Joseph. *Common Fate: Endangered Salmon and the People of the Pacific Northwest.* New York: Henry Holt, 1995.

Crutchfield, James A., and Giulio Pontecorvo. *The Pacific Salmon Fisheries: A Study of Irrational Conservation.* Baltimore: Johns Hopkins University Press, 1969.

Deur, Douglas. "Salmon, Sedentism, and Cultivation: Toward an Environmental Prehistory of the Northwest Coast." In Goble and Hirt, eds., *Northwest Lands.*

Evenden, Matthew D. *Fish versus Power: An Environmental History of the Fraser River.* New York: Cambridge University Press, 2004.

Findlay, John M. "A Fishy Proposition: Regional Identity in the Pacific Northwest." In David M. Wrobel and Michael C. Steiner, eds., *Many Wests: Place, Culture, and Regional Identity.* Lawrence: University Press of Kansas, 1997.

Goble, Dale. "Salmon in the Columbia Basin: From Abundance to Extinction." In Goble and Hirt, eds., *Northwest Lands.*

Goble, Dale, and Paul W. Hirt, eds. *Northwest Lands, Northwest Peoples: Readings in Environmental History*. Seattle: University of Washington Press, 1999.

Lichatowich, Jim. *Salmon without Rivers: A History of the Pacific Salmon Crisis*. Washington DC: Island Press, 2001.

Lundeen, Dan. *Salmon and His People: Fish and Fishing in Nez Perce Country*. Lewiston ID: Confluence Press, 1999.

Marchak, Patricia. " 'Because Fish Swim' and Other Causes of International Conflict." In Patricia Marchak et al., eds., *Uncommon Property: The Fishing and Fish Processing Industry in British Columbia*. Toronto: Methuen, 1987.

Native American Solidarity Committee. *To Fish in Common: Fishing Rights in the Northwest*. Seattle(?): Native American Solidarity Committee, 1978(?).

Rogers, Raymond A., and Catherine Stewart. "Prisoners of Their Histories: Canada–U.S. Conflicts in the Pacific Salmon Fishery." *American Review of American Studies* 27, no. 2 (Summer 1997): 253–70.

Spranger, Michael S. "Columbia River Salmon: A Resource in Danger." *Pacific Northwest Forum* 9 (Summer/Fall 1984): 51–64.

Springer, Allen L. "The Pacific Salmon Controversy: Law, Diplomacy, Equity, and Fish." *American Review of Canadian Studies* 27, no. 3 (Autumn 1997): 385–410.

Taylor, Joseph E. "The Historical Roots of the Canadian-American Salmon Wars." In John M. Findlay and Ken S. Coates, eds., *Parallel Destinies: Canadian-American Relations West of the Rockies*, 155–80. Seattle: University of Washington Press, 2002.

———. *Making Salmon: An Environmental History of the Northwest Fisheries Crisis*. Seattle: University of Washington Press, 1999.

Wadewitz, Lissa. "Competing Cartographies: Natives, Newcomers, and Salmon in the Western Canadian–U.S. Borderlands." Paper, Canadian Historical Association, May 2005.

———. "The Nature of Borders: Salmon and Boundaries in the Puget Sound/Georgia Basin." PhD diss., UCLA, 2004.

On Forestry and Conservation in the Borderlands

Alberta-Montana International Partnership. *Alberta-Montana Discovery Guide: Museums, Parks, and Historic Sites*. Helena: Montana Historical Society, 1997.

Barnes, Marc. "The Current Status and the Future of Forest Certification North and South of the 49th." Paper, conference of the Association of Canadian Studies in the United States (ACSUS), Portland OR, November 2003.

Cooperman, Jim. "Cutting Down Canada." In Bill Devall, ed., *Clearcut: The Tragedy of Industrial Forestry*. San Francisco: Sierra Club Books, 1993.

Cox, Thomas R. "Changing Forests, Changing Needs: Using the Pacific Northwest's Westside Forests, Past and Present." In Goble and Hirt, eds., *Northwest Lands*.

Egan, Michael. "Wrestling Teddy Bears: Nature, Order, and Wilderness Masculinity in the Progressive-Era Pacific Northwest." Paper, AHA-PCB, Vancouver BC, August 2001.

Gates, Paul W., and Lillian F. Gates. "Canadian and American Land Policy Decisions, 1930." *Western Historical Quarterly* 15 (October 1984): 389–405.

Goble, Dale, and Paul W. Hirt, eds. *Northwest Lands, Northwest Peoples: Readings in Environmental History*. Seattle: University of Washington Press, 1999.

Greenpeace Foundation. *Broken Promises: The Truth about What's Happening in British Columbia's Forests*. Vancouver: Greenpeace Canada, 1997.

Hermer, Joe. *Regulating Eden: The Nature of Order in North American Parks*. Toronto: University of Toronto Press, 2002.

Langston, Nancy. *Forest Dreams, Forest Nightmares: The Paradox of Old Growth in the Inland West*. Seattle: University of Washington Press, 1996.

Lothian, W. F. *A Brief History of Canada's National Parks*. Ottawa: Ministry of the Environment, 1987.

————. *A History of Canada's National Parks*. Vol. 1. Ottawa: Parks Canada, 1976.

Lower, A. R. M. *The North American Assault on the Canadian Forest: A History of Lumber Trade between Canada and the United States*. Toronto: Ryerson Press, 1938.

MacEechern, Alan. "National Parks Ecological Policy: The United States–Canada Connection." Paper, ASEH, Tucson AZ, April 1999.

May, Elizabeth. *At the Cutting Edge: The Crisis in Canada's Forests*. Toronto: Key Porter, 1998.

McKay, Donald. *Empire of Wood: The MacMillan-Bloedel Story*. Vancouver: Douglas and McIntyre, 1982.

Peacock, Sandra L., and Nancy J. Turner. " 'Just Like a Garden': Traditional Resource Management and Biodiversity Conservation on the Interior Plateau of British Columbia." In Paul E. Minnis and Wayne J. Elisens, eds., *Biodiversity of Native America*. Norman: University of Oklahoma Press, 2000.

Rajala, Richard. *Clearcutting the Pacific Rainforest: Production, Science, and Regulation*. Vancouver: University of British Columbia Press, 1998.

Sierra Club of Western Canada. *Ancient Rainforests at Risk*. Victoria: Sierra Club, 1993.

Soulé, Michael E., and John Terborgh, eds. *Continental Conservation: Foundations of Reserve Networks*. Washington DC: Island Press, 1999.

Spence, Mark. "Continental Divides: Borders, National Parks, and the Environment in North America." Paper, ASEH, Tucson AZ, April 1999.

————. "Crown of the Continent, Backbone of the World: The American Ideal Wilderness and Blackfeet Exclusion from Glacier National Park." *Environmental History* 1 (July 1996): 29–49.

Stadfeld, Bruce. "The Environmental West of Canada and the United States." Paper, conference of the Organization of American Historians, Toronto ON, April 1999.

Strong, Clarence C., and Judy Schutza. "The Birth of Montana's Lumber Industry." *Pacific Northwest Forum* 3 (Winter 1978): 11–21.

Taber, Richard D., and Neil F. Payne. *Wildlife, Conservation, and Human Welfare: A United States and Canadian Perspective*. Malabar FL: Krieger, 2003.

Weide, Bruce. *Trail of the Great Bear: International Scenic Corridor–Greater Yellowstone to Banff–Jasper*. Helena MT: Falcon Press, 1992.

Worster, Donald. "Wild, Tame, and Free: Comparing Canadian and U.S. Views of Nature." In John M. Findlay and Ken S. Coates, eds., *Parallel Destinies: Canadian-American Relations West of the Rockies*, 246–73. Seattle: University of Washington Press, 2002.

On Other Transboundary Environmental and Energy Issues

Aiken, Katherine. "Western Smelters and the Problem of Smelter Smoke." In Goble and Hirt, eds., *Northwest Lands.*

Alley, Jamie. "The British Columbia–Washington Environmental Cooperation Council: An Evolving Model of Canada–U.S. Interjurisdictional Cooperation." In Richard Kiy and John D. Wirth, eds., *Environmental Management on North America's Borders*, 53–71. College Station: Texas A&M University Press, 1998.

Alm, Leslie. "A Matter of Science: Canada, the United States, and Acid Rain." Paper, ACSUS, Portland, OR, November 2003.

Alper, Donald. "Transboundary Environmental Relations in British Columbia and the Pacific Northwest." *American Review of Canadian Studies* 27, no. 3 (Autumn 1997): 359–84.

Alper, Donald, and Debra Salazar. "National and Transnational Identities and BC Environmental Activists." Paper, ACSUS, Portland OR, November 2003.

Day, Chad. "Binational Institutional Arrangements for Environmental Management in the Strait of Georgia and Puget Sound." Paper, ACSUS, San Antonio TX, November 2001.

Eaton, David. "Managing Transboundary Water Resources: An Analysis of Canadian-American Interlocal Cooperation." Paper, ACSUS, San Antonio TX, November 2001.

Fletcher, Thomas H. *From Love Canal to Environmental Justice: The Politics of Hazardous Waste on the Canada-U.S. Border.* Peterborough ON: Broadview Press, 2003.

Goble, Dale, and Paul W. Hirt, eds. *Northwest Lands, Northwest Peoples: Readings in Environmental History.* Seattle: University of Washington Press, 1999.

Hyde, Anne F. "Round Pegs in Square Holes: The Rocky Mountains and Extractive Industry." In David M. Wrobel and Michael C. Steiner, eds., *Many Wests: Place, Culture, and Regional Identity*, 93–113. Lawrence: University Press of Kansas, 1997.

Jones, Lillia C., Pamela Duncan, and Stephen P. Mumme. "Assessing Transboundary Environmental Impacts on the U.S.–Mexican and U.S.–Canadian Borders." *Journal of Borderlands Studies* 12 (1997): 73–96.

Kasoff, Mark J. "Canada–U.S. Energy Relations." Paper, ACSUS, Portland OR, November 2003.

Kirton, John. "The Commission for Environmental Cooperation and Canada–U.S. Environmental Governance in the NAFTA Era." *American Review of Canadian Studies* 27, no. 3 (Autumn 1997): 459–86.

Kiy, Richard, and John D. Wirth, eds. *Environmental Management on North America's Borders.* College Station: Texas A&M University Press, 1998.

Lemco, Jonathan. *The Canada–United States Relationship: The Politics of Energy and Environmental Coordination.* Westport CT: Praeger, 1992.

———. *Tensions at the Border: Energy and Environmental Concerns in Canada and the United States.* Westport CT: Praeger, 1992.

Melious, Jean O. "A Breath of Fresh Hot Air: Canada–U.S. Airshed Planning on the West Coast." Paper, ACSUS, San Antonio TX, November 2003.

Meserve, Peter Haynes. "Boundary Water Issues along the Forty-ninth Parallel: The Role of Subnational Legislatures." In Robert Lecker, ed., *Borderlands: Essays in Canadian-American Relations*, 80–112. Toronto: ECW Press, 1991.

Munton, Don. "Acid Rain and Transboundary Air Quality in Canadian-American Relations." *American Review of Canadian Studies* 27, no. 3 (Autumn 1997): 327–54.

Nemeth, Tammy. "Continental Rift: The 1973 Energy Crisis and Canada–U.S. Energy Relations." Paper, ACSUS, Portland OR, November 2003.

Richards, Rebecca T., Ellen Goddard, and Kyla Rice. "Electrical Market Restructuring and Rural Development: Trans-border Issues for Montana and Alberta." Paper, ACSUS, Portland OR, November 2003.

Schwartz, Alan M. "Introduction: The Present Moment in Canada–United States Environmental Relations." *American Review of Canadian Studies* 27, no. 3 (Autumn 1997): 321–26.

Schwartz, Alan M., and Michelle Lowry. "The Canada–U.S. Environment Relationship at the Turn of the Century." *American Review of Canadian Studies* 30 (Summer 2002): 207–26.

Vannijnatten, Debora L. "Canadian-American Environmental Relations: Interoperability and Politics." *American Review of Canadian Studies* 34 (Winter 2004): 649–64.

Vogel, David, and Alan M. Rugman. "Environmentally Related Trade Disputes between the United States and Canada." *American Review of Canadian Studies* 27, no. 2 (Summer 1997): 271–92.

White, Richard. *The Organic Machine: The Remaking of the Columbia River*. New York: Hill and Wang, 1996.

Wirth, John D. *Smelter Smoke in North America: The Politics of Transborder Pollution*. Lawrence: University Press of Kansas, 2000.

Wolfe, Mary Ellen. "The Milk River: Deferred Water Policy Transitions in an International Waterway." *Natural Resources Journal* 32 (Winter 1992): 54–76.

Wunder, John R. "Pacific Northwest Indians and the Bill of Rights." In Paul W. Hirt, ed., *Terra Pacifica: People and Place in the Northwest States and Western Canada*, 159–88. Pullman: Washington State University Press, 1998.

17. Fishing the Line

Political Boundaries and Border Fluidity in the Pacific Northwest Borderlands, 1880–1930s

Lissa Wadewitz

In the waning summer months of 1895, George Webber, a U.S. customs inspector in Puget Sound, expressed his exasperation in trying to police the water border between Washington and British Columbia. In particular, he was frustrated with Canadian fishing boats illegally crossing the border to help themselves to what Webber deemed an American possession—salmon taken in the numerous fish traps at that peninsula. "If you try to get to them," Webber complained of the Canadian vessels, "they will steam away for a hundred yards across the line and then lay and laugh at you." The only way to catch them, he advised, was "to wait your chance, and the first time you can get aboard them in American waters to make the seizure."[1]

Webber's laments echoed repeatedly from his perch in the salmon-infested waters of Puget Sound as he struggled to uphold U.S. customs laws and protect U.S. fisheries from the depredations of what he perceived as fish-hungry northern neighbors. Indeed, Webber's experiences with the Canadian fishing vessels at the turn of the century highlight several crucial issues regarding the connections between political borders and environmental policies and practices that beg further study.

Borders are not merely abstract political and economic entities; they divide, restrict, and mitigate the lives of the people living along their edges. Although American historians acknowledge this phenomenon with respect to the southern border of the United States, we have not looked at our northern border with the same level of diligence and inspiration. Historians interested in the intersections of social and environmental history should be particularly concerned with how working-class or poor peoples (designations often directly tied to issues of ethnicity) interacted with their natural surroundings and how conservation legislation came to affect them and the quality of their lives. As some scholars have shown, the creation of national parks and forests and other conservation legislation in the United States interfered with poor peoples' subsistence lifeways in some areas by pushing them out of designated spaces and restricting their methods of resource procurement. Peoples living in border regions underwent similar processes, but they were able to take advantage of political realities to achieve their subsistence needs by crossing the borders between the United States, Canada, and the international seas of the Pacific; these resources included both subsistence goods and wages.[2]

The designation of the U.S.–Canadian political border and the ready access to international waters in the western Puget Sound region contributed to economic and social changes in the late nineteenth and early twentieth centuries that, in turn, exacerbated rates of environmental exploitation. The evolution of the Pacific salmon fishing industry in western Washington and in southwestern British Columbia from approximately 1880 through the 1930s provides an excellent lens through which to examine these claims. Although the creation of the international boundary had some positive economic impacts on the lives of the region's inhabitants, with the onset of conservation laws governing the fisheries, the existence of the border ensured higher catches of salmon than might otherwise have been possible. In short, the border contributed to the decline of the Pacific salmon runs while simultaneously offering the region's fishermen greater financial opportunities.

The Puget Sound Salmon Fisheries: A Brief Overview

The life cycle of the Pacific salmon precipitated many of the border tensions that have touched the western U.S.–Canadian boundary. The main species of Pacific salmon begin their lives in rivers or lakes, migrate to the oceans where they spend their formative years, and then return to ascend their natal rivers and spawn in the same place as their ancestors. The Fraser River run of salmon has been of particular interest to policymakers since the late nineteenth century because their return path passes through the Strait of Juan de Fuca—the same body of water that divides British Columbia from Washington. As a result, residents of both countries have access to the salmon before they return to the Fraser River system in British Columbia proper. This fact of mutual access has given rise to years of controversy and negotiation between the United States and Canada, and has had a significant impact on the fishing activities in the region as well as the health of the runs.[3]

Concern about the future health of the salmon runs prompted some early efforts at conservation on both sides of the border, but these early restrictions were not very extensive, nor were they effectively enforced. Stricter laws on the Canadian side of the border, together with the placement of efficient American fish traps at Point Roberts, enabled fishermen on the American side of the border to catch a much larger proportion of Fraser River salmon. Recognizing this, both governments made efforts to negotiate a fair compromise with respect to the Fraser River fish as early as the 1890s, but a successful treaty was not achieved until 1937.[4]

Border Fishing: Rules vs. Reality

Although the policymaking record indicates that Americans catching a larger proportion of the Fraser River salmon was a sensitive point in negotiations, a review of the U.S. Customs records for the 1880s through the early 1900s suggests that fishermen from both sides of the border caught and sometimes stole the salmon passing through American waters and illegally transported them across the border for purchase by Canadian canneries—often under cover of darkness and fog. In other words, fishermen were able to avoid the more stringent Canadian fishing regulations, cross the fluid water border, and retreat with their scaled booty to the Fraser River canneries.

Once the salmon started running, Point Roberts, an otherwise sleepy, largely uninhabited peninsula that juts just south of the Washington–British Columbia border into official Washington waters (see figure 18 in the afterword), transformed into a buzzing, multicultural waterscape as fishers and cannery workers from "up and down Sound" converged at her coordinates in honor of the salmon. The white, Indian, mixed-blood, and Japanese fishermen from both sides of the border came in boats numbering in the hundreds as they mingled together awaiting the cargo for which they had come. If it was a good year, the sockeye run would fill out by about the middle of July or early August, and the most intense fishing of the season would be under way. The mood was festive and somewhat frenzied as the fish were caught and delivered to the various canneries around the Sound.[5]

The U.S. Customs records overflow with tales regarding Canadian fishermen crossing the border to fish in American waters or load up with the salmon caught at the efficient Point Robert traps. Apparently this was a common occurrence by the late 1890s, by which time the Pacific salmon fisheries had become quite profitable on both sides of the border, and the Puget Sound fisheries were gaining ground versus their Fraser River counterparts. Some of the steamers coming over from the British Columbia side to purchase fish conducted the entire transaction within legal parameters, whereas others risked capture in order to avoid the hassle and time associated with reporting. The frequency of the border crossings for salmon was determined by the path of the runs, which often stayed on the American side of the line until they turned north to the mouth of the Fraser River. While smaller vessels simply crossed over to fish in American waters, larger steamers stole to the boundary line in the middle of the straits and were met by canoes or sloops loaded with fish from the traps. The scows and sloops would then transfer the fish—often numbering in the thousands—to the Canadian vessels for delivery to the Fraser River canneries.

The customs officers policing the western U.S.–Canadian border around the turn of the century had many forces working against them in their quest to control smuggling, illegal crossings, and border fishing. They were notoriously understaffed, frequently overworked, and often not well trained or supervised. These problems grew in scope as immigration and customs laws became increasingly more stringent and complex. Even when their powers were clearly defined, the nature of the border environment—particularly the fluid water border of the greater Puget Sound region—made it extremely difficult to control border crossings and natural resource usage. In addition, the fledgling nature of the force on the Pacific at that time and lack of respect for its authority sometimes prevented the customs officers from effectively performing their duties. In such cases, the customs agent had little recourse, and in at least one such instance, the "seized" vessel simply steamed away. Others continued in their pursuit of fish in spite of the presence of customs officers, and at least one group of angry Indians went so far as to confront one official at gunpoint to demand the return of their seized boat. As a result of these conditions, the U.S. Customs patrols were not very effective at policing the American border. Seizures of fish and vessels are sprinkled throughout the letters from this period, but if hundreds of Fraser River fishing boats illegally crossed the border on a daily basis during the height of the salmon runs as the records indicate, the chance of getting caught with illegal fish was low, and the rewards were worth the risk.

Border fishing linked each class of people living and fishing up and down the Sound to their natural surroundings and its resources in varying and complex ways. Many of the American fish trap and cannery owners in the Point Roberts region were troubled by the success of the British Columbia canneries in buying up Point Roberts salmon, as they frequently saw these sales as cutting into their profits. Indeed, American cannery owners were extremely frustrated at their inability to control the actions of the fishermen, many of whom were American and Canadian Indians. Yet the frustrations and concerns of the cannery men and fish trap owners must be viewed with a cautious and sophisticated eye, for the shifting nature of national capital and ownership in the traps at Point Roberts and in the various canneries around the Sound not only color their concerns as ones of complex financial interest but also suggest that the group's ranks were split in intricate ways. How these capital and national interests clashed or aligned with environmental ones is an important question that needs to be investigated further.

Border fishing was a different issue for the fishermen themselves, but it still offered both threat and opportunity. In fact, the evidence indicates that both independent fishermen and fishermen who had promised a portion of their catch to a cannery could manipulate the border fish markets to get a better price for their fish from year to year. As Customs Officer Ira B. Myers reported in August 1883, as Indian and white fishermen selling fish to Canadian canneries in that year received as much as 50 percent more for their catch, the Canadian canneries were naturally dominating the market. And the best prices were not always on the Canadian side—

the practice worked both ways and shifted with the changing economic tides.[6]

In addition to fishermen using the border to get better prices for their fish, the boundary line also offered other fish workers the ability to get higher wages for their work. White American citizens and Indians often crossed the border with the fish runs to work in British Columbia fisheries, but being white or Indian made border crossing a relatively easy venture at first. On the other hand, though usually risking deportation due to the increasingly strict immigration laws in both British Columbia and the United States, Japanese fishermen and Chinese cannery workers also used the limited flexibility that the border offered. Often these workers would cross the boundary by both land and sea in search of employment in the fisheries or at other ventures once the fishing season came to a close. For example, in his report to the Collector of Customs, Deputy Collector Walker stated he believed that upwards of three thousand Japanese fish workers would try to cross the border by stealth as soon as the Canadian fisheries closed their doors. He claimed he caught more than thirty Japanese laborers trying to cross the line in just a few days' time; twenty-six of those failed to convince him that they should not be deported. Chinese cannery workers were also in high demand on both sides of the border, but faced significant competition from Native workers in British Columbia and tougher regulations regarding their movement into the United States after the Exclusion Act of 1882. Still there are hints that their border crossings often followed patterns similar to those of the Japanese.[7]

While Indian fishermen and workers were crucial to the success of the early fisheries and the border trade, the designation of the international border held special meanings and consequences for Native American and First Nation fishing communities in Washington and British Columbia. The line dividing the United States from Canada also divided bands of Coast Salish peoples bound together via highly significant kinship ties. In addition to the emerging reservation systems and the effects of the growing salmon canning industry, the boundary obstructed Salish patterns of land and sea use, interfered with their spiritual activities, and fractured their traditional system of salmon fishing site assignment. U.S. Customs officials and Indian agents recognized that the border arbitrarily divided

Native communities, but as with the newly imposed reserve system, did not know how to reshape Indian behavior to the new boundaries. As one western Indian agent wrote of the issue, the Natives "are intermarried and visit back and forth continually, and . . . the boundary line of nations has heretofore had but little influence with them or their intercourse with each other; so that to prevent entirely their going on to that side is next to impossible." Initially, customs officials allowed Indians some leeway in their border crossing activities, although their reasons are unclear. Perhaps this leniency was due to cultural sensitivity, but more likely it was due to the fact that as the Northwest Indians were still feared and considered dangerous, officials simply wanted to avoid trouble. By the early 1900s, this laissez-faire approach to Indian crossings began to fade, and increasing numbers of seizures of Indian vessels for illegal border crossings appear in the American record. [8]

The border and increasingly strict customs officials altered the character and accessibility of Indian fisheries on both sides of the boundary. Many Native groups had long traditions of fishing at Point Roberts and other points in Puget Sound. On top of the exclusionary tactics employed by fish trappers at Point Roberts, and the discriminatory laws against Indian fishers in American waters, more rigorous border crossing rules for Indians could only serve to further exacerbate their access to traditional fishing sites. For example, when the Lummi Indians brought suit against the Alaska Packers Association (APA) in the 1890s for denying access to their customary fishing sites at Point Roberts—fishing rights that were guaranteed in the Lummi treaty with the U.S. government—the APA strategically used the border in crafting its defense. The witnesses for the defense repeatedly claimed that contrary to Lummi claims, the tribe did not have a long tradition of fishing at Point Roberts. Indeed, they insisted that the only Indians who had the right to such claims were the Saanich and Cowichan of southwestern British Columbia. Acknowledging an Indian presence on the peninsula projected the illusion of truthfulness, but arguing that such claims were limited to Canadian Indians skillfully utilized the international divide between the fishery and the Canadian Indians. Winning the suit essentially protected the company from further Indian incursions emanating from either side of the boundary line. [9]

Records of the fish sellers and poachers themselves, especially if they were engaged in illegal activities, are difficult to find. Bert Jones, otherwise known as both "Spider" Jones and "Fish Pirate" Jones, stole fish from the fixed traps that peppered Puget Sound in the late nineteenth and early twentieth centuries. According to Jones, he and numerous other fish rustlers would sneak to the traps—often in bad weather and without lights—and take fish from the traps while the night watchmen were asleep. Other times he would pay the watchmen to look the other way while he took the fish. "The watchmen figured the fish were made for everybody and they wanted their share. Everybody wanted to make money," Jones asserted. Ironically, as the efficiency of the corporate fish traps enabled Jones to take thousands of fish at a time, he had no trouble selling to a ready audience of buyers.

Although Jones apparently made the fish-rustling business pay and enjoyed the adventure involved, other factors influenced his decision to become a fish poacher. "Oh, gosh, I used to be a crook," Jones admitted. "But I wasn't any more crooked than they were. They fished their traps during the closed season and were just as bad as me." Jones' reaction to the illegal fishing engaged in by the trap owners raises important questions about local people's reactions to the rise of wage labor, the class distinctions that attended different types of gear and work positions in the fishing industry, and local people's own sense of acceptable levels of resource use. Jones apparently justified his illegal activities by the fact that the trap owners themselves refused to abide by the laws put in place to allow the escapement of salmon necessary for their future health. In fact, he was stealing from thieves himself—thieves who had no respect for the very natural resources they depended on for their wealth. As long as they obeyed the law, Jones claimed, so would he. "But if they start to steal the fish out of season," he declared, "I'll have a little hand in it myself." [10]

Conclusions

Life along the U.S.–Canadian water border in the late nineteenth and early twentieth centuries was lively, fascinating, and growing increasingly complicated with each passing year. Fishing the line held different meanings for the various groups of people living and working in the Puget Sound region, and these constantly shifted according to changes in the economy, regulations, and border policing efforts. While the border meant both opportunity and hardship for those people engaged in the region's fisheries, it meant devastation for the Fraser River salmon. Unbalanced regulations and irregular enforcement on both sides of the border during the crucial decades of unbelievable growth in these respective national salmon industries allowed fishers to use the border to their advantage to take larger numbers of fish. National loyalty and patriotic verve further exacerbated the economic competition among fishers and canneries in the region during these early years and fueled the forces behind overfishing, as Garret Hardin's tragedy of the commons seemed to play out to near perfection.[11] On the other hand, the border also provided opportunities to some of the region's fishers. The people who lived along the boundary and who fished the line may have been able to use the border to enhance their incomes and subsistence levels. But as the decline in the numbers of salmon attests, the sacrifice was great and the rewards were uneven.

Notes

This essay is an expanded version of a paper presented at the conference of the American Historical Association–Pacific Coast Branch, Vancouver, British Columbia, August 2001.

1. George Webber, Inspector, Point Roberts, to Collector of Customs J. C. Saunders, Port Townsend WA, August 27, 1895, U.S. Customs Service, Puget Sound Collection District, RG 36, box 103, file 3.

2. See Louis S. Warren, *The Hunter's Game: Poachers and Conservationists in Twentieth-Century America* (New Haven: Yale University Press, 1997) and Karl Jacoby, *Crimes against Nature: Squatters, Poachers, Thieves, and the Hidden History of American Conservation* (Berkeley: University of California Press, 2001).

3. On the salmon life cycle, see Joseph E. Taylor III, *Making Salmon: An Environmental History of the Northwest Fisheries Crisis* (Seattle: University of Washington Press, 1999), 5–6. For more information on the problems posed by the route of the salmon through the Strait of Juan de Fuca, see James A. Crutchfield and Giulio Pontecorvo, *The Pacific Salmon Fisheries: A Study of Irrational Conservation* (Baltimore: Johns Hopkins University Press, 1969), 122–27.

4. Sara Singleton, *Constructing Cooperation: The Evolution of Institutions of Comanagement* (Ann Arbor: University of Michigan Press, 1998), 61–62.

5. Charles McLennan, Deputy Collector Inspector, Blaine, to Collector Andrew Wasson, Port Townsend WA, May 5, 1892, RG 36, box 62, file 2.

6. Ira B. Myers, Inspector, (no located listed) to A. W. Bash, Collector of Customs, District of Puget Sound, August 9, 1883, RG 36, box 169, file 4; A. M. White, Port Angeles WA, to H. F. Beecher, Collector of Customs, Port Townsend WA, December 4, 1885, RG 36, box 73, file 3; H. K. Bickford, Deputy Collector, Port Angeles WA, April 25, 1893.

7. Samuel Walker, Immigrant Inspector, New Whatcom, to Collector F. D. Huestis, Port Townsend WA, September 2 and 7, 1900, RG 36, box 107, file 1.

8. Bruce Miller, "The 'Really Real' Border and the Divided Salish Community," BC *Studies* 112 (Winter 1996–97): 65.

9. *The U.S. v. The Alaska Packing Association, 1895–1897*, RG 21, U.S. Circuit Court Western District of WA, Northern Division—Seattle Civil and Criminal Case files 1890–1911, box 82, case 482.

10. "Bert Jones: Fish Pirate," in Ron Strickland, *River of Pigs and Cayuses: Oral Histories from the Pacific Northwest* (San Francisco: Lexikos, 1984), 8–11, 13.

11. Garret Hardin, "The Tragedy of the Commons," *Science* 162 (December 1968): 1243–48. According to Hardin, human beings were compelled to exhaust those resources owned "in common," as there was no incentive to inspire contrary action.

18. "The Geology Recognizes No Boundaries"

Shifting Borders in Waterton Lakes National Park

Catriona Mortimer-Sandilands

On the Forty-ninth Parallel

This is an essay about the forty-ninth parallel: the *physical* parallel, a "vista" six meters (eighteen feet) wide that the International Boundary Commission ordered, in 1925, to be regularly cleared. Specifically, it is an essay about that portion of the "border swath" that runs right through the middle of Waterton-Glacier International Peace Park, neatly dividing in two an area of land reserved to celebrate international peace (and now ecological connection) between two nations. The irony of that boundary hit me squarely when I first saw the clear-cut swath on a hike along the shoreline trail beside Upper Waterton Lake. I was not alone: There is a concerted campaign, spearheaded by the International Rotary Club, to stop clearing the swath for both ecological and symbolic reasons.

When I began to research the swath, I found a borderline of considerable interest. In 1818, the Convention of London firmly set the boundary between "the territories of the United States and those of His Britannic Majesty" at the forty-ninth parallel, from the northwest tip of the Lake of the Woods to the summit of the Stony (now Rocky) Mountains. In the midst of international political wrangling, the line was extended westward to Vancouver Island; surveyors were dispatched in 1857, and by 1861 the line was marked from the Pacific Ocean to Upper Waterton Lake. This was following by more politics and, in 1872, more surveyors. After two years of hard labor beginning at Lake of the Woods, U.S. and

Figure 17. The forty-ninth parallel swath between Waterton Lakes National Park (Alberta) and Glacier National Park (Montana). Photo taken by author.

British parties reached Upper Waterton Lake from the other direction. The dividing border was thus completed in what is now Waterton-Glacier International Peace Park.

As a border *line*, the forty-ninth parallel marks Canada's difference from the country to its immediate south. Canadians have imbued this line with huge metaphoric weight; it currently marks the end of handguns and the beginning of health care. It has also concretely offered, at different historical moments, limited sanctuary to Sioux, slaves, and draft resisters. This border is a symbolic crossing-place that marks distinction on the line and national solidity (however functional) on either side. But the place is more than the line: As a borderland, the forty-ninth parallel blends two national cultures that slop from one side of the line to the other. The borderland is thus a hybrid place; frequent crossings mean that there is a unique complexity to the border zone that is not the sole property of either side and that, as W. H. New suggests, indicates "in-between-ness" rather than difference.[1]

That this portion of the borderlands happens to include two national parks adds another layer of interest. From my side, Waterton Lakes National Park is a formally designated space of Canadian nature and nationality, yet its geology, large carnivores, and economic history, among other things, draw most meaningful links across the border. It is a "representative ecosystem" in a Canadian mosaic of nature; it is also an ecosystem that is only tenable in its attachment to a U.S. federal nature space. In this chapter, then, I would like to consider the border *line* of the clear-cut swath (figure 17) in the context of the border *land* that is Waterton Lakes National Park and also, crucially, part of the Waterton-Glacier International Peace Park. Beginning with a short history of the park, framed in terms of its shifting relations with the Canadian state and U.S. economic interests, I would like to offer that the International Peace Park and the border swath reveal clearly some of the paradoxes of the Canada–U.S. borderlands, and in particular those concerning the relationship between nation and nature in their ongoing negotiation.

Waterton Lakes: A National Park in a Border Zone

Waterton Lakes Forest Reserve was set aside by the Dominion government in 1895. Unlike Banff to the north (1887), its origins lacked the overt trappings of Canadian nationalism partly because it was understood primarily as a resource preserve for the common use of local settlers, but mostly because there was no connection between the reserve and the nation-building Canadian Pacific Railway (CPR).[2] Indeed, Waterton's early years were spent as a forest reserve, and in contrast to Banff's early publicity as the jewel of Canada's Rockies, the park saw little tourism and a great deal of resource exploration and extraction (oil, minerals, lumber). In 1909 federal forest reserve inspector H. R. MacMillan wrote a report in favor of Waterton's transformation into a national park, equivalent to Banff. His job was to convince the Ministry of the Interior that Waterton would be more profitable as a park than as a source of timber. Thus he concluded his report: "It has been stated that this territory is good for nothing but timber and park purposes, aside from the mineral value. It has been shown that it will make an excellent game reserve. . . . There is no doubt that these points together with its geologic features and its general scientific interest will render it worthy of being made into a National Park."[3]

First called Kootenay Lakes Forest Reserve, Waterton Lakes was eventually promoted from forest reserve to national park in 1911, but even then it was not so much a jewel for a nation's natural necklace as much as it was a local "pleasuring ground," an economic initiative for a region's prosperity. Crucially, Waterton was the only park (until Elk Island in Alberta in 1913) not directly linked to Canadian railway interests, and it did not attract (or attempt to attract) an eastern clientele. Its tourism was thus regionally rather than nationally oriented, which had an enormous influence on the park's development, not least because it has increased the park's reliance on a north-south access corridor: in other words, on Glacier National Park. And this regional view of the park persists. As the 1992 Waterton Lakes National Park management plan states, "The park is a scenic jewel—an 'accessible wilderness' that serves as an important seasonal tourism destination in southwestern Alberta, offering a more tranquil, leisurely paced experience than the other Canadian Rocky Mountain National Parks."[4]

By 1915 it was clear that Waterton's health hinged on its links with Glacier. Chief Warden H. E. Sibbald presented Waterton's plight in a letter to Parks Commissioner J. B. Harkin: "This Park will never be a tourist resort unless there is a railroad, but it will be used a great deal by the summer residents of Southern Alberta as a Summer Resort."[5] For Harkin, summer picnics were not sufficient. He wanted to strengthen the national parks, and this involved developing a stronger relationship between scenic preservation and economic development. In March 1915, Harkin received a letter from Chief Dominion Park Superintendent Hervey indicating that the lack of a railway was not an insurmountable obstacle to tourism at Waterton. Hervey wrote: "If we can bring the tourists from the other side over good roads in automobiles and give them excellent recreation grounds we can do quite a good business in lot rentals, etc." Harkin responded: "If we do link up with [Glacier Park] doubtless we will get many more tourists than at present and of course the getting of tourists is good business for Canada. On the other hand we have to bear in mind that such linking up would have the effect of making Waterton a sort of adjunct to the U.S. Park and on that account there might be some criticism from a Canadian view point."[6]

Both men knew well that Waterton was not just pursuing links with Glacier; it was pursuing the business of the Great Northern Railway (GNR). "The Great Northern," Hervey had written, "has undertaken a large development scheme in hand and we should endeavor to make our Park which adjoins the International Boundary part and parcel of the scheme." [7] Almost the moment that Glacier was designated as a U.S. national park in 1910, the GNR, led by Louis Hill, had begun planning and building facilities to turn Glacier into "America's Switzerland," including "tourist cabins and tee pee camps, followed later by Swiss-style chalets, at scenic points," in addition to roads and trails throughout the park connecting them. [8] Like the CPR at Banff, the CNR was overwhelmingly responsible for the early development of Glacier; like Banff, Glacier tied economics to nationalism. The first major Great Northern establishment was Glacier Park Lodge, built in 1912 at the then-astronomical cost of $500,000 and an important stop in the Railway's "See America First" campaign. Between 1912 and 1913, park visitation tripled to 12,000. The GNR can be credited with almost all of the increase. In 1913 Hill took a trip over the border. On that trip, he told Waterton Park Superintendent Kootenai Brown that he planned to build a three hundred–room hotel in Waterton. Hill did not follow through until the Great Depression; by that time, what most interested Hill was the Alberta government's repeal of Prohibition in 1923. Although Hill never specifically tied the hotel's construction to the receipt, from the province, of a liquor license, at least one reporter at the planned hotel's announcement in 1926 wrote that "the Great Northern will build a haven for thirsty American travelers." [9]

The Prince of Wales Hotel opened in July 1927. In its ersatz Swiss architecture, it entirely resembled the other GNR hotels and chalets in Glacier. In its status as a rest-stop on the grand Glacier tour, it drew Waterton into an American geographic network as the Great Northern Transport Company took visitors on buses, on horses, and in cars from lodge to chalet to lodge. One of the most famous and often-repeated pictures of Waterton originates in one of the GNR's early publicity campaigns. It has the viewer looking from above, down on the Prince of Wales in the foreground and then beyond, southward along Upper Waterton Lake, into snow-dusted mountains in the background. The gaze is directly into the United States. Infrastructurally and symbolically, Waterton became a place on the margin of America rather than a place in the center of another country.

But the hotel also influenced the development of Waterton as a Dominion Park, distinct from Glacier. A sign went up over the park entranceway for the first time to indicate to travelers that they were "entering Waterton Lakes National Park." The more the border began to be crossed, the more carefully the Dominion Park needed to spell out publicly its specificity in relation to Glacier. Thus, as the GNR was making significant incursions into Waterton, the Parks Service was busy revising key elements of its mandate on a national scale, most crucially in the areas of predator and conservation policy. In effect, these policies drew Waterton's entire boundary more clearly and connected the park to others in the system more strongly and clearly at the policy level, even through the adoption of nationalist place-names.

This apparent paradox between the increasing insertion of Waterton into a U.S.–based system of places and representations, and the simultaneously increasing weight of the "national" in Waterton, is interesting. Specifically Waterton moved, materially and discursively, from being a recreation ground for southern Albertans directly into being an international tourist destination, without a clear federally articulated sense of Waterton as a space of a particularly national nature. It was only after the place moved into a web of prominence cast from across the border that the Waterton's signification as a regional recreational site was transformed into one of Waterton as a distinctly national park. This shift is clearly indicated in a letter by W. W. Cory, deputy minister of the interior; he used GNR-inspired development of Waterton as evidence of the park's increasing national significance, and he was among the first to speak of Waterton as a particularly special site and not just a regional backyard: "One of Canada's greatest needs," he wrote, "is that the choicest . . . areas should be incorporated into Parks and given adequate protection and conservation." Waterton was now not only "good for nothing but timber and park purposes" but also a choice piece of nature with the weight of the nation behind it.[10] A 1926 article in the *Lethbridge Herald* reveals the logic nicely: "Mention to anyone in Canada or the United States the word 'national park' and it at once brings to him a picture of a scenic beauty spot, set apart by the National Government to be a playground of all the people. He knows that, if it were not beautiful, it would not have been so set apart, taken care of, and improved by the

Government of the country. 'National Park' has a wonderful significance in these days of motor tourist travel." [11]

During the Great Depression, Waterton came to be marked more intensively with a Canadian national presence. At the same time, the influence of the United States (and the interest of the GNR) shifted. After 1929, tourism in both Glacier and Waterton fell sharply. On top of an absolute drop in the number of visitors, cost-conscious travelers in Glacier were considerably less willing than they had been to pay the large bus fare that would take them, via a long route on existing roads, to the Prince of Wales. The GNR thus renewed pressure for a more direct and scenic route to its northernmost hotel at Waterton along the Belly River Road on the east side of the park; in the meantime, in the face of declining revenues, it shut its doors in 1933. The U.S. repeal of Prohibition that same year did not help business.

During this period the Canadian government developed a more focused attention on the parks as federal spaces. In the first place were legislative changes. The National Parks Act of 1930 brought all the parks directly under the authority of a separate act, effectively empowering much more stringent controls over park lands and resources than had been present under earlier legislation. Although this act did not resolve most contradictions and tensions in the parks over conservation, preservation, and recreation, it did firmly establish the parks as places subject to direct federal jurisdiction. In effect, the combination of these litigations created a more visible boundary around Waterton in relation to other lands and a more distinct and disciplinary federal presence inside the park in the form of land use, conservation, and other regulations.

Second, although federal monies for expansion of the park system dried up during the Depression, parks in Western Canada, including Waterton, were home to many federal relief work camps, which again intensified federal presence. As Bill Waiser has documented extensively, Harkin had been an advocate of using the forced labor of "enemy aliens" in the parks for road building and other construction during World War I. He was thus very quick to advocate for a similar use of the region's many unemployed men once the Depression hit, and numerous relief work camps were in operation in the Rocky Mountains and prairie parks during the 1930s. [12] At Waterton, a great deal of road building, campground, and other facility development was undertaken by these workers; they also graded streets and laid sidewalks in the townsite. At a variety of levels, these workers were engaged in the business of nation-building; on top of their considerable additions to federal lands, they were understood as building themselves as upstanding Canadian citizens.

Superintendent Herbert Knight used the availability of relief labor to advocate for the expansion of Waterton into British Columbia; he wanted to see a road from Waterton to Glacier via a western route (Akamina Pass), which would also open up the park to easier tourist access from British Columbia. Partly because of land title complications, but also because of the influence of the GNR, a different road to Glacier was eventually chosen for construction: The Belly River Road was precisely the direct route from Glacier to the Prince of Wales that the GNR had always wanted. For Harkin, the combination of the promise of greater GNR tourist expansion and the availability of a pool of unemployed workers was a perfect one. Thus in 1932 many of the men went to work on what later came to be known as the Chief Mountain International Highway.

The choice to build the road along the Belly River route involved a boundary dispute of a different kind. Specifically, the road south from the eastern portion of Waterton to the International Boundary crossed into the Blood Reserve Timber Limit "A." A reserve for the Bloods on the Belly River had been part of Treaty 7; the actual reserve, however, lacked a good wood supply, and the noncontiguous Timber Reserve "A" was added to the Bloods' area in 1893. When Waterton's boundaries were expanded in 1914 to "envelope" these lands, the Bloods' timber reserve rights became subject to contest. Where park wardens considered that the timber limit was just a timber limit and not part of the Bloods' full territorial resource, some Bloods disagreed and continued to use the land for hunting and fishing in addition to the officially sanctioned wood collection. To cut a long story short, the Bloods eventually won their case in 1936, just as the new Chief Mountain International Highway was nearing completion. Although the land was not formally withdrawn from the park until 1947 (numerous complications about the status of the road caused wrangling about park regulations to go on even longer), and although the issue of compensation to the Bloods for the roadway was not resolved until 1957, the Parks Branch did not contest the clear decision that the Timber

Limit was part of the Blood Reserve. The road was then completed with some fanfare in 1936 at the international boundary. One story has it that Canadian crews intentionally deviated from the planned direction of the road in order to give the Canadian customs house a better position on the border.[13]

The road was that important. Harkin had already tried to trade for the land necessary for the road, but the post-1930 complexities of provincial title made such an undertaking almost impossible. He had already devoted the considerable labor of the relief workers to the project. He knew that the GNR would not reopen the Prince of Wales without the road and that the hotel was an integral part of the park's development potential. Indeed, the withdrawal of Timber Limit "A" from Waterton Park was a blow to Harkin and Knight partly because they wanted the scenic new road from Glacier to run *through* the park as part of Waterton's draw. In fact, the road was also clearly related to another institution that the park was developing as part of its plan for an expanded presence in national and international tourist itineraries: the Waterton-Glacier International Peace Park.

Waterton-Glacier International Peace Park: Designating the Borderland

In July 1931, a group of Rotary Club members from both Alberta and Montana met at the Prince of Wales Hotel. At this first Rotary "annual goodwill meeting," Canon Samuel Middleton, president of the Cardston Rotary, moved that the club should petition the Canadian and U.S. governments to establish an International Peace Park to encompass both Waterton and Glacier. The Rotarians understood that Canada and the United States offered a model to the world for developing international harmony in the post–World War I era; specifically, the Rotarians saw that through the development of commercial and professional ties, a spirit of "goodwill" could be fostered between nations by increasing cooperative ventures. "What," asked one Rotarian publicly, "are the possibilities of playing together on a continental scale, as cooperating nations, in the era of readjustment which the whole world is now struggling over?"[14]

Waterton-Glacier seemed an opportune site in which to enact an international project that was at once symbolic, viable, and entrepreneurial. The Rotarians thus engaged their political connections, entreating M.P.

Brigadier Stewart and Montana congressman Scott Leavitt to take the matter up in their respective legislatures. Even for such a relatively innocuous international undertaking, the speed of the response was unusual. Although Prime Minister R. B. Bennett appeared to delay his final decision on the park until after the bill had passed the U.S. Congress, parallel legislations were passed in Canada and the United States in 1932, only one year later, despite the fact that the U.S. and Canadian governments were, in the early 1930s, engaged in a long-standing tariff war. Bennett and President Herbert Hoover were not on especially good terms. The Canadian Bill 97 read: "Whereas it is desirable for the purpose of permanently commemorating the long existing relationship of peace and good will between the peoples and Governments of the United States of America and the Dominion of Canada . . . [u]pon proclamation of the Governor in Council, Waterton Lakes National Park shall be deemed to be a part of the Waterton-Glacier International Peace Park . . . [and] shall continue to be one of the National Parks of Canada." [15]

The Rotarians looked at the GNR's developments in Glacier and saw in them space for a unified plan to develop the tourist potential of the region as a unique international playground. As local business owners in the midst of an economic depression, such development was clearly in their interest. Indeed, at that pre-Prohibition moment, the GNR supported the Peace Park idea strongly and officially, and at least one member of the Glacier Park Transport Company was heavily involved in the Rotary efforts; the Park, like the Belly River Road that would lubricate international travel, was a site of potential profit in a region that sorely needed economic assistance. On top of economic benefit, however, what helped pass the legislations so quickly was the fact that they had no effect whatsoever on the actual administration of either Glacier or Waterton. The International Peace Park was a purely symbolic gesture, designed to capture the attention of an international tourist public rather than to foster inter-park cooperation on issues of conservation, development, or even routine administration. Correspondence leading up to the park's creation is absolutely clear on this point. The Parks Branch and the U.S. Parks Service were not about to agree to any kind of joint administration. The Peace Park was in name only; all administration was to remain as legislated by preexisting acts in both countries, and all conservation and management ventures were to remain under the jurisdiction of the separate park units. With this limited meaning, Harkin was a supporter of the Peace Park, and he wrote in its favor: "Nothing is really contemplated by the Bill [other] than that the two areas shall have a common name for a definitive purpose, namely, the commemoration of the peace and good will that exists between Canada and the United States. Undoubtedly many objections would arise in either country if the proposal involved any joint administration of the two parks." He was particularly clear about the stakes of the endeavor: "It is possible that in a few isolated cases of extreme Canadianism some criticism would be offered but it would be difficult to justify any real criticism. . . . The very fact that these parks were made into an international one and that the particular reason was peace and good will would provide very much first class raw material for publicity from a tourist standpoint." [16]

The Peace Park was formally dedicated in June 1932 at the Glacier Park Hotel in Montana; a bronze cairn was unveiled "permanently commemorating the relationship of peace and goodwill between the peoples and governments of Canada and the United States." The plan was that a reciprocal ceremony would unveil a second plaque at the Prince of Wales the following year. This ceremony did not take place because, Peace Park or not, the Belly River Road was not completed and the GNR closed the Prince of Wales. The second plaque was not dedicated until 1936, shortly after the opening of the Chief Mountain Highway and the reopening of the hotel. On the occasion, the *Lethbridge Herald* stated triumphantly that "a new week-end registration record was set at this picturesque mountain playground when over 6,000 people arrived in nearly 2,000 cars, a third of which bore United States registry. Official dedication of the Canadian park as a part of the Waterton-Glacier International Peace Park and other ceremonies proved the drawing card." [17]

The influx of tourists, particularly Americans, did cause some instances of "Canadianism," mostly involving petty skirmishes over the relative importance of the name Waterton Lakes National Park and Waterton-Glacier International Peace Park, and between Waterton and Glacier over the costs incurred for any aspect of Peace Park activity. Despite the often-repeated rhetoric of the close cooperation between the parks, these disputes were almost always resolved in the direction of reinforcing the

primacy of the national parks and demonstrating the general administrative emptiness of the Peace Park as an institution. For example, when
the Chief Mountain Highway was completed, Canon Middleton tried to
have erected at the border a commemorative sign that would highlight the
Peace Park concept. Among other barriers, he ran up against Waterton
Superintendent H. A. de Veber, who was clearly uninterested in paying
for any such signs out of Parks Canada funds and resented the Rotarians'
efforts in what he considered to be his jurisdiction.

It took Middleton until after World War II to see his signs erected.
In 1947, a dedication ceremony finally took place at the International
Boundary. At the event, a Blood chief named "Shot Both Sides" presided
over a Peace Pipe Ceremony, lending a veneer of aboriginal assent to the
"international" venture while standing squarely on what was, in fact, that
piece of the Bloods' territory that had caused them so many disagreements with Waterton. The National Parks Bureau saw the dedication as
an occasion to promote not only the Peace Park but also the symbolic
joining of the Canadian and U.S. park systems: "The Waterton-Glacier
International Peace Park links the national park systems of Canada and
the United States—areas which are playing an increasingly important part
in the lives of the peoples of this continent." In this regard, Waterton's
symbolic Peace Park connections were clearly balanced against those that
linked them in the "chain of national playgrounds and places of historic
interest [that] extends from the Atlantic coast in the east to the Selkirk
Mountains in the West, and is represented in every province."[18]

In the absence of a strong political will on the part of the Waterton superintendent, the GNR came to be responsible for a great deal of
the Peace Park's promotion. For example, a new MGM ten-minute color
"travelogue" film was produced about the Peace Park in 1941, a process
clearly facilitated by the efforts of the GNR. The predominance of U.S.
tourists was also related to larger political and economic issues; in particular, between 1939 and 1942, Americans kept the Prince of Wales Hotel
open, whereas Canadians were largely deterred from visiting the park
due to the restrictions imposed by a war economy. In 1942, the hotel
was again closed in response to fuel oil restrictions imposed by Canada.
Again, however, Waterton's international success spurred new attempts
to integrate it more closely with other Canadian national parks. As Parks

Bureau Controller Stead noted in 1941, "We are hopeful that by using the whole group of mountain parks as a magnet to attract tourists instead of regarding them in a sense as competitors this ration of increase [in visitors to the parks] may be maintained." By 1943, the park's desire to attract Canadian tourists was intensified by the decline in the U.S. market caused by the country's entry into the war. More actively, at this point, nation-based sentiments were pursued as a way of cultivating Canadian tourist revenues. De Veber wrote to Stead: "The desirability and necessity of maintaining a high standard of health, especially in war time could be pointed out, showing how a holiday in the Parks could assist in attaining this end. Advertising in this connection could be directed to war workers and others working at a high pitch."[19]

In the postwar period, tourism in Waterton increased dramatically. The International Peace Park appeared then to be a way of specifying Waterton's uniqueness as a travel destination in relation to other parks in both the Canadian and U.S. systems. The GNR remained at the forefront of the Peace Park's promotion. Lucia Lewis, a publicist for the railway, advocated extending the Peace Park concept into a sort of annual carnival of international relations. She argued that the Rotary "goodwill meetings" already institutionalized in the park between July 1 and July 4 could easily be expanded into something more public. In fact, she suggested a remarkable list of events, including a ceremonial "clearing" at the international boundary, "emphasizing our friendly frontiers where we *cut down* barriers instead of erecting them"; a Peace Pipe ceremony involving First Nations participants from both Alberta and Montana; a symposium of "leading Canadian, U.S. and United Nations figures . . . [to study] the causes of friction between two countries and their peaceful solutions"; and Canada versus U.S. sporting events "to show that friendly rivalry can be as exciting as war."[20] Perhaps fortunately, none of these events ever took place, and the Canadian government refused to take up any slack in promotions resulting from the demise of her plans.

In the absence of significant administrative effort by either Parks Canada or the U.S. Park Service to give any substantive weight to the Peace Park, the dramatic increase in automobile tourism had, unintentionally, the effect of undermining the Peace Park. Specifically its single greatest asset was the GNR's advertising efforts, and the GNR was in the process of getting out of the Peace Park business. By the late 1950s, the company had experienced serious declines in revenue from rail travel due to the growth in automobile use in the postwar period. Railway hotels were simply not the choice of these new automobile tourists, who generally preferred the small and less expensive motor hotels and family campground that were being built in and around the parks. The GNR attempted to sell the Glacier Park Hotel chain, both as a whole and in pieces, and in 1960 the whole chain was sold to Don Hummel, a Montana-based businessman who pursued the interests of his hotels often in direct conflict with the two park administrations by which his operation was constrained. He had no interest in the Peace Park, and the new Glacier Park, Inc. did little to promote it.

By the mid-1950s, then, a relatively clear picture of the Peace Park had emerged. As a tool of international cooperation on park issues, even in the relatively limited domain of travel promotion, the Peace Park was a failure. Waterton Lakes National Park was an entity of the Canadian National Park system and was bound by its mandate, administrative structure, conservation rules, and even its park aesthetic and interpretive specifications. Similar restrictions were in place on the Glacier side. On both sides, the postwar expansion of the national parks was accompanied by an expansion of control and intervention by the national parks services in such areas as land use, regulation of private leasing and concession, and conservation and predator policy. Rather than promote international cooperation across the boundary, economic success had ironically contributed to strengthening national control on either side. At the same time, the Peace Park's presence as part of the public representation of Waterton and Glacier eroded, particularly on the U.S. side of the border. Although the Peace Park continued to be promoted by the Rotary Club, and although its principle of "promoting international goodwill" was included as a theme in interpretive programs at Waterton, the original enthusiasm for drawing tourists across the border through the Peace Park concept waned.

One might perhaps argue that there is thus little space for the development of a fluid and complex border *land* when the border *line* is marked so clearly by federal administrative requirements on either side. In the absence of a compelling economic interest such as the GNR's, even the formal designation of a borderland encompassing two such rigidly federal spaces seemed to falter in relation to other designations linking the parks to a different national network of spaces and representations. After the glory days of the Prince of Wales during Prohibition, and after the National Parks Act of 1930, Waterton experienced simultaneously a rise in formal federal presence and a relative decline in cross-border economic development interests. Certainly, then, one can point to particular periods in which Canadian nationalist sentiments were strong and exerted a more profound effect on the park than an earlier and more hybrid U.S./Canadian cross-border orientation.

But it is also the case that the cross-border exchanges that did happen facilitated and shifted the park's embodiment and representation of the Canadian nation. As a direct result of the GNR's developments, Waterton was able to claim a symbolic importance that allowed its superintendents to press for expansion. As a direct result of Harkin's desire to facilitate cross-border traffic with the United States, a road was built that, backhandedly, changed the relationship between Waterton and the Blood Nation. As a direct result of the formal institution of the International Peace Park, postwar tourists were encouraged at least to think about the relationship between the two park units as a symbolic representation of the artificiality of borders running through the wilderness. Although the border is actually highly visible both physically and politically, the Peace Park's emphasis on the cross-border relationship (in combination with the material artifacts associated with approaching and crossing the actual line) did have the effect of putting the border itself into fairly sharp focus. Most prominently, the border became an ecological question, as ideas of nature came to be articulated with a variety of national and cross-national positions.

"The Geology Recognizes No Boundaries": Nature in the Border Zone

Enabled by the construction of the Chief Mountain Highway, the Peace Park concept thus actually helped to unify the landscape for public consumption. Previously, economic interests had crossed the border, but until the road was built, giving a clear and relatively easy physical experience of connection between the parks, there was little everyday sensibility of the parks' similarity as parks, unless one was a backcountry warden, a poacher, or a north-south traveler on Upper Waterton Lake. In addition, the parks were not understood, on an everyday basis, as connected "ecologically." For most visitors, there was no particular representational support for an understanding of the parks as connected parts of a larger whole. In fact, in the public eye Waterton and Glacier were often represented as distinct places, their complementary differences highlighted as much as any based on similarity of landscape. A 1931 article in the *Lethbridge Herald* put it this way: "Glacier Park acts as a foil to Waterton Park. Both have beauties distinctly their own. The one makes an attraction for the other, though they are in different countries. Waterton is more restful, more idealistically a holiday resort than Glacier Park, but Glacier Park is by no means lacking in charm."[21]

The founding of the Peace Park, in the company of the Chief Mountain Highway, offered an opportunity for the public reinscription of Waterton's nature. Certainly, driving across the border, one cannot help but notice that there is no appreciable difference of scenery between one side and the other. (In fact, the clearer ecological divide is between east and west, where the prairie landscape shifts, without foothills, into mountains.) The infrastructural similarities between the parks—courtesy of the GNR—also created a border-crossing experience that gave a sense of the two parks as similar sites of consumption. There was, for example, a great deal of similarity between riding a Glacier Park Transport Company bus on the Going-to-the-Sun Road and riding a Glacier Park Transport Company bus on the Red Rock Canyon Road.

But the Peace Park afforded an ideological opportunity to drive the point home. What was the Peace Park if not a recognition of the similar natures on either side of the forty-ninth parallel? What was the Peace Park if not a ritualization of the common economic desire for nature embodied in the two parks? For example, Harkin used the occasion of the 1932 Peace Park plaque dedication to resurrect the image of Waterton's first park superintendent, Kootenai Brown, who—along with his Glacier counterpart, Henry "Death on the Trail" Reynolds—had spoken in the direction of cooperation between the two parks many years earlier. In fact, Reynolds is reputed to have said that "the geology recognizes no boundaries, and as [Waterton] Lake lay . . . no man-made boundary could cleave the waters apart."[22] When a photograph of Reynolds and

Brown standing together was unearthed at about the time of the Peace Park's creation, Harkin had it reproduced in the *Lethbridge Herald* under the title "First Chiefs of Peace Park." The accompanying caption stated that their pose "would indicate that they knew many years ago that their respective domains would be merged some day into an international peace park."[23] In this way, the Peace Park regularly invoked historical precedent to justify its existence. If the park was to appear as a recognition of a "real" and abiding relationship rather than as a mere public relations gesture as arbitrary as the border it supposedly crossed, it had to create a narrative of its existence by which its founding was simply a recognition of an already established "natural" state of affairs.

This rhetoric of the Peace Park's historical destiny included the idea that nature itself sanctioned the symbolic union of the two national spaces. The park's promotional literature repeatedly stated that the two parks were a single "natural" entity traversed by a fundamentally "imaginary" borderline that was in need of effacement. This "nature" invoked a number of themes from prevalent western "frontier" narrative on both sides of the border: freedom of movement, freedom of association, and particularly the inherent priority of nature over the artificiality of political boundaries.[24] In turn, this idea of nature appeared as a normative and naturalizing justification for the kinds of international activity that the Peace Park represented, a sort of filial "free" enterprise. As Joseph Dixon, U.S. assistant secretary of the interior, put it at the time, "We are all North Americans; we all enjoy the freedom of the great open spaces and the glory of the mountains. . . . The Waterton-Glacier International Peace Park, to our western minds, is a natural, logical development . . . [and] the act of cementing this perfectly natural friendship will serve as a model for other countries less fortunate in their past international relations."[25]

The logic by which the Peace Park was thus retroactively "naturalized" reveals some interesting dimensions. First, at the same time as the boundary between the two nations was effaced in the invocation of an inherently unifying nature, a new boundary was created *around* the Peace Park to highlight Waterton-Glacier's particular and formalized achievement of the effacement. In order for the Peace Park concept to "sell," it had to be more than just a representation of some fundamental natural unity that existed everywhere; it had to be a particular and unique representation of such unity. Perhaps to be palatable to the nationalists of both countries, the border effacement was contained and rendered a merely local rupture of a political reality that was and is potently meaningful to people on either side. In order for the effacement to be marketable, it had to be out of the ordinary, something sensationally different from the ordinary border crossings of farmers (or poachers). What better nature than a spectacular one to embody such a fetishized boundary-crossing? Thus the park spoke to a broader geographic connection between two contiguous nations by confining that connection to a single and special place, in effect domesticating the boundary breach.

Second, the Peace Park had to mark the boundary that it proceeded to cross. In order for the experience of the border transgression to be anything out of the ordinary, it had to be ritualized, and in order to be ritualized, it had to be visible. Middleton's eventual ability to erect the two boundary cairns made apparent not only the act of crossing the forty-ninth parallel—which was visible already—but also that the fact of doing so was the single most important element of the Peace Park experience. The two almost identical boundary signs read: "Waterton-Glacier International Peace Park" with the respective subtitles "Canadian Section" and "United States Section." Although they indicated a continuity between the one "section" and the other, they highlighted the place of the border over all the others in the supposedly borderless nature area. Thus nature may be boundless, but in order to be publicly represented as boundless, the artificial border was actually made even more visible than it had been.

Third, the idea of nature authorizing the connection between Waterton and Glacier was heavily racialized. The *Calgary Albertan* was quite direct on this point, noting that the founding of the Peace Park should be understood as a "gesture toward Anglo-Saxon goodwill."[26] Similarly, Middleton included in his history of the Peace Park a particularly revealing passage: "This plan symbolizes the unique relation that exists between the American and Canadian peoples. Fundamentally, this relation is based on the fact that the two peoples are to a large extent racially similar, that they are free from traditional grudges, and that their economic interests largely supplement each other."[27]

Middleton's naturalization of the Peace Park was thus based on articulating a geographic connection between Canada and the United States with an overarching assumption of whiteness. In order to accentuate the fact of the boundary-crossing "goodwill" between Canada and the United States, the Peace Park homogenized the two nations involved, making them singular, white, and unified in their interests and attitudes. In turn, this racial homogeneity was attached to an idea of unbroken U.S./Canadian "nature," effectively spreading the assumption of whiteness to an entire continent. Most immediately, the discourse was based on the foundational erasure of the aboriginal peoples from whose lands the parks were carved. This erasure was hardly unusual in Canadian (or U.S.) history, but it was particularly blatant given the immediate and visible presence of the Blood Nation, across whose contested lands the International Highway ran. Typically, the present condition of Native peoples (e.g., the Timer Limit) was ignored in favor of a ritualistic representation of native tradition such as the use of the Peace Pipe Ceremony at Peace Park events. This narrow exposure suggested that the Bloods were to take up a position "in nature" and not as a modern nation. Here the traditional ritual of the Peace Pipe Ceremony, in alignment with romantic discourses about native connections with the natural world, marked a sort of blessing on the inherent rightness of the Peace Park enterprise without interfering with the fact that there were supposed to be, in this ritual, really only two nations involved. In turn, Blood Chief "Shot Both Sides" was only able to stand at the "international" dedication as a representative of a timeless and depoliticized native-nature bond, as the racialized marking of peace was firmly bilateral.

Thus one could argue that the Peace Park's effacement of the international boundary was effected by the reification of other boundaries. Goodwill is white; goodwill is commercial; goodwill is as orderly as a bus trip across the border. More fundamentally, the idea of the Peace Park conceptually divided the apparently "naturally" connected parks from the lands around them; the two parks, despite their differences, shared the legislative mandate of being parks. Thus they shared economic and social specificity as sites for a particular kind of tourist nature consumption, as well as the growing specificity of being preserves for nature against the "outside," specifically against other kinds of resource use.

The Peace Park continues as a formal institution at Waterton/Glacier in much the same vein as its original intent. Its institution is enshrined in a "Peace Pavilion" in the Waterton townsite and in a smaller one at the ranger station at the other end of Upper Waterton Lake at Goat Haunt. At the Waterton pavilion, peace messages are repeated in many languages including hoof prints and leaf patterns, as if nature were a direct participant in the symbolic United Nations represented there. The Peace Park is also ritualized in warden-ranger "hands across the border" hikes along Upper Waterton Lake, in which participants walk the 13.8 kilometers (8.3 miles) from Waterton to Goat Haunt, ritually shake hands at the border, and take, for a small fee, the MV *International* back to Waterton. In addition, UNESCO declared the Peace Park a World Heritage site in 1995. In order to be chosen for this honor, a site must represent unique, significant, and relatively intact natural or cultural features. Waterton-Glacier was chosen because of both its geological/biological properties and the cultural institution of the Peace Park; it is, in fact, the Peace Park and not the individual national parks that merits the United Nations designation. Here the Peace Park idea has been rewritten from a cross-border model to a global one; its symbolic significance as a site of international cooperation—despite the fact that there has actually been very little—has helped to place the Peace Park on a map of global special places.

In its most recent manifestations, the idea of an inherently borderless Peace Park nature area has also been rewritten in a specifically ecological language. As the Waterton Lakes Web site describes,

> Originally, the IPP commemorated the peace and goodwill that exists along the world's longest undefended border. . . . Today, the united parks represent the need for co-operation and stewardship in a world of shared resources. This is not only reflected between nations, but also between provinces with the Akamina-Kishinena class A provincial park in British Columbia. Located on Waterton's western side and forming Glacier's northern border, this protected area was established in direct response to concerns over the management of entire ecosystems.[28]

In the first place, this passage is a considerable rewriting of history in which the parks' economic histories are painted over in ecological colors.

This retroactive naturalization of park creation is an extension of the rhetoric that was employed to frame the Peace Park as a mere recognition of a naturally occurring borderlessness. However, this passage also employs the idea that the Peace Park's creation can be tied to ecosystem management efforts and especially to the joint stewardship of the two national parks as components of a larger natural whole. Of course, the Peace Park was never designed as such an instrument. Founded only two years after the strongest Canadian park protection legislation to that date passed the House of Commons, the Peace Park could not and did not represent any shift in land management. In fact, the Peace Park existed *because* it had no teeth, no mandate whatsoever that either park would work to harmonize policy and practice. Although Waterton's economic and ecological ties have considerably bled its attachments across the border, its administrative existence ties it firmly to a raft of Canadian national parks with which it does not share any particular economic or ecological similarity. The fact is that the management of Waterton's ecology is determined by the federally based fiscal and policy vicissitudes of Parks Canada. There is an interesting split between the public representation of nature and the practical organization of nature management in Waterton; the former is oriented to Glacier, right next door, and the latter is oriented to the forty other parks in the Canadian system, the closest of which is a good four-hour drive away.

Various efforts have been made to use the Peace Park institution as a springboard to develop stronger ties between Waterton and Glacier Park practices. In 1987, for example, representatives from Environment Canada and the U.S. National Park Service met for a two-day conference under the banner of the "Waterton-Glacier Days of Peace and Friendship." During this conference, ideas developed to expand cooperative efforts included personnel exchanges and training, joint meetings, the development of a common research base and strategy, and operating procedures. None of these efforts has had a measurable impact on Waterton's management practices. In fact, the only significant joint venture currently in place, apart from the symbolic ones, concerns search and rescue operations. Ecological thinking at Waterton is not oriented, despite ecosystem rhetoric, to Glacier. Local conflicts currently in play on the park's boundaries with ranch lands—concerning in particular a planned residential subdivision and, more generally, the transformation of ranches into exurban commuter and retirement communities—draw attention to different borders, different constitutive inclusions and exclusions, and different configurations of identity and nature. In addition, recent official moves toward "ecological integrity" at the national level have placed Waterton's nature more firmly than ever within a policy frame of federal meaning despite the fact that (little) Waterton's "integrity" is only possible because of its direct attachment to (larger) Glacier. Waterton is, in the current Canadian park discourse, part of a threatened "system" of parks, and it achieves political prominence through its ecological linkage to other at-risk and precious spaces of the Canadian nation. Nature has become more national at the same time as commerce has become more international.

Conclusion: The Border Swath

In Waterton Lakes National Park, the borderline thus has multiple meanings, and the border zone has historically variable and contested constituent elements. Different practices, levels, and scales of border-nature have been produced and represented at different moments, depending on policy, economic trends, physical practices and artifacts, and racialized and nationalist discourses. One might speak of the region as a *borderscape*, an uneven collection of practices that surrounds and transgresses the boundary, giving the place particular meaning in different historical and cultural moments. One can also speak of the region as an *ensemble* of borders and signifying networks; the relative significance of the forty-ninth parallel is at least partly dependent on the visibility and significance of other borders. These include the ones between the park and surrounding ranchers; the one between the park and the oil and gas industry in southern Alberta; the one between the park and the Blood Nation; and, of course, the one between the mountains and the prairie that is so abruptly and beautifully traced inside Waterton's limits.

Indeed, the borderline as a physical place has become literally more and less visible depending on these shifts. By way of a conclusion, then, I return to the border swath with which this essay began. The International Boundary Commission mandated in 1925 that the entire border be marked with permanent cairns and that the border swath be kept clear of vegetative growth at all times in order to keep the cairns visible. The Waterton-Glacier portion of the swath was fully cut in the 1930s and recut periodically in accordance with the Boundary Commission's rules. In 1968, the swath was not only clear-cut but sprayed with Tordon 101 from a helicopter; a 1972 aerial study revealed that this herbicide had killed approximately 2,700 trees, that deformities were present in trees as far as 100 feet away, and that residual traces of herbicides remained in the soil.[29] The spraying raised concerns, but as the swath is mandated and administered by an International Commission, neither Parks Canada nor the U.S. Park Service actually had jurisdiction over the six-meter clearing around the lines: the boundary itself was not part of either country. The swath was cleared again in 1987—by hand, paid for by Glacier National Park—and this time, the Rotarians got involved. Rather than pressure the unresponsive Boundary Commission to change its mind, they lobbied their respective representatives to ask the governments involved simply to stop funding the clearing.

The swath has multiple meanings. As the Rotarians campaign actively for the eventual erasure of the boundary, park interpretive programs actually rely on the boundary for drama. Much like Middleton's signs on the Chief Mountain Highway, the "hands across the border" ceremony conducted at the international boundary every Saturday during the summer tourist season ritually *performs* the act of crossing, thus formalizing and highlighting precisely the border that is said to be so inappropriately unnatural. Performing the swath's significance as an international boundary actually enables a conversation about its meaning, its history, and its ecological significance to nonhuman "crossers." Performing hands reaching from one side to the other actually occasions a space in which U.S./Canadian differences can be highlighted and played with and *not* resolved into a bland internationalism. As W. H. New has argued, such joking is a significant practice by which Canadians obliquely express resistance to U.S. cultural dominance.[30]

As all this hand-shaking is occurring, the boundary swath is being surveyed by remote sensing technologies and reconstructed digitally in the offices of the International Boundary Commission. At the same time, grizzly bears use the swath as a convenient corridor to move from east to west in parts of the park region. At the same time, the two tiny customs posts located on the Chief Mountain Highway are told, post 9/11, to tighten security, creating a border-crossing experience significantly differ- ent from the jovial one on the hike and significantly different depending on who is doing the crossing. The forty-ninth parallel is no longer—if it ever was—simply a line between two nations; as a set of local and global practices and representations, it achieves a place in multiple stories.

Notes

This essay is an expanded version of a paper presented at the conference of the American Society for Environmental History, Denver, April 2002.

1. W. H. New, *Borderlands: How We Talk about Canada* (Vancouver: University of British Columbia Press, 1998), 27.
2. Catriona Sandilands, "Ecological Integrity and National Narrative: Cleaning Up Cana- da's National Parks," *Canadian Woman Studies* 20 (Fall 2000): 136–42.
3. H. R. MacMillan, Report on Proposed National Park, 1909, RG 84, vol. 2165, file w2, National Archives of Canada (NAC).
4. *Waterton Lakes National Park Management Plan*, 1992, Environment Canada, Western Region, 7.
5. H. E. Sibbald, chief fire and game warden, Rocky Mountain National Park, to J. B. Harkin, April 19, 1916, RG 84, vol. 2166, file w-2-1, NAC.
6. Chief Superintendent of Dominion Parks Hervey to Harkin, March 9, 1915, RG 84, vol. 2165, file w2, NAC.
7. Chief Superintendent of Dominion Parks Hervey to Harkin, March 9, 1915.
8. Ray Djuff, *High on a Windy Hill: The Story of the Prince of Wales Hotel* (Calgary: Rocky Mountain Books, 1999), 13.
9. *New York World*, March 5, 1926, cited in Djuff, *High on a Windy Hill*, 28.
10. W. W. Cory, deputy minister of the interior, to T. D. Pattullo, British Columbia minister of lands, March 20, 1928, RG 84, vol. 2166, file w-300, NAC.
11. "Call It Waterton National Park," *Lethbridge Daily Herald*, March 27, 1926.
12. Bill Waiser, *Park Prisoners: The Untold Story of Western Canada's National Parks, 1915–1946* (Saskatoon: Fifth Houses, 1995), 64–67.
13. See Frank Anderson, "Where Prairie Meets the Mountains: A Park Is Born," in Art Downs, ed., *Waterton National Park* (Surrey BC: Frontier Books, 1968), 30.
14. Frank Chaplin Bray, "Play Bridges National Frontiers," *Rotarian*, July 1934, 48.
15. Bill 97, 22–23 George V, 1932.
16. Harkin to Rowatt, February 4, 1932, RG 84, vol. 2165, file w2, NAC.
17. *Lethbridge Herald*, July 6, 1936.
18. National Parks Bureau, "Dedication of the Cairns in Waterton-Glacier International Peace Park," July 28, 1947, Waterton Lakes National Park files, International Peace Park.
19. Stead to C. P. MacKenzie, October 1, 1941, RG 84, vol. 42, file w-109, NAC; De Veber to Stead, February 8, 1943, RG 84, vol. 43, file w-109, NAC.

20. Lucia Lewis to Leo Dolan, director, Canadian Government Travel Bureau, November 4, 1949, RG 84, vol. 216, file W2–2, NAC. Emphases in original.

21. "Waterton Revisited," *Lethbridge Herald*, August 1, 1931.

22. *Waterton Resource Guide* (Waterton Park AB: Parks Canada, 1997), sec. 3, 5.

23. "Dedication of Waterton-Glacier Peace Park Brings to Light Early Picture of Kootenai Brown and Henry Reynolds, First Park Chiefs," *Lethbridge Herald*, June 25, 1932.

24. See Donald Worster, *Under Western Skies: Nature and History in the American West* (New York: Oxford University Press, 1992).

25. Joseph M. Dixon, "Joint Playground for America and Canada," *U.S. Daily*, June 29, 1932.

26. "The Peace Park," *Calgary Albertan*, June 10, 1932.

27. "Canon" (S. H. Middleton), *Waterton-Glacier International Peace Park*, n.d., 9.

28. "Waterton Lakes National Park: About the Waterton/Glacier International Peace Park," http://parkscanada.pch.gc.ca/Parks/Alberta/Waterton_lakes/english/welcome2_e.htm (June 3, 1999).

29. P. A. Murtha, "Photo Interpretation of Tree Mortality alongside the International Boundary: Waterton Lakes National Park," *National Park Forest Survey Report No. 5* (Ottawa: Canadian Forestry Service, Department of the Environment, 1972), 3.

30. New, *Borderlands*, 45–49.

19. Whoa! Canada

Environmental Issues and Activism along the Alberta-Montana Border

Todd Wilkinson

Off in the foreboding clouds of another storm, the snowy peaks of Glacier National Park rise above the invisible line of the forty-ninth parallel, reminding us how close we are to the United States of America—and yet how far away.

It's early spring, and for the last hour, we've been fishtailing on dirt roads hard-packed with black ice, just beyond the northern boundary of Waterton Lakes National Park, Glacier's sister preserve in Canada. We're feeling our way through the Castle-Crown wildlands complex in southern Alberta, headed west toward the border of British Columbia on the Continental Divide.

Mike Sawyer, a Canadian environmental activist, is behind the wheel, and he's off on an entertaining rant about how grateful Americans should be for their environmental laws and system of government.

"Canadians take great pride in reminding ourselves that we are different from you," says Sawyer, a forty-two-year-old consultant for the Castle-Crown Wilderness Coalition. "Both of our nations evolved from British ancestry. But when you came to the continent, you rose up and rebelled. We said we quite like having the Queen Mother take care of us. We like to think of ourselves as being much more polite and civil than you Americans."

"As a result," Sawyer continues, "we're a culture that is less distrustful of large corporations, and we have a natural predisposition to support our benevolent government, to believe it will look after us. This sets the context for everything you see today in southwest Canada."

What we see, as Sawyer blithely wheels around one hairpin turn after another, is a series of side roads, heading up virtually every breathtaking valley. Each leads to a natural gas well pad or logging clear-cut, an off-road vehicle trail or an old mine.

Although this rugged scarp of the Rocky Mountains rising from the high plains still holds some of the greatest diversity of plants and animals in North America, some scientists say its ecological fabric is starting to fray. For the past half century, the Castle, as it is called, has felt the ever-tightening grip of industrialization. The last decade's energy boom has accelerated development, as oil and gas companies have drained underground reservoirs in the Great Plains of Western Canada and started working their way up into the mountains.

Sawyer and a handful of activists in this province of three million people hope to slow the boom and protect the remaining roadless areas, considered by biologists to be a crucial vertebra in the backbone of the Rockies. They even dream of permanent wilderness status for the area. But they face a powerful oil and gas industry that is pumping money into Alberta's economy and a legal and political system that offers few footholds for citizens. Unfortunately, Sawyer says, Canadians are complacent about the demise of this spectacular landscape. "It's almost like we've had a collective lobotomy," he says. "All the aggressiveness has been bred out of us."

Provincial Lands

Sawyer doesn't mean that Canadians don't care about their Rocky Mountains. The country's magnificent national parks—Waterton Lakes, Banff and Jasper in Alberta—show that they do. But it is the extensive lands between the federally managed parks that have activists like Sawyer worried.

These "Crown Lands," overseen by the fiercely antifederal provincial governments, come closest to U.S. state lands. Most Crown Lands are only subject to provincial laws and are managed to generate revenue. Different provincial boards manage the various activities, including logging, oil and gas drilling, development, and recreation. Board members are appointed by the ruling party, and according to Sawyer, they often work in the industry they regulate.

The Castle Region includes shortgrass prairie in the east and lake-studded montane forests in the west. Overall it's slightly larger than Yellowstone National Park and almost entirely Crown Land.

At one time, though, it seemed destined to become part of an immense federally owned and protected landscape. Between 1914 and 1922, the Castle was part of Waterton Lakes National Park. After that, to accommodate developers and hunters, the federal government designated it as a provincial game preserve. Then, in 1954, as the postwar economic boom steamed onward, the province officially opened the Castle to development and natural-resource extraction that, except for one brief burp, has continued to this day.

In 1993, the government announced that it would set aside the bulk of the Castle as a wildlife reserve as a condition for the approval of a ski resort expansion. But a collaborative group set up by the government to come up with a management plan for the new reserve couldn't reach an agreement, and the deal fell through.

Multiple use brought intensive logging and more than one hundred oil and gas wells, with thousands of miles of roads to service them. The roads, in turn, have spurred a huge increase in motorized recreation, Sawyer says. "They all feed on each other."

Although little timber harvesting is now occurring in the Castle, activists expect it to increase when the provincial government approves a new twenty-year timber plan in 2005. The biggest pressure, though, is coming from the oil and gas industry, which can foresee the end of the reserves in the privately owned prairies to the east. Seven new gas wells were drilled into the Castle in 2001, with more in the works.

"You might say that we're taking an upgrading step," says Roger Creasey, a staff scientist with the Alberta Energy and Utilities Board, which coordinates the permitting process for new wells. "We're not necessarily going into areas that are off-limits, but development is progressing into previously undeveloped areas. We're seeing that right now."

The energy industry struts with a confident swagger across Alberta, for good reason. The entire western half of the province straddles what is known as "the Overthrust Belt," a geologic formation that extends into the Rocky Mountain Front of the United States. It is endowed with untapped trillions of cubic feet of natural gas, billions of barrels of oil, vast deposits of oil sands in the Mackenzie Delta north of Alberta, and gigantic seams of coal.

All told, Alberta and eastern British Columbia have more BTUs than the Persian Gulf. And to their south is a country with a huge energy appetite. Canada provides the United States with about 15 percent of its oil and gas needs, according to a *New York Times* article. Alberta alone exports 2.4 trillion cubic feet of natural gas a year to the United States, as well as 900,000 barrels of oil a day.

Even before the terrorist attacks on New York and Washington DC, President George W. Bush had been in talks with Prime Minister Jean Chrétien about decreasing U.S. dependence on fuel from the Middle East. Alberta figures prominently in the framework of a new North American energy policy, says David Luff, spokesman for the Canadian Association of Petroleum Producers.

Already the production is massive. Energy companies drilled 7,281 new gas wells in Alberta in 2000, an all-time record, up 40 percent from the year before, according to the province's Ministry of Energy. Energy development infrastructure in the province now includes at least 35,000 active gas wells, 37,500 active oil wells, 93,000 capped or abandoned wells, about 150,000 miles of gas and oil pipelines, and 703 processing plants that handle either gas, oil sands, or crude oil.

"There's this great glob of activity," says Sawyer, as we pull into the town of Turner Valley, which lies northeast of the Castles, some thirty miles from Calgary. The oil derrick has been a civic icon here ever since a Texas-style oil boom started in the late 1930s. Outside of town is a local park called Hell's Half Acre, the site of the province's first oil refinery, which has had a flame burning on sour gas leaking from the ground for sixty years.

Sawyer, who spent two years in the early 1990s as an oil and gas consultant for the provincial government, tells me that shortly after the company donated this site to the province for a cultural park, health officials discovered the ground was contaminated. "Where else would you get a company with a $1 billion liability giving away its burden as a gift to the people?" he asks.

Although the oil and gas industry has helped power Alberta's economy for decades, it has become a true powerhouse in the last several years. In 2000, as blackouts started rolling across California and the price of natural gas rose to record highs, Alberta hit the jackpot. The province projected it would earn $10.3 billion from leases and royalties in 2001, generating a $7 billion surplus. Applying $5.6 billion to debt repayment, Alberta expected to cut its IOUs in half that year.

Albertans have reason to be loyal to the industry, even beyond the huge employment and tax base. The provincial government promised rebate programs for the winter and spring of 2001 to help consumers pay rising natural gas and electricity bills; the rebate was estimated to average $1,680 (Canadian) per household.

"The energy industry affects the lives of all Albertans," says Murray Smith, the minister of energy. "It means we in Alberta have the lowest taxes, the strongest economy, and the highest economic growth in Canada."

Riding the boom was Alberta premier Ralph Klein, Progressive Conservative Party leader, former television personality, and mayor of Calgary. In 2001 Klein was easily elected to a third term.

"We are open for business," says Roger Creasey. "During the 1990s, we have been building a boom. In the last two years we've set drilling records. We're pretty excited about the level of business."

But Creasey says the government is concerned about proceeding too hastily. "What a lot of us want to do is ensure we don't lose quality in getting there."

Wildlife in Retreat

Conservationists say quality is already being lost in the Castle, especially in terms of wildlife habitat. The range is the northernmost extension of the Crown of the Continent Ecosystem, which extends from the Crowsnest Pass in Alberta and British Columbia to the Bob Marshall and Scapegoat wilderness areas south of Glacier National Park in Montana. It is a crucial north-south link for North American wildlife, says Arlin Hackman, vice president of World Wildlife Fund–Canada. That includes such transborder species as grizzly bears, wolves, wolverines, lynx, woodland caribou, bull trout, and redband trout—all species that are either federally protected in the United States or candidates for listing.

Fragmentation of habitat and liberal hunting laws have turned the Castle into a dangerous place for wildlife, says Brian Horejsi, an independent biologist specializing in grizzly bears. Intense scrutiny of deforestation and road building in British Columbia prompted the premier there to declare a three-year ban on all grizzly hunting. Yet in Alberta, where only five to seven hundred grizzlies exist in the whole province, Horejsi says, "You can still go out and buy a hunting license, go into the Castle, and shoot a grizzly."

It's an even grimmer tale for wolves, which can be legally shot year-round. During the mid-1990s, as many as forty-four of an estimated regional border wolf population of fifty to sixty were killed within fourteen months. During the summer of 2000, two wolves were sighted in Waterton and within weeks one was shot just outside the park.

Louisa Willcox, a Sierra Club activist from Bozeman, Montana, says it's not uncommon for bears and wolves to travel from Montana to the Castle in a matter of days, only to be shot. "Areas of southern Alberta and British Columbia have represented a bloodbath for U.S. bears and wolves," says Willcox.

"Most Americans look to Canada as this incredible reservoir of wildlife that will be a reliable source of animals forever, but that's proving not necessarily to be the case," says Kevin van Tighem, a conservation biologist with Parks Canada, the federal agency that manages parks in the country. "In fact, the irony is we in Canada may need animals from the United States to bolster our chronically depleted populations. The long-term prognosis is not good."

Looking for a Foothold

Slowing the gas boom doesn't look likely either, in the short term, according to Mike Judd, a horse packer and outfitter who has lived in the Castle's mountains all his life. Judd's house lies near a sour-gas well operated by Shell Canada, southern Alberta's biggest operator. It is visible from their driveway as we pull in. "Do you smell the sour gas?" Judd asks with a smile. "Industry will tell you it's the smell of money."

Sour gas contains hydrogen sulfide, a natural compound that must be processed out before the gas can be sold on the commercial market. Hydrogen sulfide released from gas wells in Wyoming has been blamed for the death of deer and other game animals. Over the past few years, sour-gas leaks have forced Judd and his neighbors from their home on more than one occasion. They sometimes encounter oil engineers wearing gas masks who are drilling a new hole or maintaining an existing site.

"We worry about our health, sure, but what's breaking our hearts is what's happening to the land," Judd says. "Worse than any individual well or clear-cut on Crown Land or subdivision on private land, ecologically speaking, is the infrastructure that comes with it, the cumulative effects of roads and trucks and noise and activity."

Industry doesn't take kindly to defiance, Judd says. A few years ago, he and a few friends were threatened with a lawsuit from Shell Canada for participating in a blockade to stop the company from drilling two sour-gas wells on nearby Prairie Bluff. The area is critical habitat for bighorn sheep, yet the Alberta Energy and Utilities Board approved the area for drilling.

The action against Judd and friends was what is often called a SLAPP (Strategic Lawsuit Against Public Participation) suit. A court ruled that the protesters could be liable for $100,000 each. Judd says it was intended as a warning to citizens that if they decide to take a stand, they may find themselves facing an army of corporate attorneys. In this case, it worked: Judd agreed to leave the area, and Shell Canada decided not to pursue its lawsuit.

"We have no history of civil disobedience in Alberta as they do in southern British Columbia around Vancouver," Sawyer adds. There activists have engaged in tree-sitting demonstrations and boycotts to protest the cutting of old-growth forests. "Here the police will use immediate and unkind means on citizens who step out of line. You have to remember Alberta is the most politically and socially conservative province in Canada."

Traditional approaches don't work, either. Sawyer says activists like Judd have tried to get the provincial energy regulators to hold public hearings on drilling proposals. But time and again the province has turned them down, claiming that the law only requires a public hearing if the affected parties can prove they will lose money as a result of the drilling.

When the government does hear citizen complaints, it often sets up stakeholder groups to resolve differences. "We [the Alberta Energy and Utilities Board] believe in a lot of collaboration and holding meetings in the Canadian way to pound out consensus," says Roger Creasey. "For those who accept compromise, there is some maneuvering room." But activists say that consensus almost never results in a proposal being denied.

Legal remedies are also hard to come by. Canada has no national-level equivalents to American environmental laws, such as the Endangered Species Act, the National Environmental Policy Act, and the Clean Water Act, although conservationists across the country are now pushing hard for a Canadian endangered species act. And the provincial laws governing land use are weak, says Judd.

"Every one of our provincial laws says that administrators, which ultimately means the premier, can exercise discretion in deciding the fate of land-use disputes," Judd says. "What it really amounts to is a dictatorship. Given the nature of local economic stakeholders, it's not in the political interest to support conservation."

Ray Rasker, a former Canadian citizen and a resource economist with the Sonoran Institute in Bozeman, a college town of 28,000 people near Yellowstone National Park, says few American environmentalists realize what Canadian activists face. "In a town like Bozeman there are now between 100 to 120 full-time paid environmentalists. In all of Alberta there is not more than 20. It means that industry has the run of the place and it calls the shots."

A couple of years ago, when Gloria Flora, then supervisor of Montana's Lewis and Clark National Forest, paid a visit, Judd got a stark reminder of the difference between Canadian and American conservation politics. Flora wanted to see what oil and gas development along the Rocky Mountain Front in Alberta looked like before deciding what type of development should be allowed on Montana's Front. Judd took her to the mountains outside the town of Pincher Creek. There, gas pads dot the landscape. They feed a Shell Canada refinery on the edge of Waterton Park.

The visit made an impression. A few months later, after receiving comments from across the United States and using the National Environmental Policy Act to weigh the benefits of development vs. leaving the mountains of Montana alone, Flora set the Front limits to oil and gas drilling.

"Gloria Flora said, 'I don't want the Front to look like this,'" says Judd. Flora's decision is being reviewed by the Bush administration.

Prospect for Change

Officials in the Canadian oil and gas industry say objections have not fallen on deaf ears. The Canadian Association of Petroleum Products (CAPP), which has 160 member companies that cumulatively account for 95 percent of the total oil and gas production in Canada, has funded two grizzly bear research projects, including one carried out by noted bear expert Steven Herrero, professor emeritus at the University of Calgary.

CAPP spokesman David Luff says environmentalists need to recognize that impacts are ephemeral, lasting twenty to thirty years, and then wildlands can be restored. "Our industry is there for a short period, although I recognize there will be lots of debates about whether twenty to thirty years is short," he says.

Luff says innovations, such as directional drilling and clustering of wells to minimize impact, may influence government decisions about which lands it wants open to drilling. While some areas in the mountains likely would be targeted for development, he says, others now open to leasing might be set aside for wildlife.

"I would actually say there is a lot of common ground for what Michael Sawyer is interested in and trying to achieve," says Luff. "He is concerned about cumulative effects and thresholds and targets, and so are we. There are some issues that clearly we will debate and be at opposite ends."

Sawyer says so much habitat has been degraded in the Castle that compromise is unacceptable. But that's not a view held by all Canadian conservationists.

Fifth-generation Albertan Harvey Locke, an environmental attorney who founded the Yellowstone to Yukon Conservation Campaign, an umbrella organization working to protect wildlands in the U.S. and Canadian Rocky Mountains, says it is not too late to save the Castle from overdevelopment. "The Castle is bumped and bruised, but not maimed," says Locke, who now works for the Kendall Foundation in Boston, which helps fund several Canadian conservation groups. He says any attempt by the industry to drill deep in the Castle is socially risky. "There's no question the oil and gas industry wields all kinds of power, except that it's being muted by the love of the Canadians for the mountains."

There are some signs that the country's passion for wildlands is making a difference. In the spring of 2001 in central Alberta, the Energy and Utilities Board denied a proposed sour-gas drilling project, saying that Shell Canada's operations plan would not adequately safeguard public health. It was a rare event that conservationists say was catalyzed by national publicity from renowned Canadian conservationist David Suzuki.

And in summer 2001, the Albertan government created three new provincial parks in the Rockies, totaling 200,000 acres. "These areas were not protected because the government is green," says Locke, "but because the people wanted it." Unlike the Castle, the new parks lie within a stone's throw of populous Calgary. Locke says that more people will need to become aware of the beauty of—and the threats to—the Castle before the government takes action to protect it, but it can happen. "I remain hopeful. Unlike Mike Sawyer and Mike Judd, I see the glass as being half-full instead of half-empty," Locke says.

Broadening the Battle

Ultimately, protection for the Castle may require more support from the national government in Ottawa and from conservationists in the United States. In 2000, Environment Minister David Anderson introduced a Species At Risk Act (SARA) that could be a new tool to protect Canadian wildlife. Although many Canadian scientists and conservationists have long backed such a measure, there is not much support for SARA as written; among other problems, it would apply only to federal lands, which form just 10 percent of the Canadian land base.

"It's a piece of Novocain doing nothing to repair the problem," David Schindler, an ecologist at the University of Alberta, told the Canadian press in September 2000. He and more than one thousand other scientists sent a letter criticizing the bill to Prime Minister Jean Chrétien.

Sawyer says the SARA battle shows how strong the provinces are and how difficult it will be to move them. For years, Canadian conservationists have relied heavily on public relations campaigns to advance their cause. He would like to see Canadian environmental groups and the foundations that back them adopt an aggressive strategy that includes applying pressure through the marketplace and, if possible, more lawsuits.

One place where Canadian activists could make a difference, he says, is in the ongoing negotiations over the U.S.–Canada Softwood Lumber Agreement, which has allowed cheap, government-subsidized Canadian timber to flood the U.S. market. The Castle-Crown Wilderness Coalition has joined U.S. timber companies and environmentalists in calling for a new agreement that levels the playing field.

Both Sawyer and Locke agree on the need to enlist the help of their counterparts to the south. "The Castle deserves a higher profile in the United States," says Locke. "It is part of a shared ecosystem, and its development is being driven by U.S. demand for natural resources. If anything, U.S. interest in the Castle may be coming too late." Or, as the always blunt Mike Sawyer says, "Canadians need to take an American perspective on this fight. There's hundreds of examples of groups in the United States digging in their heels and using whatever tools they have available. That's what we need to do."

Note

This essay, originally entitled "Whoa! Canada," appeared in *High Country News* 33 (October 8, 2001): 1, 8–10, and is reprinted here by permission.

Afterword

Comparing Western Borderlands and Their Future Study

Sterling Evans

There are fifty-four border crossings along the forty-ninth parallel between the United States and Canada from Lake of the Woods, Minnesota/Ontario, to the Strait of Juan de Fuca, Washington/British Columbia. The westernmost crossing, at Blaine, Washington/White Rock, British Columbia, is graced with a sixty-seven-foot-high concrete Peace Arch and flowered gardens (Peace Arch State Park, Washington) that warmly greet travelers on U.S. Interstate 5 and British Columbia Highway 99. With an inscription saying, "May These Gates Never Be Closed," the arch is dedicated to "Children of a Common Mother" (despite Americans' traditional aversion to things monarchical and disbelief that "democracy wears a crown") and to "Brethren Dwelling in Unity." Surprisingly, and despite this language of unity, the Washington Daughters of the Confederacy erected a memorial in the park commemorating, as apparently it has been named, the "Jefferson Davis Highway."

Similarly, straddling the forty-ninth in the Turtle Mountains of North Dakota and Manitoba is the International Peace Garden to celebrate the friendship and good relations between the two nations. Conceived by Ontario horticulturalist Henry Moore, the Peace Garden opened in 1932 and was further developed by a series of Civilian Conservation Corps (CCC) work camps to create a transboundary botanical garden honoring international peace. There Winston Churchill's views of the border are inscribed on the walls of the peace chapel, which is situated right on the forty-ninth: "That long Canadian frontier from the Atlantic to the Pacific oceans, guarded only by neighbourly respect and honourable obligations, is an example to every country and a pattern for the future of the world." And that two national parks between Alberta and Montana are joined at the border to form the Waterton-Glacier International Peace Park is further testimony to the people in two nations "dwelling in unity."[1] Or perhaps as former U.S. president Bill Clinton put it, this perceived unity is the result of the two nations' "common values." "Our long border, the most peaceful on earth," he wrote, "is a metaphor for all that we hold in common: a belief in human and civil rights, in free speech and federalism, in the advance of democracy and the value of trade." And former ambassador to Canada Paul Cellucci trumpeted the increased trade, much of it induced by NAFTA policies, as a reason to "overhaul" the border—to make it easier and quicker for the roughly two hundred million border crossings a year. In August 2001, Cellucci gave a speech in Ottawa in which he said the border should be thought of not as a frontier but rather as a meeting place, a "Main Street" in North America.[2]

Yet questions linger regarding the messages these kinds of words and memorials suggest. Are the commemorations at the Peace Arch, Peace Gardens, and International Peace Park misleading as to the truth about *all* peoples in the region "dwelling in unity" over the years? Have we all, especially American Indians/First Nations in the borderlands, shared a "common mother?" Can we all meet on Main Street or cross it freely? Why, as Bruce Miller pointed out in chapter 3, has it become even more difficult in the last few years for First Nations people to go back and forth across the border for cultural and economic reasons? And it may become even more difficult, for Native and non-Native Americans, since Homeland Security authorities announced that starting in 2007 for the first time in history U.S. citizens will have to have current passports to reenter the United States after visiting Canada.

The peace memorials, all located in the West and without many counterparts along the eastern sections of the U.S./Canadian line, are designed to reflect the history of it being the longest undefended border in the world, or as commemorated by western poet William Stafford, "the field where the battle did not happen, where the unknown soldier did not die."[3] There are no similar peace parks along America's border with Mexico, a border zone that has become one of the most defended and militarized in the world. Some of the bridges across the Rio Grande are marked as "friendship bridges," and Falcon Dam, which spans the border in southern Texas/northern Tamaulipas, has a similar commemoration, but there are no large international peace parks as yet. Apparently Americans and Mexicans are not "children of a common mother." And as many Mexican Americans say (which could be echoed by Native Americans/First Nations in the U.S.–Canadian borderlands), "We didn't cross the border; the border crossed us."

South of Texas's Big Bend National Park, however, a private donor is working with the Mexican government to create a new national park in the northern part of the state of Coahuila that abuts the international boundary.[4] It would be a useful opportunity for these conjoined parks to have a designation like that of Waterton-Glacier International Peace Park, but there has been no such move at press time for this book. Instead of a peace arch park with Mexico, on the border there is Pancho Villa State Park, New Mexico, that denounces the Mexican revolutionary's attack on the small border town of Columbus in 1916—the only foreign attack on continental U.S. soil between the War of 1812 and the terrorist attacks of 2001.

The disparity is likewise reflected in the practice of patrolling America's two borders. As Stephen DeLong surmises, if Americans "think about these borders at all, it tends to be in terms of proclaiming 'the longest unfortified boundary in the world' to the north, or worrying about the permeability of our southern border to drugs, illegal immigrants, or killer bees."[5]

Ideology has translated into policy. Compared to the roughly 600 U.S. border patrol agents on the 4,000-mile (8,895 kilometers) U.S.–Canadian border in 2002, there were nearly 10,000 agents patrolling the U.S. border with Mexico, which is half as long. The budget of the Immigration and Naturalization Service (INS) went from $1.18 billion in 1990 to $4.27 billion by 2000, most of which went toward enforcement along the southern border. There, the United States has instituted Operation Gatekeeper to patrol the border more effectively against the rising tide of "illegal aliens." And in the wake of the events of 9/11, the Department of Homeland Security announced that it was investigating the use of unmanned aircraft, known as "drones," that can remain airborne for fourteen hours at a time to patrol the border with Mexico. Drones, at a cost of $4.5 million each, had been tested in the 1990s, when the Border Patrol decided against their use.[6] But all of this represents an immensely fortified, militarized boundary that Americans should be mindful of when proudly boasting about unguarded borders with Canada.

There was a time, however, when policing America's northern frontier borderlands was more intense. Certainly in the years of the U.S. cavalry there was a highly armed and militarized approach to law enforcement to support the colonization efforts of pioneers and settlers against American Indians and outlaws. And as Marian McKenna, Gerhard Ens, and Michel Hogue explained in their chapters here, Canadians used the North-West Mounted Police—those red-coated Mounties who became one of Canada's most powerful icons of identity—to preclude frontier violence and to enforce Canadian policies toward First Nations and Métis. The implication was not lost on Canadian writer Margaret Atwood, who asserted that "Canada must be the only nation in the world where a policeman is used as a national symbol."[7]

Thus law enforcement on both western U.S. borders has been more for property protection, immigration policy, and enforcement of Prohibition (against liquor in the early twentieth century; against other drugs in the late twentieth and early twenty-first centuries). It has not been to deal with boundary disputes or territorial invasions by the threatening armies of hostile governments. The one exception was that of Pancho Villa's violent incursion on Columbus, New Mexico, and the U.S. response of sending six thousand troops for months into the deserts of northern Mexico to catch him—the failed Pershing Punitive Expedition.[8] The academic opportunity is ripe for scholars to compare and contrast the failed U.S. efforts to hunt down Pancho Villa in Mexico in 1916, Manuel Noriega in Panama in 1986, and Osama bin Laden in Afghanistan in 2001.

The only territorial dispute with Mexico since 1853 (when the boundary was finalized with the Gadsden Purchase in southern Arizona/northern Sonora to benefit the Southern Pacific Railroad) was in the Chamizal area of the Rio Grande in El Paso, Texas. The 1963 Chamizal Treaty, signed by presidents Lyndon Johnson and Adolfo López Mateos, settled a century-old dispute that was caused by natural changes in the flow of the Rio Grande. The treaty enacted a land swap between the two nations: 630

acres of South El Paso went to Ciudad Juárez, and 193 acres of Ciudad Juárez went to El Paso.[9]

The United States has had only one such territorial dispute with western Canada since the last segment of the forty-ninth parallel was finalized as the border in 1846. That incident, the so-called "Pig War" of 1859, concerned San Juan Island, which is located in the Strait of Juan de Fuca between Vancouver Island, British Columbia, and the state of Washington. Both British and Americans had settled on the islands, and they resided there in a rather nervous coexistence with neither recognizing the claims or authority of the other.

Tensions came to a head in June 1859, however, when American settler Lyman Cutlar discovered a pig belonging to an employee of the Hudson's Bay Company foraging in his garden. Cutlar shot the pig and refused to pay the $100 the owner claimed it was worth, prompting the British residents to seek Cutlar's arrest. The Americans then solicited U.S. military protection, and Brig. Gen. William S. Harney, commander of the Department of Oregon, sent a company of the Ninth Infantry under the direction of Capt. George Pickett to the island. Angered by the presence of U.S. forces, Governor James Douglas of British Columbia sent three British warships to San Juan to remove Pickett and his troops. Each side sent reinforcements of troops and artillery but avoided armed clashes.

When news of these potentially dangerous developments reached Washington DC, President James Buchanan dispatched General Winfield Scott, of Mexican-American War fame, to investigate the matter. Scott worked with Governor Douglas to defuse the situation; they agreed to a joint military occupation, with an "American Camp" and a "British Camp" on the island, for the next twelve years. Then in 1871 Great Britain and the United States referred the matter to Kaiser Wilhelm I of Germany as an outside party to make a ruling. The Kaiser created an arbitration commission that decided the U.S.–Canadian boundary in the strait would be to the west of San Juan Island, thus ensuring it as U.S. territory. The British abided by the decision and withdrew their troops. The peace is commemorated today at the San Juan Island National Historical Park (run by the U.S. National Park Service) and honors "the 'war' in which the only casualty was a pig."[10]

Other minor points have been anomalies more than disputes. For

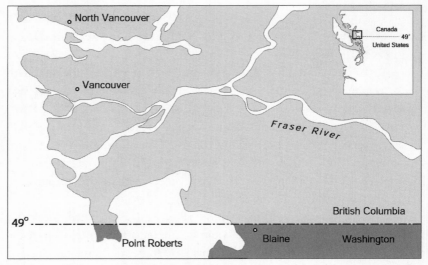

Figure 18. Point Roberts, Washington. Map by Brian Ludy and Cassie Hansen.

example, at the very western end of the forty-ninth parallel border is Point Roberts, a tiny peninsula extending into the Strait of Juan de Fuca that is physically attached to British Columbia but belongs to Washington (see figure 18). Residents or travelers have to take a ferry from Vancouver Island, British Columbia, a boat from Washington, or drive about twenty miles into Canada and then back into Washington to get to Point Roberts. The point also has a colorful fishing industry history, as pointed out by Lissa Wadewitz in chapter 17.

Another anomaly is that of the Northwest Angle—the corner piece of U.S. land attached to Manitoba but separated from Minnesota and Ontario by Lake of the Woods (named "Angle" due to the 90° northward turn the border takes away from the forty-ninth parallel (see figure 19). It was created by accident, "tethered to mapmakers' hazy conception of the origins of the Mississippi River," as Amy Radil has written. "When the river turned up south of where they expected, the border dropped down too, leaving an isolated piece of the United States up north."[11]

Although they do not live there, the Red Lake Band of Chippewa Indians owns and holds in trust 87 percent of the Angle. The rest of the land is home to about 100 Minnesotans who run fishing resorts that rely on the Lake of the Woods tourism business. The operators, fishing guides,

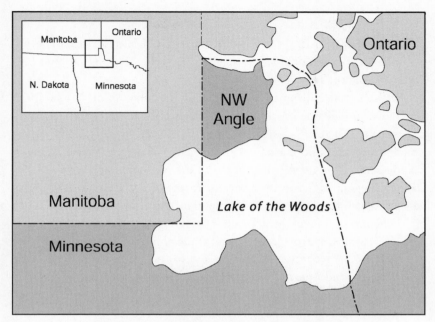

Figure 19. The Northwest Angle. Map by Brian Ludy and Cassie Hansen.

and their families (who say "the beauty of the place is without equal, and [that] living there has never been easy") have created a closely knit community over the years, and they maintain Minnesota's last one-room schoolhouse for their children. [12]

But Angleites were alarmed in 1998 when Canada enacted more restrictive border-crossing policies and Ontario legislated stricter fishing regulations for non-Natives fishing on Lake of the Woods. Amy Radil reported on Minnesota Public Radio that the issues became "a complicated dispute involving the United States, Canada, Ontario, Minnesota, and international treaties." [13] Thus some residents petitioned to secede from the United States thinking that if they were Canadian citizens they could get around the strict non-Native fishing laws. Their congressman, Representative Collin Peterson (D-MN), even introduced a secession bill in Congress, but unfortunately never consulted the Red Lake Chippewa about it, which of course angered them. The bill, eventually unsuccessful as it takes a constitutional amendment for secessions to occur, made the whole event more of a media circus than anything else. Several regional newspapers helped fan the flames, reporting that "Manitoba Wants Us,

U.S. Secessionists Insist," "Secessionist Threat Is Plea for Help," and even, in characteristic bad double-pun newspaper style, "Fishing Dispute Has Territory Angling to Secede."[14]

Without major disputes, then, policing the forty-ninth parallel ("the lamentably undefended American-Canadian border," as writer Al Purdy sarcastically called it)[15] is more of an effort of joint organizations. American and Canadian border patrol agencies, U.S. Customs Service/Canada Customs and Revenue Agency, and even the National Park Service/Parks Canada have jurisdiction over various facets of law enforcement in the borderlands of the American and Canadian Wests. In all, there are about fifty U.S. and Canadian agencies charged with some dimension of immigration, customs, patrol, security, and trade along the border.

New to this scenario and in response to the events of September 11 is the Secure and Smart Border Action Plan that both nations agreed upon on December 12, 2001. Now the border is "smart." It is a "zone of confidence," as some officials referred to how the accord commits both countries to heightened security measures and offers the option of creating possible "common security perimeters." Part of the agreement included the creation of Integrated Border Enforcement Teams (IBET) composed of federal and local law enforcement officials working together to fight cross-border crime.

There is a great deal of trade and commerce to protect. By 1989, U.S.–Canadian trade was worth US$1.3 billion a day, and it has continued to grow ever since. Eighty-seven percent of Canadian exports go to the United States, and 25 percent of U.S. exports go to Canada.[16] Thirty-eight U.S. states conduct more trade with Canada than anywhere else.[17] Not all the trade, however, is legal. Some studies show how the smuggling of marijuana and other controlled substances accounts for more trade dollars than do timber exports between the two nations. Hence the IBET units also work to combat smuggling operations. And for the first time on the U.S.–Canadian border, the antismuggling operations have become militarized. In 2004, the Department of Homeland Security established antismuggling "bases" at Grand Forks, North Dakota, Great Falls, Montana, and Bellingham, Washington. Customs agents regularly patrol the border using helicopters, airplanes, and, in Washington's Puget Sound, high-speed boats. A spokesperson for U.S. Immigration and Customs Enforcement was quoted by the Associated Press as saying that "smuggling is a two-way street. We've got cocaine and money going north, [and] B.C. bud and human smuggling coming south." The purposes of such actions were made even more apparent in the summer of 2005 when federal agents shut down a 360-foot-long drug smuggling tunnel under the border near Lynden, Washington. The tunnel, which smugglers used primarily to transport marijuana from British Columbia into the United States, was similar to numerous such underground corridors along the U.S.–Mexican line. Thus the border's status as being peaceful and undefended has started to change.[18]

There have also been changes and new interpretations in academia on how to study the western borderlands. Scholars interested in the subject should turn first to Jeremy Adelman and Stephen Aron's forum essay in the *American Historical Review*, "From Borderlands to Borders: Empires, Nation-States, and the Peoples in Between in North American History" for analysis on the discipline's multidimensional historiography and for new theoretical insights. Their definitions and discussion of "frontiers," "borderlands," and "bordered lands" over time are an essential and highly useful starting place.[19]

Equally useful were the comments of scholars of America's southern and northern borderlands who participated in an H-West Internet discussion in the late 1990s regarding their viewpoints on the directions in which borderlands history should go. Historian Sam Truett, for example, argued that borderlands represent an "alternative historical place," since their history "means different things to different people." He suggested that borderlands be considered as "hybrid spaces where sexual and racial binary distinctions falter and where new social realities flourish." That methodology, however, should not negate how borderlands narratives are studied "in relation to political identities . . . about the ties that linked region to what [Herbert Eugene] Bolton called Greater America." Thus, he concluded, "Borderlands history provides a space for 'decentering' national and imperial narratives. . . . [It] offers a framework for thinking about U.S. history *and* Mexican history . . . about American *and* Canadian Wests."[20]

Geographer Peter Morris agreed with Truett but added that America's borderlands are "geopolitical spaces" in which regional similarities transcend national boundaries. He wrote, "The most striking thing about the U.S. and Canadian Wests, at least from the perspective of the history of 'greater America,' is their similarity, not their difference." Therefore, he rhetorically asked, "Why keep telling separate stories for Montana and Alberta, or for Arizona and Sonora, when these places have long been linked, and will continue to be linked, in their historical experiences?"[21]

A scholar who has taken that very ideology to heart is historian Beth LaDow. In joining in the discussion, LaDow added that her research on the Montana/Saskatchewan borderlands showed how "the powerful forces of the natural environment largely overrode the significance of the border in people's lives." But she argued against oversimplifying the comparisons that could result in an " 'unsatisfying' similarity . . . of what 'the West' is." To augment Morris's point, she suggested that "borderlands are attractive precisely because they both acknowledge and erase differences in one fell swoop. They are poetic kinds of places—inherently ambiguous and dual—that may help us find a truer big picture."[22]

That is exactly what the goal of this collection of essays has been—to study the "truer big picture" of the history of the borderlands of the American and Canadian Wests. The essays have explored various dimensions of regionality, cross-border interactions, and historical similarities and differences on both sides of the forty-ninth parallel. And while it is important to acknowledge the similarities that have existed, the border itself has played its own significant role in shaping differences and, indeed, a national Canadian, but not U.S., identity. Canadian identity perhaps owes even more to the long border with the United States than it does to the notion of Canadians surviving a harsh landscape and climate with long frigid winters (despite the popular Molson Beer ad claiming, "Canada: where ice was born!"). As James Loucky and Donald Alper have written, "For Canadians . . . the border is central to identity. . . . [T]he border serves, in the minds of many Canadians, to maintain the distinctiveness of Canada. . . . The strong sense of awareness of this reality has for generations helped to shape a unique Canadian nationalism. This nationalism is based on Canada as 'not the United States.' As one writer [W. H. New in *Borderlands: How We Talk about Canada*, p. 6] put it, 'Canada is unthinkable without its Border with the U.S.A.' "[23]

In arguing for the importance of studying similarities in cross-border regions, however, Peter Morris wisely cautioned that we should "guard against letting 'borderlands' erase these international boundaries from view, for these borders have been some of the most important features shaping historical geographies in the North American West, and indeed the modern world."[24]

Thus, as Thomas Isern and Bruce Shepard introduced in this volume, these issues fall into all three categories for the study of this region: continentalist, comparative, and borderlands histories. And newer regional dimensions of inquiry will continue to do so. Scholars will be able to choose from a wide variety of borderlands and cross-boundary topics to research to add to our understanding of the forty-ninth-parallel West.

One aspect that will need close attention (space constraints unfortunately prevented it from being discussed here) is that of the urban forty-ninth parallel borderlands. Comparatively, there is a robust literature studying the growth of border cities and their cultures along the Mexican/U.S. boundary but only a few emerging studies for that of the Canadian/U.S. borderlands.[25] Although most of the border runs through rural, sparsely inhabited lands, the growth of near-border metropolitan areas like Seattle, Vancouver, Spokane, Calgary, and Winnipeg, and the growth of such midsized borderlands cities as Abbotsford, Chilliwack, and Kelowna (British Columbia), Bellingham (Washington), Lethbridge and Medicine Hat (Alberta), Great Falls (Montana), Moose Jaw (Saskatchewan), Minot (North Dakota), and Brandon (Manitoba) will need to be evaluated via a borderlands thesis, especially as the era of free trade expands and has impacts on these cities.[26] Likewise, with Mexican migrants moving to Brandon and other Canadian cities to work in industries like meatpacking plants, scholars will have newer continentalist opportunities to pursue.

But in the West, with the exception of Washington state, the urban growth in the forty-ninth parallel borderlands has been primarily on the Canadian side. This is not really a new development, as Canada has been for some time one of the most urbanized countries in the world with a vast majority of Canadians living in close proximity to the border with the United States. Yet, as the Loucky and Alper study points out, this has not created a unique urban-border culture like that of the U.S./Mexican borderlands and has not generated the same kind of literature or historiography on the topic. "In the northern United States and in southern Canada," they write, "the border area is not an area of uniqueness . . . there is no border culture per se."[27]

Many in the Northwest, however, are already interpreting the Vancouver to Seattle to Portland corridor as a regional, urban Cascadia that is similar in some ways to the region that novelist Ernest Callenbach envisioned in his 1990 book, *Ecotopia*—the name used earlier by Joel Garreau to define the bioregion in his book *The Nine Nations of North America* (see figure 7 in chapter 2).[28] A quick Internet search under "Cascadia" reveals efforts toward map-making, flag-designing, and the development of a Cascadia national party. One group called the International Cascadia Alliance, a consortium of thirteen Canadian and U.S. environmental organizations with the common goal of "seeking protection for the North Cascades ecosystem," devoted a great deal of time and energy to lobby for the creation of a Cascades International Park in the mid-1990s. Although the effort failed due to "vigorous opposition from property rights groups," as Loucky and Alper reported, the group's legacy has continued in the form of advocating "elaborate transnational networks to promote terrestrial corridors and protest logging practices on both sides of the border."[29]

Even more serious and successful are economists and business promoters on both sides of the line, including those who founded the Cascadia Planning Group, who emphasize the region's commonalities and who push for economic integration. Two such promoters, Paul Schell and John Chapman, epitomized the movement when they stated that Cascadia is a "shared notion, and one in active evolution. We're still inventing ourselves as a regional culture. Cascadia is a recognition of emerging realities, a way to celebrate commonality with diversity, a way to make the whole more than the sum of its parts. Cascadia is not a State, but a state of mind."[30] Along those lines, Cascadians have, as Donald Alper has written, "been successful in drawing attention to the need for thinking in regional terms in order to tackle high profile issues such as efficient transportation, growth management, joint approaches to environmental protection, and cooperative business relationships." Alper, a political scientist and leading Cascadia scholar based at Western Washington University in the heart of the region, suggests, however, that Cascadians' efforts have suffered from a "lack of institutional coherence and political support," even though they have "helped to define a new spatial context for regional action," especially with "facilitating infrastructure (rail, ports, freeways, border crossings) with the aim of encouraging shared economic development."[31]

Environmental historians, geographers, and ecologists will need to continue to study the many aspects of climate, landscape, and other environmental changes in the borderlands. One of the most pressing of such concerns will be transboundary river and watershed issues. The Boundary Waters Treaty of 1909 established the International Joint Commission (IJC) with U.S. and Canadian officials to deal with important river concerns, especially as they applied to irrigation and flood control. In the forty-ninth parallel West, these concerns were magnified when the Red River (which forms the border between North Dakota and Minnesota but flows north into Lake Winnipeg) flooded in 1997 and threatened downriver residents and businesses in Manitoba. Likewise, the Milk and St. Mary's rivers are instrumental for irrigation projects in Montana but have threatened water supplies in Alberta and Saskatchewan. Canadian concern was also expressed in 2005 when North Dakota officials started projecting ideas about problems with the Devils Lake overflow problem that could affect Manitoba. These kinds of issues, tracked on *www.ijc.org* will need more historical evaluation over time.

Leading the way on such research are faculty and students in the University of Montana's borderlands program in environmental studies, whose work will shed important data on these issues. The research will be especially pertinent as the effects of the North American Free Trade Agreement (NAFTA) become more apparent over time. NAFTA will have definite economic implications, none of which should or will be ignored, but its natural resource and environmental considerations should not get sidetracked in favor of economic discussions. This research will also need to include more on tourism—its economic and environmental impacts in the borderlands during the late twentieth and early twenty-first centuries.

NAFTA will continue to affect agricultural and industrial relations in the region. For example, a 2003 study done by economists at Montana State University showed that Canada's wheat exports to the United States significantly decreased U.S. wheat prices. This has had especially adverse economic effects for farmers in central and western North Dakota and eastern Montana, where durum wheat is a staple crop.[32] The same is true for U.S. softwood timber exports from Canada—the longtime bane of the American lumber industry. But NAFTA trade agreements did not stop U.S. authorities from halting the export of cattle from western Canada to the United States when veterinary officials discovered an isolated case of mad cow disease in that province in 2003.[33] And Canadian industrial hemp production could have transboundary implications worthy of study in the next few decades. Legalized in Canada only in 1998, but under tax prohibition since 1937 in the United States, industrial hemp will become an important fiber crop as the two nations' need to develop an alternative to replace what is fast becoming an outmoded and environmentally disadvantageous pulp industry becomes more apparent.

Filmmaking is one industry in which NAFTA policies have already encouraged cross-boundary investment. Claiming that Canada's rate of exchange and natural sunshine-lighting (especially during British Columbia's nonrainy season) make the country an economically ideal setting for shooting movies, the U.S. film industry has markedly increased its presence in western Canada. In 1995 alone thirty-five feature films, eighteen television shows, and forty-two made-for-TV movies were filmed in British Columbia (or "British California," as some bemused residents refer to it) by foreign, mainly American, companies.[34]

Likewise in the entertainment world, economists and sports historians will find ample material to conduct studies on the transborder economics and sociology of hockey, baseball, football, and other professional and collegiate sports. Topics could include the growth of hockey popularity in the United States at the expense of professional teams leaving Canadian cities and the so-called "brawn-drain"—professional and college hockey players bolting for south-of-the-border teams.[35] Will Simon Fraser University in southwestern British Columbia remain Canada's lone American-regulation college football program and continue to play teams from the U.S. West Coast?

Geographers, sociologists, and other scholars will continue to study migration patterns in the twenty-first century. Traditionally, the number of Canadians who immigrate to the United States exceeds the number of Americans who move to Canada. From 1977 to 1998, the average was 13,211 Canadians a year who moved to the States compared with 7,594 Americans who relocated to Canada. And the disparity has only increased in recent years. As free trade expanded between the two nations from 1989 to 1995, the average number of Canadians who moved to the United States jumped to nearly 15,000 a year. By 2001 this figure doubled to over 30,000, compared with only about 6,000 Americans who moved to Canada.[36]

The figures, however, do not represent "snowbirds"—those thousands of retired Canadian citizens, many in enormous RVs, who seasonally migrate across the border away from artic conditions to spend winters and billions of dollars in the sunshine of the American Southwest/Mexican Northwest and Florida—those other traditional North American borderlands. One study reports how 1.3 million Canadian snowbirds spent US$1.6 billion in Florida in 2002 alone.[37] Future studies of this population may reveal some interesting aspects of north-to-south and intercontinental winter migration patterns.

Transversely, it has only been in the post-1990s that thousands of retired U.S. citizens have crossed the border into Canada to purchase considerably lower-priced prescription drugs. Charter buses in Minnesota, with the sanction of that state's legislature, regularly transport older Americans who are tired of paying high medication prices in the States. And, of course, thousands of others are learning to purchase prescription drugs via the Internet from pharmaceutical distributors in Manitoba.

Likewise, there may be new trends on who immigrates. As mentioned earlier in this volume, the trend started by some gay Americans to move to Canada when first Ontario and British Columbia legalized same-sex marriages and then when the Canadian government legalized it for the entire nation in the summer of 2005, may increase if the United States does not follow suit (although Massachusetts legalized same-sex marriages in 2004). Likewise, the twenty-first century may see an increased migration of Americans moving across the border for what often has been viewed as Canada's higher quality of life. Between 1995 and 2002, the United Nations Human Development Index ranked Canada in first place among 175 countries for the best place to live based on educational levels, crime statistics, life expectancy, and health care. (Canada dropped to third place in 2002 and to eighth in 2003 due to a change in the way the Index evaluated education.)

Without adequate health care available to all in the United States,

Canada's nationalized system may be a pull factor for some Americans, as was reported in an Associated Press news article during the summer of 2003. [38] That will include more and more medical marijuana users unless policies become more relaxed in the States on the matter as they have become in Canada. Conversely, due to the lure of higher salaries made by medical doctors in the United States, not matched by Canada's nationalized health care system, a north-to-south physicians' exodus may continue, especially as many rural areas and small towns in the American West are in need of qualified doctors willing to relocate for better pay.

The opposite was true of academics and professionals forty and fifty years ago. In the 1950s and 1960s, hundreds of American academics emigrated to Canada when universities there could not fill vacancies with Canadian scholars. Canada also had opened new universities in response to a post–World War II baby boom demand for higher education. That certainly changed by the 1980s and 1990s when the federal government implemented a "Canadians First Preference" hiring policy for the nation's universities, without a similar policy for "Americans First" in the United States that many Canadian scholars have taken advantage of to teach and conduct research at U.S. universities.

But now in the post-1990s more and more professionals and other Americans, upset with conservative U.S. policies regarding America's on-going foreign wars, a continued blockade of Cuba, a lack of handgun control laws, the continuing refusal to be a signatory party of the international land mine treaty and the Kyoto Protocol, and many states' continued use of capital punishment, are joining gays wanting to marry legally and medipot patients needing marijuana in their relocations to Canada. One woman moving with her family from Minneapolis to Vancouver in summer 2003 told a reporter, "For me it's a no-brainer. It's the most amazing opportunity I can imagine. To live in a society where there are different priorities in caring for your fellow citizens." A New Yorker planning to move to British Columbia summed it up when he stated, "Canada has the opportunity to define itself as a leader. In some ways, it's now closer to American ideals than America is." A "New Underground Railroad" has developed to assist U.S. war resisters fleeing to Canada to avoid American military operations in Iraq. And in 2004, after what many Americans deemed to be George W. Bush's second questionable election as president, the rumors of disgruntled Americans wanting to flee to Canada grew more intense. Sensing a possible tide of American political émigrés, a Vancouver law firm set up seminars on the U.S. West Coast in late 2004 to help would-be immigrants learn how to get jobs and residency in Canada.[39] Those choosing to move will cross a more militarized border. Even the Minutemen Civil Defense Corps, that civilian vigilante group at work apprehending "illegal aliens" on the U.S.–Mexican border, has vowed to start their patrols along the forty-ninth parallel by the summer of 2006.

How these trends concerning the interaction of peoples, landscapes, and policies will be played out in the American and Canadian Wests will be the material of many future studies. There will also be new research conducted and conclusions made on older borderland topics, including more studies comparing the western U.S.–Canadian and U.S.–Mexican borderlands. There should also be more regional studies comparing the *eastern* U.S./Canadian borderlands (and for that matter, the far north 141st meridian borderlands of Alaska/Yukon/British Columbia). They will fill future volumes and will be welcome as we broaden our understanding of the trans-boundary North American West.

Notes

1. Another Canadian park in the borderlands region, Grasslands National Park in southern Saskatchewan, abuts the forty-ninth parallel on its southern boundary, but does not have an overt international peace or unity emphasis. For further discussion of the International Peace Garden, see John Stormon, "A History of the International Peace Garden," *North Dakota History* 31 (1964): 204–15.
2. Bill Clinton, "U.S.-Canada Relations: Common Values," *Time* (Canadian edition), November 17, 2003, 25. The Cellucci statement was reported by Reuters and was broadcast in a variety of media including www.cnn.com/2001/world/american/08/02/canusa .border.rent/index.html.
3. William Stafford, "At the Un-National Monument along Canadian Border," in *Stories That Could Be True: New and Collected Poems* (New York: Harper and Row, 1977), 17.
4. See Hal Herring, "How to Make Your Own Yellowstone, Mexican Style," *High Country News* 34 (November 11, 2002): 6–7.
5. Stephen E. DeLong, "'Fraid at the Edges," http://hawk.fab2/albany.edu/fraid/fraid.htm, 1.
6. Border patrol agent figures were reported in Susan Carroll, "Homeland Security Takes Over at Borders," *Tucson Citizen*, October 24, 2002. Budget information was reported

in American Friends Service Committee, "Human Rights Abuses in the El Paso/Ciudad Juárez Border Region: Behind Every Abuse Is a Community," http://www.asfc.org/border/abuserept/htm. For excellent discussion and analysis of Operation Gatekeeper, see Joseph Nevins, *Operation Gatekeeper: The Rise of the "Illegal Alien" and the Making of the U.S.–Mexico Boundary* (New York: Routledge, 2002). Drone information is from John Kamman, "Drones May Fly Patrols on Border of U.S., Mexico," *Arizona Republic*, April 22, 2003. I thank my former graduate student Dawna Knapp for alerting me to some of these sources in her MA thesis project, "Environmental Justice on the California-Mexico Border," Humboldt State University, 2003.

7. Margaret Atwood, *Survival: A Thematic Guide to Canadian Literature* (Boston: Beacon Press, 1972), 171.

8. The best account of this episode is by Friederick Katz, "Pancho Villa and the Attack on Columbus, New Mexico," *American Historical Review* 83 (February 1978): 101–30.

9. For the best discussion of the Chamizal Treaty, see Jerry E. Mueller, *Restless River: International Law and the Behavior of the Rio Grande* (El Paso: Texas Western Press, 1975), and International Boundary and Water Commission, United States and Mexico, *Laws Applicable to the International Boundary and Water Commission, United States Sector* (El Paso: International Boundary and Water Commission, 1966).

10. See Scott Kaufman, *The Pig War: The United States, Britain, and the Balance of Power in the Pacific Northwest, 1846–1872* (Lanham MD: Lexington Books, 2004); Michael Vouri, *The Pig War: Standoff at Griffin Bay* (Friday Harbor, WA: Griffin Bay Bookstore, 1999); Keith Murray, *The Pig War* (Tacoma WA: Washington State Historical Society, 1968); and www.nps.gov/sajh/Pig_War_new.htm, p. 3. For a race-based analysis on this topic, see Thomas Murphy, "Seeking a True Flag of Freedom: African Americans and the San Juan Boundary Dispute, 1859–1872," paper, conference of the Association of Canadian Studies in the United States (ACSUS), Portland OR, November 2003.

11. Amy Radil, "The Northwest Angle," http://news.mpr.org/features/199808/17_raila_angle-mn/, 1.

12. Radil, "The Northwest Angle."

13. Radil, "The Northwest Angle."

14. For further information, see DeLong, " 'Fraid at the Edges," 2–3. Headlines are from *Ottawa Citizen*, March 20, 1998, A3; *Minneapolis Star-Tribune*, March 20, 1998, 12A; and *Chicago Tribune*, March 21, 1998, News 3.

15. Al Purdy, *The New Romans: Candid Canadian Opinions of the U.S.* (Edmonton: Mel Hurtig, 1968), i.

16. Susan Bradbury and Daniel E. Turbeville, "Enhanced Trade or Enhanced Security? Post-9/11 Policy Conflicts on the Canada-U.S. Border," paper, ACSUS, Portland OR, November 2003. See also Sharon Jones, "Canada and the United States: Is an EU-Style Perimeter Viable? An Analysis of the Smart Border Accord in a Post-9/11 World," paper, ACSUS, Portland OR, November 2003; Bradly J. Condon and Tapen Sinha, *Drawing Lines in Sand and Snow: Border Security and North American Economic Integration* (Armonk NY: M. E. Sharpe, 2003; and Andre Belelieu, "Canada Alert: The Smart Border Process at Two: Losing Momentum?" *Center for Strategic and International Studies* 11, no. 31 (December 2003).

17. James Loucky and Donald Alper, "Pacific Borders, Discordant Borders: Where North

America Edges Together," paper, ACSUS, Portland OR, November 2003, 4. For more specific information on products exchanged, see http://www.can-am.gc.ca.

18. Bradbury and Turbeville, "Enhanced Trade or Enhanced Security?" Information on the antismuggling bases and the enforcement officer's statement were reported by the Associated Press and can be found at www.cnn.com/2004/us/west/08/20/border.patrol.ap/index.html.

19. Jeremy Adelman and Stephen Aron, "From Borderlands to Borders: Empires, Nation-States, and the Peoples in Between in North American History," *American Historical Review* 104 (June 1999), 814–41.

20. Sam Truett, www2.h-net.msu.edu/~west (October 11, 1998).

21. Peter S. Morris, www2.h-net.msu.edu/~west (October 13, 1998).

22. Beth LaDow, www2.h-net.msu.edu/~west (October 15, 1998). See also her book, *The Medicine Line: Life and Death on a North American Borderland* (New York: Routledge, 2003).

23. Loucky and Alper, "Pacific Borders, Discordant Borders," 7–8.

24. Morris, www2.h-net.msu.edu/~west (October 13, 1998).

25. For a rare and excellent comparative studies of the San Diego/Tijuana with Vancouver/Seattle, see Michael R. Pfau, "Looking Forward: A Survey of Cross-Border Impression Formation in the Tijuana–San Diego and Seattle-Vancouver Border Corridors," *Journal of Borderlands Studies* 16 (2001): 1–13; and Loucky and Alper, "Pacific Borders, Discordant Borders." For a broader survey on the topic, see Demetrios G. Papademetriou and Deborah W. Myers, *Caught in the Middle: Border Communities in an Era of Globalization* (Washington: Carnegie Endowment for International Peace, 2001).

26. A good starting place for this discussion is Peter Karl Kresl's book, *The Impact of Free Trade on Canadian-American Border Cities* (Orono ME: Canadian-American Center, 1993). For an historical angle on the rise of cities in the prairie provinces, see Paul Voisey, "The Urbanization of the Canadian Prairies, 1871–1916," in R. Douglas Francis and Howard Palmer, eds., *The Prairie West: Historical Readings* (Edmonton: Pica Pica Press, 1992), 383–407.

27. Loucky and Alper, "Pacific Borders, Discordant Borders," 8.

28. See Ernest Callenbach, *Ecotopia* (New York: Bantam Books, 1990), and Joel Garreau, *The Nine Nations of North America* (New York: Avon Books, 1981).

29. Loucky and Alper, "Pacific Borders, Discordant Borders," 20.

30. Quoted in Alan Artibise, "Cascadian Adventures: Shared Visions, Strategic Alliances, and Ingrained Barriers in a Transborder Region," paper presented at the symposium "On Brotherly Terms: Canadian-American Relations West of the Rockies," University of Washington, Seattle, 1996, 39. For more on the topic, see Artibise's larger work, *Opportunities of Achieving Sustainability in Cascadia* (Vancouver: International Centre for Sustainable Cities, 1994); Matthew Sparke, "Excavating the Future in Cascadia: Geoeconomics and the Imagined Geographies of a Cross-Border Region," *BC Studies* 127 (Autumn 2000): 5–44; Sparke, "Not a State, but More than a State of Mind: Cascading Cascadias and the Geoeconomics of Cross-Border Regionalism," in Markus Perkmann and Ngai-Ling Sum, eds., *Globalization, Regionalization, and Cross-Border Regions* (New York: Palgrave-Macmillan, 2002), 212–40; W. Henkel, "Cascadia: A

State of (Various) Mind(s)," *Chicago Review* 39 (1993): 110–18; M. Hatfield, "Regional Cooperation, Thy Name Is Cascadia," *Oregonian* (February 22, 1994), B7; Elaine Porterfield, "Emerging Cascadia: Geography, Economy, Bring Northwest Cities Ever-Closer," *Christian Science Monitor* (July 26, 1999), 3; Donald K. Alper, "The Idea of Cascadia: Emergent Transborder Regionalisms in the Pacific Northwest–Western Canada," *Journal of Borderlands Studies* 9 (1996): 1–22; and Bruce Agnew, "Connecting Cascadia's Communities," *Seattle Times* (July 14, 1998), 17.

31. In Loucky and Alper, "Pacific Borders, Discordant Borders," 18.

32. "MSU Economists Say U.S. Import of Canadian Wheat Decreases U.S. Prices," http://www.montana.edu/news/105218554.html, 1. For further analysis on NAFTA, see E. J. Chambers and P. H. Smith, eds., NAFTA *in the New Millennium* (Edmonton: University of Alberta Press, 2002), and Michael Hart and William A. Dymond, *Common Borders, Shared Destinies: Canada, the United States, and Deepening Integration* (Ottawa: Centre for Trade Policy and Law, 2001); and Stephanie R. Golob, "North America beyond NAFTA? Sovereignty, Identity, and Security in Canada-U.S. Relations," *American Public Policy*, December 2002, 1–44.

33. For more on the timber trade controversy, see Gilbert Gagné, "The Canada–U.S. Softwood Lumber Dispute: A Test Case for the Development of International Trade Rules," *International Journal* 58 (Summer 2003): 335–69, and George Hoberg and Paul Howe, "Law, Knowledge, and National Interests in Trade Disputes: The Case of Softwood Lumber," *Journal of World Trade* 34 (April 2000): 109–30.

34. "Facts on the Canadian Film and Television Industry," http://www.tv.cbc.ca/national/pgminfo/filmfact.html, 1.

35. For more on the historic background of this topic, see Andrew C. Holman, "The Canadian Hockey Player Problem: Constructing National Identities in U.S. College Athletics, 1947–1975," paper, ACSUS, Portland OR, November 2003; and Holman, "Playing the Neutral Zone: Meanings and Use of Ice Hockey in the Canada–U.S. Borderlands, 1895–1915," *American Review of Canadian Studies* 34 (Spring 2004): 33–57. For analysis of the internationalization or globalization of hockey, see chapters 11 and 12 of Richard Gruneau and David Whitson, *Hockey Night in Canada* (Toronto: Garamond Press, 1993). For related information, consult Morris Mott, " 'Tough to Make It': Professional Team Sports in Manitoba," in J. Welsted, J. Everitt, and C. Stadel, eds., *The Geography of Manitoba: Its Lands and Its Peoples* (Winnipeg: University of Manitoba Press, 1996).

36. "Irked by U.S. Policies, Some Americans Consider Crossing Over to Canada," AP news story reprinted in *Eureka Times-Standard* (July 20, 2003), C7.

37. See www.can-am.gc.ca.

38. "Irked by U.S. Policies."

39. "Irked by U.S. Policies." The Vancouver law firm seminars were reported on *Weekend Edition*, National Public Radio, December 12, 2004.

Contributors

Jason Patrick Bennett is a PhD candidate in history at the University of Victoria in British Columbia, and he has taught at the University of Ottawa. His research and teaching interests include North American and global environmental history, especially the role and impact of agriculture in colonial settings. His dissertation is entitled "Blossoms of Empire: Cultivating Nature and Rural Life in British Columbia and the Pacific Northwest, 1890–1950."

Theodore Binnema is a historian at the University of Northern British Columbia who specializes in First Nations and environmental history of western Canada and the United States. He is the author of *Common and Contested Ground: A Human and Environmental History of the Northwestern Plains* (2001), and is an editor with Gerhard Ens and R. C. Macleod of *From Rupert's Land to Canada: Essays in Honour of John E. Foster* (2001).

Gerhard J. Ens, a scholar on Canada's Métis, teaches history at the University of Alberta. Along with First Nations history, his interests include the history of the Canadian and American Wests and environmental history. He is the author of *Homeland to Hinterland: The Changing Worlds of the Red River Metis in the Nineteenth Century* (1996) and editor with Theodore Binnema and R. C. Macleod of *From Rupert's Land to Canada: Essays in Honour of John E. Foster* (2001).

Sterling Evans is Canada Research Chair in History at Brandon University in Manitoba. He previously taught at Humboldt State University and the University of Alberta. His teaching and research interests include Latin America, borderlands, and environmental history. He wrote *Bound in Twine: Transnational History and Environmental Change in the*

Henequen-Wheat Complex for Yucatán and the American and Canadian Plains, 1890–1950 (forthcoming), *The Green Republic: A Conservation History of Costa Rica* (1999), and edited *American Indians in American History, 1870–2001: A Companion Reader* (2002).

Leonard J. Evenden is a retired professor of geography at Simon Fraser University in British Columbia. He has published various works on metropolitan Vancouver, and his fields of academic interest include social, cultural, and urban geography and Canadian studies.

Michel Hogue is a doctoral student in history at the University of Wisconsin–Madison. His contribution here and a different article he had published in *Montana: The Magazine of Western History* (Winter 2002) were originally part of his MA thesis, "Crossing the Line: The Plains Cree in the Canada–United States Borderlands, 1870–1900" from the University of Calgary.

Thomas D. Isern is a professor of history at North Dakota State University where his research interests include agricultural history, comparative grasslands, and the transboundary Great Plains. Among his publications are *Of Land and Sky: Essays in the History of Western Canadian Agriculture* (forthcoming), *Dakota Circle: Excursions on the True Plains* (2000), *Bullthreshers and Bindlestiffs: Harvesting and Threshing on the North American Plains* (1990), and *Custom Combining on the Great Plains: A History* (1981).

Terry G. Jordan-Bychkov, a cultural and historical geographer, held the Walter Prescott Webb Chair in Geography at the University of Texas. He was the author of many books and articles on ranching history, including *North American Cattle-Ranching Frontiers: Origins, Diffusion, and Differentiation* (1993).

Renée G. Kasinsky is a professor of criminal justice at the University of Massachusetts–Lowell. Her major areas of research and teaching have been in gender, race, and class in relation to crime, corporate criminality, and media coverage of gendered crimes. She is the author of *Crime, Oppression, and Inequality: A Reader* (1991) and *Refugees from Militarism: Draft-Age Americans in Canada* (1976).

Marian C. McKenna is professor emeritus of history at the University of Calgary. Her research interests have centered on legal and constitutional history, especially comparative between the United States and Canada. Among her many publications is the book *Franklin D. Roosevelt and the Great Constitutional War: The Court-Packing Crisis of 1937* (2002) and the edited collection *The Canadian and American Constitutions in Comparative Perspective* (1993).

Sheila McManus is a professor of history at the University of Lethbridge in southern Alberta. She has specialized in Canadian-American borderlands and gender history of the forty-ninth parallel. In addition to a variety of articles, she has written *The Line That Separates: The Alberta/Montana Borderlands in the Late Nineteenth Century* (2005), and with Elizabeth Jameson has coedited *One Step over the Line: Toward a History of Women in the North American Wests* (forthcoming).

Bruce Granville Miller is an anthropologist at the University of British Columbia where he has specialized in transboundary issues of Pacific Coast First Nations. He is the author of *Invisible Indigenes: The Politics of Nonrecognition* (2003) and *The Problem of Justice: Tradition and Law in the Coast Salish World* (2001).

Stephen T. Moore is a professor of history at Central Washington University where he teaches courses on the Pacific Northwest, Canadian, and U.S. history. He previously taught at Ohio Northern University. His research focuses on the history of the transboundary Pacific Northwest, especially during the 1920s. He is the author of the forthcoming book *Of Bootleggers and Borders: Canadians, Americans, and the Prohibition-Era Northwest*.

Peter S. Morris teaches geography at Santa Monica College in southern California and specializes in the historical geography and environmental history of the North American West, particularly the Great Plains of the United States and Canada. He is completing his PhD dissertation, "Forty-Ninth Parallel Worlds: A Borderland Historical Geography of the Northwestern Plains," at the University of Wisconsin–Madison from which his contribution here and an article in *Geographical Review* (October 1999) originated.

Catriona Mortimer-Sandilands is associate professor in the Faculty of Environmental Studies and Canada Research Chair in Sustainability and Culture at York University in Toronto. She writes at the intersections of social theory and environmental politics on topics ranging from gender and sexuality to nationalism and feminism. She is the author of *The Good-Natured Feminist: Ecofeminism and the Quest for Democracy* (1999), and she is completing *A State of Nature? National Parks and Canadian Identity*.

Evelyne Stitt Pickett is a historian and is producer and director of History in Performance based in Riggins, Idaho. She is the author of the forthcoming books *James Edward Church and the Development of Snow Surveying* and, with Carlos Schwantes, *Bibliography of the Pacific Northwest*.

Paul F. Sharp is professor emeritus of history and past president of the University of Oklahoma. One of the first scholars to write on the trans-boundary West, his books *Whoop-Up Country: The Canadian-American West* (1955) and *The Agrarian Revolt in Western Canada: A Survey Showing American Parallels* (1948) and his many articles remain standard works in the field.

R. Bruce Shepard is an independent scholar, historian, and former director and curator of the Diefenbaker Centre at the University of Saskatchewan. His research interests have centered on American influence and immigration to western Canada, and he is the author of *Deemed Unsuitable* (1997) about African-American migration from Oklahoma to the Canadian prairies.

John Herd Thompson is a historian and former director of the Center for Canadian Studies at Duke University. Among his works on Canadian and North American history are *Family, Farm, and Community: The Rural Northern Plains, 1860–1960* (forthcoming), with Stephen J. Randall, *Canada and the United States: Ambivalent Allies* (3rd ed., 2002), and *Forging the Prairie West* (1998).

Eckard V. Toy Jr. is an independent scholar who lives in Mt. Hood, Oregon. He has done extensive research on the history of the Ku Klux Klan (the topic of his PhD dissertation from the University of Oregon) and other extremist groups in the Pacific Northwest. His articles on the subject have appeared in a variety of regional journals and edited collections.

Daniel E. Turbeville III is a professor of geography at Eastern Washington University whose interests are in cultural, urban, and transportation geography, especially of the Pacific Northwest and Canada. Along with many articles and papers, he is the author of *The Electric Railway Era in Northwest Washington, 1890–1930.* (1979).

Lissa Wadewitz is a postdoctoral fellow in history at the Bill Lane Center for the Study of the North American West at Stanford University. She held a Canada Research Chair postdoctoral fellowship at the University of Saskatchewan. She is preparing to publish her dissertation, "The Nature of Borders: Salmon and Boundaries in the Puget Sound/Georgia Basin" (UCLA, 2004), which uses salmon fishing to trace the impact of political borders on both the natural environment and diverse peoples who came to inhabit the border region.

Todd Wilkinson is an independent writer in Bozeman, Montana, who specializes in wildlife, environmental, and conservation issues in the northern Rockies. In addition to his many articles in magazines, he is the author of numerous books, including *Science under Siege: The Politicians' War on Nature and Truth* (1998), *Combat Biologists: The Battle for Biodiversity on Our Public Lands* (1995), and wildlife-watching guides to most of the national parks in the Rocky Mountains.

Index